M000098304

What's Next?

What's
Next?

*Exploring the New Terrain
for Business*

Eamonn Kelly, Peter Leyden
and Members of Global Business Network

PERSEUS
PUBLISHING

A Member of the Perseus Books Group

Cataloging-in-Publication Data is available from the Library of Congress
ISBN 0-7382-0760-8

Perseus Publishing is a member of the Perseus Books Group
Find us on the World Wide Web at www.perseuspublishing.com

Perseus Publishing books are available at special discounts for bulk purchases in the U.S. by corporations, institutions, and other organizations. For more information, please contact the Special Markets Department at the Perseus Books Group, 11 Cambridge Center, Cambridge, MA 02142, or call (800) 255-1514 or (617) 252-5298, or e-mail j.mccrary@perseusbooks.com.

Text design by *Brent Wilcox*
Set in 11-point Kepler by the Perseus Books Group

First printing, September 2002

1 2 3 4 5 6 7 8 9 10–05 04 03 02

To Napier Collyns,
whose passion for learning, love of ideas,
and tireless work to grow and nurture
a network of remarkable people never cease
to inspire all who know him

Contents

8 Preparing for the Long Term
Civilization and Infrastructure

Continuing the Journey
Implications

Exploring the New Terrain
Introduction

This is not your typical business book. It doesn't advocate a single point of view or unified theory of everything. It won't offer "the ten techniques for transformation" or "the seven strategies for success." It fails to prescribe what you should do next Monday morning nor does it dwell on the typical concerns of most business executives, such as improving shareholder value or increasing productivity. Instead this book suggests that no one perspective, no checklist of key trends, no single set of predictions will serve business people well as they navigate the complexity and uncertainty of the decade ahead. Rather, we must embrace multiple perspectives on the future, play with numerous ideas, search for possibilities instead of prescriptions, and explore a range of unfamiliar fields.

Just a few years ago, the suggestion that there is not a crisp new set of rules to follow would have found little favor. Think back to the late 1990s, as we neared the long-anticipated new millennium. Business gurus speculated breathlessly about a new world of opportunity and discontinuous change. Economic globalization, driven by accelerating technological innovation and enabled by the adoption of market principles across the planet, was changing everything—and for the better. Simultaneously a remarkable "new economy" was unfolding, led by global businesses, upstart entrepreneurs, and daring venture capitalists. Liberated from the constraints of old-fashioned government, they were inventing the global, postindustrial economy and society. The future was clearly in our sights.

It is tempting now to dismiss such certainty as hyperbole and misguided optimism—a consequence of our excessive times. But in fairness it is common for those in the midst of complex and accelerating change to identify—falsely—a clear, single trajectory with inevitable outcomes. In 1851, for example, when Great Britain's Prince Albert opened the Great Exhibition in London, he observed: "We are living in a period of most wondrous transitions, which tends rapidly to accomplish that great end to which indeed all history points—the realization of the unity of mankind." A nice vision—but most would agree that more than 150 years later we're still waiting. Nonetheless, Prince Albert's sense of dramatic and irreversible change was accurate enough—it was his simplistic certainty that now seems naïve. Similarly, the excitement around the turn of the millennium has properly been replaced by a more thoughtful and reflective consideration of our future—not because the opportunities are any less magnificent, but because the attendant challenges are equally profound. Perhaps the unanticipated turmoil of the first years of the new century has retaught us the lesson that the future is always more complicated, unpredictable, and nuanced than it might first appear. And that few trends ever continue on a straight line without producing unintended, sometimes counterproductive, consequences.

With that in mind, let's calmly consider our own moment in history. We do live in another era of transformation. In the last couple of decades we have witnessed an extraordinary transition from an industrial, nation-based, resource-oriented economy to a global, networked, knowledge-intensive economy. More and more parts of the world have adopted market mechanisms to promote wealth creation—from the old communist bastions of Russia and China to the emerging economies of Asia and Latin America. Corporations have been a powerful catalyst for change: opening markets, promoting privatization, and globalizing goods, services, and production processes. Millions of people around the world have gained access to new products as well as new technologies, information, and ideas. New economic opportunities have improved the quality of life for many. But there have been unintended consequences as well.

The liberation of markets, driven by the power of corporations, also created more complex, interconnected global economic and social systems that cannot be controlled and therefore cannot be predicted. The very forces—globalization, rapid technological advances, increased connectivity, mounting transparency—that businesses helped unleash are transforming the world and shaping a new and challenging environment. Global protest movements, demands for greater accountability, increasingly complex geopolitical tensions, rising concerns about environmental and social sustainability, and wider cultural divides are making the business of business even more complicated. These new realities point to a whole new set of challenges and opportunities for business in the decade ahead.

For the last 20 years businesses have focused their learning about the external world primarily on those issues that would allow them to grow and compete. In an environment of predominantly free and expanding markets, these were mainly concerned with technology, economics and finance, and similar close-to-market concerns. In the next 10 years, such a focus will no longer be sufficient to succeed. Instead, businesses must learn to anticipate and adapt more quickly to an increasingly complex environment in which many political, economic, social, cultural, and technological forces are shifting, interacting, and even colliding. This will require us to expand our peripheral vision to encompass a far broader set of concerns. We are entering a new terrain for business. And the best way to explore and ultimately understand that new terrain is to actively seek out a variety of informed perspectives. This book is designed to help you do exactly that. Here you will encounter a wide array of new views on the next decade. And for this, we are indebted to some of the liveliest minds of our time.

"No one is as smart as everyone."

Many of the ideas in this book come from a group of remarkable thinkers, most of whom have had a long relationship with Global Business Network, or GBN. Global Business Network was founded fifteen years ago on a handful of core ideas, three of which are embedded in its name. *Global* referred to the wave of globalization that would reshape economies and societies in deep and lasting ways. The word also suggested the importance of maintaining a truly global perspective in order to anticipate and understand critical developments in the world. *Business* was already emerging as the primary catalyst for change and innovation. As corporations assumed increasingly powerful roles, their actions would have greater—and far more visible—impacts. This is where the action would be centered. The *Network*, as an organizational model, seemed especially well suited to this complex and changing environment—more flexible, distributed, and supportive of shared learning than traditional hierarchical structures. What better way to explore the emerging world than through a network of global businesses?

And so GBN came together as a new kind of membership organization committed to collaborative learning about the present and shared insight into the future. It gathered many of the world's leading business corporations, farsighted public agencies, and deep thinkers to share ideas in person and on a groundbreaking online conferencing system called The WELL long before email became popular. Though the future cannot be predicted, GBN has always believed that developments can be better anticipated by combining networked learning with rigorous tools for scenaric thinking. As a pioneer in scenario planning, GBN has helped evolve this interactive process that allows organizations to explore several different futures and then create more robust long-term strategies to accommodate them.

To gain insights into the future, GBN, over the years, has created a network of "remarkable people." Russian philosopher G.I. Gurdjieff first used this term to describe thinkers who are distinguished by "resourceful minds" and a tolerance for different ideas. Pierre Wack, a visionary strategist at Royal Dutch/Shell in the 1970s, introduced this concept into the corporate world by systematically seeking out provocative thinkers to help challenge and inform the company's planning. In this sense, remarkable people are not like traditional experts or prognosticators whose knowledge is deep but narrowly focused. Rather, remarkable people are original, systemic thinkers whose boundless curiosity and passion naturally lead them to explore ideas beyond their own areas of expertise and in places where no one else looks. They stretch our thinking by pointing out issues that may be off everyone's radar screen, by reframing facts in surprising ways, and by finding connections between divergent developments.

Often articulate storytellers, these remarkable people extract and express the meaning and relevance of the most complex ideas. They both surprise and explain, sensitizing us to the new while also helping us to reperceive the old. Yet they are as interested in learning from others as they are in sharing what they know, which they do with great generosity. Finally, GBN has found that remarkable people are predisposed to optimism. They're skilled at identifying problems but are equally compelled to offer solutions.

GBN continually seeks out such people who surprise, provoke, amaze, and delight us with their intellect and their humanity. That alone is valuable. But there's also value in aggregating their insights to see a fuller range of new possibilities. One of our core philosophies is: "No one's as smart as everyone." This book is a virtual gathering of "everyone," a deep conversation where 50 remarkable people—members of the GBN network and other provocative thinkers—offer compelling views on the decade ahead.

> "A mind stretched to a new idea never
> returns to its original dimension."
> *Oliver Wendel Holmes*

The project that led to this book began in 2001. We were picking up clear signals that the environment for business could change radically in the coming decade. We wanted to look beyond the collapse of the dotcoms and the economic slowdown to explore the deeper, more systemic changes that might significantly impact business and its agenda over the longer term. Naturally, we turned to our network of remarkable people to tap into their insights and ideas. Then, halfway through the project, the terrorist attacks of September 11, 2001, occurred, raising the bar of uncertainty and urgency. Even so, the fundamental questions that we already were asking remained the same: What significant developments, key issues, and potential surprises should global businesses be watching for in the next decade? We kept our interviews deliberately open-ended and exploratory to discover what was on the minds of people in our network. We imposed only one parameter—the timeframe of the next decade—because 10 years seems to spark the right mix of creative stretch and business relevance.

Each network member interviewed made a unique contribution. And the more interviews we conducted, the richer the collective conversation became. Some of our network members help put the confusing events of the last few years in perspective. **Paul Saffo**, a well-known technology forecaster in Silicon Valley, sums up his analysis of the dotcom crash with the saying: "Never mistake a clear view for a short distance." Saffo thinks that all fundamentally new technologies overpromise in the short term, but overdeliver in the long term. We tend to overestimate how fast adoption—and the subsequent changes—will happen, while underestimating how widespread and profound the ultimate impact will be. Indeed, he says, the promise of digital technologies glimpsed in the failed business plans of the late 1990s will play out over this decade—although how they actually get delivered will surprise people. Meanwhile, **Robert Hormats**, vice chairman of Goldman Sachs International, puts the financial collapse of the technology sector in context. Anyone who considers financial markets as rational allocators of capital is mistaken—markets are never in equilibrium and always tend to overshoot. All truly transformative technologies—like railroads, the electrical grid, and now the Internet—have frenetic booms and busts that clear out many front-line investors but leave in place a new infrastructure that all businesses can productively leverage. Other network members stress keeping an eye on the long-term developments that get lost in the tumult of daily news. Economist **Roger Cass** gives a masterful analysis of the powerful economic forces that are still driving growth despite short-term turbulence in the global economy. He argues that we are only halfway through a global economic boom that has happened with cyclical regularity in modern history. To Cass the patterns are so clear that he's willing to forecast economic growth rates for the entire decade.

Many network members are preoccupied by the power struggles set in motion by globalization and fascinated by the transition from the old order of the late twentieth century to the new order of the twenty-first. Political economist **Steven Weber** points out the parallels between the current geopolitical climate and the West's struggle to articulate a new security policy after World War II. At that time, views on how best to deal with the Soviet Union varied wildly until an anonymous memo crystallized the concept of containment that would structure the Cold War for the next 30 years. The present security establishment faces a similar situation in defining the post–Cold War strategy to fight terrorism. **John Arquilla** of the Naval Postgraduate School gives a chilling analysis of the key military challenge of the decade: how to stop a terrorist attack involving a weapon of mass destruction. A portable nuclear device detonated in a major city could kill millions and cause trillions of dollars in damage to the global economy. Most disturbingly, he sets the odds of such a catastrophe occurring at one in four. **Robert Carlson**, a physicist-turned-biologist, foresees a similar vulnerability as scientists learn enough about nascent biotechnology to create devastating viruses, but not enough to rapidly counter them if they are misused or veer out of control. The imperative is to close that knowledge gap, something Carlson feels confident could happen in 10 years.

European strategists and political observers **Albert Bressand** and **Catherine Distler** argue that the coming decade will be defined by global integration, with Europeans best positioned to lead the way. By leveraging what they learned in the complicated and collaborative transitions to the European Union and the euro, Europeans can help broker global deals on the environment and other diplomatically challenging issues. Columnist **Gwynne Dyer**, an expert on the Middle East, views the tense relationship between the West and the Arab Middle East as an artifact of the ancient interactions between the two sides of the Mediterranean world and anticipates the possible rise of more fundamentalism in the decade ahead. Entrepreneur **Paul Hawken** focuses on a different geopolitical faultline: between the established economic order and the antiglobalization movement. Hawken argues that we're witnessing history's first global uprising, a movement against "the corporatization of the commons" and the power of corporations. China expert **Orville Schell** examines the overwhelming challenges facing China this decade: the largest internal migration in human history, some of the most virulent environmental damage on the planet, and the contradiction between a liberalizing economy and a repressive political regime. Schell warns businesses to beware of a possible collapse.

Many contributors concentrate on the impact of globalization and technology on people. Journalist **Joel Garreau** is testing his lag-time theory—that the cultural aftershocks of the technological and economic changes of the 1990s will play out in the decade ahead. The innovations of the 1950s—like television and the birth control pill—didn't really impact the culture until the 1960s and Garreau is convinced that cultural cross-connections from the Internet and globalization are just beginning to have very strange and important effects. Social theorist **Frank Fukuyama** warns of new culture wars that will flare up this decade in the United States and the West. The battleground will be drawn by rapid developments in biotechnology that will force some profound decisions about who benefits from genetic engineering, the demographics of life extension, and the next generation of behavior-modifying drugs. **Jaron Lanier**, the pioneer of virtual reality, explains the prospects for videoconferencing and teleimmersion, or the simulation of three-dimensional interactions over long distances. But Lanier doesn't just focus on technology. He's more concerned about the social ramifications of a world divided between vast numbers of poor, mostly young people who can closely watch the aging affluent of the West.

Other people take their analysis to a deeper human level, examining the role of values and belief systems, including religion and spirituality. **Huston Smith**, the eminent scholar of world religions, argues that the major wisdom traditions share many of the same core values, though he does not expect to see a movement towards consolidation. Cultural anthropologist **Mary Catherine Bateson**, who describes her distinguished career as the study of how people adapt to change, sees a major effort in the coming decade to sort out what is general and what is particular to all people on the planet. Inventor **Danny Hillis** takes the controversial view that the world is inevitably moving toward one global culture because in the end people share many of the same values and desires. He thinks we're in the midst of a struggle between the "globalists" and the "tribalists," who rightly fear that their cultures will dissipate. *Wired* magazine's founding executive editor **Kevin Kelly** anticipates a rise in all kinds of fundamentalisms as a practical means for people to deal with change and limit the number of choices they face. In his view of the future, there will be more of everything—all of the old choices and a steady stream of new ones—and so people will buy into groups with clearly defined "value sets" that essentially make choices for them.

Others explore the most significant technological developments of the coming decade. For many it's critical to figure out which tools and knowledge will move from development to practical applications. Some speculate that high bandwidth telecom connections could come through wireless broadband networks aggregating from the bottom up. Other network members talk about more dramatic developments like the acceleration of artificial intelligence. Computer scientist **Vernor Vinge** lays out his theory of a possible coming singularity when computers not only reach but exceed human intelligence and we may no longer be in control. We'll know by the end of the decade whether we're on that path or not. **Shaun Jones**, who heads initiatives on advanced technologies for the U.S. government, identifies some extreme yet plausible breakthroughs in nanotechnology. He makes a convincing case that we may soon use microscopic machines to journey through our bodies for diagnostics and preventative care—a cross between the movies *Fantastic Voyage* and *Tron*. The renowned physicist **Freeman Dyson** points to a long-term development that he considers inevitable: renewed emphasis on space exploration. He describes a recent, little-noticed breakthrough using lasers for space travel that might someday be seen as the equivalent of the Wright Brothers' demonstration that flight was possible.

In the realm of science, GBN cofounder **Peter Schwartz** lays out his theory that we are on the verge of scientific revolutions in physics, chemistry, and biology that are akin to such discoveries of the early twentieth century as the theories of relativity and quantum mechanics. Biotech entrepreneur **Brian Sager** sums up a range of potential developments in biotechnology, including growing plastics and mastering "directed evolution" where an organism's procreation is accelerated by thousands of generations. Science writer **Janine Benyus** thinks the life sciences might take a quite different approach. Instead of manipulating nature, which poses significant dangers, she anticipates that we will learn to mimic it. She lays out possible developments in biomimicry, including breakthroughs in our understanding of photosynthesis that will allow us to use solar energy as cleanly and efficiently as plants.

Many of the network members interviewed are deeply concerned with sustainability on a planetary scale. Evolutionary biologist **William Calvin** has a well-researched theory that contradicts the conventional wisdom about how global climate change will unfold. Calvin argues that the change will be not slow, but quick, and the resulting climate will be not hot, but cold. Calvin projects that when the global climate begins to flip, the transition could happen in the space of five to 10 years—wiping out much of European agriculture. Environmentalist **Peter Warshall** has a theory that the concept of sustainability is beginning to enjoy broad acceptance and in some ways has taken on characteristics of a religion. He sees the coming decade as having less to do with new technologies than with fundamentally redesigning everything in more sustainable directions. **Amory Lovins** and **Hunter Lovins**, co-CEOs of the Rocky Mountain Institute, are closely tracking new green technologies, many of which are much further along than the public realizes and ready to be launched at cost-effective prices. They see the world poised for the biggest energy shift in centuries—to a hydrogen economy.

Some of our network members push the conversation far into the future. GBN cofounder **Stewart Brand** is one of those predisposed to think really long term. He finds it useful to view the present as the beginning of our efforts to build a global civilization, a project that might take 20 to 50 years or more. Our challenge—to make that global system robust—requires us to address long-term, intergenerational infrastructures, from the physical to the institutional. **Katherine Fulton**, who heads GBN's philanthropy practice, offers her own persuasive theory about how building a global civil society might occur. Modern philanthropy was invented in America in the early twentieth century in response to the social problems engendered by rapid economic transformation and urbanization. She thinks that a similar set of problems is developing at a global scale and creating the conditions for the emergence of a new kind of global philanthropy. **Betty Sue Flowers**, the director of the LBJ Presidential Library, sees business providing increasing leadership on long-term issues. She thinks business leaders will shift from leadership that thinks only about tactics and strategy to wise and philosophical leadership that "wills the good."

> "All who wander are not lost."
> *J. R. R. Tolkien*

In the course of conducting the interviews upon which this book is based, we gradually developed a way of framing the new, broader terrain that businesses must explore and understand for future success. We have captured this in a map (see figure on following page) that is intended to help you navigate the wide range of issues, some familiar, some much less so, that will shape the business environment in the coming decade. This new terrain map also defines the structure of this book, with a chapter dedicated to each of the eight specific territories we will explore.

There are four major realms, or quadrants, within which the interview excerpts are arrayed. The realm of *Power* includes the traditional areas of politics and government, as well as economic power expressed through wealth creation in an increasingly global financial system. In *People*, the focus shifts to issues and trends at the societal and individual levels, in-

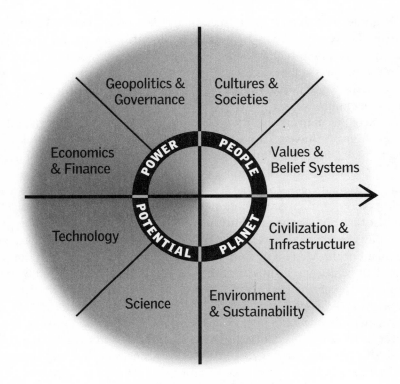

The New Terrain Map

cluding those involving cultures, values, and beliefs. *Potential* concerns the evolution of scientific knowledge, as well as its practical application through new technologies. The final realm, *Planet*, covers topics of long-term, universal significance, from the state of the natural environment to the development of sustainable human systems.

Within each realm, the new terrain map is further divided into two domains, with each domain corresponding to a chapter in this book. Two of these domains, *Economics and Finance* and *Technology*, have long been a critical focus for business and will remain important in the decade ahead. These more conventional preoccupations cluster around the left end of the horizontal axis. As you move toward the right you encounter other domains that we think will become increasingly important over the next decade.

Following that logic, we move from the familiar turf of *Economics and Finance* to *Geopolitics and Governance*, which many already see rising in importance to business. New tensions, conflicts, and alliances in the world of geopolitics will have enormous implications for the future of our increasingly interconnected and interdependent global economy. Moreover, a renewed focus on governance, perhaps at a more global level, is probable given 20 years of deregulation and the liberation of market power. But understanding these developments also will require a deeper familiarity with diverse *Cultures and Societies*. Even these relatively stable arenas are now in flux as our economy becomes increasingly global. Today different cultures are simultaneously integrating, clashing and diverging, and evolving in their own unique ways. However, cultures and societies are rooted in *Values and Belief Systems*, which are even slower to change but fundamentally shape people's desires, behaviors, and relationships. In the coming decade businesses will need to tune into all these areas and better understand both the diversity and commonality to be found in people across the planet.

A similar logic works for the other side of the map, starting with *Technology*. Developments there and in *Science* are more intimately related than ever before. Science, accelerated by better tools and higher levels of communications between peers, is expanding its knowledge base faster than ever. The speed at which new scientific discoveries are enabling new technological applications that are being taken into the marketplace is also accelerating. At the same time scientific knowledge is enhancing our understanding of the impact of human activities on the planet, thereby deepening our concerns about the *Environment and Sustainability* and increasing our awareness of the need for systemic and long-term solutions. That naturally segues into our final and usually least-explored domain: *Civilization and Infrastructure*. How well are we preparing for the problems of the twenty-first century? How do we build systems of all sorts to sustain not only a global economy but a growing global population? What kind of physical and intangible infrastructure, including civic institutions, should we create to respond effectively to our mounting challenges and seize our new opportunities? And what role will businesses be expected to play?

"It is not the strongest of the species that survive, nor the most intelligent, rather, it is those most responsive to change."
Charles Darwin

As you explore each of these domains with us, we hope you will encounter a variety of ideas that resonate, startle, and even entertain. You may disagree with some ideas and discover others that stimulate further inquiry. Ultimately we hope you begin to think differently about the future. If so, this book may leave you with an overarching question—now what should I do? We don't pretend to have all the answers, but we do have some thoughts about how organizations and individuals might respond. In short, in the face of massive complexity, take a tip from Mother Nature. Learn to adapt.

Over the last 20 years every effective business has been involved in systematically building *competitive advantage* for sustained success. This has primarily focused on developing a deep understanding of the marketplace. In the coming decade businesses will have to also focus on the development of *adaptive advantage*, based on a deep understanding of the world. As many of the challenges of the coming decade unfold in the world external to business, companies will need to be looking much farther afield. They will need to anticipate and understand key developments in the world at large earlier and more accurately so they can act quickly and more effectively. Developing this adaptive ability will prove just as important in determining long-term success. The final chapter of the book highlights some ways to begin building adaptive advantage through thinking differently, learning differently, and acting differently.

But for now let's start exploring the new terrain and enjoy what is in essence a field trip into the future in the company of 50 highly informed and opinionated people. To make the journey as stimulating and lively as possible, we have not set out the ideas of each contributor sequentially, but have clustered passages from many of them around some of the core issues that are shaping our times.

These are the thumbnail sketches of the cast of characters that you will meet throughout the pages of this book. For more detailed information on each person look to the full bios in the back of the book.

Laurie Anderson
Performance artist, writer, and musician

John Arquilla
Professor of defense analysis and netwar researcher, The Naval Postgraduate School

W. Brian Arthur
Economist and complexity theorist, Santa Fe Institute

Mary Catherine Bateson
Cultural anthropologist, educator, and author on adapting to change

Janine Benyus
Life sciences writer and biomimicry advocate

Stewart Brand
Cofounder of GBN, The Long Now Foundation, The All Species Project, The WELL

Albert Bressand
Economist specializing in Europe, globalization, and capital markets

William Calvin
Neurobiologist, University of Washington; writer on evolution and climate

Robert Carlson
Scientist at Applied Minds, a research and invention laboratory

Roger Cass
Economic historian specializing in long-wave analysis of economic activity

Catherine Distler
Strategist focusing on European integration and telecommunications

Gwynne Dyer
Global columnist; historian of the Middle East and military affairs

Esther Dyson
Technology writer/publisher; Eastern Europe venture capitalist; founding chair of ICANN

Freeman Dyson
Physicist; writer on science and religion; professor emeritus, Princeton's Institute for Advanced Study

Betty Sue Flowers
Poet, scenario writer, and educator; director, the LBJ Presidential Library

Francis Fukuyama
Professor and theorist on political economy and public policy, Johns Hopkins University

Katherine Fulton
Partner at GBN-Monitor specializing in the futures of philanthropy and media

Joel Garreau
Geographic demographer; journalist and cultural revolutionary, *Washington Post*

Gerald Harris
GBN scenarist, specializing in energy, utilities, and community development

Paul Hawken
Environmentalist, educator, author, and technology/sustainability entrepreneur

Michael Hertz
Corporate law partner; cofounder of Pro Bono Net, a public interest legal organization

Danny Hillis
Inventor and computer scientist; cofounder, Applied Minds, a research and invention laboratory

Robert Hormats
Economist and vice chair, Goldman Sachs International

Shaun B. Jones
Navy captain and surgeon specializing in advanced technologies and national security

Kevin Kelly
Founding executive editor, *Wired*; cofounder of The All Species Foundation

Jaron Lanier
Composer and musician; computer scientist; inventor; virtual reality pioneer

Amory Lovins
Energy and sustainability visionary; cofounder, Rocky Mountain Institute and Hypercar, Inc.

L. Hunter Lovins
Natural capitalism visionary; cofounder, Rocky Mountain Institute; founder Windstar Land Conservancy

Michael Murphy
Author and pioneer in human potential and transformative practice; cofounder, Esalen Institute

Jay Ogilvy
Cofounder, GBN; philosopher; writer on values and normative scenarios

Walter Parkes
Hollywood movie producer; president, Dreamworks SKG

John L. Petersen
Futurist; founder of the Arlington Institute; writer on national security and wild cards

Jeffrey Rayport
Economic historian, Harvard Business School; founder, Marketspace, a Monitor e-commerce strategy company

Richard Rodriguez
Essayist on culture, ethnicity, and social change; cultural memoirist

Paul Saffo
Director, Institute for the Future; technology forecaster

Brian Sager
Scientist; biotech/nanotech venture advisor; composer, new classical music

Orville Schell
China scholar; dean, Graduate School of Journalism, University of California, Berkeley

Lee Schipper
Physicist; codirector, EMBARQ, the WRI Center for Transport and Environment

Peter Schwartz
Chair and cofounder GBN; former head of scenario planning, Royal Dutch/Shell

Alex Singer
Film and television director; consultant on technology and entertainment

Huston Smith
Religion and spirituality scholar-educator; author and documentary filmmaker

Bruce Sterling
Science fiction writer; catalyst, Viridian Green, a virtual environmental design movement

Hirotaka Takeuchi
Dean, Graduate School of International Corporate Strategy, Hitotsubashi University, Tokyo

Dorothy Q. Thomas
Global human rights and women's rights activist; MacArthur Fellow

Nirav Tolia
Internet entrepreneur; cofounder and CEO of Epinions

Kees van der Heijden
Director, Center for Strategic Planning and Future Studies, Strathclyde University, Glasgow

Vernor Vinge
Science fiction writer; emeritus professor of math and computer science

Peter Warshall
Biological anthropologist and naturalist; consultant; editor, *Whole Earth* magazine

Steven Weber
GBN scenarist on globalization; political economist; professor, University of California, Berkeley

Lawrence Wilkinson
Cofounder, GBN; investment, business, and media advisor; vice chair, Oxygen Media

Part 1

Power

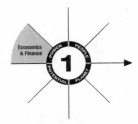

The Evolution of Wealth Creation

Economics and Finance

"The dotcom bubble trained a whole generation of young entrepreneurs. They rode it up, they rode it down—they came out. They're still 32 or 33 years old, with their whole careers in front of them. I think we just forged what will go on to be the greatest entrepreneurial generation of the last 50 years."

Paul Saffo

"It should plot out like this: 1994–2000 was the initial boom expansion of the long wave; 2000–2002 will be the transition phase as we move into the next level of these technologies, which are driving the expansion; and 2003–2008 will be another dramatic phase of economic growth and productivity around the world."

Roger Cass

"In business, it's not just action that counts—it's also the interplay among hypotheses as to what's going to happen next."

W. Brian Arthur

"One of the things that is still unresolved in my own mind is if you made a model of the ideal global economy, does it make the most sense to have only a few specialists make the things we need and have them ship those things to wherever they're needed, or does it actually make more sense to have many local origins for those things?"

Kevin Kelly

"The economic is really the heart of the tremendous crisis we are in. The clearest evidence is that, by my understanding, the rich are getting richer and the poor are getting poorer. The question is: is anybody at the helm? I'm talking about businessmen."

Huston Smith

We start exploring the new terrain for business from the familiar turf of economics and finance—obviously vital to all businesses and traditionally watched very closely. The central importance of this domain won't diminish. In fact, the state of the global economy and financial system in the coming 10 years will help define the larger picture. For example, a high-growth economy that's spreading prosperity will create a very different foundation for political and social innovation than will an anemic one. Equally, the style and form that economic globalization takes will have significant implications for the geopolitical and cultural tone of the coming decade.

Given the tumultuous economic events of the past few years, it's also useful to anchor our exploration of the future in a better understanding of the present and recent past. Many of our network members talk in detail about the causes and ramifications of the dotcom collapse, the stock market deflation, and the global economic slowdown that followed. We share their ideas in the first section of this chapter: **Whatever Happened to the New Economy?**

Looking ahead ten years, there are very significant questions surrounding the long-term potential and direction of the global economy. Some network members argue that underlying economic forces, driven by new technologies and globalization, are still strong and will pick up where they left off last decade. Highlights of this argument, based largely on the thorough work of economic historian Roger Cass, form the second section, **Getting Back on Track.**

Economist W. Brian Arthur tempers their optimism, however, with some cautionary comments on economic forecasting. He reminds us that the future is fundamentally unpredictable partly because it is created out of all of our actions, which are based on our expectations about what will happen next. We can't know beforehand how the complex interplay of many economic players acting on their own hypotheses will play out. Arthur's compelling argument forms our third section, **The Inevitability of Uncertainty.**

As if demonstrating Arthur's thesis, other network members speculate on how the global economy could follow trajectories quite different from those of the past. For example, we could see a radically decentralized global economy or an even more highly integrated one. The next big economic boom in the United States may be led by biotechnology and proceed with a greatly reduced need for foreign trade. Or entrepreneurial disruption might soon be replaced by a long period of consolidation and industrywide lock-in. These intriguing prospects are explored in **New Directions Ahead?**

Finally, several of our contributors pose questions about the global economy and financial system that reflect growing social and geopolitical concerns, especially related to the gap between those who are doing well and those who are not in our new economic era. This last section we call **Reframing the Challenge**—and it introduces an important recurring theme for this book.

Whatever Happened to the New Economy?

Busts and Booms Are Equally Irrational

Bruce Sterling ∘ I think that things tend to work in terms of bubbles and busts. The thing about busts that's interesting is that people in busts are every bit as irrational as people in bubbles. After the bubble, they devalue the bubble. They sort of grind it underfoot and say, "Well, we were completely delusional then. How could we have ever believed that of ourselves and our future?" But the bust is no more practical and hardheaded or realistic than the bubble is. In a bubble you can get money for anything, and in a bust you can't get money for even really good ideas. People freeze up. If you've got a choice, you want to bet on bubbles. Booms last 17 or 18 years, while busts don't last more than two or three years before people start shooting each other. Historically, if you've got a choice, which is the human customary mindset, we're generally in a bubble mode.

The Fundamental Reality Underlying the Bubble

Paul Saffo ∘ One of the most important lessons I learned as a forecaster was as a young child. A rancher down the road shared a folksy saying that has stuck with me and become something of a mantra. He said, "Son, never mistake a clear view for a short distance." That's what happens in a bubble like the one we just went through. People are so overwhelmed by the potential of what they're seeing. They think it's so obvious that it's going to arrive overnight.

It was obvious that the dotcom bubble couldn't sustain itself and that valuations were totally out of whack. I was also convinced that it was not like the South Seas bubble or tulipmania—it was a much more participatory bubble and informed by an underlying reality. To me the only uncertainty was the nature of the deflation. Was it going to pop explosively, or was it going to deflate like a bicycle tire with a slow leak? Now we know.

The real question is: What are the lessons that we take away from this? In the case of tulipmania, the underlying thing had no intrinsic value. In this case, there is huge, society-shaking, intrinsic value in the technologies and the processes that were going on. We obviously have seen that stuff continue quietly; it's still building. It's like watching a tsunami coming in. A tsunami can be very big in the shallows, but if you're out in the deep ocean, it passes under you unnoticed. We're still in the deep water here, and I think it will be a while before this stuff starts washing up. Next time, it will be more gradual.

The Ultimate Transaction Cost: Just Getting Online

Kees van der Heijden ∘ I don't believe that the technology market was wrong in everything it did before the crash. I don't believe that this was simply a speculative bubble. The bubble model can only lead to the conclusion that the "new economy" has gone away. I don't believe that. I think the basic economic models and business models that were being talked about made a lot of sense. I think we overlooked one detail, which came back to haunt us. We overlooked that these economic/business models could only work provided that most people were online and that they were not incurring other transaction costs by doing so. That simply was, and still is, not the case. People will only engage with the opportunities offered if they don't experience this upfront transaction cost. That means that the technology must become entirely transparent. And that's about much more than keyboards. The whole technology has to get out of the way; it must be invisible or people experience it as a barrier.

Transaction costs include everything that creates friction in the process of making economic actors informed actors. Transaction costs determine how the economy runs. They include what happens inside the company and what happens between actors in the marketplace. Until a year ago, the expectation was that these transaction costs were going to be progressively reduced. This meant that everybody would have increasing access to knowledge about all aspects of transactions that until now had been privileged. There is no doubt that such a development would completely transform the economic scene.

I think that potential's still there. Technology can remove transaction costs from the economy, and there are some areas in which it's actually happening—a good example is in the business-to-business area. And when that happens, enormous economic opportunities open up.

You have to go back a long time to find anything that's comparable to what we've just gone through. Even so I don't think we've seen anything like it happen so quickly. It was only five years ago that it was all blue sky. And then there was a sudden boom in valuation, quickly followed by a collapse. Companies went from being worth billions to being wiped off the map in a period of one year. I think it is a unique experience, a huge and interesting experiment in intervening in the economics of the marketplace. The world will learn from this. We'll gain new insights about the laws of the marketplace.

Social psychologist Kurt Lewin used to say that if you want to find out about a system too complex to understand by taking it apart, you have to give it a big kick, and carefully watch what happens. By comparing what happens with what you were expecting to happen you learn something new about the system. Well, we've just given the world economy a big kick. This is going to be food for thought for years and years to come.

The Dotcom Bust As Creative Disruption

Peter Schwartz ∘ As for the crash of Internet startups and turmoil in new economy companies, I've always maintained that economic transformations of this kind are never easy. Creative, expansive disruption brings with it upswings and downswings, and a lot of the ideas that are created out of that are not good ideas. Evolution is like that. I am not the least bit concerned. Clearly the dotcom boom got out of hand. It was crazy, a boom of excess. Having said that, issues like accessibility of broadband are important. The fact that there was a bust isn't important.

There is abundant capital. There are lots of new startups and a lot still going on. The froth on the surface simply went away. Pets.com was probably never a good idea, but eBay is still around, Amazon is still around, interesting new innovations in the consumer space are still around. A movement toward new communication and media via the Web, new Web distribution models for music—all of that is still going on. It's barely begun. This was the first ripple in a mounting wave.

The Meltdown Was Mainly in Financial Markets

Jeffrey Rayport ∘ The meltdown is a myth—except, of course, on Wall Street. How do we know that there has been a meltdown? We know because of the Nasdaq crash on April 16, 2000. We know that there have been something like 200-plus dotcom bankruptcies among public companies since that time. We know that really big-name players, like Webvan and Kozmo and Furniture.com and Garden.com, have disappeared. We also know that there's more private equity in venture capital that's been raised and is sitting in funds today than ever in the history of human life on earth, and yet it is flowing at one-fifth the rate that it was flowing in 2000.

So how do we know there was a meltdown? Because there was a meltdown in the financial world, of publicly traded equities on Wall Street, and in terms of private equity in venture capital. The reason I say it's a myth is that if you look at the trend lines regarding the impact that Internet-related technology or IT generally is having on life among the 2 billion people who live in the industrialized world, the answer is that nothing's changed. Until the courts finally shut Napster down, its growth rate to a high of 80 million users was absolutely unprecedented. ICQ, the instant messenger service owned by AOL Time Warner, has just passed the 100-million mark. Its growth rate hasn't slowed down at all. AOL Time Warner's subscribers on the AOL side are now above 30 million. Individuals' use of the Web continues to climb. The growth of shopping on the Web is down a little bit, but it's still growing, compared with a decline in the overall retail sector.

So the curious phenomenon is that it's completely schizophrenic or, at best, bimodal. On the one hand, you have the financial world, which says that every bit of the promise is a myth and this stuff was all charlatanry and it was a flash in the pan. The technology may matter, but it certainly didn't matter to the capital markets. And then you've got the world of consumers, who are consuming both the products and services at rates that are completely in keeping with what we saw in the glory days of 1996–1999. And for that reason, I think that Wall Street has blown it. I do think we took too many companies public in too short a time, and many of them didn't have viable economic models. When you take 150 companies public in 1998 and 200 more companies public in 1999, and have a 500-company run rate until the meltdown of April 2000, you may indeed have to do triage to figure out what's worth keeping and what's worth pulling the plug on. So I see this very much as a financial correction. But the fact that consumption patterns have withstood the negative publicity about the financial correction is testament to the power of this technology in terms of its increasingly (not decreasingly) profound influence on society.

The Blurring Line Between Venture Capital and Public Markets

Robert Hormats ◦ The startups were usually clear about the fact that they weren't going to make money in the near term. Companies were saying they needed to build up their franchise and develop their branding. The first generations of investors were willing to pay for that. The companies themselves figured they could go back for cash whenever they wanted it and it would be there, so they generally didn't manage their money well. When the economic downturn occurred serious questions were raised about whether there would be profits in the future. The next round of financing wasn't there. Most companies couldn't go back to the market a second time. Many didn't have a good business plan to begin with. Many would have failed even had there been no downturn.

A venture capitalist will stick with you for a while. Public markets are much more fickle and don't have that allegiance to companies. If the companies don't deliver, investors in public markets tend to take their losses and move on. For a while investors were long-term thinkers. They invested in a certain technology even if it wasn't making money at the moment. They figured it would eventually do so, so they put their money into it. For a while investors weren't actually looking at current profits. In fact, they moved away from companies that had very good current returns to companies that didn't, but the expectation was they'd be big long-term winners. They knew that a few would fail, but if you go for several, the thinking was one will connect and be a grand-slam home run.

In effect, the public equity market became a venture capital market. In the history of American capital markets, most companies didn't come to the public market until they were making money or were about to make money. They got money from banks before that. Very few companies came to the public market without some sort of track record. After the IPO successes of Amazon and Netscape, many companies came to the market with no profits and only the expectation or hope that they had medium-term prospects for making profits. So the average investor in effect became a venture capitalist, buying companies at a much earlier stage than he or she would have 10 to 15 years ago. A lot of people regarded this as get-rich-quick, and really didn't have sufficient appreciation of the risk involved. They were becoming venture capitalists without the sophistication. Most people have learned their lesson and won't go back to buying those kinds of stocks very soon. Average investors will steer clear of most startups for a long time to come.

There are some events that shape eras. The high-tech market collapse will shape the thinking of an entire generation of investors. They'll be more cautious and they'll have much more diversification in their portfolios among categories of stocks, and between stocks and bonds. It will slow the whole startup process down. I think it will make equity capital-raising much more difficult over the next 10 years.

The Lessons from History on Discontinuous Technology

Jeffrey Rayport • Every single time there has been a discontinuous moment of innovation, it has changed the possibilities for business. I'm not talking about disruptive technology; I'm talking about something truly discontinuous. The Internet is not disruptive technology; it's a new grid in the world. It's a grid like the transportation grid or the power grid. And each one of these grids has changed the way business is organized, the way business makes money, and the scope and scale with which business can operate.

It's absolutely the case that we saw a bubble in the mid-1990s similar to the bubble we saw in the mid-nineteenth century with the telegraph. There were literally dozens of telegraph companies that licensed the Marconi technology and were trying to make a go of it. They figured that if this technology was going to "change the world," then an ISP equivalent was needed—in this case a telegraphy office with a mom and pop who were transmitting messages and boosting signals. And some major financial panics drove a shakeout that wiped out the excess capacity, leaving Western Union to consolidate the industry by 1866.

The last big financial panic of the nineteenth century happened because there was a buildup of 200 railroad companies that were essentially building the information highway of their era, an infrastructure for the transportation of both raw and finished goods across the U.S. The capital requirements for building that nationwide infrastructure were so huge that they almost literally invented the modern financial markets. It was the need to finance big railroads getting built, the Pennsylvania, the B&O, and so forth, that created Wall Street, that created the New York Stock Exchange. In that era, a bunch of people got very wealthy—the so-called robber barons, the Jim Fisks and the Jay Goulds and the Cornelius Vanderbilts, who all had a part in building the financial markets and running these railroad companies. Some widows and orphans got crushed in the financial panics of the 1880s and 1890s, but after those two panics, the telegraph and railroads not only survived but also flourished.

We saw the same thing with the shakeout among car companies. At the industry's height, in the late 1910s, there were 560 independent automakers in the United States. By 1927, when the River Rouge plant was churning out Model Ts at $350 a pop, there were only three companies worth talking about and a handful of others that were competing for share.

In each one of these cases, a new infrastructure technology came along and a bunch of people said, "Communications could change the world," or "Transportation could change the world," or "Automobiles could change the world." We saw the same thing to some extent with the microelectronics revolutions after World War II. But the bottom line is that in each case, first came the realization, then came the excitement, then came the new business creation, then the froth in the market that created a financial bubble, and then the collapse of the bubble. In each case, after the bubble collapsed, a long period of growth began, and the growth was predicated on the very technology that had caused the bubble.

I think that we have emerged from a similar kind of bubble, for the simple reason that the statistics we were just talking about would certainly convince me that the impact of the Internet is much greater today than it was three years ago. And yet three years ago, the so-called Internet sector was worth 20 to 40 times what it is today.

The Legacy of Transformative Technologies and New Models

Robert Hormats ∘ One of the key points of a transformative technology is not that the individual people who develop the technology make the money. Some do, some don't. The key is that it enables many other people in a variety of sectors to become more productive and make money. Often it's not the first mover that profits most; it's those that use the technology most effectively to improve their own existing business models.

We are in and will continue to be in a period of very substantial technological progress. And remember the "new economy" wasn't just about technology; it was about better management practices, better business models, more efficiency, accelerated globalization, increased international labor mobility. The knowledge we have gained in adopting these new technologies plus breakthroughs in technologies themselves have been dramatic. Someone once said to Thomas Edison, "Mr. Edison, you have done 50 experiments and haven't developed a light bulb. Are you concerned about these failures?" Edison said, "What failures? We have learned 50 different ways not to make a light bulb." We learn by our mistakes.

Vested Interests Tried to Contain the Internet (But Can't)

Bruce Sterling ∘ I think profit motive is one of the most powerful forces in the world. I think it's the ace of spades in the deck of social change at the moment. You can trump almost anything by saying that there's no money in it. That's sort of what's being said about the Internet now. You've seen over the past year and a half a really powerfully financed and pretty well thought through campaign to damage the Internet, or at least to limit its spread to areas of profit margins and other industries. Microsoft sees Linux as a cancer, a destroyer of intellectual property. They see it as something of an ant bed. The ant bed kills the cow and you are left with a pasture that has ants, but you need a cow—a cash cow.

It's very interesting to see this stuff come out in this bald way because the classic reaction of a liberal capitalist society to a genuine innovation is co-optation. "Yeah, we'll market it! We'll sell it to the kids! We'll put it in the Gap!" This has happened so many times so far across the board that it's become a law of nature. Yet we saw this tremendous force wash up against the Internet and recoil. It's like they couldn't co-opt it. "Quick, stop the damage!

Dig the trenches! Put up the whorl wire!" Maybe they can actually stop it, in which case it kind of shrinks down to this hobbyist thing. Development was really pushed by people who were willing to invest absurd sums of money. It was like a co-optation mechanism gone haywire. Anybody who was anywhere near it was being buried in money. It's very funny to see that stuff just sort of melt away like the dew and leave what are really old questions for the Internet in command of the field.

Does information want to be free? Can you do business there? Is it commercial or is it non-commercial? Is there or is there not free speech? Do we copy software or do we let it wander around loose? Who's in command of the desktop: the operating system or the guy who owns the machine? These are some of the oldest questions in the computer industry. People tried to finesse them, to bury them beneath heaps of cash, thinking that something will work out and it will all be OK. It ain't all OK. It's not working. You can dismiss it but if they were just dismissing it they wouldn't be nearly as afraid of Linux or Napster as they are. They are genuine threats to the established order. They had to be killed. They couldn't be bought off or invested in. But it's gonna be hard to make those things disappear.

We'll Find New Business Models That Finally Do Work

Nirav Tolia ∘ We saw more innovation in the last three years than we've ever seen before. Things like Webvan failed miserably and took billions of dollars down the drain, but as a result, at some point in the future you will be able to get groceries delivered to your home. There have been great innovations, the majority of which went away because we couldn't find a business application for them.

The next 10 years are largely going to be about finding the business applications of those innovations. There is a Rubik's Cube of different technological advances and ways the world can work out there; we just have to keep turning the cube and figure out which combinations work. Innovation cannot exist for innovation's sake alone. It's got to exist hand-in-hand with application. That's what I think the next 10 years will be about.

The next five years will be about taking glimpses of the things we've seen and putting them into practice. The first example of that is Napster. Napster opened up a Pandora's box, but do you think there won't be file sharing and digital downloads as a result? We'll figure out the business model. Napster will never go away. It will be the predecessor. It's more like an evolutionary thing to me than a big bang.

Silicon Valley Will Rise Again

Paul Saffo ∘ The way I explain the crash in Silicon Valley to friends on the East Coast is that our kind of crash is really different from the kinds of crashes New York has had. In New York in '29, things went down and people jumped out of buildings. We have an architectural advantage: Our buildings are two stories high and they're surrounded by grass.

The valley is always in danger of drowning in the waste products of its own success. We need failures like this in the same way that the hills above the valley need regular brushfires to clear out the chaparral and make space for fresh growth. The thing that was really worrying me wasn't the fact that the collapse was coming, but that it was taking so long to come. We reached a point where there was no cheap office space for startups. It was hard to hire people because nobody was going anywhere. Everything was stagnating. What we need is this constant refreshing. Now we've got cheap office space and we've got lots of people with time on their hands and ideas, and they're recombining. We have venture capitalists who are starting to invest again. This failure is essential to the success of the valley.

Why did the World Wide Web take off as a commercial phenomenon in Silicon Valley? After all, it was invented by an English researcher, Tim Berners Lee, on the Swiss-French border, who thought he was developing a groupware system for academics. Here's why: Just before the World Wide Web arrived, we had an industry collapse in Silicon Valley. It was the interactive TV industry. People were transfixed by the 500-channel universe; they put hundreds of millions of dollars into companies that eventually failed. When they failed, all that was left was a financial crater big enough to be seen from the moon without field glasses.

There was one other very important thing. A whole bunch of skilled employees were thrown onto the street—skilled C++ programmers who had just been paid salaries to develop very refined media sensibilities by experts from Hollywood. Suddenly they had no jobs. They were on the street, looking around, and they said, "Hey, look at this cool thing called the World Wide Web." They discovered that all of those media sensibilities they had learned, plus their C++ skills, were directly relevant to doing things on the Web.

That's why the Web took off here and nowhere else. All of these people came out of failed companies and the same thing's happening now. The dot-com bubble trained a whole generation of young entrepreneurs who got in early. They rode it up, they rode it down—they came out. They're still 32 or 33 years old, with their whole careers in front of them. I think we just forged what will go on to be the greatest entrepreneurial generation of the last 50 years.

\

Getting Back on Track

More Computation, Communication, and Globalization

Kevin Kelly ∙ It may be that we've just come through a period where there was a convergence of forces and alignment, where the change was very obvious as it was happening. And that might not be true right now. Part of our confusion is that it's not as if the forces of the digital revolution and globalization have stopped. They're continuing. The story of the next decade is there's going to be more of the same. There's going to be more and more of it: more computation, more communication, more globalization. We say, "Well, that's not the story," because that's what's going on now. But in fact, more of that is the story.

Beyond the Uncertainty: How We Might See the Boom Resume

Peter Schwartz ∙ There's no doubt that the uncertainty surrounding the coming decade has increased. I think the fundamental mechanisms for a long boom, a vast global economic expansion, are still right, but September 11 may have been a direction-changing event. Either it was a speed bump on the road toward modernization and globalization affecting no fundamental change, in which case we're back on the long boom track fairly soon, or it was a critical moment in history and will push us in a completely new direction, for good or ill. It's too soon to know. But there's no question that in the short run, our uncertainty has increased enormously.

Still, our fundamental economic engines are very strong. The real question here is geopolitics and the war: Will we be dropping bombs and fighting a long, protracted war that becomes bigger? Taking the current trends, you'd probably say that it's going to be over soon and will on the whole have been manageable and not catastrophic. If you really believe that the economics are fundamentally sound, which I do, then once you get this war out of the way those engines begin to kick back into gear as the dominant set of forces. There are signs afoot of deeper forces of globalization and integration by Asian countries, China, and Russia. These were maybe even accelerated by the war and its coalition building.

Biotechnology, new energy technologies, and nanotechnology are moving faster than we thought. Fuel cells are advancing at least as fast, maybe faster. In fact, most of the underlying technological changes are indeed happening as fast or faster than we anticipated. The underlying economic engines of growth that were significant before are still very significant—as long as the politics don't disrupt them. That's why the war is so important. A big rise in terrorism is one of our big scenario-killers.

A Long-Wave Theory Explaining Vast Economic Expansions

Roger Cass ∘ Let me try to summarize the theoretical basis of long booms. The conventional long-wave theory—the Kondratieff wave—is based on a price cycle. Kondratieff was a Russian economist who lent his name to these theories and chronologies on long waves, price cycles, inflation, and deflation and who died in the 1930s. My view is quite different; I don't subscribe to the price cycle. It worked well in the nineteenth century when commodity prices affected economic behavior substantially. But the work I've done in the past 30 years revolves around two other sets of data. One is trends in global liquidity: the availability of liquidity in the global system as measured by money supply, international reserve assets, and international bank lending or cross-border lending. You can measure those pretty precisely for a hundred years or so.

The other data set is waves of technology—technological innovation—which have been measured in various ways by various studies. For example, the Dutch and the Germans have done some richly detailed studies on patent filings and other measures that show peaks of creativity or innovation in the middle of down cycles. It's the theory of "necessity as the mother of invention"; as entrepreneurs are thrown out of work or are forced back onto their own resources, they tend to become incredibly creative. We've seen this in the 1980s and the 1930s, in the 1880s and the 1830s.

Once you begin to see such innovation happening, usually within about a ten-year period as you move toward the end of the down cycle, the funding and venture capital to turn those innovations into commercial products begins to expand. Of course when the economic cycle turns up, bank lending becomes more available and interest rates in real terms start to come down rather than going up, which is perhaps contrary to conventional wisdom. This combination of the innovation that occurred in the down cycle and the liquidity and increase in venture capital of the new expansion cycle fuel the next generation of technologies. Innovation and liquidity are really combined because if you don't have the financing for innovation then it simply doesn't get commercialized.

Usually the technology cycle runs about ten to fifteen years in terms of its impact on capital investment. Then after the midpoint of the expansion cycle, you get an excess of capital investment. Expansion cycles end through excesses of one form or another. As economic activity outruns available resources, price pressures build. Too much capital investment has been put into place and satisfies underlying demand for a period of years. You begin to see—and in the last expansion cycle we saw this around 1965 or so—the capital investment boom beginning to slow down before the actual cycle ends.

You can look at patterns within down cycles and up cycles that occur with unfailing frequency in all the prior cycles. A down cycle, just to give you an idea, is marked by an initial severe recession, like the one that occurred in 1974–1975, right after the oil shock. Then you have a bounce of about three to four years, as in 1976–1979, followed by the central recession, or depression, which occurred at the end of the first 10 years. That was the global economic downturn in 1980–1983 when we were as close to depression as we have come since the 1930s. Next you have the secondary recovery and then the final washout recession or "clearance sale" when bad assets are written off; that took place about 1990–1992. Once you get that final washout recession then you are ready for the next boom, the next long boom, or the next long expansion.

I've also looked at how the stock market behaves in expansion cycles and down cycles. What I've found is pretty interesting. Usually if you buy equities in the midpoint of a down cycle, and sell them at the midpoint of an up cycle, about 10 to 12 years in, you will make some nice returns. The converse is true with bonds. You sell bonds at the midpoint of a down cycle and buy them at the midpoint of an up cycle. Your asset allocation switches quite dramatically somewhere along the midpoint as you get into these periods.

We began a bull market in 1982, which was the midpoint of the last down cycle—which went from 1973 to 1993. Since then we've had one of the greatest bull markets in history. The Dow has gone from 1000 in 1982 to 11,000, with similar increases in the S&P and even bigger growth in the Nasdaq. Now the sell point comes at the midpoint of the up cycle. I'm talking about the up cycle beginning in 1993, and ending sometime around 2016 or thereabouts. We're talking about a peak in this market around 2006 or 2007, which is my top for this bull market. In the interim, of course you don't go straight up. You have periods where the market gets ahead of itself. This happened at the end of 1999.

A Positive Scenario of Sustained Global Growth

Roger Cass • The up cycle is marked by extended expansion, which occurred in 1994–2000. There may be brief recessions or downturns, usually because we've generated some excess in the financial markets or in capital spending. In this case high-tech capital spending ran for five years at a 20–25 percent annual rate, which was simply unsustainable. The other key factor is redundancy in terms of high technology. Because these booms are so creative and dramatic, the new generations of technologies become like breeder reactors and create new technologies. Today you're going from legacy systems to next-generation systems in the fiber optic and telecommunications areas. You see companies that get behind the curve in terms of their fundamental technologies, like Lucent and Nortel and Cisco, being penalized dramatically. Other companies that are on the leading edge of the next generation of technologies, like Ciena, ONI Systems, and some smaller companies I can mention, are going to do well over the next six or seven years. Those are the companies you should focus on.

What is key in a period like 2000–2001 is disinvestment—noninvestment—the creative destruction. The key to the dynamism of the American economic system, as opposed to those of Japan and the Soviet Union, is that those economies never disinvested; they never bit the bullet. In those cases it happened for political and ideological reasons more than for economic reasons. In our country we have a free market and capital markets that work. Businesses are penalized in the financial markets unless they bite the bullet, take their write downs, go through their layoffs, get costs under control, and move on to the next stage. That's what we're going through now, in my opinion. We're in a transition period that will extend from 2000 probably into the first half of 2002, maybe a little longer in some areas of high tech. But the economy in general is not in bad shape.

Unfortunately there seems to be a prevailing view that the glass is half-empty right now, rather than half-full. Too much focus is on the 8 percent of GDP that is high tech, rather than the 75–80 percent that is consumer spending, housing, and other areas of the economy that are holding up very well. We're beginning to build the confidence and the economic data that will support higher market levels. Then we'll move into the next phase of this great technology boom that will extend for the best part of another decade. This is not only telecoms and fiber optics—it's biotech; it's nanotech; it's all of these things combining to create an explosive increase in living standards. It's a global technology cycle this time around that's not limited to a few industrial nations. We're seeing the benefits of the technological revolution in Asia, Latin America, and around the world.

It should plot out like this: 1994–2000 was the initial boom expansion of the long wave; 2000–2002 will be the transition phase as we move into the next level of those technologies, which are driving the expansion; and 2003–2008 will be another dramatic phase of economic growth and productivity around the world. After that things will begin to slow down. Markets don't turn down necessarily, but we won't have the same kind of rapid growth. Capital investment begins to reach a saturation point sometime between 2010 and 2015 or so. Inflation rears its head again as we begin to stretch the limits of scarce resources. The productivity gains begin to diminish. We begin entering the phase that will lead into the next down cycle, beginning, in my view, sometime between 2015 and 2020.

There's usually a catalyst for these cycles—some identifiable event that triggers the next down cycle. I don't know what is going to trigger the one 15 years or so from now—perhaps an environmental problem.

Projecting Global and Regional Growth

Roger Cass • The last long up cycle from 1947–1973 was the golden age of the global economy. Between 1947 and 1973 you had real GDP growth annually of 4.8 percent, and 5.5 percent in annual industrial production. Then from '74–'93 you see the difference in the rates of growth. Industrial production, which had grown at 5.5 percent in the expansion cycle, grew at 2.4 percent in the down cycle. Capital spending globally grew at 5.9 percent and 2.7 percent respectively, and world trade at 8.7 percent and 4.4 percent. Consumer prices doubled. The big thing is liquidity growth shrunk to zero in this period from 5.9 percent annually in the expansion cycle.

In our expansion from 1994–2000 the rates pretty much emulated 1947–1973. GDP, industrial production, capital spending are very similar. Trade compares: 8.5 percent to 8.7 percent. Liquidity compares: 5.1 percent to 5.9 percent.

Going forward for the next 20 years, I've got Europe growing overall at 3.1 percent from 2001 to 2020, the United States and North America at 4.3, Japan at 3.8, Australia and Australasia at 3.6, and the OECD overall at 3.7 percent. So Europe is the laggard, but that's pretty good compared with growth of 2 percent in the '70s and 1 percent in the early '90s. It's certainly not as high as the post–World War II reconstruction growth that was 5.2 percent annually.

The focus will be on Asia because that's where the huge populations are with the most potential for economic growth. The two largest economies in the world in terms of population are China and India, both growing at over 6 percent. Imagine if they can keep that up and we can get the benefits of the technological revolution in both countries. India is fascinating to me. It's potentially one of the most dynamic economies in the world if they can get out from under government regulation. India has a very sophisticated high-tech work force; we've been employing them in droves in the U.S for software and programming. India could become one of the world's dominant economies.

Asia certainly has the potential to regenerate rates of growth of 6–7 percent. The average growth rate from 1994–2000 was 6.6 percent. For the prior 30 or 40 years it was 7–8 percent. I've got 6.7 percent as my Far East projection for the next 20 years vs. 4.3 percent for America. When you've got one billion people in China and one billion in India, that's a third of the world's population in two countries alone, both growing at a rate of 6–7 percent. That's a hell of a potential for the global growth rate. My forecast for the aggregated global growth rate is 4.7 percent on a purchasing parity basis, and 4 percent simply on an exchange rate basis.

Global Labor Markets Now Open for Service

Nirav Tolia ∘ We have started to farm out a lot of our labor-intensive tasks to India. It's two dollars a day to get someone to do the same thing that you'd otherwise pay an American worker $40,000 a year to do. In these third-world countries you have two things going on: overpopulation, which means the value of human labor is way down, and a currency that is largely devalued. The whole cost of living is lower. Here, we pay customer service reps $30,000 a year, and they can hardly afford to live in the Bay Area. Pay someone in India $2,000 a year and that person is rich.

A huge market for human labor is going to be opened up. On the Internet, you can do stuff without being in the same place at the same time. As an entrepreneur, I'm thinking there's a huge opportunity to go start a company in India. Those companies will be able to take their natural asset, which is human labor, and be a lot more efficient in deploying it. In a way, it's the new generation of manufacturing—made in China, made in India. You're going to get a customer service email from Amazon.com, and at the bottom it's going to say "Made in India." That's the way this stuff is going to work. In most cases, it's a win-win.

The Next Wave of Productivity Growth in the Service Sector

Roger Cass ∘ So far the impact of technology on productivity has all been in the manufacturing sector, where productivity growth has been close to 5 percent. In large chunks of the tertiary or service sector, which is actually 70 percent of our economy, the official figures are not showing any productivity growth. That's partly because they haven't managed to measure it properly yet, but it's also a function of the learning curve. When productivity growth rates in retail, banking, and financial services catch up with manufacturing, the U.S. economy will blow through 6 percent GDP growth. We'll be growing at the rate of third-world or developing countries. I think that's entirely feasible within the next 10 years.

Productivity growth is there, but it's not being measured in the official data; it doesn't show up. We're understating real GDP growth and overstating inflation. Some revisions are starting to trickle through: productivity growth in the service sector was once lumped into five or so broad categories and now we're developing 20, 30, 40 subcomponents to measure it effectively. As these come through in the official numbers that are accepted by business and the public at large, then we'll see that our economy is growing far faster and with less inflation.

In addition to not measuring the current state of affairs accurately, we have to recognize that another productivity bonus will develop as we move up the learning curve in terms of technology. Generally, it takes 10 years or more to use new technology effectively, although this periodicity is also shrinking rapidly. In past technology cycles the acceptance took far longer; it took 40 or 50 years to get automobile use up to 50 percent of the population. Now new technology is accepted within five or ten years on a mass basis. Obviously the productivity gains from these inventions are going to accelerate.

The Inevitability of Uncertainty

The Theoretical Problem with Forecasting

W. Brian Arthur ∘ I am interested in models involving forecasting. There are a lot of examples in economic systems. The stock market is one where the behavior you take—whether you buy or sell Intel or Cisco—depends very much on what you think Intel or Cisco stock will be worth in three days or three months or in a year's time. Nobody's disputing that. Similarly, you buy a house based partly on what you think it might be worth in 10 years' time. It may seem that forecasting is straightforward. But it isn't when you are trying to forecast what other people are also trying to forecast.

Here's an example. There's a bar in Santa Fe I used to go to called El Farol. On Wednesday nights it used to have Irish music. But the bar gets stuffy and crowded if too many people go. So this inspired the following problem that became very famous as the "El Farol Problem." Imagine 100 people are thinking about going to El Farol. The bar only holds 60 comfortably, so each one is trying to forecast how many people will be there that evening. So you have 100 people separately and without communication trying to figure out if they should go to El Farol that evening. Each one obeys the same rule: If he thinks fewer than 60 will show up, he goes. If he thinks more than 60, he doesn't go.

Now let's imagine that nearly everybody is forecasting that it will be crowded tonight. Nearly everyone won't go, so that will negate that forecast. Let's say that nearly everyone—85 people—are expecting fewer than 40 to show up. Then those 85 will show up, which will negate the fewer than 40. So in this case if people have similar forecasts—and economics is built on this notion, that we all will do the same thing under the same circumstances—those similar forecasts will negate each other. You then have a Yogi Berra situation. He remarked about Toots Shor's restaurant in New York, "That place is so crowded that nobody goes there anymore." For me the theoretical problem was: How does one form forecasts in a situation where if we all formed the same forecast, that forecast would be immediately negated? The outcome is basically formed by our forecasts.

This applies in the real world. Let's say there are 100 firms in technology laying fiber-optic cable. If they all expect that they will lay too much cable, they will not want to lay much the next year. These sorts of problems come up all the time. You have to expect that the demand will be there, whether it's in high tech or anywhere else, before you want to make a product.

A great deal of business operates on forecasts. Not even formal forecasts. I want to grow soybeans. I may not have a formal forecast, but I'm not going to grow them unless I think I can get decent money in the market and that there is a demand for them. So all over the economy you find that actions are taken because of what we expect is going to happen in the future. I wanted to get the simplest model of forecasting that was interesting. So I chose one in which if everybody believed the same thing, all of those beliefs would be negated. If all 100 thought that only 24 people would come, they would all show up. They would have forecasted 24, but the actual would have been 100.

The point I wanted to make was that in business, it's not just action that counts—it's an interplay among hypotheses as to what's going to happen next.

There Are No Correct Answers in Envisioning the Future

W. Brian Arthur • El Farol is a well-defined forecasting situation with a bad outcome. But high tech is worse. Its situation is inherently ill defined. Imagine that the CEOs of high tech are thinking of going into wireless or proteomics or genomics—something trendy. All 50 of these people are on the prow of the ship. There is a fog of technology, like a fog of war. Some have bad vision through this fog and some have good vision. Bill Gates, by the way, is one of the top vision people for seeing what's coming next. Why should there be a fog of technology? Basically, if you're getting your company positioned, there are a

lot of things you don't know. You don't know how well your technology is
going to work. You don't know who else is going to be in the game or who your
competitors are going to be. You don't know how their technology is going to
work. You don't know whether the public or other businesses will be interested. You have ideas about all of these things, but none of these are particularly well known. High tech entrepreneurs live in a world of indeterminacy.

So go back to the CEOs on the prow of a ship. They are moving toward a
city, if you like; the city is the future. As the ship moves forward through the
fog they can start to see the outlines of the city. But actually the city is created, or the future is created, by the actions the other CEOs are going to
take, and those are predicated on their beliefs. So you're a CEO trying to
form beliefs or forecasts or more generally a vision about a situation that is
forming from the visions of others. Formally and logically, in this situation,
forecasting is indeterminate. The more high tech the economy becomes, the
more we are in a situation where there is no correct answer.

I want to make this point very strongly: There is no correct answer. In
business, people think that if only they were smart enough they could come
upon a correct answer. That is, if we all had immense IQs, were wise and had
plenty of experience, breadth, and depth of vision, we could see through the
fog. But in many cases that does not mean that there will be a correct answer. In high tech—this sounds theoretical or even philosophical, but this is
a practical point—if you're strategizing at the strategic level here, management ought to be confused.

The Casino of Technology Strategizing

W. Brian Arthur • I have this metaphor of a casino of technology. Imagine
all technology strategizing takes place in a big casino. There are gaming tables
everywhere, and the Larry Ellisons and Bill Haseltines of the world are all
wandering from table to table wondering which game to join. There's a new
game forming—let's say it's broadband or digital banking. Bill Haseltine, who
runs Human Genome Sciences, is the first to the table and he says, "I want to
play this game." The croupier says, "Fine, Mr. Haseltine. You can play."

Haseltine says, "How much will it be to ante up?" The croupier says, "For
you it will be $4 billion." Haseltine says, "Fine, who else will be playing?" The
croupier says, "We do not know until they arrive." So Haseltine says, "OK. What
products are we going to be playing with?" The croupier says, "We do not know
until we see them." Haseltine asks, "How well will they work?" The croupier
says, "No one knows that until the future." Haseltine replies, "What are the
rules?" The croupier says, "The rules will be formed when people sit down."

Haseltine has to decide whether to play or not. If he waits until the game is fully in progress, it will be too late. Under a condition like that, whether you take very smart people like Haseltine or Gates or Craig Barrett, there is no correct answer. So what a CEO in high tech has to do is figure out scenarios or figure out backup strategies.

It's very much like driving a car at night. You can only see as far as your headlights and you can easily run off the road. You have to react to things as they unfold. But nevertheless, to drive safely at a reasonable speed, you do have to have a picture in your mind that you won't round the corner and find a brick wall. For these reasons, high tech is different from what went before.

New Directions Ahead?

Growth Without Globalization Through a Biotech-Led Boom?

Steven Weber ∘ The conventional way to think about the next big phase of productivity, economic growth, and new production in the West is that it will be like the old one, except bigger and better. So it would be extensive. It would be export oriented. It would be trade oriented. That sort of economic growth and the expansion of the global economy go together. And that's been true for the past 45 years.

It was a little less true during the mid-'90s because a lot of what we were doing was actually investing in stuff that was happening here in the United States internally. But still, you always see global trade growing faster than global economic growth, and that's been the paradigm of mid- to late-twentieth-century, late industrial capitalism. And I think if we go back to that kind of growth paradigm, then it's hard to see jump-starting that growth phase without settling some of this geopolitical stuff. We need a modicum of stability because growth would be dependent on vibrant export markets and stable foreign exchange markets.

I've been toying around with an alternative picture where political instability on a global level is a parameter for 15 to 20 years. Could the United States have a paradigm of intensive growth that would not be constrained to the same degree by instability around the rest of the globe? In other words, could you have a new sort of paradigm of growth without globalization? And that's what brought me to this notion of an intensive biotech-led economy. Think about it. For an auto-led economy or a steel-led economy to grow it has to become globalized at a certain point. That's even true to a significant degree for information technology. But I wonder if it's as true for some of the stuff in biotechnology.

Advances don't need to be exported. Pharmaceutical companies lose money when they export drugs. The most sensible thing for them—and in a sense they're trying to do this—is to disconnect foreign markets. Their nightmare, the reason they don't want to sell drugs at cost in Africa, is because they're afraid that those drugs are going to get re-exported back into the United States. So they have no interest in globalization, in a funny way. Their only interest in globalization is getting the biological property that's out there in the Amazon, and they probably won't need that for very long either because it can eventually be created in a test tube.

So is there a new paradigm of growth? Up until recently my view was like everybody else's, which was that the way forward was towards an increasingly frictionless global economy. That now has a whole new set of transaction costs: increased security, more difficult to travel, shipping is slowed considerably. So that means trade becomes more expensive. That's the sand in the wheels of the global economy, and probably the consensus view is that it reduces global economic growth.

But I started to wonder if that was necessarily the case. Could it actually increase the incentives for people who want to develop a different paradigm of growth, that perhaps we don't need the world economy in the way we thought we did because all this import/export stuff is messy and difficult? A lot of the stuff we want to do in biotech, for example, doesn't require import/export and, in fact, could be done in an intensive fashion at home. More than 15 percent of our gross national product gets spent on health care. What happens if that becomes 40 percent? That could be a huge source of intensive economic growth, which would, to a considerable degree, be delinked from the global economy.

It's unilateralism becoming isolationism: we're engaging on our terms, and you need us more than we need you. There's some truth in that. That's Condoleeza Rice's view of the world—and she's not wrong. It may not be the best long-term political strategy, but from an economic perspective, the U.S. has a track record of doing that.

A Radically Decentralized or Integrated Global Economy?

Kevin Kelly ∘ We're moving from this theory of globalization to the actual living of it, and trying to grapple with the specific issues of what it really means to be global. One of the things that is still unresolved in my own mind is if you made a model of the ideal global economy, does it make the most sense to have only a few specialists make the things we need and have them ship those things to wherever they're needed, or does it actually make more sense to have many local origins for those things? If you were to invent the ideal global marketplace, does Indonesia specialize? Should all the forks of the world be made in Jakarta because they make them best, and then be shipped everywhere? Or should forks be made in every city in these little tiny micro-fork plants that can make forks or spoons or whatever it is that you need? Or doesn't that matter? We don't know. There is some ecological advantage to having things made locally, but there's also some ecological price to having things made locally. So, in other words, if you think about the earth as one large system that is all interconnected, what would be the ideal, efficient way to do things?

That's a critical uncertainty in global manufacturing. Does it become intensely specialized, with global specialization? Or does it become globally distributed? And you can see it going either way right now. Or it may come down to the economics of a particular thing. Maybe you centralize or specialize all the chips, but you do plastic locally.

Heading into an Economic "Lock-In"?

Lawrence Wilkinson • For the past seven years or so, my hobby has been to look for signs of lock-in, to see if I could see it coming. Simply defined, lock-in is when an industry moves out of the rough-and-tumble of many competitors and much more innovation into a more stable structure, and a handful of companies emerge to dominate for the long haul of the lock-in. A classic example would be the big three U.S. automakers—GM, Ford, Chrysler—in the postwar boom.

The problem with signs of lock-in is that there are lots and lots of false positives. But we're in a moment now where the massive consolidation that's happening in the wake of the downturn of the markets, in the Western world anyway, is aided and abetted by what's called deregulation. There are lots of things that might lead you to think, "Ah, we're on the down ramp now." Then you look around and you think that perhaps this is not over yet, that the center of gravity is simply shifting from the tech sector to life sciences.

Even then, I don't think that the full flower of the impact of information and telecommunications technology, for instance, has been felt. Last night, I started riffing through the companies that offer very elaborate mathematical techniques for maximizing value chain operations. Now, if a fraction of what these guys say is true—and I have reason to believe that more than a fraction is—and if it spreads broadly, then it will have a revolutionary impact on everything from reordering the retail hierarchy through to a complete change in the operating economics of industries at large. This hasn't begun to be felt yet, but since that genie's out of the bottle, it will be.

We're at an interesting moment that has symptoms that are unfortunately characteristic either of the transition into a lock-in or the gentle water between rapids. When you're in it you never know, if you've not been down the river before, whether it's the gentle water after the rapids or the gentle water between. That's where we are right now—not that this could be characterized particularly as exactly gentle.

The real question is: What's the pace of innovation going to be? The big difference between the transition and a lock-in is that in a lock-in, the ability of the people in control to manage the pace of innovation holds. What you get is a lot of incremental innovation—planned obsolescence, as it were. What you don't get is a lot of leapfrogging of generations or dueling standards—all the sort of stuff we've lived with. On the one hand it's great to live with all the sort of stuff we've lived with for the past 20 years because it's been so exciting. On the other hand, it's a real pain in the ass. So, there are "advantages" in either case. And either way, neither is a world in which change stops; innovation simply has a different pace, a different character.

I suspect that we may not get an economywide lock-in, but rolling periods of transitional economic lock-ins. So we may see the whole healthcare arena explode into transition even as telecom implodes into some kind of lock-in. Now I don't know that that's going to happen, but it's possible. We'll know that we're no longer in a transitional position when concepts like planned obsolescence make sense again.

Some more traditional consultants with whom I've worked have a maxim that all markets tend toward "rational competition." It's a euphemism for oligopolistic behavior; it's the rule of three. All markets tend toward there being three competitors, which manage the market together under the leadership of the number one competitor. So all three are profitable, but with profits growing disproportionately relative to their rank in the oligopoly. It's classic Econ 101 stuff—and the essence of lock-in. It will happen at some point; it's just that the path and the pace from here are murky, and I'm not sure we're there yet.

Still, it's useful, I think, to try to identify the players who might succeed in grabbing the leadership in a lock-in—leadership that's very hard to dislodge once it's set—because they, and their behavior, can help us understand the forces that might propel us out of transition.

Reframing the Challenge

Our Global Economy Is Different from Anything Before

Kevin Kelly ○ I think that one of the surprises we have not absorbed yet is the fact that a single global market is qualitatively different than a world of national markets, starting with vocabulary. Almost all economics talks about things like imports and exports, which almost becomes meaningless if you have one global market. We don't talk about imports and exports from California to Nevada. It's not a very useful way of looking at our economy, to divide up all the states and see how they're doing.

But trade and all these issues revolve around things like the idea that you could have competing national economies. I'm not saying that economies don't compete any longer, but when you have a global market, I think there's an entirely new level of dynamic that takes place. It's like when you say, "There's no place to dump waste." When you try and throw something away, there's no "away" in a true global ecology. There is also a sense in which there is no outside. To me, a lot of economics has this sense of there being an outside, there being somebody who's not in your economy. And I think that's the difference—with a true global market there's no one who's outside of it.

A global economy may be more robust. But it may not be, or I should say, it may have other weaknesses that we haven't yet explored. One of the problems with having a single economy, of course, is that if it does get bad, there ain't anything else. And this is why I'm not so quick to say that it's robust. If it gets sick, that means everybody in the world's going to get sick. What we need to do is explore how a single global economy is different from a world of many national economies. And I don't think we've done that yet.

This is quite bold—I may come to regret this one—but I think that the global economy might allow us to actually make economics more of a science. I could imagine a renaissance in economics coming from a serious study and exploration of a single economy rather than multiple economies. In other words, I could imagine the field of economics being revived by theories and observations and understanding built around the fact that there is only one economy, ignoring the artificial segregations of national economies.

How Capitalism Must Evolve to Survive

Robert Hormats ○ There is less confidence that globalization is the right answer. There is more pushback and less acceptance of the centrality of the U.S. business and economic market. A lot of countries have, in effect, rebelled or exhibited resistance to American economic influence even though they have not rejected free market principles. We see in Europe today resistance to U.S. pressure on environmental issues, trade, and a whole range of other concerns. There is a growing self-assertion on the part of the Europeans, the Japanese, and others. The notion that the unfettered global market is the unifying economic idea of our age has now encountered resistance. It's not the orderly, unified, market-centered, America-centered world many expected to see.

These forces of resistance are not necessarily permanent, but in a way they are almost a logical reaction to what seemed to be the centralizing, homogenizing set of features and ideas of the system. The Europeans, the Japanese, and others are becoming less accepting of the unfettered free market; you get a lot of people saying globalization infringes on their culture and causes great uncertainty in their economies. The dotcom collapse and Enron have soured the atmosphere regarding the American financial model.

It's not just the Seattle or Genoa effect; it's more "the market is good, but we need our own homegrown domestic institutions." These cannot be swept aside by globalization, although they have to change to accommodate globalization. Globalization without strong domestic institutions, such as an effective social security system, laws to protect intellectual property, good financial regulation, and sound corporate governance, make countries less prepared to deal with globalization. You need social cohesion and stability at home. Globalization that disrupts this is very troublesome to countries and societies. Laws and institutions cannot be imposed from abroad. They must be homegrown and enjoy a reasonable level of domestic support.

What caused the change, in no particular order, is that the U.S. was seen as excessively arrogant, sort of in-your-face, if you will, about its success, like high five-ing in the end zone. It was a little too much for the rest of the world. The second was that the changes in technology were so breathtaking that there almost had to be a pause to catch up. A lot of technology has been seen in emerging nations as benefiting the few relative to the many. There is, in a way, almost an inherent tension between capitalism and democracy in the near term. In the long run, capitalism and democracy work very well together, because capitalism allows more and more people the opportunity to succeed. It underpins democracy in that sense. It also enhances pluralism and empowers more people with a wide range of opportunities to improve their lives. But during a transitional period to capitalism, it benefits relatively few people very quickly. Many people appear to be left behind. It happened in the beginning of the 1900s, too. Society eventually catches up. But the lag leads to frustration and populist pressures.

While that transition is going on, there is a feeling that a few people gain a great deal while many others do not. This has caused some people in emerging nations to doubt the broad benefits of capitalism, new technologies, and globalization. There is a divergence in incomes, too much widening of the income gap. The people who want to catch up have the feeling that their lives are being disrupted. Trade should benefit large numbers of people, and does in time. But certain people seem to be the quick winners and others perceive themselves as the losers.

In the long run, capitalism and democracy are mutually supportive. The freedom of competition, to develop and explore new ideas, opens up vast opportunities for people to succeed economically. Capitalism is an inclusive system, and brings more and more people into it. Growth means you hire and train more people, and more people have the opportunity to become entrepreneurs. It fosters economic and social upward mobility. But prosperity doesn't go in a single seamless line.

In the dramatic spurts of growth in the late eighteenth and early twentieth centuries, capitalism seemed to be beneficial to relatively few people. It took a lot of time for the others to catch up. There was a great deal of fear. There were laws enacted against chain stores, for instance, due to the fact they were disruptive to the ma-and-pa stores. Workers felt that powerful companies tread on their interests. Many companies did abuse their power. And the government acted to counter that. In the current period what will enable others to catch up is training and education for the new jobs and opportunities for the current century. That was essential to U.S. growth and social stability a hundred years ago—the education of large numbers of people.

I have been reading the history of other periods of transformation. In 1815, Britain was at the peak of its game; it beat Napoleon and pioneered the Industrial Revolution. They were the America of that time, untouchable. What happened? There were a lot of things, but the most troublesome to their future was the British elite's failure to understand that they had to help educate the children of the lower-income groups; whereas Germany, then later the U.S., spent a lot of resources on education. That's how people catch up and feel more powerful. Americans who feel disenfranchised and have their lives disrupted will feel much more comfortable if they or their children can be educated for the new jobs of the century. That means ongoing adult education plus improved education for younger people, particularly minorities. Current minorities are going to be the fastest growing portion of the labor force over the next two to three decades. If they are not well educated, the entire economy will suffer—and social stability will as well.

The Despair of Samson As a Parable of Our Times

Huston Smith ∘ Mahatma Gandhi once said, "When people are on the brink of starvation, the only way that God can appear to them is in the form of bread." In a way, religion is a shell until we have the economic and political context. So you come to me seeking wisdom on the infinite, the eternal, and things like that, and I want to double it back to the business community, saying, "Look, the ball is primarily in your hands now."

Politics follows the dollar, who gets what, when, and where, and how and how much. That's what politics is really about. So the economic is really the heart of the tremendous crisis we are in. The clearest evidence is that, by my understanding, the rich are getting richer and the poor are getting poorer. The question is, is anybody at the helm? I'm talking about businessmen. Is anybody running this show, or is technology so out of hand that no one even knows how to turn this around? By turning it around, I mean lessening the gap between the rich and the poor.

Technology brings us invaluable benefits. I would be in a wheelchair today without my surgical hip replacement. We know about the benefits of technology, but one of the ways in which the world turned over on September 11 is that it punctured forever the myth of historical progress through technology. We've been living that pipe dream for 300 years, even though the writing has been on the wall for a long time. Now there's nowhere to hide. We've never suffered a direct attack. We've assumed that two oceans and neighbors on either side left us secure. Now we know that's an illusion. By upping our security forces we may catch the first 24 attempts, but there will always be a twenty-fifth attempt. Now we're talking nuclear and germ warfare. It's a tremendously scary time.

Now what could turn this around? My tentative answer is to give hope to not the third world, but the "two-thirds world," where UN statistics predict that there will be 5 billion people living on the verge of starvation by 2025. Give hope to the Middle East. The reason for the Islamic terrorists' fury isn't religion—it's economics. Within the Muslim world, there is despair. If people are in despair, they're going to lash out, and even their own individual lives don't count for anything.

I think of the story of Samson, in the Hebrew scriptures, chained to these huge pillars of the temple. He's helpless. Since there's no hope, he might as well bring the temple down even on himself, so he pulls the pillars in and he dies, but the temple collapses too. It's a parable for our time.

Toward a New World Order
Geopolitics and Governance

"If we don't decisively defeat transnational terrorism, we're looking somewhere in the next 10 years at a strike with a weapon of mass destruction, and that will change everything forever."

John Arquilla

"The Middle East is, in a weird way, the other part of the West, the other half of the Roman Empire and of the Mediterranean world. They have known us for 1,400 years and have been at war with us for most of that time. Until the eighteenth or nineteenth century, they thought they were winning—and usually were."

Gwynne Dyer

"This narrow globalization, this product-based globalization, has now reached a threshold where the intimacy on the economic side is such that if we remain miles apart culturally and politically and institutionally and legally, we are schizophrenic. It is like sharing a house with someone you don't trust. Can you do that? No."

Albert Bressand

"Ichiro Suzuki, the Seattle Mariners baseball player, is a good example of what the Japanese need to do—go overseas for success. Take risks like Ichiro and you will be rewarded. Until now the Japanese were very intolerant of failure. They need to try new things, perhaps fail at a few, and accept it."

Hirotaka Takeuchi

"The Chinese have the needle in their arm in terms of the information technology revolution. They use information for business, but they don't want it to infect other areas of life in a way that might undermine one-party rule. But information tends to be unruly."

Orville Schell

"I think we're seeing the first worldwide uprising. We've never seen one before . . . It is not as yet a political movement. It's a social movement. And we're seeing just the beginnings of it."
Paul Hawken

We may finally be emerging from the post–Cold War era into a world that will be defined positively for what it is, rather than what it is not. Indeed, several network members suggest that this period is analogous to the years immediately following World War II when the West reframed its understanding of the ongoing security threat and set in motion a Cold War that lasted for more than 30 years. Today, transnational terrorism may be the new threat accelerating changes. And globalization, rather than World War, is the deeper force that has disrupted established power configurations and launched new struggles over the shape and control of an emergent world order.

The terrorist attacks of September 11, 2001, may have been the catalyzing event that redefines geopolitics and marks the beginning of the new era. But they may not have been—and we cannot allow them to eclipse other long-term dynamics at play. In this chapter we step back and look at the major developments in geopolitics and governance that stand out today. There is no attempt to achieve completeness in our broad sweep across this domain. Some regions of the world are not covered here, though they are discussed in other chapters. Instead, we focus on six highly uncertain and underexplored areas undergoing structural change, around which we have organized this chapter.

The first is **Terrorism and Security**. Just how dangerous will the next decade be? Some answers are hardly reassuring: a possible proliferation of terrorists, suitcase nuclear bombs, biological weapons, and potential damage—physically, economically, and psychologically—far in excess of anything experienced before. The slightly better news: a range of defensive countermeasures is likely to emerge to minimize the risks. The second, related theme is **The Future of the Islamic Middle East**. This section is informed by a deep historical perspective on this once-powerful region, which may shed light on future developments. With that in mind, some of our contributors fear that more fundamentalist regimes are inevitable while others argue that the shock of September 11 and subsequent developments will spur the region into a decade of rapid modernization and democratization.

The third theme is **The New Roles of the United States and Europe**. While the Islamic Middle East witnessed the gradual loss of power and influence over the last several centuries, the United States and Europe saw a dramatic rise in theirs. Indeed, the United States is becoming so powerful that, for the first time in history, the conditions might be created that prevent the rise of a rival power bloc. As one member speculates, if no one can beat the United States, then everyone might join them. Others warn, however, that the United States could emerge as a "rogue superpower" countered even by allies. Some European network members argue that Europe's experience of the last decade has better prepared it for the challenges of the next: increasing integration beyond economic ties. Europe may provide world leadership in how to politically, legally, and institutionally integrate between nation states. It might even lead the way toward more global governance and a global civil society—themes that will be explored more fully in the final chapter on Civilization and Infrastructure.

Next our network members reflect upon **The Plight and Potential of Japan**. We start by discussing the depth of the problems confronting that country and its rapid descent in recent years from a model worthy of emulation to an object of anxious concern. But a couple of contributors also affirm, with some optimism, the strengths that may serve Japan well in the coming decade. The fifth theme is **The Emerging Powers of China, India, and Russia**. The West's relations with emerging powers, especially its former Cold War enemies, China and Russia, remains in considerable flux—as do these countries themselves. While making obvious efforts to integrate into the global economy, they also face daunting internal challenges in rebuilding and reorienting their societies. These efforts pose huge risks and huge opportunities—not only to themselves but also to the world at large.

Finally, as globalization disturbed the power relations between nations, it also helped create a transnational force with no geographic home. **The Anti-Globalization Movement** provides our final theme. Some define this amorphous movement as youth or the progressive left in the developed world who seek to rectify the damaging side effects of globalization. Others consider the movement as giving voice to an even larger group: the poor billions of the developing world who are powerless and suffering in the new global economy. A case could be made that this movement is not anti-globalization but anti-corporatization. If so, the backlash could be increasingly directed toward business corporations. As one member speculates, it's even possible that in ten years' time, the anti-globalization protests that began in Seattle will be considered as significant as the fall of the Berlin Wall, and as far-reaching in their ramifications.

Terrorism and Security

September 11: Tragic Moment or Historic Turning Point?

Peter Schwartz ◦ I don't think we should take for granted that September 11 is a big deal, because it might not be. It was an excruciatingly painful thing that happened, but history may not see it as terribly significant. It may turn out that what we're dealing with is, in fact, a small, crazy cult that collapses and disappears in its consequence because we've knocked out its supporting government and we catch and/or kill Osama bin Laden and the other key players. And nothing happens again.

Something similar happened in 1986 when Ronald Reagan was in office and Libya was involved in an attack on American soldiers in a West Berlin nightclub. We dropped tons of bombs on Libya and Qaddafi just quieted down. If that's the case here, it will have once again demonstrated U.S. military superiority. This enemy might not be nearly as nasty as we expected, in which case the interesting question is, What did this event trigger that might be positive rather than negative?

If it's not a big deal, one of the significant outcomes is the new relationship with Russia and, to some extent, China, and, to a lesser extent, Europe. Russia has, in effect, joined NATO, with the United States' active support. China has been collaborating and working with the United States—particularly on the intelligence side—and has made all the appropriate supportive noises. What we have are the beginnings of a political realignment of the key geopolitical actors in the world. This is a very good thing.

The alternative is that this is, in fact, a big deal, and there are a large number of young men out there, particularly in the Arab and partly the Muslim world, who are hungry to die and kill us in the process. They want to foment revolution throughout the Islamic world; they want to march on Europe; they want to have a victory of radical Islam over the West—in which case it's a very different scenario.

The Potential Economic Costs of Further Attacks

Peter Schwartz ◦ One of the lessons of September 11, which was reflected in bin Laden's tape, was that they got more bang for their buck than they expected. They didn't expect to bring down the towers; they certainly didn't expect the catastrophic damage they did to Manhattan. The biggest effect that they achieved was economic. They took a weakening economy and pushed it over the edge—the grounding of airlines, the disruption of the airline industry, and the secondary effect on Boeing et al. rippling outward. All of this shifted the cost equation and we're now in a deficit. It'll probably cost us a trillion dollars—not just the few billion dollars in direct effects.

These guys are now wondering, "What else can we do that would be really disruptive? Suppose we drop 10 planes over the mid-ocean?" If that happens, who's going to fly? If you can't fly, can you run worldwide businesses? It could trigger a global depression. That wouldn't displease terrorists in the slightest. They have it within their power to do that. No airline security system can prevent it—the systems are designed to make people feel better, not to stop terrorists. If they want to take us back to the seventeenth century, these are the things to do. That's the dark scenario. And if that happens we're in deep trouble. The question is, do they now have the means? Have we so disrupted their network, are they so small, that they can't actually pull it off? If the network still exists and it's bigger than we think it is, the consequences of what they do can be catastrophic.

Ramzi Yusef is in jail for the first World Trade Center bombing in 1993. One of his plans, in fact, was to drop 10 planes over the mid-Pacific. They found files on his PC that said he had carried out a test where he assembled nitroglycerin in the bathroom of an airplane going from Hong Kong to Taiwan to Tokyo or a similar route. Yusef hid the bomb in the bathroom onboard, and then got off in Taiwan. The plane traveled on and the bomb went off. It killed two people and collapsed the floor of the first-class cabin into the cargo hold, but didn't blow up the plane. The plane was able to make an emergency landing. His notes said, "The bomb was too small. We need more nitro." The lesson was not that it was a bad idea. The lesson was to make a slightly bigger bomb that could bring down the plane. He went on to say that the terrorists should, on one day, make 10 planes disappear over the Pacific Ocean. They're invisible on radar. Nobody can see them. Poof—plane's gone. Each sinks before it can be found. A plane on its way from San Francisco to Sydney—gone! Vancouver to Hong Kong—gone! They can't find any evidence of who did it or what's going on. If that happened, every airline in the world would shut down. On the day 10 planes disappear, no one will fly again for a decade. The world economy will grind to a halt. It's possible—and the airline security system does nothing to prevent it from happening.

If it turns out that we get rid of al-Qaeda but a new al-Qaeda, as it were, arises and does something equally nasty, over time it will have a significant effect. You move into a high-security society and all that is implied by that: the friction costs, the trust costs, the privacy costs. It will be extremely difficult to deal with, and it will significantly change the future in a darker way.

The Risk of an Attack by a Weapon of Mass Destruction

John Arquilla ∘ September 11, as horrible as it was, did only a modest amount of damage. After Pearl Harbor, Japan went on a spree of conquest that lasted six months. After September 11, bin Laden and al-Qaeda went underground as much as possible. So the psychology of these two attacks is very different.

Much of the retributive action taken against al-Qaeda and the Taliban in Afghanistan may have the unintended consequence of reducing demand for radical change, because it appears that we're doing quite well at this point. That makes it all the more important to understand the lessons of the field operations in Afghanistan. This was not a story about pure mass brute force winning the day—this was about small, nimble formations empowering the more massive capabilities that we have. That subtle point is generally lost on our own people in the Pentagon, and I think will be generally lost on the American public.

So there is a risk, and I think it's a terrible risk. If we don't decisively defeat transnational terrorism, we're looking somewhere in the next 10 years at a strike with a weapon of mass destruction, and that will change everything forever.

What we see is the culmination of a century-long trend that began with high explosives at the turn of the last century. We've seen this growing destructive and disruptive power of the small group. That's going to extend right down to the individual in the coming years. That trend will only increase. For me, our number-one war aim in the struggle against terrorism is to prevent terror with weapons of mass destruction. There is already abundant evidence that they are trying to acquire such capability, and I have no doubt that al-Qaeda would use a nuclear weapon if it had one.

The scale of the damage would be staggering. If the World Trade Center had been hit with a sizable nuclear weapon, three million could have been dead instead of 3,000. It would be three trillion dollars in economic disruption instead of perhaps one trillion dollars. Think also of the psychological effect of having a vulnerability that can never be redressed.

This, more than anything else, calls for a fundamental change in mindset. When you and I go to bed each night, neither of us worries about the fact that the Russians have 7,000 strategic nuclear warheads still in their arsenal. Would you and I sleep well tonight if we knew for a fact that Osama bin Laden had one or two or three devices? We'd be terrified. A terrorist organization can't be retaliated against with nuclear weapons, so deterrence doesn't work anymore.

I'm worried that we've arrived at another of those points where, as Karl Marx put it so well, "All that is solid melts into air." All of the basic constructs about national security from the Cold War are under great pressure and falling apart. Mutual deterrence is meaningless with nuclear weapons in the hands of a transnational terrorist group that's actually living in your country and doesn't have a country of its own to be retaliated against. It seems to me that against such a threat, the finest field armies, the best aircraft carriers, and the most far ranging bombers are of little moment.

This is where we have to get our minds. We have to understand that a fundamentally different kind of capability must be created to secure ourselves. That capability resides partially in our military and partially in law enforcement and in intelligence, but to a great extent it resides in our own people watching, listening, becoming part of a sensory organization that includes ourselves, our allies, and people around the world. People need to watch what goes on and to put up the red flag when some terrible crisis is occurring in a failing state, because that's going to be a breeding ground for such capabilities. It will be a place where some disgruntled scientist is trying to sell a suitcase nuclear weapon to a terrorist organization.

The fact is there is an existential chance that an attack with a weapon of mass destruction will occur. If I were forced to put a figure on it, I'd say there's a one in four chance—a one in three chance at the most. But that's still pretty high and it should make us think about negotiation now. Because if there is a darker scenario out there that has a remote chance of happening, we need to consider alternative strategies now. There's no better time than in the wake of our great success in Afghanistan. We would not be negotiating from weakness, but rather from strength. This would be a time to try to achieve a diplomatic solution.

Every other war in history has generally had some kind of negotiations that went along with it. Even the Third Punic War, which ended with the entire destruction of Carthage, was subject to extensive negotiations. This is a time when we ought to be thinking about some form of negotiations. We have to figure out whom to talk to, and how. It could be almost like we envisioned interstellar warfare, where the negotiations take place by subspace radio because you don't meet physically with your opponent. We don't want to think about people sitting around the same table in Paris, but we may want to think about something being mediated through CNN or Al-Jazeera.

The implications of an attack with weapons of mass destruction are so great, and the tradition of negotiating war termination so strong, that it behooves us to think about how this war might end. Otherwise, we think only about an unending war, which inevitably will result—in 10, 20, 50 years— with a weapon of mass destruction being detonated on American soil.

The Devastating Psychological Impact of a Nuclear Bomb

John Petersen • People talk about nukes missing from the former Soviet Union. Guys like Saddam Hussein and Qaddafi have been trying forever to buy such devices or find them or steal them. I asked a friend who used to be a very senior person in the Department of Defense about the likelihood that some of those nuclear devices have worked their way into the United States. He hesitated, then said, "I don't know how you could think that it hasn't happened."

It's been kind of a fiasco watching officials try to get anthrax spores out of the Hart Senate office building. They evacuated everyone and then gassed the whole thing. That didn't work so they gassed it again. Now after three months these people can go back to work. Now imagine a small nuke being set off in downtown D.C. or radioactive fallout all over Manhattan— no one will go back for five years. It would be extraordinary. If you think September 11 was a body blow to the psyche of the United States of America, just wait until somebody sets off a nuke.

Our Current Window of Vulnerability to Bioterrorism

Robert Carlson • The problem we should be concerned with is that within just a couple of years we will be seeing modified organisms that have much greater destructive potential than anthrax. The lab that you're sitting in could probably make a bug that is incredibly destructive within six months. And if a bug like that was released, we don't have the ability—we being scientists, biologists, the public health system—to do anything about it. We do not have the ability to find the bug, to isolate it, to understand its biology, to develop a response in time to do anything about it if it's sufficiently virulent. The skills exist today to make that bug. They don't exist to do anything about it. I'm not worried about any of the labs that have the capacity today to do that, but in two or three years everyone is going to have that capability if they want it.

Here's a horrific example. Let's say a bug popped up today that grows like tuberculosis, which means that it takes at least two weeks to grow the bug in the lab to the extent that you can do any biology with it. Let's say it has about as many genes as E. coli does, because if you were going to completely twist an organism into doing something bad, it's probably something like E. coli with a bunch of genes we've never seen before. Not all of those need be real genes—some of them might be noise. We don't have a way to find out quickly which of those proteins actually does whatever it does to make the thing pathogenic. It might not even be an artificial pathogen—it could be like Ebola or some other bug from the jungle that we've never dealt with before.

We can't do anything about it. It takes a long time for us to go through the motions of sequencing the genome, doing the rough biology to find out how the organism works in order to cure it. We have to develop the ability in the next few years to go through that process much faster, to be able to look at how the biology interacts with its host, to look at what proteins are there and what they do differently that we've never seen before.

We won't always be under the gun and struggling to catch up. There will be a time when it will be OK that people will screw up or that people tend to make mischief, because the technology will exist to solve those problems and solve them quickly. But we are already in a danger period where we can manipulate biological systems but we can't do anything about those manipulations—we can't go back and fix things.

In five years we will have a model in the Molecular Science Institute lab that accounts for the behavior of 10 to 20 proteins in a quantitative, predictive way. The fruits of that effort will include new measurement tools, manipulation tools, modeling tools, and simulation engines. It becomes a set of tools that are immediately applicable to every other biological system. There are other people elsewhere in the world, attempting to do the same thing, without necessarily having the exact same goals. So in five years we in the field are going to have a very diverse set of capabilities both in understanding and manipulating biological systems. But there will be a period where we can enable more mischief than we're able to fix—there's no question about it.

The Need for a Radically Decentralized Civil Defense System

John Arquilla ∘ We're an open society and will change little of that, even to defeat international terrorism. An open society, quite simply, has too many stadiums, too much infrastructure, too much commerce that's done by vulnerable media. These vulnerabilities won't go away.

We are also looking at an era in which our potential adversaries must realize that there is no advantage in trying to replicate the forces we have. It's extremely costly, and it takes decades. By the time they did it, we would be generations ahead in conventional weapons anyway. If I were an adversary of the United States or the industrialized West, I would be looking at cyberwarfare—at netwar. I would be looking at all these odd new ways to engage Americans and their allies because the Americans seem so ill-prepared for it. That's why I suggest that we're moving into an era of increasing vulnerability. It's as simple as that.

The entry costs to becoming a terrorist or someone who can engage in irregular warfare against the United States are quite low. You don't need to have enough resources to build a carrier battle group or a main battle tank—you simply need to have interconnectivity and people willing to give their lives to the cause. Then you can ride the rails of advanced Western technology and free Western ways to strike at the West.

That said, there are ways to limit the kind of damage that can be done. This goes from physical security to information security to global security. Our first step is to organize ourselves into networks. I saw the organizational chart for the Office of Homeland Security the other day, and it was a 1950s-style line diagram from top to bottom. That's not the answer. The answer is to build a network. We might do better at homeland security if we didn't have a director for it and simply created a network where people got to talk with each other on equal footing and work together to solve problems.

I greatly favor a tremendously decentralized defensive structure, organizationally as well as operationally. I think that all Americans should see themselves as part of a sensory organization. The terror war that's being waged has no front line; the front is everywhere, and we are all on it. So we all have to be sentinels. The plane that went down in Pennsylvania is one of the best examples of getting remarkably good intelligence about the attackers and of people acting on the spot to deal with the problem. Advanced information technology does a great deal to empower a decentralized defensive force, whereas in the nuclear age civil defense was something of a joke. Nuclear warfare is so destructive that the living would likely envy the dead. Civil defense then was basically a few basements in large buildings stocked with moldy crackers. But civil defense in an information age can make a profound difference.

We need to think about empowering people with the ability to pass information. They will act whenever they have the chance because, quite simply, we don't have enough forces to be everywhere or to anticipate where attacks are going to be, and we will almost always be defending against the last target set rather than the next target set. We have to rekindle a kind of frontier mentality. In the nineteenth century, the individual homesteader had a great stake in his own security. I think some of that sense is going to be coming back.

The Future of the Islamic Middle East

The Historic Roots of Current Feelings in the Middle East

Gwynne Dyer ∘ The Middle East is, in a weird way, the other part of the West, the other half of the Roman Empire and of the Mediterranean world. Even though Iraq isn't in the Mediterranean, most of its empires had Mediterranean coasts. As recently as 800 A.D., these countries were part of the West; Turkey was until the fifteenth century. And they perceive that they've always been in contact with the West.

The Chinese had never heard of the West until the fifteenth century except for travelers' tales. Similarly, we erupted into Southeast Asia and Latin America all of a sudden, coming by ships over the horizon. That's not the case with the Middle East. The Middle East has known us for 1,400 years and has been at war with us for most of that time. Until the eighteenth or nineteenth century, they thought they were winning—and usually were. Advances on one front, defeat on another. They lost Spain, but they were on the border of Budapest as recently as 1688. They still held the Balkans 75 years ago, all of it.

For the rest of the world we came from Mars. Suddenly here we were with our superior technology, better organization, huge wealth, and frightening, ferocious discipline. We came, we conquered, we left again, and they picked up the technology and started using it, Japanese style. Eventually they will democratize not because we are democratic but because if we give them those technologies they will do it for themselves. It goes back to a basic principle: Human values are in fact egalitarian.

For the Middle East, the perception of the West was very different. They believed that they were both culturally and morally superior. They believed that they were technologically superior down to the late nineteenth century; in fact they probably lost technological equality around 1750, but this wasn't recognized. Then in 1918, long after the rest of the world had been colonized, long after even Africa had been colonized, they're suddenly colonized. It is that recent, within living memory.

They were still believing that: "We are the other half of the Mediterranean, morally superior civilization. We are suffering minor technological handicaps at the moment but obviously we always win in the end." Suddenly there are European troops in the streets and they're reduced to colonial status. The huge disaster is still resonating in the collective memory in these countries in a way that the experiences of Robert Lord Clive in India or the Muslims in Indonesia don't resonate in modern consciousness. Their relationship to anything that we do and our artifacts, both political and technological, is far more ambivalent than anybody else's. They believe that these are the poison gifts of the people who, unfairly, and against all the dictates of right-thinking history, somehow won. There has been an enormous ambivalence toward taking on Western values, even if that gets you Western goods and power. The whole thing is much more fraught emotionally.

The generation that came out of World War II attempted to shove Western technology—and all the things that come with technology, because you can't really separate it—down the throats of populations who were already deeply ambivalent. The rulers were facing great Western arrogance and intervention. They can only overcome that by bootstrapping themselves into a better economy and a more technologically competent society.

So what you now have is a generation of people whose first-level analysis is: Western equals corrupt/imperialist/doesn't work. Must return to root values/Islam and so on. At the same time, of course, they want cars, their kids to go to university, and their countries to be modern, powerful, and respected in the world. And their own families in their countries are prosperous, comfortable, and secure. They even want democracy, but unlike the Filipinos or the Indians, they can't simply pick up this model and say, "That's culture-free, we'll use that." For the Middle East it isn't culture free; it is laden with negative symbolism.

So the fundamentalists, first of all, are dedicated to tearing down the structures they see as being imposed by people who are lackeys of the foreigners, whether the former Soviet Union or the West. But they do want to build afterward. They are in a real intellectual bind. Look at Iran, which is the classic case for 20 years running. It had a democratic revolution: 69 percent of the population voted for Khatami in the last election. They want to have values that they think of as their own and yet transmute those into a democratic political system. This is not impossible, provided they let things like hierarchy go. But there are people who like the idea of hierarchy because they are at the top of it.

I think Islamic fundamentalism is a culturally necessary detour around the obvious road to modernization and democratization—a necessary but conceivably very uncomfortable, lengthy, and ugly detour.

The Risk of Broader Conflict

Peter Schwartz ∘ The goal of the radical fundamentalists is to re-create the caliphate—that is, to create a set of Islamic regimes across the Middle East, from Pakistan to North Africa. In this case, it would mean rebellions in three key countries: Pakistan, Saudi Arabia, and Egypt. The Syrians would naturally come in. The Iranians would find themselves in an awkward position—on the one hand being supportive but on the other being opposed to the particulars of it. They're Persians, not Arabs. There's a deep and historical divide there.

A key question is Iraq and Saddam Hussein. We can get everybody onboard to attack al-Qaeda and the Taliban, but it's harder to get support to attack Hussein unilaterally. Bush might do it anyway. If that were to happen it could trigger revolts in Saudi Arabia, in Egypt, and in Pakistan. It's not assured that an attack is necessary to trigger revolts, or that there would even be revolts if we attacked. There are a lot of mini-scenarios about how the

Middle East could play out. What happens with the Arabs and the Israelis? What happens with Hussein? What happens in Saudi Arabia? What happens in Egypt? What happens in Pakistan?

The Probability of New Fundamentalist Regimes

Gwynne Dyer ∘ I don't think that the fundamentalist movement has spent its strength yet. This is about the Arabic and perhaps Farsi-speaking Middle East; it's not about the Muslim world as a whole. I wouldn't make the same analysis for Pakistan, let alone for places like Indonesia, or even Turkey, which has its problems.

Most countries in the Middle East are losing per capita income every year. The population is growing faster than the economy in most of these countries, so that there's a gradual slide in living standards. Obviously, we all know about Iraq, but it's also happening in Saudi Arabia. The average incomes have been halved in Saudi Arabia in the last 20 years—admittedly from quite a high level, but still halved.

In places like Egypt, we are looking at very decrepit political systems. These emerged either from military coups long ago—though they've adopted various disguises since—or from very old ruling-family monarchical systems, which are attempting to carry on as though nothing has happened.

In the Arabic-speaking Middle East, and in Persia and Iran, you had a generation of people emerging from the military. Even the shah's family was ex-military; they came to power in a coup and then called themselves kings. In a few cases like the shah and the present Saudi royal family, it's a Western-oriented modernizing model. In many more cases, including dictatorships like Syria and Iraq, it was a Soviet-oriented model. They weren't communists, because that would be godless, but both Assad and Saddam Hussein come out of the Ba'ath movement, which is communism with God.

But the problem is they have not delivered the goods in terms of prosperity and consumption. Perhaps equally important, they haven't delivered the goods in terms of dignity and respect for their countries in the world. This is particularly measured by performance against Israel but is a broader issue as well. Modernization in the Western mode, whether American-oriented or Soviet-oriented, has failed.

Almost all these regimes are still in power—except in Iran. But if we assume they will go under in the next 10 years, who is going to replace them? In most cases, it will be fundamentalists. The other folks are discredited. This is a part of the world where things are very screwed up.

The Possible Fall and Rise of Iraq

Roger Cass ∘ Iraq is a tribal society, very much like Afghanistan and Saudi Arabia. A lot of the tribes are very dissatisfied with what has been going on under the regime. I'm sure we're working with those tribes, as we did in Afghanistan with Special Op forces, to rise up when the situation is appropriate. In my view, the defeat of Saddam Hussein will take even less time than the defeat of the Taliban once we make our move.

The other thing that is not understood is that the Iraqi economy is in a state of total chaos. There's 80 percent unemployment. The dinar has collapsed. A few years ago there were three dinars to a dollar; now there are something like 2,500 to 3,000. The currency is just plummeting and there are no jobs available. And so I think when Hussein is overthrown, it'll be very popular with the people at large.

Iraq obviously has enormous oil reserves, the second largest in the world and they're vastly understated. They only report, I think, 10 percent of their actual reserves, as proven, and then even it's about 110 billion barrels. Iraq could be producing around six million barrels a day within two years and 10 million barrels a day within five years. They're producing at two and a half right now. Once we establish a democratic government in Iraq and get Western technology and Russian technology working with the Iraqis to develop the oil fields, we'll be able to vastly reduce our dependence on Saudi Arabia.

The Danger of Saudi Arabia Going the Way of Iran

Roger Cass ∘ Saudi Arabia is the world's largest oil producer with the world's largest reserves. It's currently producing slightly under eight million barrels a day. It has the capacity to produce around 10 million barrels a day. Official reserves are around 260 billion barrels. And imports from Saudi Arabia are still very important to the U.S. and the West. But this is a regime that has basically run the economy into the ground over the last 20 years. They've been essentially in recession or bordering recession since 1990. Budget deficits have been running anywhere from 5 to 15 percent of GDP per annum because much of the money is frittered away by the royal family. It's been estimated $400 billion has been siphoned off by the House of Saud over the last 20 or 30 years. And it's an economy where per capita incomes have fallen by two-thirds since 1980 to about 7,000 dollars per capita, which puts it as one of the lowest per capita incomes of any of the Gulf States.

For 20 or 30 years or more, it's been a given that Saudi Arabia was critical to American national interests, that they should be regarded as one of those nations where it's important to maintain good relations. We've reached the point where we're beginning to think this support has been counterproductive.

If we continue to support an unpopular regime, it's likely to go the way of Iran. Instead of encouraging democratic forces that would liberalize society, we have continued to support the Shah. In many ways, Saudi Arabia resembles Iran in the late 1970s. You've got a buildup of the more radical mullahs. In Iran there were two mullah factions in Qom and Teheran. In Saudi Arabia you've got one group in Buraydah and one group in Riyadh, moderates and extremists. And you've also got the two armies, the regular Army and the Saudi National Guard. Unless we move preemptively within Saudi Arabia and take a more active line in supporting moves toward democracy, we're going to wind up with the possibility of a radical Islamic regime taking over.

Now, I think what has happened since September 11 has also neutralized some of the forces of Islamic fundamentalism within the region because it has failed. Jihad has been a failure. And the Arab street is revising its support for the more extreme form of fundamentalism because it's become a blind alley. They cannot compete militarily or economically against the West. There's a growing sense within the Middle East that they have to moderate their views and change their way of thinking.

September 11: The Last Gasp of Reactionary Politics?

Steven Weber • Was September 11 the shot across the bow, or was it the last gasp of reactionary politics? My original thought was that it's the shot across the bow that we've been fearing for so long. And now, to be provocative, I think you have to pose against that the possibility that this is the last gasp of anti-globalization reactionary politics.

Blowing up the World Trade Center is an act of desperation. Which for a lot of people—including people in the Arab world and leaders in the Arab world—has discredited the opposition to globalization in a really profound way. That forces people to make a choice. With all its problems, would you rather live in a world of liberal capitalism, or would you rather live in a world of crashing airplanes into civilian buildings?

One has to be careful about Western or American triumphalism, but you can interpret what happened as the last dying gasp of a reactionary civilization that has failed to keep pace with the modern world.

The New Roles of the United States and Europe

The Striking Parallels Between Today and the Early Cold War Era

Steven Weber ○ There's a very interesting parallel between today and the immediate post–World War II era. It was clear as early as 1943 that the Allies were going to win, and they were already arguing over the shape of the post–World War II world. And it took seven or eight years to figure out what that was actually going to mean.

So from 1944–1950 there was an interesting debate going on about what matters in this postwar world. What do we have to pay attention to? Who are our friends? Who are our enemies? How important is technology? How important are people's beliefs? Who in the world actually matters to us? Who in the world doesn't? A whole set of questions about the world order was being thrown out on the table. And you could watch the way different organizations and people switched their views and started to construct a set of beliefs.

In 1947, in the midst of all this fervent uncertainty, George Kennan, then a bureaucrat in the U.S. Embassy in Moscow, anonymously wrote "the long telegram" back to the State Department. He later published it as an article in *Foreign Affairs* called "The Sources of Soviet Conduct." That was the Mr. X article in which he clearly laid out the major contours of the post–World War II world—this Cold War—and a strategy for dealing with it, which he called containment. And people just cottoned onto it because finally, in the midst of all this noise—does Greece matter, does Turkey matter?—there was a guy who had a very clear, coherent argument: this is the problem; this is what we should do over the long term; and in the end, if we do it, it'll work out OK.

The debate immediately centered around that iconic article. People started to ask, "Is this right? Is this wrong?" It still took two or three years for everyone to sign on and to agree that, yes, in fact, we were now living in a period called the Cold War; it had these characteristics; and the United States needed to take certain steps in order to prosecute that war to a desirable outcome.

What brought it all to a head was the invasion of South Korea by North Korea. That allowed Truman and others to push forward a set of policies that they had had in the back of their minds for some time but, in fact, couldn't get people in the Senate, particularly Arthur Vandenberg, to go along with. So when North Korea invaded South Korea, that changed everything. They basically took all this intellectual apparatus that was building up for this Cold War and put it into a document called NSC-68, written by

Paul Nitze, which became its political manifestation. That's when budgets rose and the whole thing really started.

Before the events of September, there were debates about a similar kind of transition going on. People were moving slowly from "OK, it's no longer a Russia-dominated, Cold-War world" to "It's a world dominated by other kinds of threats, issues, worries, concerns, and beliefs." And September 11, like the invasion of South Korea by North Korea, brought all that stuff to the fore and allowed it to work through the political system. The dynamic's very similar—people had been talking a lot about what we're now doing but there had been no political momentum behind it.

Now I get the sense that President Bush is trying to define a core message for this era, which is essentially good vs. evil. It's organized Western democratic states against the forces of transnational terrorism. It is as clear in that manifestation as the message of the Cold War, which was the West against this transnational, ideologically driven phenomenon called communism, which was represented by the Soviet Union.

You can see all the parallels, statements like "It's going to be a long war," "We're in for the long haul," "It's an ideological phenomenon," and "It's not just a state." This was the same message people were sending out to justify why we had to fight a war in Vietnam. It wasn't a war against Russia; it was a war against communism. It's going to be fought all over the world. It's going to go on for a long time. It's going to require long-term vigilance and sacrifices by the American people. I think the messages are very similar.

The Emergence of the United States As a Rogue Superpower?

Peter Schwartz • The Hart-Rudman Commission developed a scenario of the United States as a rogue superpower. The United States, because of its great success, would be seen as the Microsoft of the world: hugely successful, triumphant, proud to let everybody know that we're number one and prepared to play rough when we don't like what you do. Nobody much loves Microsoft, and nobody much loves us. This is a world in which we end up isolated rather than isolationist, because the rest of the world aligns against us.

The U.S. recently took a very big step backward by renouncing the Antiballistic Missile Treaty. This is a first in U.S. history—to renounce a treaty that we helped create. This is an act of unilateralism in the extreme. We are seen throughout the world as an arrogant superpower caught up in the excesses of its own power.

George Bush has carried out an act of enormous diplomatic damage that simply will not be reparable for decades. There is no reason anybody should sign any kind of arms control agreement with the United States ever again. We are not trustworthy. We have just demonstrated to the world that you can sign an agreement with us and, at our convenience, we will renounce it. A Republican president negotiated the ABM treaty, and every other president since then has actively supported it with the exception of George Bush, Jr. It is "rogue superpower" in the extreme, and with consequences that will last decades. The United States has just proved itself unworthy of being a treaty partner.

The Unprecedented Possibility of No Balance Against U.S. Power

Steven Weber • There's a core realist notion that international politics is about a balance of power. It says that states tend to join a weaker coalition rather than a stronger coalition and this happens for two reasons. One, because it's the more powerful side that threatens them, so they want to join the other side. Two, because their contribution will be more valued if they join the weaker side rather than the stronger side. That's been the guiding realist view of international politics for a long time, and there's pretty good historical evidence to support it.

The only time that dynamic tends to be undermined is when people have no choice. That's the story of Stalin joining with Hitler in 1939. But what if you move into a world where one country is so much stronger than other countries, purely in a military sense, and there is no possibility for other countries to come together to balance that power effectively? I don't think that's ever been the case.

At least for modern international relations, it's a little bit terra incognito. And I don't think we know how countries will respond. The obvious argument is that people would oppose the United States. But are the other major powers in the world better off trying to oppose the U.S.? Or are they actually better off trying to join with the United States and get some of the fruits and benefits of the power the U.S. exerts around the world? People might do that because, frankly, the U.S. really is different than Nazi Germany in terms of its willingness or desire to control the territory of other countries. We piss off the Europeans about lots of things, but even the French know that we're not going to invade France. That was not the case with Nazi Germany or with any other great power throughout most of history.

The risk of opposing the United States is that it is almost an individual choice in Washington to allow your government to survive. I think the U.S. has demonstrated that if it wants to, it can probably bring down most governments in the world, outside of Europe and Japan. It can be done financially and it can be done militarily. The reason someone like Hussein is still in power is because the United States permits him to be in power. If the U.S. wanted his government to fall tomorrow, it could do that. The question about what comes after and whether it would be better or worse for the U.S. is a different story. But the choice is with the U.S., not with Hussein. And that's really a fundamental difference.

In the past, you could have plausibly done something to protect yourself from a threat by combining with other great powers. Now, if you can't beat them—and you really can't beat them—you might as well join them.

How the United States Must Help Create a Global Civil Society

John Arquilla • Nearly 80 years ago, Teilhard de Chardin wrote in *The Making of a Mind* that the world began as a rock, a geosphere. Heat and moisture came, and it became a biosphere with the arrival of life. He said, "We are now at a point where the geosphere and the biosphere will be completed by the rise of a noosphere, a realm of the spirit." He was an eyewitness to much of World War I, as both a chaplain and an ambulance driver. He thought that the horror of the war demanded that the world be changed. The change he called for was one in which there would be free people and prosperity, brought about by the great powers constraining themselves in the cause of all mankind. I think it's never been stated better than that.

The noosphere and what I call noopolitik are about giving first loyalty to freedom and human rights and to some sense of economic equity in the world. For Americans in particular, it means a willingness to constrain ourselves, to put ourselves in the judgment of this civil society. When I see the reluctance of the United States to sign up for something like the International Criminal Court, I shudder, because the International Criminal Court is civil society in the making. It says that if you commit crimes, you will be punished. How can the United States say, "We will not be held liable in such a court." How can we be fostering this civil society if we won't obey its own rules?

The creation of supranational bodies on environmental issues would be another case. The United States says that it's very concerned about environmental issues, but doesn't want to give up any of its sovereignty. The basis of a noosphere is a willingness to concede sovereignty in some areas and to constrain one's own use of power. That also means military interventions would not take place in unilateral ways, but rather on the basis of international consensus for action. I think the 1990s are a good model of the ability to gain consensus for many interventions—including in places like the Balkans, where there were such sharp differences between us and the Russians and even the Chinese. They did not step in the way of that intervention. So it seems to me that is the sinew of civil society—this willingness of the great power of the time to constrain itself.

Whether we like it or not, the United States is a great empire, like any other that has come along in history. Great empires have risen, have persisted, and then have declined and gone away. Most of them have collapsed in a heap of rubble. Some of them have retreated somewhat more skillfully—Great Britain being a good example. The British went from empire to commonwealth. That was a lovely concept. I think the United States wants to create a kind of information commonwealth in which its values, ideas, and products are shared freely and easily throughout the world, and that is a lovely legacy to leave behind.

Let us accept the fact that American preponderance is already being undermined, not by Russian missiles or Chinese military forces, but rather by irregular terrorists and criminal organizations. We'll have to fight endlessly, like the Romans trying to deal with the problem of the Barbarians, if we think we're going to tamp down terror forever. When did the tribal wars of the Roman Empire end? They never did, until the empire was overwhelmed. Now is the time for us willingly to let go of our grasp of superpower and to share that power with others and put that power to use in the service of a global cause. That's all that will strengthen us against chaos.

This world would be shaped by a global civil society. The nation-state does not have to go away, but it gets transformed. It is the civil society itself whose values are adhered to in all of these nation-states. All must constrain themselves to protect individual rights. I think this civil society is empowering itself whether we help it or stand in its way. But the timing of the rise of such a system is going to be affected greatly by the attitude of the U.S. We ignore it at our peril. Good strategists should right now be thinking about how the U.S. can work with this movement and take advantage of this trend, not only to maintain American national security, which is our job, but also to improve the security of the world.

What will grow very apparent over the next 10 years is that security is indivisible in nature, or what David Ronfeldt and I have called "integral"—something that cannot be broken apart. Either all will be secure or all will be insecure, because the world is so interconnected that in any of those insecure areas the most pernicious of threats can rise.

Concrete Steps Toward Forming a Global Society

Albert Bressand • There is a very strong generic American perception that the U.S. is relatively far apart from the rest of the world, relatively self-sufficient and on top of most processes, and therefore not threatened. What September 11 has shown is that we are no longer in a world where "domestic" can be separated from "international." The people who committed these terrible acts used the resources of American society. They used the training, the flight schools, and the commercial airliners to inflict tremendous pain and damage.

This is an iconic example of the threats in today's world. They are the threats of the global society. They are not the threats that you have when you have well-sheltered nations, each behind its borders, and yet we have not made the adaptation. We have not adjusted our mindset to the fact that there is indeed such a thing as a global society but it is simply not recognized as such. We have not developed institutions for it. It is grossly lagging behind the global economy in terms of the attention it receives and the efforts to regulate and govern it in the proper fashion.

There are some key issues to be addressed if we're to move toward a global society. Let's start with the market itself, where globalization is a well-established and ongoing process. A genuine "single market" requires shared transparency around common international accounting standards. The U.S. has said repeatedly that it cannot compromise the quality of investors' protection by adopting non-U.S. standards, even if these international standards were developed with a lot of U.S. participation. What the Enron failure shows is that there is no country that has a perfect standard. The U.S. standard, known as U.S. GAAP, is now recognized as having loopholes. Enron couldn't have happened under British standards. It couldn't have happened under the International Accounting Standard (IAS).

Next are remedies. The World Trade Organization, for example, is the one institution where decisions can be made by the multinational panels. Once a country has complained about another, such a panel is appointed and they reach a decision, and that decision is binding. The U.S. accepts this decision but is really dragging its feet and feels there is something totally unjustified about this international panel telling Americans what they should do. Moving a little further from the market, antitrust law has to be more integrated than it is today. You cannot have the same market and differing definitions of competitive behavior.

After these market-related issues, there are other issues that are international in nature including the environment, war crimes, drugs, and money laundering, to name a few. The Bush administration was very reluctant at first to put any pressure on offshore centers. Now they've discovered that al-Qaeda money goes through them and they're suddenly thinking, "Maybe we could a take a closer look after all." But do they really understand that it should not be a short-term remedy? It is not about going after al-Qaeda's money. The issue is that offshore centers are inappropriate for a global economy. How can you have organized black holes in what is supposed to be a global market?

How Europe Might Lead the Charge Toward Global Governance

Steven Weber ∘ It's easy for outsiders and even Europeans themselves to see Europe and the European Union as this incredibly slow-moving, ponderous bureaucracy. It can't make decisions, it's retrograde, it has inflexible labor markets in some places. It's easy for us to have this vision of Europe as this old-style, ancient regime, a constrained dinosaur that just moves incredibly slowly.

I think it is worth considering the alternative viewpoint, to look at what Europe's been able to do in the last 10 years as a region. They have built, as imperfect as it is, the most extensive supranational governance system for a globalizing economy of any part of the world. The EU is a new thing. They've gone from the European coal and steel community to quite an elaborate supranational governance structure for a large number of countries in 45 years. Twelve countries in Europe now have a common currency and look how easily they transitioned to the euro, even with all the predictions of doom. In the next few years the EU will expand to include some subset of the former Eastern European countries. Imagine, 12 or 13 years after the end of the Cold War, these countries will become members of the European Union. That supranational governance structure will then internalize a kind of north/south divide, because many of those countries really are fundamentally developing countries. Imagine what it would take for the United States to do that with Mexico!

I'm just painting the picture of Europe as an extraordinarily dynamic region that is in some ways way out ahead of the rest of the world in figuring out how to govern a globalizing economy. Way out ahead—no one's even close. This is a region where, at least within the Schengen region, people don't need passports to go across countries, where there is a public transit system that moves people efficiently across borders like nowhere else in the world, where products move across borders without tariffs, and where there is a single currency. Financial markets are increasingly integrated and will become substantially more so over the next few years. I think you can tell a story in which Europe is the leading edge of the world polity.

If you think of the globalization process as inexorable, then at some level we'll be looking for the European experience to be writ large. Imagine being part of the British monarchy in 1797 and coming to Philadelphia to watch the Constitutional Convention of the United States. You would have said, "God, what a bunch of buffoons! Democracy? They sit around and argue with each other. They can't make decisions. They're writing a constitution?"

You'd see it as a messy, stupid, inefficient, retrograde way of governing. But, in fact, they were creating a governance system for the next generation of political and economic growth. We look at the EU as the *ancien regime*. And maybe we're the *ancien regime*.

The Need to Acknowledge That No One Country Holds the Truth

Catherine Distler · Sometimes it seems that the U.S. forgets it is a nation of 50 states, and the integration of those states has not always been so easy. The problem is that the integration is accomplished now, and nobody can imagine that Cuba may ask to be the next U.S. state. What would you do in that case? The only vision of integration that the U.S. seems to have is a bit unilateral—"I have the truth and you have to adopt my own view of the world."

At Prométhée we have fostered discussions about what is a very powerful concept in Europe, namely mutual recognition. In many ways, we have the feeling that there is no one truth and if something is acceptable in one country, maybe the other countries should consider accepting it. It's not always like that. You have discussions, and you have minimum standards that have to be agreed upon by all of the members. Integration doesn't always mean uniformity. You sometimes also have to acknowledge that you have one truth and it may not be the universal one.

The Potential of Europe As a New Kind of Political Entity

Albert Bressand · If something emerges in Europe that could be called a state, it is very likely to be different from any other state we have seen, not only because of the complexity and the diversity of the construction but also because of the different trade-offs Europeans are likely to strike between the local, national, and EU levels in different fields.

Europe is very far from being no more than a common market with a single currency and no political backbone. Let me surprise the British reader who awoke to Europe the day the euro failed to flop: The reality of political integration in Europe already includes most of the characteristics of what we call a state today, including a parliament, a common court of justice above national courts, and a tightly integrated regulatory framework for most economic activity, as well as a number of social norms. Much less convincingly, it also has begun to develop elements of a common security and foreign policy. Now this is a bit like Magritte's famous painting (now at the Los Angeles County Museum!) that shows a pipe with the caption, "Ceci n'est pas une pipe"—this is not a pipe. It is not a state because the whole strategy—the "Monet method" by the name of founding father Jean Monet—was to use economic and technical cooperation to advance the ideal of political integration that they saw as the only buffer against other Franco-German wars, and to do so in the least controversial manner possible. Now 50 years later, the pipe exhibits furious resemblance to—surprise!—a pipe.

There is a possibility of bringing these elements together in a U.S.-style federal system. Indeed, such is the question presently being debated by the constitutional conference that will make proposals as to the Union's "final state" by 2004. But it is not the only way the European experiment can evolve and a number of the participants in that constitutional conference see it as a last opportunity to roll back Brussels and its army of bureaucrats who, incidentally, number fewer than a middle-sized national ministry.

As these debates show, there is still strong resistance to political integration; in many countries there are still very strong nationalistic forces. In some countries, like the U.K., it's a minority, but a vocal minority. Therefore, it is possible that integration continues for another 10 years, just as it has in the past, without the splashy aspects of a fully fledged federation. Nevertheless, and provided the fabric so patiently woven does not unravel, the reality is one of full economic integration and of a political integration far beyond what people usually perceive. Now if the fabric does unravel, we'll see interesting times with little Le Pens of all shades putting their nation first, calling for their money back, and teaching foreign investors and cosmopolitan bureaucrats the type of lesson our ancestors were so good at giving that it took us two world wars to unlearn them.

Why Europe Will Never Be a Superpower Like the United States

Kees van der Heijden ∘ Europe is a very loose coalition of powers that just happen to have been very successful in creating this huge common market. It is important to remember that since then they've been trying to build on this in terms of political unification and have been utterly unsuccessful. The thing that works is economics. The common currency is probably the boundary, as far as they can possibly go. And beyond that, you see the continent forever falling apart in difference of opinion. It is interesting that the resolution of problems in the Balkans fundamentally required American intervention. The Europeans are just too complex a system to take a quick and efficient view on these sorts of matters. So Europe is not a power like that. We don't have any structure in place. Put the European leaders together in a room and they won't agree on anything. There is no common point where opinions and notions come together and where arbitrage can take place about where things should go. Interests are different; political traditions are different. Each of these countries has such a different identity. Their histories are different, they have different stories. And there is no structure that pulls these things together.

The idea that Europe would be a sort of superpower: It sounds very, very unrealistic from where we sit here. People have talked about political integration for years and at the moment it's being talked about quite a lot. And there's been zero progress. I think the market's helped to some extent in that it's created "good neighbor" attitudes and some degree of goodwill. So heads of state meet together regularly, they talk, and they manage to, most of the time, solve day-to-day problems. But there isn't a central leadership point. So I certainly don't see anything being created in Europe that would be able to stand up. If there is going to be a counterpoint to America in the world you have to look at the places where there is still some political leadership—perhaps China.

Integrating Europe: The Aging West and Young East

Catherine Distler ∘ One problem we face is that a dozen candidate countries from Central and Eastern Europe and from the Mediterranean region are knocking at the Union's door, and we know that we have to take them onboard. They know that they have a lot of work to do in order to enter the Union, like swallowing the thousands of pages of regulations the EU put in place in the last 50 years or so. It is a lot of work, a lot to swallow, yet, at the same time, they know that this provides them with fantastic possibilities to leapfrog by simply importing, for instance, the stock market regulation that has been put in place at the European Union level, or the food and drug rules that allow for export of value-added agricultural products rather than just bushels of wheat. If 15 countries consider that it is a good regulation for the European environment, it should be for the Czech Republic or Poland. It's ISO 9000 certification at the power of a whole economy.

We know that we will have to work with those countries. We are not only working together to set up regulations to improve cross-border trade, we are also helping other countries to adjust, to do what's necessary to join the club. It's a huge project—to accept a country is one thing; to be sure that they will be comfortable being a new member is another thing. Europe understands that nobody can afford a failure.

Another key issue in Europe in the next decade will be the aging population and the fact that something will have to be done. However, most of the candidate countries have a younger population than we do. The day they enter the European Union, the people will be free to settle where they want. It's not only the freeing up of capital and goods; it's the freeing up of people. A German could be elected mayor of a French city without any problem.

The immigration challenge is greater in some countries than in others. The population is aging more rapidly in Italy, for example, than in France or Ireland. The need for immigrants will be different for different countries. Yet we will have to reconsider the immigration policy and the historic links many of our countries have with different regions of the world and agree on a common policy.

Europe's Comfort with Shifting from Globalization to Integration

Albert Bressand ∘ This will be the decade of integration. People believe globalization has happened, and we believe it has not. What has happened is a lot of trade, a lot of financial flows, a lot of manufacturing across continents, a small number of world products—iconic products, not very many, actually. Go beyond the economy and look at the society, and ask yourself, "Are these societies truly globalized? Have they integrated in a meaningful way across borders?" The answer, in many ways, is "no" or "not yet."

On the positive side, what we see with September 11, the Balkans, Enron, the euro, and several developments is that there now is a possibility of deeper cross-border integration of the workings of societies. What does that mean? Well, this spells the end of the narrow view of globalization that stops at trade and foreign investment but expands to the rules, regulations, and laws of these societies, and possibly some political institutions and courts of justice. Americans don't like international courts of justice, but there is one now, in front of which Milosevic has been brought. Deeper integration means also institutions in the field of the global environment, including the Kyoto project. Kyoto may not be perfect, but it is at least an effort to put our institutions in accordance with the global nature of the economy and the ecology underlying it.

So integration is the one word we as Europeans would pick to describe what could happen in the forthcoming decade—the shift from globalization to integration. We believe that Europe is at the forefront because you have 12 countries that have happily thrown in the wastebasket time-honored currencies with all the historic baggage that goes with them. Europeans practice deeper forms of integration than the U.S. free-trade zone concept.

Here's the deeper question: Is the story of globalization beyond Europe simply about buying one another's products, or is it about trustful relationships? The latter calls for accepting the person on the other side of the border as a legitimate partner on his own terms, in his own legal environment, with his own cultural baggage.

We would claim that the difference between European-style globalization and the mainstream brand is that in the mainstream brand, the trust stops with the product. You trust the product and you can buy it, but you do not trust that the laws or currencies or central banks or courts of neighboring countries are good enough to be applied to you. They are good for the others over there with their laws and their institutions, but not on your side of the border.

Every time something like the Kyoto protocol is proposed where we would share in the same law, the U.S. says, "We don't accept that. We just want the products. Keep the laws; keep the culture; just give us the product." This is the deeper issue beyond currency. The euro is not there just as a monetary measure. The euro is there because we trust one another.

This narrow globalization, this product-based globalization, has now reached a threshold where the intimacy on the economic side is such that if we remain miles apart culturally and politically and institutionally and legally, we are schizophrenic. It is like sharing a house with someone you don't trust. Can you do that? No.

Do we trust one another as fully fledged beings or as homo economicus? If we trust one another as homo economicus, we are interacting through a set of global markets for capital, goods, and services, but we are not in a global society. We are a set of domestic societies sharing a global market.

The Plight and Potential of Japan

Japan's Number-One Problem: The Need for Massive Immigration

Hirotaka Takeuchi • In the twentieth century, corporations had to solve an economic problem and did a pretty good job of it. In the twenty-first century, corporations will also be solving social problems. The number-one social problem for companies everywhere will be immigration. Japan is no exception, with the birthrate being as low as it is. Twenty years from now, Japan will need 600,000 immigrants each year to maintain its current work force level. According to statistics, right now there are currently 630,000 non-Japanese working in Japan.

That will require Japanese society to rethink fundamentally its attitude toward non-Japanese workers. They cannot self-sustain their work force unless there is such a tremendous improvement in productivity that less than half the current work force is needed 20 years from now. But if you assume the current productivity level and assume you will need to sustain the current work force, those are the numbers they will be faced with. There is a huge bias among Japanese against immigrants. Companies need to do something about that.

Japan's Range of Challenges and Slippery Slope

Robert Hormats ○ With Japan, I don't think you can expect much. They are on a very slippery slope demographically. They are going to have fewer people 30 years from now then they have today. Unlike the United States, which benefits from dynamism and immigration, they don't have immigration. They are borrowing very heavily, so when the old-age crisis hits, it will hit them harder than anyone, with the possible exception of Italy. Unless they are able to make some significant changes in their economic practices, which include deregulation, restructuring a lot of inefficient corporations, and restructuring banks, they will be a weak economy for a long time to come. The only ray of hope is that they have a new reform-minded prime minister who is pushing for major bank and corporate restructuring.

The Younger Generation and the Prospects for Sustained Reform

Hirotaka Takeuchi ○ Koizumi is the first political leader in the last 20 years who has told the public in a very straightforward way, "We need change." The past didn't work; therefore, we need a major reform to achieve change in the future. That message was a relief to the public. The Japanese public had been waiting for change. They knew that the old system was not functioning properly. His strongest card is popular support, which seems to be sinking. He has given a very clear-cut message: Things will be tough. The public already knows they will go through two to three years of tough times before there is fundamental reform. The Band-Aid approach that has been used in the past hasn't done anything for Japan. We need something stronger, like surgery.

There is an opposition Democratic Party of Japan. The leader is Yukio Hatoyama. His thinking is very close to Koizumi's thinking. In fact, if Koizumi gets kicked out of the Liberal Democratic Party (LDP), Yukio Hatoyama will take on Koizumi's ideas. There are also similar-minded younger politicians that share Koizumi's thinking. There is likelihood that if the LDP stalls Koizumi's reform plan, they can always regroup and form a new reform party. Koizumi is not playing the game alone. There are enough younger, reform-minded politicians. It will be like watching a tug-of-war the next few years. If we go back to the old politics, there is no future for Japan.

Reasons for Hope: A New Japan in the Making

Roger Cass ∘ The situation in Japan is so dire now; they've got huge fiscal deficits. This country was the epitome of fiscal probity 15 years ago and now they run the biggest government deficit in the world: either 8 percent of GDP or 20 percent, depending on how you measure it. If you throw in the public agency debt and the stuff that is buried in footnotes in the government accounts, they have an enormous debt overhang problem. According to recently released numbers, non-performing bank loans are in excess of one trillion dollars, not the two or three hundred billion they'd been claiming for years. Now they'll offload it into a resolution trust or common corporation to get it off the bank balance sheet so they can lend again.

If Koizumi can sustain himself and push his reform program, which I think he will, we'll begin to see public confidence recovering. Then I think the real estate market will base out. It's basically been going down for 12 straight years, back to early-1980s levels. When that occurs the collateral against many of these nonperforming bonds will begin to stabilize and hopefully move up again. So I think that Japan is on the verge of a new Meiji Revolution. The corporate sector is finally getting it. Business executives in some of the key Japanese corporations are partly under the influence of outside financial advisors from the U.S. and Europe, who are advising them on how to restructure, to write things off, to get away from lifetime employment. They're opening up the financial markets.

I think you've got a new Japan in the making. They're definitely going to have a recession or near recession this year and maybe even next. I anticipate no growth until fiscal 2002 and maybe even later. But once you get a sustainable move up in the stock market, and once the public sees that the value of their property is basing out and stabilizing and become confident that they have a new generation of leadership, it will transform the whole situation for Japan. Along with the corporate restructuring, this will allow profits to soar and the stock market will take off, maybe more than any other stock market in the Western world.

Japan, to my mind, is the best bet you can make right now. The NIKKEI is close to 20-year lows and isn't going to go much lower, maybe a thousand points at the most. The upside is double or maybe triple after the next 5 or 10 years. With that, Japanese growth will resume. They aren't going back to growth rates of 7 or 8 percent like in the '60s, '70s, and early '80s, but I think that Japan can very quickly regain 4–5 percent growth.

Ichiro Suzuki As the Symbol of a Globalizing Japan

Hirotaka Takeuchi ∘ The Japanese industrial model has worked well in the last 50 years but has run its course. There has been too much success. Folks were pounding their chests and boasting about how successful Japan has been, but those times are over. We need to be realistic and realize there is a new form of competition. It's a new game and we need to remember it is a global game. The best metaphor for this is Ichiro Suzuki, the Seattle Mariners baseball player. Baseball fans used to swarm the stadiums for Ichiro. But domestic baseball's popularity has decreased immensely now that they've seen what the game can be. Japanese media company NHK is broadcasting all the Ichiro games, and the public thinks, "Oh, that's baseball."

Ichiro is a good example of what the Japanese need to do—go overseas for success. Take risks like Ichiro and you will be rewarded. Until now the Japanese were very intolerant of failure. They need to try new things, perhaps fail at a few, and accept it. That's what we need to do to compete in the global marketplace. Look at the acceptance of Ichiro in the U.S. If you are good, the U.S. accepts anyone, regardless of race or color of skin. The Japanese are saying to themselves, "There is something to this open society here."

The Emerging Powers
of China, India, and Russia

China As a Wild Card: A Creative Engine for the World?

Kevin Kelly ∘ China is the wild card. China can go either way. They could become married to us like Japan did, or they could become our enemy like Russia did. And if they decide to be an enemy, they could be very disruptive around the world and seriously divert things. Beyond that, they have the potential in the next decade, like Japan, to start to throw off pieces of the future. I think they have the ability to actually start to generate components of things that we will find a central part of our lives.

For example, the Japanese decided that they were masters of the miniature and craftsmen, so they made the consumer electronic gadget world possible. And whereas part of the society is very archaic and medieval, they were way ahead of the future there. I think China has that capability. I don't know what the arena will be. But I think they have the potential to leapfrog forward and wow the world with something that we don't have.

I'm sensing potential. I'm sensing armies of highly educated, extremely hard working, and in many ways very creative brains, a workforce eager to make money. And when they are enabled to do things, I think they'll do something. I'm into wild guesses: maybe they do something with wireless. Maybe they do something with material science. Maybe they devise a new way to set up a company. I don't know. There are just so many of them—so smart, so eager, so hard working, and so much wanting to be part of the future—that we have to give them some slack.

China's Unpredictability and Massive Slate of Challenges

Orville Schell ∘ What makes China difficult to prognosticate is that different and quite opposite scenarios for the future are almost equally plausible. If you look at Sweden or Australia, even at a country like Thailand, there is a relatively narrower spectrum of possibilities, give or take a meltdown or a change of governments. In China the opposite is true. I could sit here and argue the "collapse scenario" and be utterly convincing. I could argue the "peaceful evolution" scenario—slow, piecemeal reform—quite compellingly as well. I don't think that there is any country of consequence that is so unresolved. Japan is in stasis, paralyzed. Taiwan vibrates to markets around it. The Philippines is kind of a permanent low-grade basket case. Indonesia is very uncertain. India is always teetering on the brink, but always seems to survive. But China, to use a metaphor that is seemingly quite crude, is like somebody who decides they want to undergo a sex-change operation and then in the middle of it decides, let's just stop right here! They're neither he nor she.

This is where China finds itself today. It has a Leninist system adopted during the Stalin era in the early '50s that is pretty much intact, but it has an economy that is radically altered and reformed and is all fired up with the marketplace, incentives, entrepreneurship, and bottom-line mentality. One has to stand in great awe of China's ability to have unleashed these very dynamic, tectonic market forces and still maintained the amount of political control that they have. Will it last? That's the million-dollar question. And if it doesn't last, what then? You do have to respect the way in which this juncture between economics and politics has not yet tipped the whole apple cart over. Having said that, there are a lot of very, very severe and ever-tightening contradictions that, in my view, are going to be very difficult for the Party to overcome.

The problem of China's internal migration is quite staggering. China is now host to the largest migration in human history: 150 million people migrating from the countryside into the cities to pick up work with no welfare, no schools, no healthcare, no houses, nothing. In cities like Beijing, Canton, and Shanghai, roughly 30–40 percent of the populace are what they call "floating population." This works to China's advantage in certain economic ways, namely, by providing low-cost labor to build freeways, tunnels, buildings, infrastructure. But it works to China's disadvantage if there's an economic slowdown, because suddenly you then have tens of millions of displaced people. There is no context for them. They can't go back to the land.

Another huge problem centers around environmental degradation. You'd have to point to the staggering environmental cost of this development, the degradation of almost every aspect of life—air, water, estuarine life, forestry, grasslands. I suppose there were some places in the Eastern Bloc during the Soviet period, but that was mostly old-fashioned coal pollution, and drying up a river or the Aral Sea. In China, you have much more fundamental forms of resource destruction. An aquifer is pumped way down. Rivers stop flowing. For instance, the Yellow River effectively doesn't flow anymore. It used to be called "China's Sorrow" and washed away millions; now it's so dammed up and pumped out that it's basically, in the lower regions at least, a great big sewer. Water resources are in a terrible state. So is air. Twenty-five years ago you had one beautiful blue day after another in Beijing, even though they were burning a lot of coal. Now there's automobile exhaust pollution too; you don't see the sky sometimes for a month. And there's the flooding of the Yangtze because of the destruction of forest habitat in the foothills of the Himalayas. These are the costs of keeping growth rates high and the economy going.

And then there is the problem of the banks, which are effectively basket cases. They're cash registers that the state has used to bail out state-owned enterprises. It's a huge problem and China doesn't know what to do about it. They've tried to contrive an asset management regime, sort of like what we did with the savings and loan crisis. But the money has to come from someplace. And China's financial markets are rigged lotteries, manipulated by people on the inside. There's no fiduciary trust or real regulation. There's no way for investors to have confidence that they're not going to be skinned alive by a bunch of manipulators who are out to play the market. Until China gets financial markets that aren't so corrupted and poorly regulated, they will not be able to generate sufficient domestic capital to keep the economy going.

A Fundamental Collapse of Chinese Values and Ideology
Orville Schell • China is suffering from a collapse of values and ideology. Nobody believes in the Party. People are flocking to Christianity, Falun Gong, Buddhism. They are also flocking to materialism, but that doesn't quite do it. So there's a massive crisis of belief. In China, they're discovering

that when you redecorate your bathroom and get ten pairs of platform shoes and a nose job, you're still unhappy.

In China, there's no founding ideology that people can now believe in. Look at all of the fawning over Jefferson and Adams in the U.S.; it's actually quite inspiring stuff. But there are no foundation documents in China anymore. Mao Zedong is just an old ideological pirate. People can't say, "This is really inspiring; these are the stars we steer by." They have Mao's portrait up, his body stuffed in Tiananmen Square, but it doesn't do the trick. So there's a fundamental crisis of belief and ideology. There is also a crisis of spirit and values. How does one be a parent? How should one treat one's employees, one's boss? How about one's leaders? How should they behave? How should one be a citizen? There is no guide. There's no church. There's no ideology. There's no family-values structure. Chinese grab a little here and they grab a little there, but it is hardly coherent.

Their value system got reamed, steamed, and dry-cleaned in the revolution. During Mao's revolution, there was a cultural break in the link of grievous proportions, and of several generations. Whether you're talking about art, the classics, Confucian values, propriety, whatever, there was a break. It's almost as if in China's genetic code, some genes got removed. It's not enough to say, "We'll just go back to Confucius." It's like American Indians saying, "We'll live in a trailer in a parking lot and eat at McDonald's, but then we'll go back to the old ways." It's not so easy.

The Generational Shift of Power to China's Modernizers

Gwynne Dyer • There will be change in China. There is no way they can keep this bicycle moving down the road for another 10 years without it wobbling off track in one way or another. Get out of the main cities and look—Shanghai, Guangzhou, any other city. All they need is an economic downturn and they're in such deep trouble. There are an awful lot of people living on the edge. There will be huge change there.

I keep travelling back there, taking the pulse and wondering if the old regime is dead yet. The answer is, the ideology is dead as a doornail, but the system of power has not been dismantled. There is an attempt to police the Internet in China, but with, frankly, very little success. Anybody who is interested can find out anything they want. The firewalls don't stop that. They've completely given up attempts at thought control. You can think and say anything among yourselves as long as you don't stand in Tiananmen Square and put it on a poster. There's no longer any attempt to control this. In that sense, they've given up the attempt to control the information flows. You can't turn off fax machines without unplugging the whole national telephone grid. As long as the goose goes on laying the golden eggs, the old system can stagger on, but I don't really believe that it'll be there in 10 years' time.

A debate is going on inside the Chinese Communist Party now that is essentially an argument by those who believe that the party is standing with its back to a cliff and that one step back means it's dead. But there are those who say: "No, no. What people want now is prosperity, freedom to travel, and freedom of information. Stop treating them like children. Give them democracy. We can do that and hang on to power for a generation. All you have to do is abolish the Party's monopoly on communications and political power. Go to a free press, to free travel and elections. We'll win because we get the credit for it. More importantly, we'll win because we're the only party—and will be for a generation—that has a political organization in every one of the villages where 70 percent of the population live." If you want an example of how this is done, look at the Liberal Democratic Party in Japan.

In the long run, it is very likely that the modernizers will win and the last-ditch people will lose. If you analyze this—and obviously, you can't do it statistically; it's impressionistic—the bitter-enders are older than the compromisers are. It's a generational issue. Simply the turnover of a half a generation will deliver enough people who will push through the argument into the positions of power. The Party will make the jump in the interests of its own survival and the prosperity of its members.

The Dangers of Mainlining Information

Orville Schell • The Chinese have the needle in their arm in terms of the information technology revolution. They use information for business, but they don't want it to infect other areas of life in a way that might undermine one-party rule. But information tends to be unruly.

How the West Should Relate to an Ascendant China

Robert Hormats • China will be the great economic story of the first part of the twenty-first century. It has shown an enormous dynamism. With all the concerns about unemployment, the banks, and inefficient state enterprises, it has performed far better than anyone had dreamed. In the '70s, when it started to open up, there was no one who could have imagined what has happened. They have improved the living standards for hundreds of millions of people. They have improved diets, longevity, education, and health for more people in a shorter period of time than any nation in history. It's the spectacular social and economic success of our time. They have enormous problems in their state enterprises and banks and growing unemployment, but if their good policies and momentum continue, then China will remake Asia, and then the world.

It's always hard for old powers to cope with the emergence of newer powers. France ceded its power to Britain with the Napoleonic Wars. It was an uncomfortable transition from Britain to the U.S. a hundred years ago. Although it didn't involve a war, there was a lot of friction between Britain and the U.S. until World War II. China won't be the dominant power soon, but it is an up-and-coming player economically, politically, and militarily. Traditional powers are always uneasy with that process. The question is, do we work with the Chinese in an orderly way, trying to accommodate their interests and ours and building on whatever commonality of interests exists, or do we instinctively see them as a threat? That is a big question for the United States.

The one thing you can predict is that if you treat China as an enemy, the probability is it will become one. If you treat it as a country you want to cooperate with, the odds are it will respond in a way that is cooperative. It may not work that way, but at least you have a better chance if you do it that way.

The Race Between India and China

Gwynne Dyer ∘ India is the world's most unremarked miracle. Compared with China, India has one huge handicap. Eighty percent of Chinese speak the dialect of Beijing, Mandarin. There is no majority in India; 40 percent speak Hindi, but that's as good as it gets. But India has learned to deal with its huge complexity and has already crossed the hurdles. It is democratic; it is united; it recognizes its diversity; and it's got mechanisms for dealing with it. It is a federation with a lot more power at the center than, for example, the American or Australian federations have. The central governments can literally dismiss state governments in India. Yet it has held together for 50 years now.

China has a number of hurdles it hasn't crossed yet, and I think they are coming up. China at the moment has a higher per capita income than India, and it certainly looms larger in the world's consciousness, partly because it scares us more. But China hasn't dealt with democratization or the politics of redistribution in a democratic society, which India, however incompetently, has been dealing with for a long time. "How come you are that rich and I am that poor?" is a subject that hasn't been addressed yet in China, but as soon as you democratize, it will be. China hasn't dealt with decolonization either. I don't know if Tibet will ever get its independence, but if so, it will be precisely at the point when China democratizes.

India, even with all of its problems and many handicaps, is over those hurdles. Its performance has been improving, certainly in terms of political turbulence. I would say that India could be at least as prominent as China in the global scene.

India's Cultural Advantages and China's Economic Ones

Orville Schell ∘ India is the most diverse, dynamic, cultural festival I have ever seen in the world—good and bad. This country has not been culturally defoliated as China was. China had the double-whammy of a Cultural Revolution that did everything within its power to expunge traditional culture. And then, just as the situation loosened up, in came the marketplace, which can also have a very deleterious effect on traditional culture. Whereas India is just thriving with linguistic, religious, ethnic, and cultural distinctions to the point where it's a jumble of pieces. No one side can quite create a tyranny over the others. India's a bit of a mess and a bit chaotic. But if you believe as I do that people do not live by the Nasdaq alone, that they also need things like family, religion, culture, history, and values, then in a sense India is a more coherent society in its incoherent way.

Would I prefer India to China? Certainly, if I had money, I would. India has a much more relaxed attitude toward the outside world. It's not fraught with pugnacity. It has a huge cheap labor force and a very good education system. It's an English-speaking country for educated people. Yes, the transportation system isn't great. There are terrorists. There's some real strife. But India is going to be a great experiment.

It will be interesting to see if India or China wins the race, whatever the race is. In a funny way, I think China is ahead, purely economically. But for me that isn't enough. I think that's the great fallacy of economic planning. A host of things about what it means to be human don't calculate into the equation. I think human beings just don't like to be suffocated. They don't like to be poor either. So there's something to be said for an authoritative government that can feed people and let them have the basic necessities. But that's not my vision of the good life.

Russia As the "Lab Animal for the Twenty-First Century"

Bruce Sterling ∘ Russia had more twentieth century than anybody else. Every time the rest of the world got a cold, Russia got pneumonia. If there was rigid fascist stuff going on, they would have pogroms. If there were ethnic difficulties of some kind, they would deport entire populations. If there were attacks of McCarthyism, they would shoot all their authors. They carried out things in a kind of grandiose Slavic extreme. I look at the future of the twenty-first century, the downside of it, and I think of Russia as a kind of great lab animal. Everything is dysfunctional. There's a catastrophic loss of faith in their institutions, also a catastrophic loss of a sense that improvement is even possible. The immediate reaction to that seems to be very visceral. People stop having children. The health system also collapses. They're losing half a million people a year, and those are rates of population loss unprecedented in peacetime.

If your situation is in a visible decline and there doesn't seem to be any way to turn it around, people get a sense of learned helplessness. I don't think we've ever seen a society on the planet where that kind of thing has so profound an effect demographically as it does in Russia, and I worry about that.

Russia's Stabilization and Economic Turnaround

Roger Cass ∘ Russia's institutional and regulatory framework has been very weak but my perception is that there's quite a bit of progress being made. Putin is aggressively addressing the old robber-baron oligarchic controls of some of the larger companies and getting them to improve management practices and transparency to foreign investors. The Russian stock market was probably the best stock market in the world in 2001. Crime is still an enormous problem. But I think Putin is going to do a better job of dealing with it and limiting the influence of the Mafia than did Yeltsin and prior post-revolutionary administrations.

Russia isn't finished: Look at the broad context of an economy that is moving slowly toward stability, getting money, getting their tax collection under control. Capital inflows have been so strong that the Russian Central Bank has actually intervened to hold down the appreciation of the ruble, which is a total turnaround from the massive depreciations just a few years ago. They are reforming the tax system in a very responsible way by moving to a flat 15 percent tax rate, which is encouraging tax collections.

Putin is something of an enigma but he's also a pragmatist. He realizes that Russia is tied to the West. I think they're making most of the right economic moves; whether he can sustain political support in the Duma is going to be a question mark. But I like the chances for Russia.

Russia's Forward Momentum and Long-Term Rebuilding

Esther Dyson ∘ I think Russia is moving forward. In 1998 they had their equivalent to the year 2000 bubble and in both cases you just looked at the market and thought: "What are these guys smoking?" The valuations of the dotcoms were totally nutty and so were the interest rates the Russian government was paying. The government doesn't produce anything, so how can it pay interest rates of 180 percent? The whole thing collapsed and a lot of the money and Westerners fled.

Many of the Russians who had been working for Western businesses lost their jobs. Then they looked around and said, "Well, our currency is way devalued, we can't afford imports, yet people still need stuff." You could call it a boom—suddenly local manufacturing began to be profitable again. People had to deal with reality. It was a really tough time, a lot tougher than it is for these guys in Silicon Valley who may have to get a job doing something they don't like.

But it differed from the early 1990s in Russia in that there was now a large community of people who were trained in how to run a business. They had begun to understand the basics of management, administration, and production of the market economy. When the support of the VCs, capital markets, and foreign money withdrew, people started to deal with reality.

Now Russia is a very difficult place to operate; it is still corrupt. There are still a lot of problems, but some people understand that and actually want to solve them. Even some of the more corrupt people realize that it's probably better to run a business efficiently so that it makes money, because eventually they will run out of oil or whatever so they should build something that is productive. If I want other people to invest with me I have to make it reasonably transparent and honest, even if it might be simply a greedy business reason that makes me be honest. I wouldn't say they are necessarily honest but they're behaving more honestly, because they know they will develop a reputation, one way or the other.

When people ask me if they should invest in Russia, I say, "Look, if you want to spend the time getting educated, I say absolutely. But don't just throw your money over there, because what they need is education and training. They don't need just money; they need many other things. They have the resources to create stuff; what they don't have is the infrastructure and the experience to do it. It is changing slowly, but it takes an awfully long time."

The Anti-Globalization Movement

Moderating Globalization to Ensure More Winners than Losers

Orville Schell ∘ I think globalization is happening and it's not going to be stopped. It's such a powerful force because of information and transporta-

tion—the world is really shrinking. The logic of the bottom line is in-
eluctably pushing toward cheaper and cheaper labor markets. So I think we
are going to be inextricably bound up. The questions are: How do we prevent China from becoming a sewer to keep K-Mart well stocked? How do
we make globalization work to the best possible advantage of everybody?
There are many things about it that I find repugnant. But there are other
things that are positive and almost always irresistible.

This is powerful stuff, and we are living in a mercantile era the likes of
which the world has never seen. We are almost drugged on the virtues of the
market. I think we are forgetting some major things in this equation that
make life meaningful. If you look at it that way, it's sort of like sex: You cannot stop it, but you can civilize it. You can make people not rape and pillage
and hurt people. I think the best we can do with globalization is to try to
modulate some of these bad effects that we've got to identify. I'm not sure it
will be successful, but you can't just give up.

I don't think we're going to get this genie back into the bottle. So then the
question is: How do you make more winners than losers? I think the protesters, the backlash, the Ruckus Society, is a very primal howl of disease.
People don't quite know why, but they're not feeling good. It's important not
just to listen to what they say, but to listen to the fact that they're expressing some sense of being strangled and unhappiness.

The First Worldwide Uprising

Paul Hawken ∘ I think we're seeing the first worldwide uprising. We've
never seen one before. We saw proto-fascistic movements like communism
and Marxist-Leninism, but they're the opposite of what we're seeing right
now. They had charismatic, white male vertebrates leading them. The global
movement resisting corporatization doesn't have leaders that way. There is
no single leader or group of leaders. It is not organized. There are intellectual leaders, to be sure, and some heroes. But it is not as yet a political
movement. It's a social movement. We're seeing just the beginnings of it.

Sooner or later we are going into a long period of economic trials due to
the excesses of the '80s and '90s. A lot of people are going to pay the price
for these excesses with unemployment. People will call into question those
leaders and policies that preceded what they're going to experience both in
this country and the rest of the world. I'd say we're seeing the beginning of
something that's going to affect the world for a long time. At the same time,
there will be responses. There will be corporate responses, there will be governmental, institutional responses, and we don't know what those re-

sponses will be. It's hard to predict outcomes too far out because you never know whether corporations will figure it out or whether the invalidation of the IMF and the World Bank will simply create new super-institutions or whether the massive delegitimation of these institutions will create a kind of vacancy—a period of chaos in which there are no legitimate international institutions that can implement global policy.

We may be going into such a period. As long as the institutions in question see as their mandate serving corporate interests, I don't think there's any chance they will reattain legitimacy. We have to be charitable in a sense that those institutions grew out of a world that had seen the painful effects of economic nationalism that both precipitated and abetted World War II. There were enormous losses of life and suffering. Bretton Woods and the General Agreement on Tariffs and Trade and the International Monetary Fund and the World Bank were founded with values that were meant to ameliorate the conditions that preceded them. But like the Chinese adage, you become what you hate, they've become the very thing that they tried to eradicate, only this time it is economic supranationalism.

What I can imagine will happen is what is overlooked: There are 100,000 non-governmental organizations in the world today, most of them very small, who are reimagining how our world can work with 6.17 billion people, going to 9 billion by sometime in the latter part of the century. There will be a need in the next 50 years to feed and clothe and house and educate more people with limited resources than we ever have before in the history of the planet.

I think there is going to be a recognition that the solution cannot come from on high, that it cannot come from policies that are set by theory and then implemented by force. I think there is going to be a change. I think what you're going to see from an economic and social point of view is a turn toward trying to see what's actually working out there. There are a lot of things that are working well and they don't fall within the domain of international banking; they don't require massive investments. Many times they require no investment whatsoever, but they're entirely localized and self-sufficient, like the Grameen Bank micro-lending programs in Bangladesh.

I do think you are going to see some maturity in the world. Rather than trying the same thing that didn't work before, institutions might ask, with a little humility, "What is working?" It doesn't mean you can take what works and just implement it in the next village or county or valley; it means that something's working and there are deeper issues as to how that came about. There are structural and fundamental aspects about education, trust, and leadership that aren't replicable. Hopefully we will begin to understand how you create the conditions for a healthy society. In a garden, you create the conditions for a healthy plant; you don't make a healthy plant. The conditions have to do with putting the right plant in the right place and spending a lot of attention on the soil itself. The rest of it, making sure that it doesn't dry out or get overwatered, is rather simple.

The same thing holds with respect to developmental issues, because globalization is about development. There is this idea that, as Bush and other people were quick to say in Genoa, the 200,000 protesters are going to lock out the poor and consign them to lives of misery. Nothing could be further from the truth. The questions that need to be discussed are: What are the models of development? Whose idea is it, and who benefits? It doesn't mean the progressive movement or the anti-globalization movement has the answers—they may have some, but it is really people all over the world that have answers.

The answers are not in money—they are in listening. Answers have to do with imagination, design, respect. They have to do with empowering women. They have to do with healthcare and taking care of children. Essentially, they have to do with creating a world in which people do not feel insecure. That cannot be done through the coercive implementation of so-called free trade.

The Paradox of Calling Elected Officials Undemocratic

Robert Hormats ∘ Undemocratic—that word always amazes me. Demonstrators in the street, who are elected by no one, are arguing that the U.S. and other Western governments are undemocratic. The argument they might make is that what these governments are doing is unresponsive to their particular concerns—but not that it is undemocratic. They are frustrated, but by and large these are democratic governments who think what they are doing is representative of the interest of the majority of their people.

If the protesters want to have an influence on the government, they ought to go through the political process and vote to exert their influence. There is a long tradition of demonstrating publicly your opposition to a government policy, and they certainly have focused a lot of attention on these issues, but the actual decisions will need to be made by governments in the context of their own democratic governmental procedures. The notion that activists are somehow going to go around the government by appealing to big international institutions for change is folly.

The "Corporatization of the Commons"

Paul Hawken ∘ What is the commons? People have commons in their villages or towns or cities—shared spaces are a commons. The commons is the climate and the sky. Nobody owns it. The commons is the flow of resources that exists in forests, oceans, coral reefs, and wetlands. The commons is traditional medicine, traditional healing, and traditional remedies. The commons is music and culture. The commons is water, rainfall, pollination, rivers, and oceans. The commons is wilderness and wildness. These are some of the things that are the commons.

The people who are arguing most articulately and vociferously against globalization are protesting the corporatization of the commons. The commons that are being corporatized include the human genome, seeds, water, food, airwaves, media, and if the draft agendas of the World Trade Organization and the Free Trade Area of the Americas are passed, much more. The commons includes stories, music, and culture as well. It includes place and self-determination. It includes the ability for people to decide what is and what isn't acceptable as a product in a certain locality or region or place. It includes tradition. All these areas are also being taken over or corrupted by corporations.

Corporatization is caused by the unending and pressing mandate for corporations to grow their capital. Not so long ago, if a CEO led a company with a 7 or 8 percent ROI, that was considered to be a credible performance, and they could keep their job. Now if you make a return on investment of 7 or 8 percent, you're not a real man and you will be quickly replaced by someone who promises greater returns. What kind of world is it where, in the words of Hazel Henderson, capital is divine? It's a world where capital has the right to grow, and it has a higher right than the rights of people, of cultures, of place, of qualities that historically have been our commons. What happens is you have a corporate sector that is way overdeveloped, way overcapacity.

Corporations are seeking new areas in which they can grow and that just weren't imagined before. Bechtel, the Suez-Lyonnaise des Eaux and Vivendi in France, and others want to privatize water the world over. Aventis and DuPont and Monsanto want to control 90 percent of the germplasm of 90 percent of the caloric food intake of the world. Ted Turner said that in the end there will only be two media companies in the world and he wants to have a stake in one of them. Rupert Murdoch thinks the same way. McDonald's opens up 2,400 restaurants a year. Right now one out of every five meals in the U.S. is fast food and they want that to be the case everywhere in the world. Coke says that it has 10 percent of the total liquid intake (TLI) of the world and its goal is to go to 20 percent. Or is it 30 percent? These are fabulous—and I say that in the pejorative sense of the word—and absurd and devastating goals for corporations.

They are being answered by people who are suffering, not simply by white middle-class protesters in Quebec and Davos and Salzburg and Genoa and Seattle. In many places in the world where corporations are trying to implement their visions of how to grow capital, they are meeting resistance. They will continue to meet resistance from the world as long as they try to essentially colonize what people have held in common for the history of humankind.

The Strange Bedfellows Forming the New Movement

Kees van der Heijden ∘ If you look at the coalition that's behind the anti-capitalist movement, it's extraordinary to see what people have been brought together there. You see trade unions, underdeveloped countries, environmentalists, and other unlikely partners sort of working together. It's extraordinary. These people don't belong together in any traditional scheme of things. But we probably cannot express the situation all that effectively in traditional terms. We will have to invent new concepts that cover this new thing. It's such a strange combination that people have great difficulty putting a label on it. But basically it is about people who used to have power but have lost it.

The market, of course, has distributed this power over many, many hundreds of players. And while in the past a trade union or an environmentalist movement could take on a government, now they have to take on the global market, thousands of companies. National markets are so much easier to fight than the global market. I think they are looking for ways to make their adversaries more identifiable than something vague and untouchable like the "global market."

I think the real battle is between local power and the open systems. I think the open systems are the ultimate adversary. The corporations tend to benefit on the globalist side, so they're probably in that open system camp more often than not. But they're not the camp itself. For example, if Motorola fires you, then obviously Motorola's the enemy. Right? But Motorola will explain the situation: "Look guys, we can either fire 6,000 Scots or we can go broke altogether. What do you want? If we fire 6,000 Scots, then we have another 6,000 left in work, right? But if you don't allow us to do this, then what will happen is we will go broke, and then everybody's out of a job."

This disempowerment is the great frustration that people are feeling. They are up to this amorphous thing called the global marketplace. And that makes it entirely impossible to fight the system in any sort of way. So, people come to the conclusion: "OK, so we don't want this global system, because it prevents us from doing anything about what we really think we ought to do."

The Perception That Most Governments Serve Big Business

Paul Hawken ∘ In order for people to exercise democracy, there has to be a democratic unit. There has to be a place, a locale, a community, a village, a city, a county, a shire; there has to be a place in which democracy happens. If there is no place, there is no democracy. To say, as the WTO would argue about its members, that those who make these agreements are representatives from democratic countries that have been appointed by their government, so therefore this is a representative system, is nonsense.

Name more than a handful of governments in the world that are not corrupted, that are not bathed in corporate money, that aren't oligarchies, that aren't influenced heavily by corporate spending. Some of the European countries do well in this regard. The rest of world does not. Look at Dick Cheney and U.S. energy policy. He still won't release the documents about whom he met with and who had access to the vice president's office prior to the formulation of our national energy policy. The public doesn't know which oil, nuclear, and coal companies and their lobbyists met and determined what U.S. policy would be. Environmentalists were out. Scientists were out. Constituencies within the renewable energy industry were not consulted. Until corporations understand that they are spearheading a kind of commercial fascism, they're going to find that resistance will grow.

It's fascist in the sense that it is an attempt to create a meta-order for people, with the assumption that a small group of people knows better than the larger group; therefore the large group does not have to be consulted. Whether it was Marxist-Leninism or Mussolini, fascism has always been informed by the vanity that a few know more than the many. What is the WTO trying to bring to the table? Rules, order. But whose rules? Whose order?

The Imperative of Decentralization and Diversity

Paul Hawken ○ I'm not completely at odds with corporations, but I won't sugarcoat what I'm saying. The way to create healthy, vibrant economies and societies is through diversity. We know that scientifically. Any system that loses its diversity loses its resiliency and is more subject to sudden shocks and changes from which it can't recover. The corporatization of the world is the loss of diversity—it's forcing uniformity upon people. As Arnold Toynbee said, the sign of a civilization in decay is the institution of uniformity and the lack of diversity.

And that's exactly what we're seeing, only it is called "harmonization." The degree to which a company or a corporation honors and then allows diversity to emerge from a place, a country, a locale, a culture, a tribe, a city is a good thing. The degree to which it tries to enforce a one-size-fits-all formulaic solution to diet or media or agriculture is, in my opinion, going to be seen in hindsight as just as much a criminal act as the deracination of indigenous people by the Spaniards, the genocide of Native Americans, or the enslavement of African Americans. We look back at those things now and feel ashamed. We will look back at what we are doing right now to the world and see it as a violation of humanity.

The economic principle of subsidiarity says that decisions, whether they be economic or political, should always be made at the smallest or closest unit relevant to the issue at hand, because those are the people who not only have the most at stake but who also have the experience and knowledge with which to make an intelligent decision. Rather than globalization we should instead be talking about the localization and interdependence of economies, and those corporations that help with localization should do very well. For example, energy companies should introduce technologies to create local sufficiency with respect to energy to the degree that it is possible. Whether it's a global company or not, it is a company that is helping a region, a locale, a city, or a village. Any company that goes further and teaches things that allow self-sufficiency is even better. Any company that wants to dominate local economies—to buy out, take over and make that economy or country dependent on them—to me is violating what I would call humane economic principles.

The Possibility of a New Era of Social and Political Innovation

Katherine Fulton ◦ I believe the next era began with the protests in Seattle two years ago. I think we will look back on that moment the way we look back on the fall of the Berlin Wall from the previous decade. If you think about it symbolically, the wall fell and it unleashed a lot of energy. To some degree, what you saw in Seattle was a backlash against what had gotten unleashed by the Berlin Wall, the acceleration of the movement of global capital. So we had this sort of lag time of the more bottom-up social response to the consequences of the ascendance of business.

I do think it is entirely possible that the story line of the next 10 to 20 years is social and political innovation, driven by the convergence of a young generation and an aging generation facing a growing urgency of challenges. This is not a prediction but a scenario that depends on economic times not driven by fear. If the primary driver isn't fear and scarcity, then people who have ridden a 20-year business boom will be out looking for meaning and how to make a difference. They won't all be billionaires; these will be people who are just changing careers and doing different work. Then there will be the generation coming out of college, especially post–September 11, looking around and wondering what really matters in this new environment. Some of it depends on the ability of the younger generation to see themselves as citizens of the world in a new way.

Part 2

People

The Challenge of Change
Cultures and Societies

"The influence of women is a humanizing one. It tends to bring back the human dimension into very esoteric or abstract discussions, and in doing so, it reemphasizes to everybody that at least half of that human dimension happens to be female."

Dorothy Q. Thomas

"I know people in Los Angeles who believe that they are reincarnations of Indians, but who are the great, great, great, great granddaughters of pioneers, and who have Indian housekeepers who are in fact evangelical Protestants. This is a time in which we are beginning to trade off identities."

Richard Rodriguez

"The old Soviet Union was killed by television. I think part of South Africa was killed by television, too, because while I think that print and literacy would probably have killed both regimes in the end, television in both cases made the lies so vivid."

Gwynne Dyer

"You can't have part of the world where there's a small, aging bubble of Western elites and then this massive, throbbing, younger, and increasingly impoverished group of people."

Jaron Lanier

"Once rich people can genetically engineer their kids to be smart, that's a formula for conflict. I don't know that it will lead to a tiering of the human race, because before that can happen everybody else is going to get so mad that the result will be a lot of social conflict."

Francis Fukuyama

"I think one of the characteristics of this kind of situation where you have to adapt and learn all the time is a need to move toward a greater value on listening and the realization that we can't control all of this complex process of change."
Mary Catherine Bateson

Cultures and societies have been changing throughout human history—sometimes evolving slowly, at other times churning rapidly; sometimes fusing and integrating, sometimes separating and disintegrating; sometimes changing with ease, and often with painful friction. You can probably see all of these tendencies occurring simultaneously somewhere in the world. But there's also a growing sense that television, travel, transparency, and myriad other factors have accelerated and broadened social and cultural change. This chapter explores some of the causes and implications of this change—and the unique challenges they pose for the decade ahead.

We start with **The Changing Status of Women**, a profound structural shift that has already spread through the West and is now poised to transform other societies, both socially and economically. One member argues that, as the transition from agricultural and industrial work to knowledge-based work continues, pressures for equalization between the sexes can only increase. Another makes a case that successful economic development is inextricably tied to improving the rights of women, even though there may be a price to pay in terms of social disruption.

Our second section, **The New Cultural Fusion**, examines how cultures may come together in new ways. One network member sees a built-in lag time between technological and economic changes and their full social and cultural ramifications. If so, we should soon begin to see the deeper impact of the technological innovation and globalization of the 1990s on the world's cultures and societies. Many speculate on what life will be like as communication spreads and the boundaries blur between countries, cultures, and individuals. One believes that the frontier of imagination for people in the United States has already surreptitiously shifted from east-west to north-south—in other words, Americans are starting to realize that they're part of the Americas. Another says that in this decade new global cultural trends will begin outside the West, particularly in the vibrant developing world. Others speculate that we may soon see new hybrid identities that have little precedent.

We then explore **The Deepening Power of Global Media** as a key social and cultural driver of our recent past and immediate future. Many parts of the world have already experienced deep societal change partly due to television. One contributor argues that television accelerated change in the former Soviet Union and that uncensored television will have a similar impact as it reaches new regions of the developing world. Another network member counters that, on the contrary, this simply creates more opportunity for manipulation through propaganda. At the same time, continuing developments in communication technologies, such as next-generation videophones, will change how individuals connect across distances. Ultimately, advances in teleimmersion and virtual reality may challenge our definitions of what's real.

We then look specifically at some deep concerns about the coming decade of cultural and social change. In **Faultlines and Friction** we explore the growing divides and tensions within and between regions of the world. The special plight of much of Africa is a case in point: There, small, often warring ethnic tribes have yet to fuse into larger, more cohesive social groups. However, as another network member argues, the diverse societies of the developed world also are finding it increasingly difficult to reach consensus on social and cultural issues. And yet another speculates on what happens when the largely young and poor populations of the developing world can closely watch the aging, affluent populations of the developed world, an advancement that could prove to be highly combustible.

The next section focuses on **The Cultural Dilemmas of Biotechnology** that will enter the public debate this decade. We cover the scientific and technological advancements in later chapters, but here, led by social scientist Francis Fukuyama, we look at some of the major social controversies likely to surround these developments. What will happen if much more of human behavior is found to be rooted in genetic predisposition? Will we identify those predisposed to violent behavior or perhaps reengineer them? Or will the affluent be the ones to first reengineer their children and give them advantages for life? Or take a more modest but immediate and potentially widespread problem: How will businesses cope when older workers live longer and don't retire to make room for younger blood?

Finally, we turn to the topic of **Adapting to Change**. Cultural anthropologist Mary Catherine Bateson takes the lead in explaining the complicated dynamics of change that we experience in our personal lives (e.g., growing older, moving homes) against the backdrop of rapidly changing technologies and social norms. Within this context, she argues that people of all ages can adapt most effectively by honing their abilities to listen deeply and learn continuously.

The Changing Status of Women

The Information Society and the Transformation of Women's Roles

Francis Fukuyama ∘ I've been sort of optimistic about the United States because over the last few decades we've gone through a huge social disruption that's basically a byproduct of the transition to an information society out of a more hierarchical industrial order. So over the last decade, most social trends in the United States have been ticking upward. That's probably going to get screwed up by the recession, but I think the basic trend is good.

I'd look for this to happen in other countries. Japan is going to be the great test case because it is now going through a big-time 1970s-style American deindustrialization. They're going to move a lot of jobs overseas, which means that all the male heads of household will lose what they thought was a commitment to lifetime employment. There is a huge underutilized labor force of women in Japan. I think that out of sheer necessity either women or immigrants will have to be hired, and I think for the Japanese it probably will be easier to put women into the workforce. But then that's going to have a lot of the same social consequences as happened in the United States.

I think the single biggest change in social norms that was occasioned by the transition to an information society was the change in the role of women. In my view, living in an information society means that productivity is based on mental labor rather than physical labor. Women are a more natural part of the workforce in that kind of world, and that led to all sorts of changes in the family and social norms and relationships between the sexes, a lot of which were quite destructive. They were very disruptive in terms of what they did to children. In the end, society norms itself and it adjusts to various kinds of technologically driven destruction. We are coming out the other end of it now.

The countries like Japan that do it later have the advantage of seeing what happened in the countries that did it sooner, so that history never quite replicates itself. But it's just a hard thing for any society to go through.

The Impact of the Global Women's Movement

Dorothy Q. Thomas ∘ At the beginning of the 1990s, there was a lot of women's rights activism going on in different parts of the world. Out of several large UN meetings a conversation began among women's rights activists from all over the world that it was necessary not only to work within their countries but to work regionally and globally. That awareness was escalated by the onset of globalization and by a number of other factors that ultimately led to a vast scaling up of the level at which women's rights activists from different parts of the world were collaborating and conducting their activism—not only within their own countries, but at a global level.

For example, if you looked at the World Conference on Human Rights in 1993 as a kind of watershed, the first world conference on human rights in almost 50 years, the initial agenda made no mention of women. By the time that conference was over, the notion of women's rights as human rights had been thoroughly ensconced in the conference documents. There was an agenda setting forth the need to protect and promote women's human rights as a core effort of the global human rights enterprise.

That is a fundamental shift in perspective on women, on women's status, and on the relevance of women's issues that occurred in a roughly three-year period. That change was attributed entirely to the fact that women were globally organized and present at that conference and were refusing to accept second-class status. They would not accept that what they experienced was less than what any other human being experiences, that it's somehow OK to abrogate their rights because it's a cultural thing or a personal thing or a family thing, whereas it would not be OK to abrogate the rights of a man in a similar situation.

The influence of women is what I would say is a humanizing one. It tends to bring back the human dimension into very esoteric or abstract discussions, and in doing so, it reemphasizes to everybody that at least half of that human dimension happens to be female.

Empowering Women Spurs Development—And Resistance

Dorothy Q. Thomas • If you empower a woman to make better decisions— say you enable her to own land and to manage that land, or you enable her to make reproductive choices and to manage those choices free of violence— you affect not only that woman, but you're very likely to affect her family and her community. If you went through a similar process with a man you would not have that extensive of an effect because their relationships are different. The woman is more responsible with respect to the family and community than a man, and exercises her influence accordingly.

Amartya Sen, the Nobel Prize–winning economist, has shown the degree to which the neglect of the rights of women has impeded, if not utterly retarded, development in different parts of the world, and that addressing the rights of women is an essential component of successful overall growth. His argument is that rights are a crucial component to any kind of effective long-term growth and the rights of women cannot be neglected in that regard.

I think that message has been pretty widely received. I don't know how well received. There was, and continues to be, enormous resistance. For the same reason there is enormous resistance to globalization. If you talk about enhancing the power of women, you're basically talking about re-structuring every social organ, from the family on up. Everybody's power relationships are going to change. The resistance to that is profound, as profound as the resistance to any kind of transformation in the area of na-tional identity or sovereignty. In fact, it attacks pretty much the same un-derlying principles.

The New Cultural Fusion

At the Threshold of a Cultural Revolution

Joel Garreau ∘ In the 1990s, I was assuming that any technological revolu-tion of this magnitude has to lead to a social upheaval of similar magnitude. Yet when you look at the '90s in the United States, it's a really boring decade socially. It was peace, prosperity, and Monica Lewinsky. That was the news. We were not seeing the social upheaval that we could rationally expect.

So that leads me to my current hypothesis, which is that the '90s were like the '20s or the '50s. The '20s were a period of great technological up-heaval: the widespread adoption of refrigeration, telephones, automobiles, radio, and any number of things. And yet it was a pretty frivolous decade, which was followed by the massive social upheaval of the '30s. Similarly, the '50s had everything from television to the atomic bomb to birth control to mass-produced suburban housing. The litany is endless, and yet it, too, was a really boring decade—the Eisenhower decade—which was followed by the cultural upheaval of the '60s. So my working hypothesis is that the '90s was that quiet decade, and this decade that we're heading into is the period of seismic cultural upheaval.

Actually, it's Betty Sue Flowers who gave me the first decent explanation of what I'm doing in terms of this whole cultural revolution hypothesis. Her argument is that the '30s were about justice, especially economic justice. That's what the upheaval was about. The '60s were about authority: the civil rights revolution, Vietnam, who's the daddy, who's in charge here. She argues that this new cultural revolution involves figuring out how we fit together into a larger picture. The reason we're having so much trouble is that we don't have a common frame of reference anymore as to what constitutes truth or beauty or logic or anything. It's been going downhill since the En-lightenment, but hasn't hit a crisis situation until now. What I'm seeing suggests that we've been pushed to think outside the box for so long that we've lost track of what value a box has.

It's the search for the box, which is the search for a new framework to understand reality. Why bother? We need the box because it's difficult-to-impossible for different parts of society to work together toward a common goal if they don't have some common framework—something as basic as what constitutes reality. It's a collective project. So obviously, the great irony is we're talking about getting back in the box. That's what this cultural revolution is about: how everything fits together that now appears disconnected.

Even the current economic view is sort of holistic. The conventional wisdom is that everything is connected to everything, that the guy working in the Nike factory in Malaysia really is connected to you in some important way. In economics, it's increasingly clear that you can't have any one activity in China without having multiple effects on the larger network, many of them unintended and unanticipated. That economic notion, that everything is stuck together, comes as an overlay on top of the environmental view, which has a similar take: that everything is connected to everything else, that each piece of the puzzle has value. So some obscure snail in the middle of nowhere has a value because it is part of the larger network. That's what we may be trying to head for—trying to figure out where we fit in this network because it's getting stranger all the time.

Where things fit. How things fit. How I fit. It's about identity. Who am I? Who am I relative to these other people? These people sitting next to me, these people in Iran, these people in France. I'm not talking identity politics the way it's used now, which is that you base your claim to fame on how aggrieved you are because you're a left-handed transvestite Laotian or something like that. That may be part of the early indicator, that we are getting this weird identity politics that is tearing us apart when, in fact, the project is trying to figure out how we fit together.

It's the search for coherence in what is increasingly incoherent. We're trying to get into the box. We are trying to create a new box. Thinking outside the box turns out to be so yesterday.

Global Diversity Represents an Opportunity to Learn

Mary Catherine Bateson ○ To the extent that globalization reduces diversity, it is destructive. The issue is whether we can move toward a sense of globalization that includes a value for diversity of all kinds and a valuing of the distinctive things of particular cultures and traditions.

When I first heard the word globalization, my immediate response was, "Wow, that can only be a good thing." But if globalization produces uniformity with a huge loss of knowledge and species and all of that, then it's not a good thing. It's being part of a global community in which there's a huge amount of difference and diversity and opportunity to learn from others. Diversity represents an opportunity to learn.

America's Shifting Axis from East-West to North-South

Richard Rodriguez ∘ When I think of globalization, I think of that new line in the American imagination, which is the line that was missing. We'd always written the American history book like Hebrew, east to west, against the page, which is why we couldn't tolerate the Chinese in California. We were deeply threatened by people who came to the continent from the other direction. They were coming and telling us that California is how America began. We were going through our melodramatic insistence that Venice Beach was the end of the road and here were all the Chinese kids going to Berkeley from the other direction. During World War II, of course, we couldn't stand it. What else could these people be but subversives? They had to be linked to another reality, and in fact, they were. They were insisting that the map went in the other direction. Those lines now that come west to east and north and south are really the beginning of our globalization, and they are not easy math.

For all the insistence on CNBC about global business, Americans have not reconciled themselves to the Americas yet. We are just beginning to discover the Americas. That we exist within this hemisphere is still a relatively new idea to us. We understand business, we understand oil in Venezuela, and we understand that Mexico drinks more Coca-Cola than the United States does. We understand that Americans now consume more hot sauce than they do catsup, which, if there is really any indication that this society is in the advance, I think that's it. But we don't understand fully that we are a country now, not as in the Irving Berlin song, between coast and coast, but between hot and cold. We know that is a dangerous place to be, on the plains in the middle of summer when the cold draft comes off the Canadian expanse and meets the warm flow from the Gulf of Mexico. We know that's a very dangerous place to be, between hot and cold. We are driven ideologically between these two extremes.

Americans are using globalism as an abstraction. When you're talking about globalism, then we really have to start wondering what it is that we're related to, where we are globally in the world. This idea that America sits within the Americas is an idea that most Americans are resisting. As recently as 10 years ago, there was a statistic that one in three San Diegans had never been to Mexico. These are people who live right on the border. It is interesting to me that we could be so uncurious about a place that is so proximate to us. Almost every teenager in Mexico is bilingual. Everybody knows what movies are playing in the United States. No American can tell you what television shows there are in Tijuana, what they listen to, or what they do that's Mexican.

Why Americans Must Engage Differently with the World

Mary Catherine Bateson ◦ I feel that Americans cannot limit our interaction with the rest of the planet to commerce and technology and warfare. If we engage in commerce, we should also be thinking of all the places we do business with as developing societies, and societies with distinctive contributions to make. To the extent that we are exporting technology, we should be listening and importing ideas and learning from other countries. To the extent that we are engaged in a military campaign, we should already be planning now for peace and for a way for Afghanistan, a miserable country, to be prosperous, self-confident, and peaceful. If America wants to be isolationist, we should stop exporting weapons. Do you see what I mean? The trouble with globalization is that it's one-sided. We are withdrawing from global responsibility on things like Kyoto without withdrawing from interfering, exploiting, and things of that sort.

It's really important that American citizens know more about the world and know more about what American corporations are doing in the world and the effect that we're having and what human beings in other places want, and how they live. We might understand why so many of them are angry with us. Interdependence is an empirical fact. To make it work, we have to make it work at every level. If we are deeply engaged in the world, let's engage in every possible way. If it were possible to pull back and have nothing to do with the rest of the world, I might argue that that was a very dull choice, but it would be a makeable choice. But it's not.

The Proliferation of Great Films from Around the World

Alex Singer ◦ That good films are coming out of Iran or Korea or Mainland China seems extraordinary. I remember when the picture *Rashomon* came from Japan, and the impact that had on me. And I understood something without even trying to put the words around it. Once the Japanese could make *Rashomon*, they were going to be part of my world in a way that I could not anticipate. This obscure, beaten, ruined country was somehow going to be in my face. And I knew that because they couldn't have made *Rashomon* in the early 1950s unless that were true.

Japan was the most devastated country in World War II, in terms of the atomic ruin of major cities and the destruction of the old order. The changes in, say, Germany were relatively cosmetic compared to the changes that were happening in Japan, in terms of concepts of governance, for example. That they could produce such a work was for me a signal.

There are countries in Africa that I can hardly name that are producing films now, and there's Iran and Iceland and so on. So it's no longer the province of the Western industrial countries at all. We're ignoring India, of course, by saying Western industrial countries. Film as a universal form— film you can export and that will be understood and that will move people from another society, that's the kind of film I'm talking about. Those kinds of films will generate fresh ideas, which is what *Rashomon* did.

The Human Impulse to Absorb the Stranger

Richard Rodriguez ∘ That impulse to absorb the stranger begins as early as 1492, which is when the Indians see Columbus. They come to the water's edge to look at him. That impulse of taking the stranger in is what I would argue is one of the great annotations one must make to whatever Marxists say about colonialism. You cannot explain what is happening in the world right now without understanding that impulse, that absorption of the stranger. I would call that a feminine impulse, or maybe even an Asian impulse. I say Asian because the strength of the Asian impulse in my cosmology has always been in its willingness to imitate, take you in, absorb you. In the very broader sense, it is the contemplative rather than the active European, Hellenistic impulse.

In the 1950s, the Japanese, having been defeated by the male principle in history, happily so, came to see Detroit make automobiles. They came over with their cameras, which we thought was amusing because they were always taking pictures of things. They came over in groups, which we thought was even more amusing because we are solitary creatures. Then they went back to make the Toyota. We still don't know what happened. We still don't get it. How does that work? How is it possible in the process of taking to turn it around? How is it possible that maybe the greatest writer in my generation in English right now is a brown man who writes about India in snowy Toronto?

We don't understand that, so we don't understand these Mexican kids I met in Tijuana, Mexico—the city we think we invented, and we did, we Americans, out of our lust. Forty years later there are these boys who belong to a group called Victory Outreach, which is an evangelical group along the Mexican-U.S. border. They are evangelical Protestants that work with kids, usually with very serious drug or gang problems. They were telling me that they were about to go to Europe to convert Europe back to Protestant Christianity. I thought to myself, nowhere in the *New York Times* or the *LA Times* or the *Washington Post* was there mention that there were four-foot-tall Mexican Indians going to Europe to convert Europeans to Christianity.

That impulse in the world right now that I see in some very powerful way is really off the radar of most Americans. I just don't think that we understand what's going on around us. We are desired. But to be desired is also in some sense to be embraced. I keep trying to teach kids that instead of keeping yourself separate, if you really want to get involved with the dynamics of the world right now, you have to start stealing cultures. That includes Americans.

This Decade's Big Trends May Blow in from Outside the West

Kevin Kelly ∘ In the next 10 years some of the most important trends and developments for the U.S. will come from outside the U.S. This may be a bit of a blow-back phenomenon, or it may actually be something wholly original and creative. This is very hard for us to imagine, but we had an example recently: the Islamic suicide martyr. That terrorism definitely came from the outside and had a huge effect on our country. But I'm not suggesting that these are always going to be insults to us. It could be a completely different way of doing business or some kind of political movement started in Eastern Europe or an ideology. It could be a youth movement that began in Latin America—something substantial that is not just going through America, but going through other parts of the world.

California's Gold Rush As an Early Implosion of Civilizations

Richard Rodriguez ∘ It was Karl Marx who said about the California Gold Rush, "It would be the great modern event of civilization." What Marx understood about the California Gold Rush is that for the first time in history, with the discovery of gold in California, the entire world would come to one place. That had never happened before in the history of the world. Even though the Roman Empire had gathered its known world to its center, in fact there are vast parts of the world that didn't come. With the discovery of gold in California it was exactly at the moment of possible movement that you could have the Malay, the Australian, the Scotsman, the Peruvian, the Chilean, the Chinese, the Japanese, the Frenchman, and the African converging on one point. I think he was talking about that implosion of civilization on one place, which is what we're seeing now.

Where Will the New Cultural Revolution Happen First?

Joel Garreau ○ My area of interest and expertise over the last 20 or 30 years has been North American culture and values, including Mexico and Canada and the Caribbean. There are a couple of sound reasons to be interested in this culture. One is that for 400 years, the future has tended to show up here first.

The American Revolution was ahead of the French Revolution, which was ahead of the Russian Revolution. Yes, the Industrial Revolution started in England, but right quick the American system of technological, mass production took the fore. We're always grappling with the new.

To this day, the Americans are unique in world civilization. They have the power and the money and the freedom to do whatever they think best. They don't wait for the government to come in and tell them what to do. "It is God's will"—that is not from our language. "Que sera sera"—that is not from our language either. I'm interested in watching the people with the money, the power, and the freedom to change the world, and if it happens to be Americans, I'm interested in that.

There isn't any place that I find more interesting right now, but this could be lack of imagination on my part. The best argument I've seen against my position is that I haven't heard a Bob Dylan. I haven't yet heard the music of this revolution coming out of America. I keep waiting to hear the 2001 equivalent of "The Times They Are A-Changin'." I keep waiting for that voice.

I'll admit that I'm wrong and accept that the Cultural Revolution is being born outside America if confronted with the right facts. Here's what I'm waiting for: a Bolivian rock-and-roll band to get to the top of the charts in South Korea without having gone through an American music company and have it all happening on the Web. That would do it for me. That's the "aha" moment. That's the "times they are a-changin'" moment.

The Strange Swapping of Identities

Richard Rodriguez ○ I know people in Los Angeles who believe that they are reincarnations of Indians, but who are the great, great, great, great-granddaughters of pioneers, and who have Indian housekeepers who are in fact evangelical Protestants. This is a time in which we are beginning to trade off identities. The Indian is the Christian and the European is the pagan. The Puritan may end up being the Brazilian and the Bostonian may end up naked in Tahiti.

The Deepening Power of Global Media

The Beginnings of True Globalism As We Finally Connect All

Kevin Kelly ○ For the most part, globalism has been mostly theory and abstraction but what we're headed into is a period of real globalism, where we have different cultures truly impacting people all around the world at once. It seems very hard to believe that we could possibly connect every person in the world and not have more phenomena and more experiences sweeping through the entire world. I can't believe that we can have every person on the Internet, watching TV, or having a phone and not experience global phenomena for good and bad. That's the point that we have to realize. I think some shocking things will happen, sometimes shocking in a horrible sense and sometimes shocking in a fun cultural sense, all because you've got everybody connected together. That just seems to me to be inevitable.

The power of communications at its best, and this is of course the difference between the Internet and TV, is that you have a generative ability. The Internet gives every person in the world the ability not just to consume everything simultaneously, but to generate something, to send out, to make. That's the new territory. We've seen what happens when everybody in the world consumes, whether it's Dallas or the Olympics or a video image, but what about when they're all making something or they're going to march somewhere. Like Woodstock—a million people are going to appear at some corner of the globe. They'll collectively have this idea to meet for some reason and come together at one spot from every country in the world because of this communication medium. Who knows what they'll do? But the world will wake up and say, "My gosh, how did that happen?"

In the year 3000, they'll look back to this time and marvel, "Oh man, to have been alive then, because that was the first time in the history of the world, of this planet, when it was wired up for the first time, when they connected everybody together." That only happens once. And as that's happening, we are able to exchange information, exchange value, communicate in hundreds and thousands of new ways and new directions that were never before possible.

As we amplify and enhance communication, making it simultaneous and global—exploding the power of communication around the world and linking everybody up for the first time—we are creating this vast territory of possibilities for new kinds of institutions, new industries, new kinds of business, and new ways of doing business. That to me is like coming to the New World for the first time. This is a frontier. So much is being discovered in this next couple of generations and the effects will last thousands of years, just like the town structures that we set up as settlers came to the New World.

The Power of Media in Spreading Propaganda

Jaron Lanier • I think that World War II was a media war. Humans weren't yet used to moving images well enough to be able to deal with them in a balanced way, so propaganda was too powerful. If you look at Nazi culture, it was essentially a culture of media and media events. For us today such media wouldn't mean that much because we are inured to it, but for them it was so overwhelming that people became stupid. With the fall of the Soviet Union, it came to light that Stalin spent an unconscionable amount of money on a Manhattan Project for new media to do propaganda. He was essentially working on forms of virtual reality very early without success; he had this vision of simulated reality to masses of people as a way to influence them. Had it worked, I think it would have had the effect that he hoped for.

The thing about this is that it's all relative. Brains adjust. We're adaptive creatures. For us in the West, we've already been through World War II and media is no longer as powerful to us. We can accept it in proportion. The kids who grow up on MTV would not be as swayed by war propaganda because they're like, "Eh, I've seen it all."

One of the reasons that the peace process didn't lead to an agreement in the Middle East in the last couple of years is because a lot of people in that part of the world are seeing real propaganda for the first time and haven't been able to adjust to it. There is, for the first time, Arab television that just makes people nuts. It's really striking. I think that it might take a generation for them just to get used to it, to be able to say, "Ah, that's just TV. This is stupid."

Television Allows People to See Things for Themselves

Gwynne Dyer • The old Soviet Union was killed by television. I think part of South Africa was killed by television, too, because while I think that print and literacy would probably have killed both regimes in the end, television in both cases made the lies so vivid.

You can trace the spread of literacy and printing around the planet. You can explain a great deal of the democratization of the third world by the fact that you first get a mass vernacular press in the old ex-colonial countries in the 1960s. Give it a generation to work. Of course they're going to get on with this, but it will be the 1980s or 1990s by the time they do.

Now they've also got television. Television has huge penetration. There's no Indian village where you can't buy a satellite hookup—somebody is illegally taking it down from a satellite and selling connections. I think that television is a wonderful medium because it makes it so hard to lie. Television requires pictures for every single second of sound, meaning that there always have to be pictures germane to the subject under discussion on the screen. The real world is very hard to fake. You can change the camera angle, you can edit out the bits that don't fit your story, but you've got to go with the pictures you can get.

By the late 1980s there had been 70 years of absolutely Orwellian control of the mass media in the old Soviet Union—to the extent that they would send out new pages to paste into the encyclopedia when history changed. What they used to say in the Soviet Union at the time was, "The future is known, but the past changes." Since about 1970, almost everybody in the Soviet Union has a television set, but they didn't relax the censorship until about 1987. The 24-hour shower of lies continued completely unaltered through all of that time, yet when you went into the kitchens of people in Moscow, everybody knew everything about their own society. They could tell you as much as the *New York Times* could, maybe more.

I think they did it by watching their own television and reading their own newspapers, but viewing and reading between the lines and filling in the blanks. That is actually easier to do with TV because there have to be pictures. The pictures won't always go with the lying words that are superimposed over them. Once you figure out that you're being lied to, and you watch a half-hour of this every night, you begin to join up the dots and discern the shape of the truth. It was a sort of collective, national project of deciphering the truth, which worked amazingly well. They knew everything. Increasingly you find this in other societies as well.

Hollywood: The Perennial Global Messenger

Walter Parkes ∘ For the past 100 years, Southern California has been the center for the world's image-making machine. It's been that way for decades and will continue that way for decades, and it is strangely not subject to the vicissitudes of the economy. It siphons social ideas and incorporates them into its messages. It's at times prescriptive and mostly reflective. And it has historically had the role of being the dream machine for the world.

Even so, things have changed a lot; it's becoming a far more international market for movies. That's not for every kind of movie. They have to be more archetypal big pictures, ones that tend to have strong iconic values. You don't get that sort of thing on, say, most American comedies, which are very culturally specific.

The first consideration when you hear a movie idea pitched is whether there's something that rings the bell in the room on some kind of deeply intuitive level. Then, as you try to justify how much you plan to spend on the movie, you tend to look at what its box office potential is. We tend to make movies according to how we assess their value around the world.

We recently considered a very interesting project. It was a merging of a Western and a samurai movie, about a Civil War officer who goes into hard times for the 10 years after the war. He's found by an agent and is brought to Japan to help the emperor build an army, at a time when the army outlawed samurais. He leads an army against this renegade samurai, and he realizes that as a character he's more like the samurai, a man left out of time. He eventually goes over to the side of the samurai.

In a movie like that, because it's going to be expensive, you want to find a market where you feel reasonably sure of its success. Japan would top that list. We then said, "Wait a minute. How is a Japanese audience going to react to a Western cowboy who comes in and becomes a hero for a samurai?" And on top of that, it has an American director.

I called up our distributors in Japan and had this conversation. Are there built-in cultural problems with this story? Even if we do the best possible job of it, are there issues that that culture will have problems with? And, sure enough, there were. We ultimately decided that the budget it required was too risky to go ahead. But it literally had to do with seeing the market as a global market, seeing within that global market a particular place where the movie should be robust, i.e., Japan, and realizing that this particular story might have cultural problems in that market.

Why Communication Technologies Might Displace Travel

Jaron Lanier ∘ Telecommunications is interesting. The first tests with very crude analog videophones were done in the 1960s. For the last four decades, there's been a problem, which is that people don't like them. There are various reasons, the most obvious being that, until recently, it was impossible to create a videophone where people could make eye contact. Because the camera and the screen were in different locations, it was impossible for people to look at each other, and that was upsetting.

A secondary reason was psychological. I hope not to be pounced upon for this, but women more than men were overly self-conscious at being exposed visually. What's interesting now is that, in order to deal with bandwidth restraints, we're doing visual communications with high-level control points rather than transmission of bit maps. The eye-contact thing is easily solved so that people can look at each other. Also, since we are reconstructing what people look like, it's possible to change their hair and what they're wearing. The level of exposure is tremendously reduced. We can have pseudo-realism instead of perfect realism. With those two features, I think it will start to take off.

Telecommunications is driven by two primary demographics: One is businesspeople and the other is teenage girls. Businesspeople typically communicate at large distances as an alternative to traveling those distances; teenage girls communicate at short distances just because that's what they do. That's pretty much cross-cultural.

For businesspeople, the competition is essentially between telecom and air travel. Air travel is not pleasant at this point because the volume is already beyond the comfortable capacity of the existing infrastructure. There's also a psychological factor here. In my mind, commercial air traffic safety is one of the greatest technological triumphs in the whole history of our species. Having said that, there is an inevitable error rate in any technology. When there's an error in a commercial aircraft, hundreds of people die.

These are all indicators to me that, as our technologies improve, there will finally be more of a sense that the businesspeople I was talking about will start to use teleimmersion—or near teleimmersion—as an alternative to air travel. The implications of that are enormous. It will create more of a sense of locality because it means that people will stay in one place more often than we now do.

How Communication Technologies Will Boost Travel

Paul Saffo ○ The essence of cyberspace is this: In cyberspace, there is no distance between two points. Now that has very surprising consequences. Some people still hold on to this quaint notion of travel substitution—that we're going to trade airplane seats for computer screens and we'll travel less because we'll videoconference more. Absolute hokum.

I have the statistics to back me up. When you talk to someone electronically, if you talk to them long enough, inevitably it leads to a face-to-face meeting. Once you meet face to face, you want to continue the conversation electronically in-between, so that more electronic communications lead to more travel, and more travel leads to electronic communications. In fact, if you run the statistics out, travel miles and telecommunications minutes have been chasing each other upward for the last half-century. But now what we're getting is not travel substitution, but travel shifting. By having more communication and travel options, we make both more convenient— we end up doing more of both.

I know where this ends up. We will spend all our time on airplanes. The plane will never land, but we'll never notice because we're so busy video-conferencing with our virtual travel agents scheduling our next trip.

The Dangers of Addiction to Next-Generation Virtual Reality

Alex Singer ∘ The development of immensely more sophisticated virtual realities introduces a new form of complexity to our society. It's not just another kind of game. I know this from my own experience when I was involved 12 years ago in the development of Jaron Lanier's head-mounted displays of virtual reality. At a very crude level, I found them immensely intoxicating. And the notion that if it were improved a thousand-fold, could I measure out a healthy level of participation? The answer is, I don't know. I haven't been tempted with that.

I think VR will have a truly significant impact on the fabric of societies. It will be similar to what the Internet has done by capturing a significant population who do things that are, for example, not healthy for either their physical bodies or their somatic systems, or for their relationship to the people immediately around them. That phenomenon is growing.

We are an addictive species. I don't know whether it's also true about the whole phyla of mammals, but certainly this primate is highly addictive, and to any number of things. These are deeply addictive things that can intrude on our physical operations as individuals. It can intrude on the fabric of the social order. And I'm talking about the whole globe, not just America. Because the vulnerability to these things is universal to the animal. We're dangerous to ourselves. We're dangerous to others. And addiction is one of those phenomena. And it does represent a wild card.

It also represents all the incredible potentiality of the Internet, and those virtual-reality journeys can and almost certainly will produce phenomena having to do with the way we understand ourselves, the way we understand art, the way we experience the universe. I think it may affect our spirituality in profound ways, so that you're now on the edge of a precipice that we simply have no experience with.

Faultlines and Friction

Growing Gaps Create Mounting Instability

Jaron Lanier ∘ This is a terribly unstable world. I'm actually quite worried. This is where the long boom falls apart for me. I look at Mexico City and I look at Islamabad. What are these people going to do? They're going to be ultra-screwed by the end of the carbon fuel cycle. All these people who are just frustrated and miserable are watching media and seeing these old people resting on their laurels in the West. It's hard for me to see nice scenarios come out of that.

Now maybe there could be some. If I want to construct a happy ending to this story, one might be: sure, they're not well educated but it doesn't matter because there are technologies that allow them to be as effective as if they were well educated. You don't need to be literate anymore—the computers are smart enough to understand you. Maybe there's some happy scenario where things do work out and all of those many people find fulfilling lives. Maybe. But you can't have part of the world where there's a small, aging bubble of Western elites and then this massive, throbbing, younger, and increasingly impoverished group of people.

Here I have to talk about the absolute and the relative. In absolute terms, there's been a decrease in abject poverty in the last 20 years. The rising tide does raise all boats. However, if the top rises at a faster rate than the bottom, then the difference between them will be getting larger, not smaller. That's the system we're in.

We still tend to think in terms of this opposition between the two competing ideologies. At one end you have the Left's ideology, which is a zero-sum game with the poor needing to battle the rich for any gains. Then there's the trickle-down ideology of the neo-conservative Right, which is that the wealth trickles down and raises everybody. Neither of those models is correct. What's actually going on is the poor are doing better but at a slower rate than the rich, so the separation is getting greater and greater. No established ideology reflects that third circumstance, which is the one that we're seeing on both a national scale and an international scale. That missing ideology needs to be articulated.

Remember that human psychology is driven by relative perceptions. There are peoples for whom the ability to live at all would at one time have been a tremendous achievement. Now they also demand dignity and autonomy and all sorts of things. Our desires are relative. There's a wonderful quote of Jefferson's that says something like 90 percent of human experience is based on expectation rather than actuality. Even if the poor are rising, if they perceive that the difference between themselves and the rich is getting even greater, they might subjectively think of themselves as being more screwed rather than relatively better off. It's absolutely essential to recognize that.

In an era of biotechnology, at some point there's just a break. People become different. The people who are much better off have so many different biological options that they are in a different status. I don't really know if their brains are different, but they certainly have vastly different life expectancies and possibilities. With some control of major diseases and a bit of genetic tweaking, certainly the life span of the elite can be increased. Let's say that the average life span of somebody in a poor country goes from 50 to 60 in 10 years, but it goes to 200 for some elite people in the West. The distance between 50 and 80 is less than between 60 and 200. When it gets to 60 and 200, it's really like two species. I think at that point there's war, even if the other people are still improving.

Africa's Unique Social Challenges

Gwynne Dyer ∘ There are 51 or 52 countries in Africa, depending on how you view it. Africa, counting North Africa, has about 15 percent of the world's population but it is more chopped up and divided than Europe. That is very fundamental to Africa's problems, but not in the classic analysis that the colonial borders have carved up Africa without attention to ethnic groups. That's true, but hardly unique; have a look at the Hapsburg Empire sometime.

The problem is more fundamental: People live in relatively small groups that have a long history of not liking their neighbors. There are 600 million people in sub-Saharan Africa. I can only think of three ethnic groups in Africa, south of the Sahara, with more than 10 million people, including the Horiba and the Zulu, who are probably closer to 9 million. Then there are at least 200 ethnic groups of over a million and that means the average size of ethnic groups is very much smaller than it is elsewhere. Even then you could argue all day about what an ethnic group is, where you draw the borders, are people part of the same ethnic group if they speak two dialects?

This predates colonialism and significant European contact. Nation building and democracy become very difficult when you are that carved up. The contrast is huge, if you look at the rest of Eurasia. Eight ethnic or at least linguistic groups account for 75 percent of Europe's population. Three linguistic groups account for half of Asia's. In the Americas, only three languages are spoken, four if you count Haiti and Quebec. Yes, there are some complications, because of mestizos and Indians. But basically these are very large societies, big units.

Whereas in Africa, the average ethnic linguistic unit is tiny, and it has been that way forever. In the rest of the world, except Africa, all of these little tribes with their dialects, traditions, history, and grudges got ground together by the great imperial powers into much bigger groups. When Caesar invaded Gaul there were 40 different tribes. Now there's the French. The same is true with Germany, China, Britain, Italy. Although this process continues into the present, it was mostly accomplished a thousand years ago.

If you look at North America before the European conquest, it looks just like Africa, with 500 tribes. We swept them aside and now they live on reservations or have integrated into the larger society and are no longer a political problem. But if North America had modernized with those 500 tribes and there'd been no European invasion, America would look just like Africa. Politically it would be a mess.

Africa didn't go through the imperial process of grinding together because large empires never arose there. I believe it's because of disease. If you can't keep horses—and they die without modern medicine—you have no mode of power beyond human labor to build your empire. Then the empires don't arise and the little groups don't get ground together into bigger groups. Apart from the very southern tip of Africa, disease kept European settlement out. Although conquered politically, Africa is the only bit of the pre-1500 world outside of Eurasia to make it into the present more or less intact.

But now what do they do? They are trying to modernize their economies and create inclusive political systems with far more ethnic complexity than exists elsewhere. Africa makes the Balkans look simple. It is a canard that the borders drawn by the colonial powers are to blame; there are no borders you could draw to fix this problem. Do you want 200 countries?

Africa's solution is to move beyond identification with one's own ethnic group, and that is a lot to ask. There aren't a lot of examples of really multi-ethnic countries that work well, even in the West. We're expecting Africa to come up with a solution, and it will have to. This is a hill no one else has had to climb. So I am not very hopeful in the short term about Africa. Because until it climbs that hill it's not even going to develop economically.

Anything Could Happen in China

Kevin Kelly ∘ China and India are vast and, culturally, I think their transition to the modern world will surprise us for its speed and its weirdness. It's like Germany and Japan making a very rapid transition from being war-torn nations or Taiwan transitioning from a third-world country to a very cash-rich, developed nation. The astonishment in China is going to be huge.

I think there will be some horrors. They could range from China fragmenting like the Soviet Union, to China becoming weirder than the Communists, in the sense that they become very authoritarian. You could have strange things happening like Taiwan actually wins and China becomes completely mercantile like Hong Kong, only more so. Or we could see the resurrection of communism or something like the Falun Gong could set things off. It's almost an open book in terms of what could happen in China.

Seeking Consensus in a More Diverse, Complex Society

Frank Fukuyama ∘ It's always been the case that culture and social norms are difficult and slower to change than technology, so it's not as if this is a new problem. In many ways, the kinds of social changes that took place in the United States between 1850 and 1900 were more momentous than the changes that took place between 1950 and 2000. That's when everybody essentially moved from the family farm to the city to work in factories. I don't think that the Internet even compares to that kind of change in people's lives, or the kinds of norms that accompany this different kind of urbanized industrialized life.

What's new is more cultural diversity and a bigger and more complex society. That makes it extremely difficult to generalize about what's going on. You can get pockets of different kinds of cultural adaptations or cultural stasis and they all coexist in the same society. People who don't like the change will simply wall themselves off and live in a community where they don't have to deal with it. You have a lot of geographical diversity in this country, so it's possible to do that pretty easily, which means that characterizing the society at all culturally is just really, really difficult.

Getting society-wide consensus on certain issues is much less likely now than in earlier generations. The difficulties are largely at a cultural level. Politically, the world is getting more unified. You have more democracy and more democratic legitimacy around the world. Below the level of politics, you have this incredible cultural diversity and disagreement.

The Cultural Dilemmas of Biotechnology

Why Biotechnology Will Prove Highly Contentious

Frank Fukuyama ∘ About six or seven years ago, I began to realize that the biotech revolution was, in the end, probably going to be a lot more consequential than the information technology revolution. I started thinking through some of the ways in which biotechnology could have unanticipated social consequences and what some of those might be. I have to confess I'm not a techno-libertarian. There's the *Wired* magazine–type perspective that says that anything technology produces is going to be great. I think you could make the case that IT has produced very little social harm that anyone can identify. But the potential for biotechnology doing a lot of things that we may not be that happy with is, I think, a lot higher.

For example, greater knowledge about the heritability of characteristics will have definite political impacts. We've already had this big fight over things like the Bell curve, and the larger discussion about the heritability of intelligence and the difference between races. My view is that it's an unresolved issue. There's going to be more empirical scientific work done, and it's going to be hugely controversial: We'll be able to connect genes to different kinds of social behaviors, not just intelligence but alcoholism, crime, and aggression.

There's a lot of history behind this. At the beginning of the century, under the impact of crude social Darwinism, people thought that virtually everything was hereditary. There was a big reaction to this, which got a further stimulus from the Holocaust and Hitler. By the middle of the century, most social scientists thought almost nothing was heritable and that everything was simply socially constructed. The pendulum has swung back very heavily toward the heritability side because of the revolution in genetics and a much greater understanding of the actual mechanisms that link genes to behavior. The psychological profession now thinks that intelligence is about 50 percent heritable, which means genes account for 50 percent and other environmental factors account for the other 50 percent. Fifty years ago people would have put the heritable number much lower.

With neuropharmacology, you're at the beginning of a period where you'll be able to alter behavior with drugs. We already have things like Ritalin and Prozac. Ritalin is basically used in many cases as a mechanism for social control. Prozac has very deep impacts on personality, identity, and behavior. And this is just the tip of the iceberg.

In fact, I think most of the things people are anticipating being able to do through genetic engineering will occur first as a result of drugs. There is a lot of concern over designer babies, genetically engineered children that will be smarter, taller, sexier, whatever. I think that's probably further off than people realize and before it happens you'll be able to change behavior through drugs in similar ways. If you want a smarter kid, there will be a pill for making your kid smarter.

Can Next-Generation Psychomedication Shift Human Nature?

Jaron Lanier • Human nature is still the biggest driver. And so the biggest change would happen if human nature, on the average, shifted in some fundamental way. There are some prospects for a wild card along those lines. What I'm thinking about is universally sanctioned psychomedication or some other technology a bit down the road. There is already increased pressure on parents to choose Ritalin for their children at an earlier and earlier age. There are even cases where parents have been sued for not putting their child on Ritalin because other parents thought their child was being disruptive and harming the classroom experience.

Some people have asked seriously whether the prevalence of Prozac and other antidepressants had something to do with the dotcom bubble. A large enough percentage of people who had a decrease in fear were investing that the bubble increased beyond what it might have sustained. The market correction has not been as traumatic as one might have expected, either. People haven't been jumping off roofs. Everyone has been rather mellow. I think we might be seeing some effect of psychomedication.

There's an interesting question about why violent crime has gone down in the U.S. in the last decade. The most convincing theory I've seen is demographic: the reduced percentage of adolescent males. The rise of certain drugs might also be a factor. Let me put it bluntly: What if Prozac became popular in the Middle East? What if it became popular in Ireland?

The Ramifications of Life Extension

Frank Fukuyama ∘ Just think through the demographics of life extension. There's a certain amount of political correctness in celebrating the fact that everyone is living longer and that older people have got these new opportunities open to them. But it really could be a very bizarre world that emerges. In about 50 years, the median age in virtually every developed country is going to be about 60. If it's lower than 60, it's only because these countries let in huge numbers of third-world immigrants. The United States is already fairly far down that path, but for Europe and Japan that's a very destabilizing political scenario.

For example, in Italy, the median age for the native-born population will be about 60 by the year 2050. If they let in substantial numbers of immigrants from Africa or the Middle East, their median age will be about 20, and they will be of a completely different culture. You already have political backlash against that. It's very hard to see how that won't lead to a fair amount of social conflict.

For businesses, the most important issue of this demographic development has to do with age-graded hierarchies. You had this lifetime employment model where you got an education in your twenties and then stayed at a job for 40 years. That education was supposed to last you that entire period. I think a lot of the downsizing that took place in the early 1990s was about that model increasingly ceasing to work. It obviously had other causes as well, but a lot of the skills that middle managers in their late forties and fifties had acquired were no longer relevant or necessary for the economy.

I fail to see how you can avoid a lot more of this in the future. The need for retraining and learning new kinds of technical skills is going to increase rather than decrease. Older people are going to stay healthier and mentally active longer than previously. All corporations are going to have to figure out how to get people to accept a kind of demotion in social status, and be willing to retrain and therefore to compete against younger people rather routinely.

Experience and age are often rewarded because there are things that older people have to offer. I guess the real problem is that they get better in certain ways and worse in others. There is a saying among economists that the economics profession advances one funeral at a time. It's unfortunate that intellectual progress and innovation often are generational things.

People grow up and the life experiences they have as young people pretty much shape their worldview. If you grew up in the Depression, you have a certain attitude toward savings and you tend to be a bit scared about the future. That's different from people who grew up in the baby boom in a period of extended prosperity. Almost nothing that happens subsequently in your life can disabuse you of that kind of general framework, which is why big political changes usually take place in 25-year cycles. It literally requires enough people dying off in a generation to really affect a major paradigm shift.

The aging of the baby boomers is really going to change a lot of things. There's been a fair increase in social conservatives because baby boomers all have kids and families. And now they're going to be worried about their retirement and issues of that sort. This generation has caused a whole lot of trouble as it has grown up and aged. It's probably going to continue to do that, but now the concerns will be more those of older people.

Youth Culture with Geezer Bodies

Kevin Kelly ∘ In many ways America has been youth culture. The typical American male is an arrested adolescent who is still in many ways living a teenage life. Probably females are too. What's interesting in America is that at some point the youth culture will die off and we'll have an old culture and old demographics. The question is whether we'll have a youth culture with old demographics. Youth culture, geezer bodies—does that work? We're going to find out.

Other countries of the world—Sweden, Poland, Japan—are also going through a major graying. I think this is really significant. Maybe we don't have north-south divisions among countries; we have old-young. We may have one set of countries that have made the reverse demographic transition to geezer demographics and geezer culture and all these other countries that are still in the global teenager mode—a pyramid with a huge number of teenagers at their base.

It's going to be new; people are living longer, they've got better health and money. Sometimes they still want to work. And there are things for them to do—lots of things for them to do. If they become a majority, if it becomes a geezer boom, then exactly what does that look like?

Why Genetic Engineering Will Need New Regulation

Frank Fukuyama ∘ Genetic engineering will be a big problem. You'll have elites being able to embed their advantages genetically in their offspring. We need a regulatory system for human biotechnology to prevent people from using it for enhancement purposes as opposed to therapeutic purposes.

Once rich people can genetically engineer their kids to be smart, that's a formula for conflict. I don't know that it will lead to a tiering of the human race, because before that can happen everybody else is going to get so mad that the result will be a lot of social conflict. It could lead to a revival of state-sponsored eugenics, because people will think that elites are getting away with this. They're either going to want to stop them or have it made more broadly available to everybody else. The way to deal with it is pretty simple. You just regulate it.

The Possibility of Children with 20 Genetic Parents

Vernor Vinge ∘ For the first half of this century, bioscience is going to proceed along but in a patchwork, chaotic way. In other words, you really are going to get some extraordinary things that affect the man on the street, but you have to be very careful to pick your right fatal disease.

There will be disease that's totally wiped out so that it's no more inconveniencing than a common cold. Then right next to it will be disease that still kills you. It's like the reverse of what happens when you're sitting in a city that's being bombed—in that instance, if you're in the wrong place you get hit by a bomb. Well, in this case, if you're in the right place, you get hit by a glorious fix. There's going to be a tremendous number of people whose lives are saved.

But the ethical issues will be overwhelming. Issues like abortion are completely simple compared to issues in bioscience like stem cells and cloning. It will become more and more of a hassle to the extent that laws are made for not doing it. Then the question is, How universal can these laws be made? What sort of countries are not going to obey those laws? We could have all sorts of wonderful things happening, and at the same time all sorts of tragedy and social turmoil over it.

Consider reproduction. We're on the verge of having so many different ways to have a child. It looks like parthenogenesis is possible—reproduction without having males involved. A simple way is cloning. Cloning or parthenogenesis—well, how persnickety are we going to be about how people have children? If a single mother doesn't want to deal with males, if it were possible to have a child and not have any male involved, is there going to be a law against that?

What if it were possible to have a child that got its genetic material from more than two parents? What would it be like to have 20 parents? Each of those 20 parents would only be related to you one-tenth as much as a normal parent. Would you still want to have a child if it were not 50 percent you? I think most people think it's immoral if you want to have a child that is more than 50 percent you—i.e., a clone. Do we also think it immoral if you want to have a child that is less than 50 percent you?

Biotech Could Reorder the Political Landscape

Frank Fukuyama ∘ I think biotechnology is going to split the existing Left and Right, right down the middle. You can see this in Europe already. A large chunk of the environmental movement has gotten very anti-biotech and there's some potential for that happening here as well. On the Right, biotechnology is forcing this utter split between social conservatives on the one hand and libertarian conservatives on the other. So you'll have this funny reorganization of the politisphere where you might get an alliance between the social conservatives and the environmentalists and then another alliance between the libertarian conservatives and the more pro-technology people on the Left.

Preparing the Public for the Coming Biotech Debates

Paul Saffo ∘ We have a huge education problem, and we've got 10 years to fix it, probably less. A functioning democracy depends on an engaged public that is fully informed and capable of critical thought. The hidden, slow-moving, glacial disaster in our society has been the decrease in quality education. Here we are, in the middle of a biotech revolution, and we have people saying there's no proof of evolution. Well, evolutionary theory is foundational to the biotechnology revolution. We've already seen practical spinouts of evolution, and yet substantial parts of the American public don't believe that evolution happened. This is a crisis.

The good news about biotech is that all the extravagant claims being made now, like life extension and genomic drugs, are going to take a while to happen. Never mistake the clear view for a short distance, remember? We could make them accelerate, but for the most part we're going to be talking about the same things on the horizon in 10 years that we're talking about today. In the 10 years after that, that's where get the inflection point and things start arriving under our social Christmas tree. We have time to educate; I think we really do have time here. We need the equivalent of a Sputnik event, which did so much for science education in the early 1960s. We need something to shock people into saying that we need to do biology education in this decade.

Adapting to Change

The Complexity of Adapting to Many Levels of Change

Mary Catherine Bateson ∘ As a cultural anthropologist, my focus has been increasingly on how people adapt to change. There are a variety of different kinds of changes. There are the changes that happen to all human beings over the course of the life cycle, growing up and moving through different social roles. That's true for all human beings. You have to learn how to be a 12-year-old, then you have to learn all over again to be a 16-year-old. You have to learn how to be 60, too. So that kind of change is a constant in all human communities.

To that we've added very rapid cultural and technological change that requires constant learning. We've also added to it the set of changes—which are comparable, in terms of their adaptive demand—that have to do with such things as immigration. In other words, you've learned how to be a 16-year-old. You can't just learn how to be a 30-year-old, you have to learn how to be a 30-year-old in a country that has had 14 years of very rapid change since you were a 16-year-old. And quite likely you're not in the same place in that country, or you're in a different country. So you're learning how to live the next stage of your life with an even more radically different culture. I would add one more piece to it, which is that the effect of demographic and biomedical change means that even while the world is moving faster, we are living longer and have to adjust to more years of difference in that world. Moreover, change is constant. I know people who have adjusted to living in a new country three times. Each time they had to deal with language and learning the culture and coping mechanisms and so on.

This process of change means that the nature of authority is changing all over the world. It used to be, in human experience, that old people knew more than young people and that this was the basis of their authority. They had lived more years and had a deeper familiarity with a stable culture. And so when junior argued about something, granddad could say, "I know because I've lived longer." That's no longer the case. The relationship between who learns and who teaches has been a relatively stable one in human cultures for millennia: You looked at the previous generation to learn how to live yourself. That's no longer possible. Today you're finding 12-year-olds teaching their grandmothers how to use computers so they can exchange emails. That's the small example. There are many larger ones. This is an issue in politics, it's an issue in religion, it's an issue in business.

The Vast Potential of the New Global Generation

Betty Sue Flowers ∘ I am both hopeful and puzzled by the generation of the last four years. That is, I am hopeful because they are supple and flexible and their minds are more scientific in a sense. I am puzzled because they don't have much content in their minds. I think it is because they are truly global. They see things from so many perspectives. It's not just relativism; it's multitracking. In the same way they can listen to the radio, watch TV, and work on their computers all at the same time, they can have different versions of the world in their heads at the same time. They also have multiple personalities going. I am now talking about well-educated college kids. Many are playing games online in which they have different identities. They also travel enough that they have different identities with different groups of people.

This isn't necessarily a bad thing; it is neutral. This simply is the most neutral generation I have ever seen—and also the one with the most capacity. Watch out! They have such wide peripheral vision. It is almost as if they were designed for this world.

Cultural Change Will Pull People in Different Directions

Mary Catherine Bateson ∘ What happens in culture change is not that you get one group of people on one side of the change and another group on the other side, but that almost everyone is pulled in two directions. From time to time there may be a clear polarization between them, but that's not what's going on most of the time. If you consider the abortion debate in this country, there are people who feel passionately that abortion should be available at any time upon demand, and there are people who feel that it should be completely outlawed, but the great majority of Americans stand somewhere in between. They don't like abortion, but they don't like outlawing it because they care about individual choice.

I think that's a much more typical way that things come out. People want to give their kids computers because they feel that will enrich their lives and increase their earning capacity later on, but they're nervous that they'll be finding things out by the computer or getting on to pornographic sites. One day, we hear one preacher warning about pornography on the Internet and we want to control the whole thing. The next day, somebody is advertising the computer we should give our 7-year-old for Christmas and we go out and buy it.

Shifting to a Global Mindset

Dorothy Q. Thomas ∘ A friend of mine says of human rights, and I'm sure it pertains to a lot of other issues, "Human rights is a revolution of the mind with application in the real world." I think that what is at stake with the globalization of everything is as much about consciousness as it is about anything else. Something is obviously going on around you, but you're seeing it through an established lens that cannot accommodate it.

I have had conversations with all types of people about the relevance of global human rights to their domestic activism in the United States. With all types of people—grassroots, elites, all classes, all colors—I can see this moment of hesitation, even if they might get some of the practical benefits of reframing their work in more global terms. They may even think, "Wow, that really is pertinent. There is solidarity with people who are experiencing similar things in other parts of the world." They might glimpse all of those potential benefits of seeing themselves less as purely Americans and more as global citizens, but at the same time there is a very profound resistance that has to do with, "What does this mean for me? What does it mean for my work? What does it mean for my community? What does it mean for my country?" I think the way those questions are ultimately answered is that it has more cost than benefit.

Instead of being maybe a large fish in a relatively large pond, you're going to be a somewhat smaller fish in a much bigger pond. I think that takes adjustment for everybody concerned. Your power structures, your identity, your ideology, everything will be transformed if you decide to supplement your existing largely domestic, local, national, whatever-it-is frame of reference with a more global one.

You're almost asking somebody to jump in the river before they know how to swim. Their first reaction is going to be, "There's no way I'm going in there, and if I did I'd probably drown." The challenge is to get folks to swim, and swim in a way that makes them feel as though they're going to survive and flourish, not swim out to the middle of the ocean only to find a lot of other swimmers, and three-quarters of them are going down.

Listening As a Core Competence in Times of Change

Mary Catherine Bateson ∘ To thrive under conditions of change, you have to be learning all of the time. Therefore, the relationship between the manufacturer and the customer is different; the manufacturer has to listen in a new way. The same is true of political leaders. Then you have the phenomenon happening in various places where people are trying to stop this pattern of change and reestablish traditional hierarchical models of authority, where the people at the top can say, "Don't trouble me with facts; my mind is made up." If you do that in the world today, you're going to get into trouble.

Clearly some people are stressed out by the nature and pace of change. But if I look around the United States, I see a lot of signs of very successful adaptation. People are getting used to the fact that under circumstances of change and longer life expectancy they may make major career shifts in the course of a lifetime; they go back to school and learn new skills. They're defining their identities in much more fluid ways that reflect their learning. I think one of the characteristics of this kind of situation where you have to adapt and learn all the time is a need to move toward a greater value on listening and the realization that we can't control all of this complex process of change.

More and more young people are growing up in homes where their parents are used to adapting to change and used to being helped by their children in that process. More and more corporate structures are taking account of this, so that you have people at the top who value their own capacity to learn and to listen rather than assume that they are there to lay down the law.

End of Story: The Cultural Sea Change

Vernor Vinge ∘ When I was a kid, the novelty of science fiction for me was that there were stories where the world was different at the end of the story than it was at the beginning. Those are hard stories to find. Occasionally you'd find cheaters, where it turned out to all be a dream. Nowadays, I think the average man on the streets expects that the world will be different at the end of the day, in the general sense of the term, than at the beginning. That is really a cultural sea change.

The Search for Deeper Meaning

Values and Belief Systems

"One of the great issues that we're going to have to keep discovering and exploring is the relationship between that which is general to all human beings on the planet and that which is particular."

Mary Catherine Bateson

"I believe we are heading toward a single global culture. That's a very scary thought to most people because they see that if they're not part of the dominant culture, then their culture will be wiped out, their values will be wiped out, the things that are important to them will be wiped out. Yet, I think that it is absolutely inevitable. The reason I think it is inevitable is that people are basically the same."

Danny Hillis

"When you have a zillion options, you have to have different ways of cutting through. One of the ways you cut through those options is you use value sets. You have a set of values that enables you to navigate, because it automatically says, 'Don't bother with these choices. You don't have to worry about these.'"

Kevin Kelly

"One of the striking things about the last 20 years is the rise of fundamentalism. It's true of all religions and in fact all ideologies. Even capitalists now are more capitalistic than they used to be."

Jaron Lanier

"In some ways we seem to be devising a new religion in this decade in which people say that they aren't religious, but they are spiritual. They're basically inventing a new religion comparable to the great awakenings of the early 1800s when Americans invented Jehovah's Witnesses and Mormonism and Seventh-Day Adventists and all that."

Joel Garreau

"I would be more confident looking ahead not 10 years, but 50 years. Then I would say, almost certainly, we are going to have social institutions emerge to support transformative practices."
  Michael Murphy

"We are the ones who make up the new story. It comes out through us. The new story has got to be global and its values have to be coherent in relation to our new identity. Inherently, it is also a new story of who we are, what the good is, what health is, and I mean that in the widest sense—spiritual, emotional, and physical."
  Betty Sue Flowers

The previous chapter explored how people connect, clash, and interact in communities. This chapter overlaps with the last around the common theme of "people," but looks more closely at the underlying values and beliefs that drive our behavior and inform our relationships.

We start with a very brief but important section on **Understanding and Valuing Difference**. It is very difficult for any individual to set aside his or her own values and beliefs when looking at the customs of others, and yet we are highly conditioned to view with suspicion all that is deemed to be "subjective." With the help of an anthropologist and a philosopher we present several frameworks for considering the rest of this challenging chapter.

The process of economic and social globalization exposes us all to the diverse cultures and societies of others while at the same time pushing us toward greater fusion and, potentially, less difference. Here we build upon this paradox and consider: **Are Values and Beliefs Converging?** Are there certain needs, desires, core values, and beliefs that all people hold? Are these becoming more similar? Opinions vary. One contributor identifies common values dating back to ancient, more egalitarian times. Another sees them as modern values that are a function of societal development and not dependent on particular cultures. Another views them as increasingly Western, for better or worse. Still another considers them global and says that convergence is inexorable—and will bring the demise of subcultures that are fighting to remain intact.

Next we consider the evolution of **Identity in a Changing Environment**. One set of reflections could be considered globalist: How do you define yourself in a system where no group can really be considered outsiders, let alone the enemy? One network member contends that are there are limits to identifying with everyone because each individual can only extend his or her circle of empathy so far. Another set of reflections might be called tribalist. An intriguing development to watch in the next decade is the rise of tightly defined value sets that people can adopt wholesale, as a practical alternative to dealing with the myriad choices bombarding them.

Fourth, we consider **The Evolution of Religion** as an important indicator of our changing ecology of values and belief systems. Opinions are split about how important traditional religions will be in the coming decade. Huston Smith, an eminent scholar of world religions, outlines what is common across all the world's wisdom traditions, but believes it's far-fetched to assume that they will eventually be subsumed into one world religion. Other network members anticipate a proliferation of many new religions, some composed of strange blends of the old. Several contributors consider fundamentalism to be an extreme form of traditional religion as well as a more general reaction to change. They also think it is likely that fundamentalism will be on the rise in the coming decade.

Next we look at **New Expressions of Spirituality**. Some network members see people's frustration with traditional religions leading to increasing interest in many forms of spirituality in the decade ahead. One suggests that America might be in the midst of spiritual rejuvenation analogous to what is known as the Great Awakening in post-colonial times. Another lays out several ways new and hybrid forms of spiritual practice might arise to help make meaning out of the world's crosscurrents of ideas.

That leads us into **The Outer Reaches of Human Potential**. Will we witness a greater belief in and reliance on our own human capacities? Here we draw largely upon the insights of Michael Murphy, a pioneer in transformative practice, to better understand extraordinary or supernormal functioning. This encompasses extrasensory perception, the sixth sense, and other abilities that science simply cannot explain. Murphy points out that all cultures through the ages have reported cases of individuals—from shamans to yogis to saints—who have performed extraordinary feats of healing, strength, or revelation about the future. He has even documented and classified the range of such abilities from the distant past to the present. Even from a scientific perspective, we're likely to understand and appreciate these abilities more fully in the coming decade.

We conclude this chapter with reflections on **Finding a Way Forward**. Here we consider how understanding which values and beliefs are changing—and which are not—might prove useful in the future. For example, there are practical business reasons for ensuring that your organization looks attractive to the growing numbers of people who yearn for a sense of mission. And at a deeper human level, we can all participate in the creation of new stories—new myths—that help us make better sense of our world in the present and the future.

Understanding and Valuing Difference

Getting Beyond Cultural Relativism

Mary Catherine Bateson ∘ One of the great issues that we're going to have to keep discovering and exploring is the relationship between that which is general to all human beings on the planet and that which is particular. We're going to have to keep looking at these models and asking how far to push on them, and try to be more consistent and more loyal to them ourselves.

I think what we do is we look at a piece of another cultural tradition and we say, "Horrors!" instead of asking where it fits in. What are the highest values it serves within that tradition?

An example would be that old Mohammed had a lot of wives. He lived under circumstances of warfare and he repeatedly married the widows of his generals when they were killed in warfare. One origin of polygamy was, in societies where women were dependent, to protect them. Now, we say polygamy is terrible. In fact, missionaries traditionally have gone into societies and said that if you want to be a Christian, you can't have two wives; throw one of them out in the street. If we say, "You have a social institution whose goal is to protect the weak," maybe there are alternative ways of doing that that we can agree on.

Another example is infanticide. Among many, many human beings, for instance, if an infant is born deformed, it will be killed because the community really has no way to support and look after it. Or if a child is born too soon after a previous child and survival depends on the mother's milk, the child may be killed, because only by killing one child can the other children survive. This is the custom. What is the value behind that custom? Maybe with modern medicine or infant formula, there are alternative ways of doing this.

In the process of sorting out the value systems and listening respectfully, it's possible to move toward ways of adapting and changing. I don't want to go so far as to say that all cultures are identical at heart or to say that there are no institutions that I would like to see eliminated. There's a lot of change I would like to see happen, but the way to make that change happen is to move up to a meta-level and try to understand what it is that this group of people really cares most about, not what they do that I disapprove of.

When I'm teaching about what is sometimes referred to as cultural relativism, I make a distinction between cultural relativism and cultural relativity. Cultural relativism is an "ism." It's an ideology that says that anything that anyone else in another culture does is OK because their culture says it's OK.

That is not the position that I would take. The position that I would take, as an anthropologist, is to suspend judgment on the particular institution until you understand how it fits into the culture. In other words, see the institution of, say, polygamy in relation to the state of warfare, interdependence of the family unit, etc., in that society and in relation to what people value in terms of protecting the weak. You might then say that a particular behavior has to change, but you could then advocate a change in the context of understanding what it is people want through that behavior.

If we say that our consumption of fossil fuels has to change, it's not enough to say that this entire American nation is immorally destroying the resources of the earth, which is a great deal worse than polygamy, my dear. We have to look at what fossil fuels mean in terms of mobility and choices and see if we can make them available in some other way. We have to look at what people are trying to achieve by having huge cars or whatever it is. We have to say that mobility and virility are values in American society. Maybe they can be achieved in some other way. Maybe they could even be achieved with vehicles that don't guzzle so much gas. Maybe we could introduce some other values that people care about and get them to make better choices.

A New Kind of Ethical Pluralism

Jay Ogilvy ∘ If you look at the history of philosophy, you will see that when you make a sharp distinction between subject and object, between internal and external, you will see going along with that a distinction of facts as objective, values as merely subjective. They get trivialized as merely subjective. You cannot get good ethics out of this. Values get subjectivized; they become mere tastes, mere whims. You get this subjective relativism. That's why I want to reject this set of dichotomies; in the real world they're all tied up together.

In the next decade we'll be looking for a cultural competency that goes beyond manners—being rooted in your own values to where you can comfortably hear someone else's differences. Pluralism is a competency, not just mere subjective relativism, ethical pluralism. In the past, there's a sense that if it's ethical then it has to be hierarchical and monistic, and if it's pluralistic, it's amoral or relativistic. I say no, that somewhere between there, there is an ethical pluralism. There's a way of holding on to your values and letting others have theirs that doesn't say "whatever."

Are Values and Beliefs Converging?

Mass Communications and the Egalitarian Beliefs of All Peoples

Gwynne Dyer ∘ A number of people have noticed—how could you not?—that there's a much larger multilateral and global context in which things are happening. There's a whole lot more globalized decision-making than used to be the case, whether you're talking about G8 summits and nonsense like that, or international criminal courts or the World Trade Organization. There's been a shift in the level at which a lot of things are done. They're not done unilaterally anymore. I think the reasons for that aren't getting explored very much. The world is, in a way, becoming a more unified place, not just economically but in its political values—its moral concerns, you might say. What I mean is that between 1988 and now we have seen an enormous shift from a world where most societies were totalitarian or old-fashioned military dictatorships to a world where most societies are more or less democratic with freedom of speech and relatively open communications to the rest of the world.

I know people who will deny that, but they're the sort of people who come up with a list of 135 wars that are going on because they're hired by the arms industry to make things look bad. You just have to go around the world and notice how the secret police follows you in many fewer places these days. Of course there has been a huge shift from a world where dictatorship was the norm to a world where some kind of open society—with many flaws and corruption—has become the norm.

All of a sudden good guys are in the majority. The good guys actually are in power in the majority of countries in the world now. That means a whole lot of things that you couldn't do in the past because the bad guys were in the majority, suddenly you can do. Why since 1990 do we have international tribunals going after war criminals? Why do we have interventions to stop genocides? Not every time, and we didn't do well when we intervened, but we wouldn't have dreamed of doing that before. Why do we have an attempt to create a structure of international human rights? This is, of course, what dictatorships would never accept, but it's the first item on the agenda for every democracy. If you're a majority, it becomes a global agenda. That is enormously important in terms of determining how the world works. The point of departure for people has become different. The sets of assumptions are different.

I think the reasons for that have to do with the globalization of information. Two hundred and fifty years ago, there wasn't a single mass society on the planet where people were legally equal. Why is that? I begin to think that, at a very fundamental level, this has got to do with the ability to communicate across large numbers of people.

In the early to middle 1990s, I started talking to anthropologists and even primatologists. What the anthropologists say is that if you go to the smallest societies, the ancestral societies, the hunting and gathering groups—almost invariably these are egalitarian. Nobody has the right to give anybody else orders. A lengthy, time-consuming, rather boring process of discussion and consensus generation makes decisions. Things are shared. Meat is shared, but not equally; the hunter—the guy who brought it down—gets the best bit.

Although these are essentially egalitarian societies, it doesn't mean they're pretty. These are also societies where everybody is armed and they've got a real problem with impulse control. So I'm not saying that ugly things don't happen here. I'm saying that the fundamental behavior patterns of hunter-gatherer societies throughout the world are essentially not democratic in the modern sense, but egalitarian, which is the foundation for democratic values. We are all, in principal, equal.

Then you go into mass societies, which we did between about 7,000 and 2,000 years ago, depending on what part of the planet you're talking about. The numbers go up from the low hundreds to the hundreds of thousands and into the millions. The first thing that's going to happen is that the society's old ways of making decisions and allocating resources are going to collapse because they can't deal with the numbers. A hundred thousand people can't talk to each other. There's no way.

After you get into the hundreds of thousands, centralized decision-making by a tyrant is the only way that works. This is universal in every society in every part of the planet for thousands of years, down to about the eighteenth century. And it's just as true of Western culture as of Chinese culture. Louis XIV was definitely a man with Asian values.

Suppose that, first of all, through the printing press and literacy and later on through electronic communications, you get back the ability to communicate across the society so that everybody can be on the same page of the book. Everybody can know the topic of the discussion and take part in it, at least passively. This had not been possible for thousands of years, since we left the little hunter-gatherer groups. So, if default-mode human values are hunter-gatherer values, which everybody shares from the past, and if you give us back the ability to communicate even though we live in these vastly larger societies, it's quite likely that we are going to go back to the original value system. If we can, we probably will.

Through the 1990s, that's what I began to think was happening. In fact, the United States is the leading example—it was the very first mass democracy in the history of the planet. I would argue that the American Revolution happened when it did and where it did—late 1700s and in what became the United States—because the U.S. was the first country on the planet where over 50 percent of the adult population was literate. You could communicate. You could actually dispense with the top-down tyrannies and move toward an egalitarian-based society. Now it took 150 years before everybody was equal. Women didn't get the vote until the 1920s, but there was a huge leap made right away in 1776.

If you look at what's going on there, it is the technology of mass communications that made the American Revolution possible. When the second Continental Congress met in Philadelphia in 1775, nobody thought it was going to go for independence. It was actually Tom Paine's pamphlet, which was read by about half the population in six weeks, that shifted opinion. All of a sudden this very large society, three million people at that point, can act as equals and make a collective decision.

The point is if you extend this possibility technologically to other societies through printing and literacy or through ease in electronic media why wouldn't they do the same? I really think that you can account for the way that democratic values have spread around the world over the past 200 years simply by tracking the course and speed with which mass communications have spread around the world.

Trending Toward One Culture Because All People Are the Same

Danny Hillis ○ This is a very unpopular point of view, but I think we are going through a time in which one of the basic dynamics is globalism versus tribalism. It tends to appear in a lot of different guises—American or cultural imperialism, for instance. I think that's a matter of tribalists being afraid of the global culture. That's a good cheap shot, to label it as American.

I believe we are heading toward a single global culture. That's a very scary thought to most people because they see that if they're not part of the dominant culture, then their culture will be wiped out, their values will be wiped out, the things that are important to them will be wiped out. Yet, I think that it is absolutely inevitable.

The reason I think it is inevitable is that people are basically the same. I don't buy into the notion that there is something about the Japanese race that makes the Japanese aesthetic better for them, or something about the French that makes being French better for them, or something about people living in New Guinea that makes a certain kind of dress better for them. The things that are good for me are, in fact, exactly the same things that are good for a Frenchman and for a Japanese and for somebody in New Guinea.

That's not to say that there aren't elements in many different cultures that are going to get preserved as part of the global culture. I'm sure I would be better off if I had certain things from the New Guinea culture and the French culture and the Japanese culture in my culture. What I see as the global culture is not American culture, but taking elements of every culture and putting them on the menu for everybody.

What's frightening is that people think of global culture as being uniform. In fact, I think it's much more diverse than tribal culture. People can mix and match elements from lots of different cultures. There's individual diversity, but the diversity isn't going to be determined by who your parents were or where you were born—it's going to be determined by the creative forces of people's choices and combinations.

It used to be, in tribal culture, that everything came as a package. Who your parents were determined what your religion was, where you lived, what language you spoke, which set of ethical rules you operated on, interaction conventions with people, what kind of food you ate. You took the total package, and it had some good and some bad in it. There were many packages available in many different tribes, and each was in some respects better than the others and in some respects worse than the others.

The American melting pot is an example of how this global recombination might work. You could put all of these elements together and deconstruct them, not take them as a package. I can eat sushi for lunch, Chinese food for dinner and bacon and eggs for breakfast. I might have Islam for my religion. I might speak English. I might live in Europe and have Buddhist vegetarian dining habits. I'm sure that there are lots of people who have that particular combination. In a sense, there is more diversity of possibilities.

The Constant Amidst 2,000 Years of Change

Paul Saffo ∘ The constant amidst all the change is our behavior as humans, the way our behavior expresses in different ways. I suspect you could go back 2,000 years and find that our basic desires and needs, the things that animate us, have not changed all that much. The way they express themselves outwardly can change very dramatically.

Why a Static Multiculturalism Is Untenable

Danny Hillis ∘ We all want a roof over our heads. We all love our children. We all respond to music. We all laugh at jokes. The best kind of roof to put over your head and what kind of music moves the human spirit are not determined by where you're born. It may be different from one person to another, but it's not different for somebody born in the United States and somebody born in Japan. To believe anything else is basically a kind of racist view of how people think and what people want.

I think that multiculturalism—this notion of preserving all cultures and letting them coexist—is a fundamentally untenable standpoint. Where does it lead? If you think that what is right is holding your culture together as a package—your way of life, your religion, your food, your language, everything has to stay as a complete intact package—then you are genuinely threatened. The world culture is genuinely your enemy because it is going to wipe out your way of life. I understand why a lot of people are feeling very desperate right now. There is a real conflict here. It's not a misunderstanding—in fact, it's a very accurate understanding of what's happening.

The second real conflict is between rich and poor. The resources of the earth are extremely uneven in their distribution. Large portions of humanity don't participate in the same system that you and I do. While the system gives you and I an opportunity to prosper, and I'm talking economically right now, it just plain doesn't give that opportunity to a lot of other people. Aside from any issues of culture or cultural imperialism or preserving traditions, there's the substantial, real issue that poor people want to have resources that they don't have and, in fact, should have.

People confuse those two issues because the world culture tends to be the rich culture too. I think that the world culture should win, but I don't think that means that the rich people should stay in control.

Modernization Doesn't Require Anglo-Saxon Values

Gwynne Dyer ∘ We have vastly underestimated the degree to which people have common political as well as economic aspirations. There are people who insist that there's going to be a clash of civilizations, who try to keep the old game going, the Samuel Huntingtons of the world, trying to find the next great enemy after the Soviet Union, which so inconveniently vanished. Those people who insist that culture is somehow the bedrock of human behavior would insist that neither economy nor communications could eradicate the differences and shift them from one path to another because humans are just different.

On the contrary, I would increasingly say that, no, they're not that different. Both politically and economically, aspirations in Syria, Omaha, and Burma are about the same, or at least, given exposure to the same opportunities, they would be the same. Opportunities for information, for economic activity or upgrading. When you get this technological lurch into a global economy—and earlier than that, global communications systems with real reach—then the behaviors of people become, in a weird way, more rational and more predictable, from my cultural perspective, than they were before.

There is an old set of assumptions, such as that the Soviet Union had control of the people's communications and minds for 70 years so Russians could not think themselves free from that. Or that Islam creates a whole different set of expectations and values and so the people cannot democratize or modernize their economics because they're trapped in this different world intellectually and culturally. Together with that is a deeper set of assumptions—that modernization is something only Westerners do. If you don't have Greeks in your family tree, if you don't have Anglo-Saxon values— mind you, the French Revolution wasn't committed by English speakers— or if you don't at least have Western European roots culturally, then you can't do a modern economy. You certainly can't do a full-scale democratization of your society. It's not just, "Cultures are different." It is implicit in a lot of the commentary and analysis that the only culture that can deliver you into modernity and democracy is this one: Anglo-American, with Western Europe coming along for the ride.

I think this is bull. It's like Asian values. Give me a break. My father and certainly my grandfather had exactly what Lee Kuan Yew of Singapore is talking about when he talks about Asian values. This is not a cultural distinction. It is, if anything, a generational and temporal distinction. They're not yet in their generation where I am in mine. There's a 50-year lag. It isn't going down a different track; they're just further up the track.

The Propagation of the Modern Western Mind-Set

Kevin Kelly ○ I think it's a fair bet that what we would call Western values will continue to propagate and expand through many countries in the world, generally through the elites in that country as they become more modern. Maybe we should call them modern Western sensibilities, the whole suite of democracy, free markets, privacy, private identity, a sense of science. There's a whole palette of attributes and mind-sets that would be part of that. I think we should also expect a fairly significant alternative to that—value sets that are either based in religions, new religions, or quasi-religions, or are a-religious.

Identity in a Changing Environment

The Search for a New Identity When There Is No "Other"

Betty Sue Flowers ∘ Where we are today is not about solving problems but about starting to think in a new way. I could see that happening within a decade. You can see how all these issues are aligned. We are having a big debate now about the identity of human beings and who we are. It's playing out in this country around the stem-cell issue. What are human beings? What is our relation to each other? And to the unborn and born? What is a frozen embryo? Is that a potential human being or a potential healing source for other human beings? Where does possession start and stop? All these issues are connected into a sense of identity. Who are we individually, and who are we together as a species?

Our whole sense of identity is shifting in the same way that the identity of human beings shifted in the nineteenth century when we realized we were descended from the apes. The whole anti-slavery debate changed with Darwinian theory. With the new knowledge, we saw that we were all one family, descended from the apes. It was very difficult to think that any human being could be the slave of another, because we saw ourselves as a species for the first time.

In the past, almost all cultures have developed ethics for the citizens and ethics for the barbarians. They are two different things. You can murder your enemies, but not your family or friends. Now the sense of identity—the whole issue of who are our neighbors, who is our kin—is coming up in a new way. Every time there's a shift in ethics, there's a shift in the answer to that question, and you can no longer define some people outside the circle. If the circle of inclusion gets wider—if humanity includes women, slaves, and others—your behavior will be different.

And that has economic consequences. It did with slavery, for example. Today we haven't even begun to articulate what our economy is built on based on who we think our neighbors are. In fact, we are beginning to see that earth itself is an "other." Plants and animals are part of our survival, too. The idea of saving species at some economic cost would have never occurred to the Victorians. But now it occurs to us that some species deserve to be here on this earth just because they are—not for any function or purpose that serves us. It's a different sense of inclusion. That's not to say that we don't eat or use them, but we are taking them into account in a way that we hadn't before.

There have always been forerunners and prophets who have seen ahead of the rest of us. Then it reaches general consciousness, so that saving species is generally accepted as a good thing. That's been fairly recent. Now we see that this whole definition of the "other" is getting problematic. What really is "other"? It's all one big system. If we can't make something "other," then how do we get by in the world? Because we have always operated with an "other." It's how we've defined ourselves.

The Circle of Empathy

Jaron Lanier • Let me describe a framework that I've been using to try to understand events. I call it the circle of empathy. The notion of the circle of empathy is that people draw a circle around themselves where inside the circle are things that deserve empathy and outside the circle are things that don't. Now most people, when they're young and idealistic, tend to want to draw the circle pretty large. Indeed it would be lovely to draw it really, really large, to be able to live life in such a way that one caused no harm at all.

Essentially what happens is that if you're in some distinct clan it heightens a sort of circle of empathy distinction. So, if you see a child that seems to be a member of your clan, you feel that child should receive medicine and should be educated. However, if the circle is kind of fuzzy and there are all these children that don't really look like you, you're less likely to include them, for one thing because the circle grows large.

Right now we have global telecommunications. All of us are aware of how awful it is to be poor in a big city in India and how miserably short life is. We're aware of how many people die from malaria. We're aware of what's happening with AIDS in Africa. We're aware of what will be happening in all likelihood with AIDS in central Asia. We know all of that, and yet our capacity for empathy is simply exhausted. We have empathy fatigue.

Unfortunately there's another problem with this. The more partial or one-sided our communication is with people who might be within our circle of empathy, the more vulnerable we are to have our empathy degrade into vanity. I believe that is precisely the process that's defeated leftist ideologies since their inception.

Speaking generally, the difference between the Left and the Right is that the Left is attempting to expand the circle of empathy and the Right is attempting to contract it. Since there are real costs to maintaining a circle of empathy, the Right is sometimes correct. Now, some of the classic struggles have been, Should blacks be allowed in the circle of empathy? The Right at the time said, "No," and the Left said, "Yes," and more or less the Left won, to some degree. In the American Left in the '70s and especially in the early '80s, we transitioned through a wave of revelations about who should be included in the circle of empathy. We moved from blacks to women and then to gays and other groups. There was this sense of, "Wow, there's this other group of humans whom we were excluding from our circle without really thinking about it. They shouldn't be excluded."

There are those who then wanted to expand it further than humans. One example is artificial intelligence, which asks that we extend it to computers. Another is the animal rights movement. When we crossed over this species barrier to animals, we redefined empathy. We moved to one of the Buddhist notions of empathy—"this is another sentient being so it deserves our sympathy," not "it's a being with potential that isn't realized." That's a very different circle of being: a circle based on potential versus a circle based on some notion of sentience or simply, life.

Unfortunately there are real costs for empathy. It's a thing we should spend carefully if it's going to mean anything at all. Real empathy is expensive. No matter how much telecommunications we have in the world, the amount of time we have in a day does not allow us to develop a profound empathy and communication with a poor person in India or the Sudan. Our level of communication with them is actually inferior to our level of communication with our dog—thus the empathy gap. All the telecommunications in the world won't improve that, because we still have only so many hours in the day.

African Americans' New American Identity

Gerald Harris ∘ In the next 10 years I don't think there will be a "black agenda" or a minority agenda that is any way distinguishable from the American agenda for what I would call poor people. We've moved to an economic class issue. It doesn't have anything to do with whether you're black or white. Look, you've got your Oprah Winfreys and Michael Jordans and Bob Johnsons who have millions of dollars. The system is open for people to participate. It's really—Do you have the skills? Do you have the drive? And if you have all that in America, you're an American, and you just need to play that game.

There are poor people who are from all different groups. In fact, you already have in this country classes of blacks that have nothing to do with other classes of blacks. If you are a black doctor in the suburbs, your kids don't know anybody in the inner city. They may wear the same style of clothing, baggy pants and sports jerseys and hats on backward and all that because they see it on TV or in a magazine or walking down the street. But they don't hang out together.

The big issue to look at is, what will it ultimately mean when we are all Americans? The real rub in that issue is not on the minority; it's on the majority. How will the majority of Americans and the majority of white Americans finally come to an accommodation around diversity and stop things like "we've got to move out of the neighborhood because Joe Black, who's a Harvard lawyer, moved in." Will white America get over it? I think a lot of white Americans have gotten over it—they don't really care.

We're always going to have our little enclaves and our little social gatherings that may be racially or ethnically restrictive. So I'm not one who thinks we're going to have this great mixing bowl and everybody's going to do everything together. There are going to be places that are very diverse and places where people get together with their own groups. And I don't think that's a bad thing. It's called identity. Identity gets bad when people want to use it against you—you're not one of me, so therefore, you can't have the same rights that I can have.

The Rise of Value Sets in the Face of Burgeoning Choices

Kevin Kelly ∘ One of the stories that I would expect to see in the next 10 years is a reaction against technology of some sort—a counterforce to continued adoption of new technology. In other words, I am forecasting, based on very little evidence and just a lot of hunches, that we will develop cultural ideas or movements about dealing with the increasing numbers of options and gadgets and information that we have. Right now it's a vague feeling, with some folks like the neo-Luddites who get no respect, but I think that can change. I'm reading a paper called "The Tyranny of Choice" by Barry Schwartz. I love the title. The idea is that total freedom actually may be toxic. For America, land of the free and fundamental freedom lovers, there actually may be too much freedom.

This plays into zillionics. When you have a zillion options, you have to have different ways of cutting through. One of the ways you cut through those options is to use value sets. You have a set of values that enables you to navigate, because it automatically says, "Don't bother with these choices. You don't have to worry about these." It restricts the boundaries of your choices so you can actually evaluate them, and you write off things outside the value set.

When there's a huge abundance or overabundance of choices, you have to compete on making fast choices or not choosing, or relying on a set of values that allows you to make choices so that you can get through a lot of choices a lot faster. Some of the attraction for these values, maybe even fundamentalism to a certain extent, is that there is a set of guidelines that allows one to make a choice by saying that we will constrain the choice set to this territory here. That makes it possible to feel in control, to not feel overwhelmed, to feel that you are able to shape some identity.

Religion and family values and all these kinds of things, I think, will continue to be important and play a role, and we may also come up with more technological values. I continue to be fascinated by the Amish. It's not that they've stopped adopting technology, but they say, "We'll only evaluate the technologies or consider adopting ones that fall within this realm—the ones that bring together our community—and anything else that doesn't, we're not even going to mess with. We just say no."

With genetics, the animal rights people and the deep ecologists are kind of leaning toward some value set. Basically, here's a set of heuristics we're going to use for evaluating technologies: Do they enhance nature? Do they cause killing? If they meet the criteria, then we will consider them. If they don't, they're out.

The Evolution of Religion

What the Great Religious Traditions Hold in Common

Huston Smith ∘ We know that the religions have some things in common and some not. One can say that all of them are against greed and therefore value generosity, and therefore value justice as opposed to injustice. The ego is our biggest addiction for all human beings and we have to get rid of that as much as possible. In Christian terms, we should learn to rejoice with those who rejoice and weep with those who mourn, which means that what they're feeling we should make our feeling. They all say this is an ideal. Whether you call it original sin or forgetfulness or ignorance—those are favorite terms for different religions—the common denominator is that there is something awry in the human heart. It's clear as day: They all say that.

Talking about commonalities among religions, William James put it in a sentence. He says if we were to take the phenomenon of religion in human history, what we would hear it saying is the best things are the most enduring things, and say the final word. It can and does say that to the individual. If you stand up for what is right, justice and the rest, that will count in the long run.

Now, they couch it in terms of another life. But however you couch it, the language always has to be mythical because the depth cannot be mapped into ordinary language, no more than in quantum mechanics. God is at least as strange as quantum mechanics, and that's an understatement. It's not going to map into this language.

None of them say that little drops of water, little grains of sand, will add up to the fact that we will have a just world on this plane of human history. They don't say that. They all pitch their hope for beyond history. This is a mixed world. The Hindus put it most explicitly: 50 percent happiness/50 percent unhappiness, 50 percent wisdom/50 percent ignorance, 50 percent dark/50 percent light, and so it will always remain.

This gets us back to the myth of hope. In my youth I interviewed Reinhold Niebuhr on progress. I was a young man then and I believed in progress, but I knew that he was critical of it, so I kept pressing him: Has there been any progress? The most I could get is, "Oh, sure, in certain areas."

"Like what?" I'd say. He'd respond: "Well, how about plumbing? Or dentistry." What he would not allow or grant was that there has been any net progress. Every item of progress carries its price tag. We develop antibiotics, a great progress in health, and immediately we are handed the population explosion. We're handed nuclear energy, nuclear reaction, which we thought would solve our energy problem, and then we have the problem of nuclear waste, to say nothing of the atom and bombs. We discover pesticide and we think it will take care of the food problem. It's been said that it takes about 35 years for the full consequences of a major breakthrough to come. So, 35 years later, we have Silent Spring and endangered species.

Today I do not believe in historical progress. But that's all we have. Secularists, as we basically are, don't think that there's another world. Everything has to make sense in this domain, including hope. But hope is the ultimate resource of the wisdom traditions. They say this is not the only world, which throws this world into a different perspective.

I use one of my favorite analogies. In this world, we are in a gigantic balloon. We have flashlights. The flashlight is a metaphor for the scientific method. We can shine it on anything inside the balloon that we want to, but there's no way we can get the flashlight outside the balloon to see what's outside it or if indeed there is anything outside it. Now, modernity and secularism says there's nothing outside of it.

All the wisdom traditions say—and it's why I have given my life to the study of them—they all say with a single voice, "This world is the shadows on Plato's cave, which are created by the light outside the cave." And I think that's true.

The Potential Proliferation of New Religions

Kevin Kelly ○ Many people are talking about religion making a resurgence. I don't know if resurgence is the word because I don't think that it ever went away. I think that it will continue its appeal. We're thinking in an abstract sense of the notion, this is only one of the appeals of traditional religion. One of the appeals of traditional religion is this thing I was talking about of constraining the options, which I think lots of different value sets share. I think traditional religions have other things that make them attractive in addition to that. Community, for one thing, which some other traditions also serve. I think the appetite for a belief in someone greater than yourself, a creator, is an incredibly fundamental need and yearning for humans and that is also what traditional religions will feed into.

But I also suggest that there will be new religions that will also come about to try to feed that. History seems to show that we have continual bifurcation and specialization. There are new religions all of the time. So, I would say there will be a persistence of traditional religions and an increase in the number of new religions and an increase in other dogmas, things that are not quite a religion, but have many of the attributes of religion.

It's even possible that in the next 10 years we'll see a new global religion. New religions are invented all the time. I have long predicted that in the former Soviet Union, the next wave of new religions would erupt, because they have all the ingredients for generating this: an innate spiritual aptitude and hunger, which is centuries old; a susceptibility to religious beliefs; and the complete collapse of their former value system. So you have a bunch of people who need religion, and they don't have one, and so I think they're going to invent it.

My recipe for the future is generally "all of the above"—and in everything. It's very little of the old going away and the new coming, so you have basically more, more choices, more varieties. Very, very seldom does the future bring fewer varieties, less diversity of things, fewer choices. So religions? More religions.

The Improbability of One World Religion

Huston Smith ○ I often get asked if there is ever going to be one religion. My answer is, "I don't know, but I feel very sure that if we were to have one world religion tomorrow, there would be two the next day."

We live in a multiple world. To follow up that line, there are some people who would rather be number one in a sect of 200 members than number two in the Vatican. So the individual outreach and ambition comes into that. I don't know what a new religion would have to say of importance that the old religions don't have if we winnow them carefully.

The Baha'is tried that—let's have a new religion. They included a number of admirable planks that are not in other religions—Esperanto, a world language, world government. In 1949, as a historian of religion, I went to a large Baha'i rally. One of the speakers predicted the entire world would be Baha'i in 1964. So much for predictions. No, there will be innumerable new religions. There have been 500 in Japan since World War II. But they don't get anywhere.

I think the only religions that have amounted to anything in history are revealed. It's not out of the question. Muslims read the Qur'an as saying that Muhammad was the last prophet, which is another way of saying there will be no more cosmic revelation. That was 1,400 years ago, and the Qur'an has been right about that so far. Islam is the last world religion, the last major religion in history.

When Latin America Becomes Evangelical Protestant in 2070

Richard Rodriguez ∘ If the conversion rates remain what they are now, the projection is that by the year 2070 Latin America will be not only predominantly Protestant, but evangelical Protestant in its majority. It becomes the moral force at time in which Americans in our own secular moral vacuity insist on describing the South as the region of our temptation, the place where the white powders come from, the place that is lawless. We are not used to describing that place as being the place where the Puritans are going to come from. Nor do I think that we really understand that within that so-called Hispanic community may come a force that we are not used to—a moralistic force that is not going to be nice toward us and is going to be as judgmental as any Old Testament prophet.

Fundamentalism As a Response to Threat

Huston Smith ∘ There are two places where fundamentalism is a problem today. One is the United States, which is very different, but the underlying phenomenon is the same. Fundamentalism is always the consequence of feeling threatened. That's even true in the United States. The religious right claim Christian fundamentalism goes back to New Testament times, but they don't know their history at all—it's only less than 100 years old. It came into being in the 1920s, when two things came up to threaten conservative Christians.

One was Darwinism, which seemed to say that we're the result of chance, a mutation, rather than being created in the image of God. Secondly, they were threatened by the higher criticism, which treats the Bible in critical analysis as any other book, a secular book. That led to the Jesus Seminar, with scholars researching the authenticity of Jesus' life. The conservative Christians weren't wrong actually. They were farsighted, because those two things have reduced the status of Christianity in America.

For Islamic fundamentalists, the underlying problem is they feel threatened, but the reasons for the threat are very different. They feel that this modern world will keep on pushing Islam into the background and marginalizing it. The modern world has two things in it: the haves get richer and the have-nots get poorer. That plays out so well because the haves, their profits increase not through constructive work that they do, but because of the dividends for their investment. The Muslims, according to their beliefs, don't have any investments so they have to work with their hands for everything they get. Meanwhile the wealthy go sailing on further and further ahead. That's one threat.

Then they are also threatened by the takeover of the Western culture. Not just the economy, but the culture, the ethos. There's the dissolution of the family and the sociologists are backing them up on that. They see a moral decline in sexual standards. The standards have all gone. It's just individualism plus the pleasure principle.

Well, they're threatened by the modern economy, which the haves get, and they're threatened by our culture, a moral slough. We leave them no out. That's our greatest fault. If they have no out, they have no hope and find themselves in despair. They would rather bring us down, even if it brings them down, than let it continue this way.

Fundamentalism As a Reaction to the Hubris of Technologists

Jaron Lanier ∘ Treating non-linear things as if they were linear, pretending that computers can become intelligent in any planable timeframe, that the human genome can be mastered, that pills can create creativity—all of those are examples of exactly the same mistake. This practically counts as an ideology in itself; it's the characteristic delusion of our times.

That delusion is broadcast daily when there are articles in legitimate science magazines proclaiming that computers are feeling emotion, as if emotion were some simple thing, or that a gene's been discovered for something like intelligence or loyalty. When such headlines appear, even in legitimate sources, it's natural for people to feel as if their inner selves were being somehow conquered or exposed. It's as if what used to be sacred, unattainable, and unknowable has been turned into a resource—essentially, as if their inner lives have been commoditized.

When people hear these false claims stated with such authority and confidence, they must find a way to respond. They don't want to lose themselves; they don't want to become commodities. The only channel that most people have available is traditional religion. One of the striking things about the last 20 years is the rise of fundamentalism. It's true of all religions and in fact all ideologies. Even capitalists now are more capitalistic than they used to be. There's this kind of blood-to-the-death feeling that you find even in religions like Buddhism that haven't had much of it historically. Now there have been Buddhist wars and terrorists. That's not even to mention all the other religions. We're seeing a fanatical Judaism that we haven't seen since Roman times. We're seeing various sorts of Christian militancy around the world. Historically Islam has not been as mean-spirited as it frequently is now. While the Hindus in India have always had a crazy split with the Muslims, they're nuts now. The Sikhs too. The list goes on.

There are also identity issues. The notion of Chinese blood, Chinese soil as a concept would have been unthinkable 15 years ago, and now you hear about it in all of the different Chinas. There's a retreat into identity and old ideologies just to have some anchor, because people feel that this digitization and reduction monster is about to swallow them whole. It isn't, but that's the perception and the fear.

Unfortunately, there's sort of a self-fulfilling prophecy. If you're willing to contort yourself enough, to make yourself stupid enough, you can make a machine seem smart. You can make yourself seem reduced and contained by all of this stuff. You can make yourself linear. For example, if you can hypnotize students and parents into believing that the IQ test means something, it might as well be important.

I think Hamas is a reaction against computers as much as it is against Israel. I'm sure they see the news and they feel terrified of all of this stuff, like their soul is being overtaken by these elite Westerners. Fundamentalism is a response to false linearization because it's saying, "No, there is something special and sacred and unattainable about my soul." I wish they realized that they can be right about that without having to turn to violence and traditions. In the mid-twentieth century, we were starting to get a balanced approach to traditions. You could be Jewish and a believer but you could leave other people alone about it. But that's not good enough if someone is saying that your soul can be computerized. Then it's like, "Hell, I'm going to blow you up, and then we'll see." Frankly, I think I'd be the same way. If I really believed that these reductions were valid I would join a terrorist group, because I believe in my soul and I would be angry enough that I would be violent.

I don't want to say things that offend people. But soft and mushy today turns into gun toting tomorrow when the chips are down. People have to have a belief in their own spirituality. The difference between the Taliban and New Age is not as great as it might seem because I think in both cases what they're saying is, "I'm going to mystify myself. I'm going to say that there's something fundamentally unattainable about my soul. I'm going to make a statement about it in defiance of rationality because rationality as it's been presented to me lately and as I understand it is something that would threaten and overtake my soul." There's nothing really new about that. That's always been the problem with rationality since the Enlightenment, and indeed earlier. There's a different cast to it now because that was always abstract and remote; this is very personal and specific.

I think we underestimate the impact this has on people. There's been an enormous worldwide rejection of the Enlightenment in the latter part of the twentieth century that nobody foresaw. In the West it's in the form of crystals and flying saucers or, in many cases, fundamentalism. In other parts of the world it's just fundamentalism. Right now the Enlightenment has gone off-course on this confusion of linear and nonlinear systems. So we bring it on ourselves.

I listen to some colleagues talk about how "they're building a computer with emotions." They don't know what emotions are. A scientist who tries to study real emotions in a lab still can't characterize them. He appreciates the complexity of emotion and that there's something irreducible about its complexity. Yet some computer scientist who doesn't think deeply about what emotions are can say: "I have a computer with emotions." That same person who did this bogus piece of reduction wonders why people believe that they've been abducted by flying saucers or why they take up arms in defense of their religion. The two events are intimately connected. We in the sciences and in engineering and in technological-capital management bring it on ourselves.

New Expressions of Spirituality

Aligning with the Natural Forces That Determine Our Lives

W. Brian Arthur ∘ We're looking for a world in which there are bigger forces than us that we are aligned with and in which, to some degree, we can control ourselves. We want to feel that we are aligned, that we are headed in the right direction. Let me put it this way: I'm not sure what the future of standard religion, Islam or Christianity or anything else this century, will be, but I am quite convinced that human beings operate from deep instincts. You could call them spiritual or a yearning for magic, but it's a yearning to align ourselves with the natural forces that determine our lives.

America's Deep Spiritual Current and Restless Questioning

Laurie Anderson ○ One of the things I think is very important to remember about America is that there's a dominant string of spirituality. It's one of the reasons that Buddhism does so well there. America is its new home. My sense is that a lot of people are fed up with this consumer approach to the world and the idea that to be a good global citizen you have to just keep buying stuff. George Bush says, "Let's go out and shop!" to help us out of this slump. Of course, I'm not stupid, I know what he's saying. But there are other things he could also say and I feel angry that he's not. Here we are as Americans who have a tradition of asking questions in other ways, a genuine spiritual tradition.

I do think when you look at our greatest books, they're very questioning. I'm thinking of Twain and Melville and Hemingway and guys who left the mainland to look back from some piece of water, like the Mississippi River or the ocean. Maybe they were just dreaming and it wasn't really what they saw, but I'm going to say it's what they saw, because I'm naïve. I think that we have, as a relatively young country, a beautiful naïveté. It's one of the things we're known for. It's not just Hollywood. It's not just this kind of funny optimism that we also have, which I love. But it's another thing—call it a spiritual current. I see that in a lot of people who love art and music particularly and are willing to say, "I want to pay attention to this."

I think the thing that makes us great software designers is the same thing that is telling us to ask questions like, "What are we doing here?" We don't live in a particularly sensuous society. We have a lot of stuff, but we don't really know what to do with it. We're not relaxed with it, even though there's a veneer sometimes, a Napa Valley veneer of, "Yeah, we appreciate it." There is always some unrest going on underneath that, like "How can we make Quark better? What should we do now?" It's that, but it's not just that.

Whenever I find something that has a vivid edge to it, I always look for the flip side, so fear has desire right next door to it. Love of stuff has hatred of stuff right next door to it. When I'm thinking of something like belief/religion, then on the other side is safety/money.

Spirituality and the Rise of the Internet

Joel Garreau ∘ At Christmastime I ended up writing about how could the market for dotcoms have totally cratered while the Internet was so clearly booming? The answer is, essentially, that the Internet was created as a gift. Tim Berners-Lee and everyone else basically gave away what they learned. If you were of a Christmas sort of mind, you'd believe that they were doing it for the greater glory of God.

This leads to one of the real pieces of weirdness that has happened in this last year, which is how surprised I am at how often values and even spirituality end up right smack in the middle of pieces I'm trying to be really hardheaded about. Like why was the Internet growing while the market collapsed? That was meant to be a totally hardheaded look. All of a sudden I find myself in the gift economy, which takes me to Jesus.

The notion was that in the early days of the Internet, there was no particular attempt on anybody's part to come up with personal gain for what they were doing. They were all contributing for free—their ideas, their code, their whole attitude toward how to build a Net. There is a notion that there's such a thing as a gift economy—a way of exchanging goods and services without getting either the market or the government involved. This notion is based upon "bread upon the waters," that if you do something good in a general way, like create a Web site, good things will come back to you, and you can count on that, even though you can't describe what it is going to be. You have this vague sense that good things will happen if you give things away.

And actually, it pretty much works. But when you start trying to get at what that economy is about, then you start getting into some very weird spaces: What the hell is a gift economy? Where did this gift economy idea come from? And, of course, it's a very ancient idea—the underpinning of Christianity and probably a bunch of other religions, too. You have all sorts of references in the Bible: spreading the bread upon the water, the loaves and fishes. I guess it's the idea of selflessness.

Tracking Three Major Trends in Lifting the Human Spirit

Michael Murphy ∘ Religions are not up to the job. They have delivered incalculable goods into the world. The world has been lifted up by the great religions, obviously. But once I got to Stanford and heard about evolution, it was very hard for me to get very excited about the Virgin Mary anymore. I had thought I was going to be an Episcopalian priest when I grew up. I lost all interest in the Trinity; it didn't make sense.

It was the same with college kids all over the world, in every faith. I was looking at some interviews with these kids in Kabul. How sophisticated they seemed about Islam! I was blown away. Already there is sophistication ready to pop in Afghanistan. It's everywhere in the world. It's spirituality, exploration into our greater nature beyond the strictures of formal religion. That's been going on a long time—since Voltaire, for Christ's sake. This has been in full gear for 250 years at least, and in partial gear for 400 years—since the birth of the scientific awakening, certainly since the French Enlightenment.

This general lifting of the human spirit has to be accompanied by a conceptual framework that is adequate to the modern experience. Modern writers like Huston Smith have moved to a perennialist viewpoint to look for the common ground in all religions. But this coming to terms with our spiritual depths and with the mystical insights and with our larger human nature in a modern and postmodern world, that's part of the challenge here.

What's happening and is going to continue to happen has at least three levels. First, as all of this stuff comes into the modern world, people will continue in their traditional faiths while informed by the new. Let me take an example of a person in a traditional religion. Father Arrupe was the head of the Jesuits, arguably the most powerful order in the Catholic Church, certainly the biggest one politically. Father Arrupe, every day, did Zazen meditation on a cushion because he was in Japan. He said that out of meditation and sitting on a cushion, he came to a different state of mind than on his knees in prayer. He also did prayer.

There are so many people like that. They go back to a traditional religion, or they stay in it, but they bring in these new modern understandings. In Berkeley, there are all these liberal Protestant churches where people regularly practice Zen and do biofeedback and who are in psychotherapy. In Marin County, not only do they go to church, not only are they in therapy, but they also have to be in a somatics class.

The second level is the new religions, as Jacob Needleman has written about. For example, there are two teachers in the Bay Area who are very popular now and extremely sophisticated. One is Hameed Ali of the Ridhwan School. It's a great marriage of modern psychology and therapy with the contemplative lore. He's a Kuwaiti. His younger buddy has now split off and started his own school, which has the same sort of combinations. These are the most sophisticated guys, with an extremely sophisticated following.

It's built out of traditional stuff and modern. Our Esalen group can be seen this way. There are these modern expressions of this new, emerging, pluralistic worldview.

The third level that I see is a kind of general set of shared insights. There are great truths in all religions; we all sit around and agree to that. There are tremendous bodies of lore in each tradition. You could list scores of assumptions that are going to come to be more and more universally shared by more and more people, even if they don't go back to or stay in a traditional religion, and even if they're not in one of these new quasi-religions or philosophical kinds of groups. You're going to have this three-level system all over the world. I would argue we have it now, and that it will continue to develop as a triple-layered system.

A Different Syncretistic Spirituality Is Coming

Richard Rodriguez • I do see a new kind of religious sensibility, a different spirituality coming. I don't think our theologians are anywhere near this. I don't think the churches know about this. I meet kids like this all the time. A girl in Atlanta, Georgia, comes up and she says, " Do you know what I am?" I say, "No, I don't know what you are." She says, "I'm an African-Korean." I say, "That's nice." She says, "Well, that's not half of it. What I really am is a Baptist-Buddhist." Now that interests me. I thought being a Malibu Buddhist like Richard Gere was interesting, but being a Baptist-Buddhist is really interesting. I think she's going to create a theology we've never heard before in the world.

I know about the history of Hispanic Catholicism enough to know that the brilliance of Catholicism in the sixteenth century was that it was syncretistic. It was able to absorb aspects of the Indian culture. So I think that the religions that are going to be syncretistic in that way are going to be the religions that will really thrive in this era. I don't see that within the Christian churches right now.

America's Third Great Awakening of Spirituality

Joel Garreau • In some ways we seem to be devising a new religion in this decade in which people say that they aren't religious, but they are spiritual. They're basically inventing a new religion comparable to the great awakenings of the early 1800s when we Americans invented Jehovah's Witnesses and Mormonism and Seventh-Day Adventists and all that. It was called the second Great Awakening. I think we're in another period like that right now.

The Science At the Core of the Contemplative Life

Michael Murphy ∘ The key thing that makes scientific study empirical is that you follow prescribed disciplines, whether in chemistry or whether in the contemplative life or whether in sport. You follow these procedures, then you get disclosures. Something happens. But then what you discover has to be verified by a community of people adequate to judge what the hell is going on. You or I would have a hard time confirming the observations of a particle physicist looking in a cloud chamber. Is that a muon or a pion? I wouldn't have the least idea. It's just a very few people who can tell.

The same is true of the contemplative life. You have to be a master of the contemplative life to recognize the signs of a mystical disclosure. Mainstream scientists will debunk the claim of the Zen Roshi, the highest order Zen master, that this is a science, and they will just say that it's a matter of your faith. I am saying that this is all empirical in fundamentally the same sense. It's a disciplined inquiry that reveals data but has to be communally verified or shown to be false. Your assertions have to be falsifiable in principle. Otherwise, you're just in the realm of revelation and faith, you see? This is where religion meets science, you could say. This is one place it meets, in the knowledge quest.

I want to argue strongly that in the contemplative life, in the gut of these religions, you can get beyond dogma, beyond belief systems. You can get to this core experience that make it a valid knowledge quest. This goes beyond mere faith and mere belief systems into valid mystical knowledge, clairvoyant knowledge. These are extensions, expansions, enhancements of our universally shared human capacities and attributes.

The Outer Reaches of Human Potential

The Power of Revelation Across All Enduring Cultures

Huston Smith ∘ Human history has shown that there are intuitions within our makeup that in various ways have pierced through what the mystics call "the cloud of all unknowing." All of a sudden one sees.

One gets glimpses of this in the exquisite moments of life. Maybe even sex at its best: total love by two people, where what one wants the other wants most to give. Music can do it. Art can do it. It's this rift in the clouds of nascence or unknowing. They are moments of grace, you might say. The world's great geniuses have them and can hold them in place longer than the hoi polloi can. They are like numbered dots on a child's puzzle and you put the pencil through the dots in the right sequence and a giraffe emerges. Those are moments of revelation—the word revelation etymologically means "ray vellum." Vellum is a veil, and ray is to withdraw or move.

So we have two great windows onto the big picture, the whole of things. One is the scientific method, and the other is this capacity built into the human self to see and glimpse, but we can't hold it in place. These moments of revelation are like the dots and then all you have to do is draw the line through those revelations and you get the religious view of reality. Theologians have played an important part in those revelations. And that happens across almost all cultures. I would probably say all enduring cultures.

We do the best we can to describe this with words, to put multidimensional reality into the flat surface of our ordinary language. But ordinary probes cannot capture this larger world isomorphically any more than our round planet can be depicted on the flat pages of a geography book. Those are only two dimensions, whereas our planet is three. Poets come closest using language, also musicians, composers. Great artists and religions are pretty close to the same thing.

A Natural History of Extraordinary Human Functioning

Michael Murphy ◦ I consider my research to be a kind of natural history of extraordinary human functioning—the theory and philosophy of the further reaches of human potential, and also the ways and means of bringing it about, or what I call transformative practice.

I use these terms interchangeably: supernormal, meta-normal, and extraordinary. Quite simply, it is functioning that is markedly beyond the typical functioning of most people living today. That is a relative term. In times past, for example, writing and reading would have been a supernormal activity; at times I think, in America, it is getting to be a supernormal activity again. In Egypt, for example, the scribes said only a very few people could read and write.

Attempts have been made throughout history to organize this data, particularly in the religious and shamanic traditions. In the Hindu-Buddhist tradition, they talk about siddhis—these are the yogi powers that appear. In the Catholic tradition, they're called chrisms—the supernormal capacities of the saints. In the Sufi tradition of Islam they are called adornments of the man of light. In shamanism, these are shamanic powers. All of these traditions have catalogs of these powers that have been observed over millennia. In modern times, there have been all sorts of studies of this as well. It doesn't form any distinct lineage—there is no natural history of extraordinary human functioning. It's time to name this as a field, however hit-or-miss it has been.

How, then, do you make sense of all of this? The move I've made is to see them all as evolutionary or emergent expressions of universally shared human attributes, which in turn arose from our animal ancestors in the course of evolution. I broke it into 12 sets; I am now expanding that. Perceptions of the external world was one of the sets I used. All living creatures have vision, hearing, taste, touch, and smell. Each of these has all sorts of supernormal expressions. What I have discovered in my research is that there is a whole bunch of this stuff, particularly in sport and high adventure, that is kind of in-between—you don't know whether it's a hyperacuity of the senses or clairvoyance. Another set is kinesthesis—the ability to read our own insides. There's an immense lore of supernormal kinesthesis in the yogic traditions. Sometimes people are geniuses at communication but we don't fully appreciate the nuance, the very supernormality of it. We take it for granted. I'm fascinated by how great orators or comedians or poets or novelists can invoke emotion in an uncanny way.

Let's remember that all of science began as natural history. Before you get to the mechanisms, you simply collect the specimens and experience. I would argue that we're in the natural history phase of supernormal functioning. I've made a classificatory move by saying that you can map them all as supernormal expressions of universally shared human attributes, which, in turn, were inherited from the animal kingdom. So it's a simple move. But then once you do that, the next question is, how do they arise? Obviously now they are not arising by natural selection. These things emerge through a process of natural selection in the animal kingdom, but among humans, they can be enhanced through transformative practice. So the vector continues although the modality is different.

The Rigorous Study of the Supernormal

Michael Murphy • When you look at the emerging field of this natural history of supernormal human functioning, it's been largely a hit-or-miss process; you get a burst of activity and interest and then it tapers off, starting in the 1830s. It flowered in the 1880s and '90s when the British and American Societies for Psychical Research published journals, proceedings, annals—thousands and thousands of pages on telepathy, clairvoyance, apparitions and the evidence for the survival of bodily death, psychosomatic changes, the abnormalities of genius, etc. With World War I and behaviorism all that comes to an end. To my knowledge, the first truly scientific study that was published in any kind of journal was in 1937 by a graduate student at Yale who did a physiological study of a yogi. There were some very brilliant studies in the '50s in both Japan and in India. In 1970, three key articles were published—one in *Science*, one in *Scientific American*, and one in the *American Physiologist*. The field exploded and particularly crested out in the 1970s and 1980s. In 1987, Steve Donovan and I published the only existing bibliography of all the meditation research literature that's in existence. I wrote a brief history of the field in *The Future of the Body*. Interest tapered out in the 1990s.

Now you could say, "What about New Age? What about all this literature on human potential that is all over the place?" It's thin. It's shallow. It has not made any appreciable influence, in my judgment, on academia. It has run on a kind of parallel track since the '60s in the popular culture. All through American history and all through the history of Europe there have been similar popular movements of mysticism. If you go back to the nineteenth century to Rosicrucianism, if you go back to the eighteenth century to the Masons. George Washington, Benjamin Franklin—these guys were all Masons. It was their New Age stuff, so to speak. The only point I want to make here is that in every age in modern times there has been this popular occultism and mysticism—now we call it New Age stuff—that has not had any depth of practice or any greatness of realization. It never has produced a single great mystic. America has never produced one, nor has modern Europe.

Saint John of the Cross, Saint Theresa—we don't have them anymore because the culture doesn't value this. If you start to practice like this they think maybe you should go to a mental hospital. There are monasteries, but there are so few. The thing I'm after, there's no basic constituency for it. There's no national association. There's no international association. There are no university departments. There are no university chairs. There's also the law of numbers in this. One of the reasons Americans are so good at sport is that every kid does sports in high school, and you are bound to get some good football and basketball players. And it's so prized. In other words, there's a pyramid of achievement and a vast cultural celebration and reinforcement of it. Every culture gets what it prizes. India has gotten great mystics. Not now, though—now they're getting great software programmers.

Sixth Senses, Intuitions, and What We Do That Computers Don't

Laurie Anderson ∘ We live in a culture so tilted towards hard information and people who are tied to their workplaces—they are tied to their laptops. Even more so than when they were tied to their desks—always, always, always at work. I think it's a real tip-off that some of the things that are being made to make life at your laptop easier are the same things that are being designed for paraplegics. My biggest fear is that what we're really good at is going to atrophy.

Sixth senses. Seventh senses, eighth senses. In my new piece *Happiness*, there's a short section about that—I use silence as an example of what we can do that computers can't. You know, what happens in silence, in an awkward silence, for example. When people stop talking in a meeting or at lunch and it's like "Uh oh." Your antennae go out. You become aware. You're feeling around, looking, taking the temperature, and figuring out what to do next, until somebody goes, "Uh yeah, I saw a great movie the other night."

If you're working on your computer it's either there or it's not there. It's on or it's off. Silence is interpreted as nothing going on and it shuts down. That's it. They are just boxes, you know? They're not doing a fraction of what we can do. And the things that we can do—our intuitive abilities, even our physicality— are beginning to disappear, I think, because we worship these computers.

The Future of Transformative Practices 50 Years Out

Michael Murphy ∘ What's ahead? What's next? I don't know. Evolution meanders more than it progresses in all domains, as far as I can see. I would be more confident looking ahead not 10 years, but 50 years. Then I would say, almost certainly, we are going to have social institutions emerge to support these transformative practices. Inevitably it has got to dawn on us that we can get more systematic about this, because this is, for me and for a lot of people, a more interesting frontier than virtually anything. To transform our very nature itself. I could see astronauts getting out in outer space and being bored silly, but to stay here and open your senses so that suddenly you look at a wall and it's more like a gold lamé sari, where you can meditate and you suddenly shift—and my God, it's shifting every minute. You don't need a drug for that. Learn how to see this way. This kind of love comes up for people when you're in this state.

I've seen this at Esalen for all these years. They start to make some discoveries about themselves and suddenly they look at everyone and suddenly everyone looks like a character from a Tolkien trilogy. Everyone is just enchanted. This is the power of Esalen, the power of enchantment for at least two days. Then they go home; they're high until about Tuesday. Then they gradually forget what it was and they are very inarticulate and they say to their friends, "God, I really had a great time." That's about it. They can't remember the nuance of the experience very well. We don't have a language. If we had a longer time horizon, it's almost inevitable that this stuff would break out more and more.

Religious Myth As Premonitions of Our Future

Michael Murphy ∘ The myth of the resurrection, all of these myths of the transformed body, I think, are premonitions of further possibilities. I argue that many religious myths can be seen much like Jules Verne years before Jacques Cousteau-Verne kind of invented the submarine before there was a submarine. Or let's say these balloons that could travel around the world, like in *Around the World in Eighty Days*. Jules Verne imagined all sorts of things. So did Leonardo da Vinci—he imagined an airplane and had started to work on the helicopter. These are premonitions of what could be.

I'm saying that in religious myth, a lot of this is a premonition. The human race or the human imagination has the capacity to see into the future. Arthur Clarke envisioned the geosynchronous 24-hour satellite. He had that 40 years before reality. Just as science fiction has anticipated technological advances, I argue that a lot of children's cartoons, fantasy literature, and religious myth do the same.

Finding a Way Forward

Attracting Knowledge Workers with a Deep Sense of Mission

Jay Ogilvy ∘ I think that good people—and here I mean in the sense of smart and successful, those who will add to your bottom line—are also going to want to think of themselves as good people, ethical people who have made the world a better place than the way they found it. I do think that it is a very important and strong motivator that's going to be a bigger and bigger deal when the economy gets back on track. To get the best talent in an organization, it will be important to put a vision out there that says, "When you get up in the morning to come to work here, it's something you're doing for more than the paycheck."

I heard this wonderful line from somebody awhile ago. You've heard of people calling in sick? A guy from Intel told me: We're having a problem with people "calling in rich." The money just isn't the motivation anymore. If there isn't some flying of the banner, in a sense a crusade, a sense of meaning and purpose, people don't show up energized. I think that's pretty obvious. But it's easy to forget about and say, that's touchy-feely California. Well, maybe. I'm sure there are a lot of people for whom greed, achiever values, and just winning is enough. But I think there's an increasing number of people with a bit of a mission, who need a sense of purpose.

Beyond Profit: Businesspeople Seeking the Spiritual

L. Hunter Lovins ∘ We were sitting with a bunch of young corporate executives, trying to pitch our sustainable natural-capitalism thesis, and we were talking about how this can increase their competitive advantage. It can increase their profits. It's the basis of competitiveness in the coming decade, and it's profitable right now, and it'll be more profitable later. Profits, profits, profits, which we thought would be the basis on which a business audience would be interested in this stuff.

After a while, one guy stood up and said: "It's good that you talk about profits. Yes, we're interested in that. But we care about more than profits. We care about things like leaving a legacy, like why am I doing this? What is all this money to me?"

What he was really talking about were spiritual values. There are an increasing number of conferences titled things like "Spirituality and Business." You look at the business section of a bookstore, and there are an increasing number of books on spirituality and business. It is, I think, a phenomenon that is going to increase, not decrease.

I sit on airplanes and look at the books that the guys sitting next to me, the corporate executive male types, are reading. They're not about how do I make even more money. It's the various personal growth, religious, or spiritual books. I ask the guys, "Why are you reading this? I would think you'd be reading the *Wall Street Journal* or Jack Welch's autobiography." They get a puzzled look, but they say, "Well, right now this is more what interests me." I think it is gaining traction.

The New Meta-Values Supportive of Adaptability and Change

Mary Catherine Bateson ∘ We are gradually learning to think of change as a constant. I would say that in the last 10 years the word "change" has become much more positive in its connotation. Listening to ads, for instance. It used to be that if you said to someone, "I'm going to make you different from what you are now," they'd dig in their heels. Now you say it and it sounds like a makeover, it sounds like reinventing yourself. And all of these things have become part of our conversation. Instead of people thinking of their identities as fixed, they're thinking of them as fluid. It begins to be a cultural value.

At the same time we have to be asking what other tenable constants there are. We're going to want a society with values related to change and adaptability and listening and responsiveness. But then we're going to need to identify those as meta-values and look for constants within them. If you say that listening and learning are going to be the values, they carry with them a respect for other people, for instance. Some version of that respect for other people has to become a meta-value—that I believe you may tell me something worth knowing. You could be the Laotian who moves into the building next door or you could be a Hare Krishna devotee in the street. You could be my three-year-old child. If my take on the world is that I am a constant learner, I need to be able to listen respectfully to all of the above. All of a sudden, constant learning becomes a way of constructing a form of respect for other people across difference.

Another feature is the meta-value on diversity and conserving diversity. The slogan I use is, "You are not what you know but what you are willing to learn." That's what I have on my Web site. At that point, you care about the preservation of all biological species. Each one represents highly evolved information. At that point, you begin to respect other cultures and their differences because they can teach you something.

The Willingness to Learn

Mary Catherine Bateson ∘ I have argued that the willingness to learn is the foremost spirituality. It is a stance toward the universe when you say, "I treasure each part of the creative world because it has something to teach. It's part of the overall pattern. Therefore, I approach all with a degree of humility, because there's so much I don't know."

I think a lot of different kinds of spirituality are rising that look very different on the surface. I'm sure that few people would easily make the connection that I'm making. It seems to me that one of the things that people do mean by spirituality is listening for an inner voice, a contemplation, a kind of openness to deeper meaning. All of those are aspects of listening and learning and exhibit a willingness to let go of particular formulas and absolutes and be guided to something else.

One of the things that I see is that it's striking a lot among women. I see women who are talking about spiritual search. They are also going back to college and getting degrees that allow them to start new jobs. They don't necessarily connect these two things. I would connect them as both being ways of saying, "I am open to change and listening and looking for deeper meaning."

I see the emerging phenomenon as lifelong learning. I see lifelong learning as manifesting itself at many different levels, some of them just practical, like learning how to use a cell phone. One of those levels is a level of spiritual development and deepening. It may or may not be labeled that way.

To me, it seems analogous with many things that are specifically labeled as spiritual. Spiritual means not material. That's all it means, literally. So I'm searching for something that is not material, that is in some sense a mental experience. If I search for the experience of learning, if I'm curious—that's a spiritual trait. It's a spiritual trait from which can be derived a set of attitudes toward other human beings and toward the natural world that in the past have been regarded as religious and spiritual attitudes.

The Need for New Wisdom About the Common Good

Betty Sue Flowers ∘ Organized politics and religion are still working on another model, an old paradigm. So I don't see leadership coming from that direction. The reason politicians are in such bad standing is that their story is patently not the real thing and yet they're still telling it. They'll talk about working for the common good, and people don't believe them.

Today if you lean in to listen to the tone and energy of the conversation, it sounds like very old-time religion. It has to do with moral righteousness, so that either party arguing against each other is arguing as if from a pulpit. That is the old time. We can't speak from a pulpit and tell the world that the other guy is going to hell anymore. It doesn't have anything to do with the future. The future is not about who is going to hell and who is going to heaven. We are all in it together. It is not about who has it right. It's about what the best next step is, which we can only take all together.

Maybe politics can change. Politics, unlike some other fields, is very sensitive to an individual's coming on the stage in a way that business isn't. Business is more of a communitarian endeavor. Interestingly enough, even if you have a charismatic pope, religion is a much more institutionalized thing. But politics is very much about leadership, and a different voice or galvanizing presence can make a huge difference.

Most great political leaders articulate a message that somehow has risen from some other source, not themselves—but today we don't have those other sources of wisdom, so whatever that new message might be has not been articulated. And I don't see an articulator coming on the scene anytime soon.

For example, think of the founding of this country. Thomas Paine wrote *Common Sense* and that prepared the ground for the Declaration of Independence, which then galvanized the will for a system to be developed, which is enshrined in the Constitution. Jefferson, Hamilton, and all those leaders weren't just packaging Paine's or John Locke's ideas. They felt these ideas so deeply, they actually birthed the "new." The future emerged through them.

I don't have a prediction because you never can tell, but it is possible that within five years some germ of a new thought will emerge for us. It depends a lot on what happens with the economy; it depends on wars and events and a conversation around ideas that change the background against which we talk, so that a new common sense emerges.

Creating the New Global Story

Betty Sue Flowers ○ We are at a pause of will. If we had what we thought was a good story about where to turn our will, then it wouldn't matter if things went up or down. We would explain them in terms of our story and keep going. But since we don't have the new story, we can be thrown by whatever negative thing happens, or we can be thrown into illusion by whatever positive bubble happens, like with the dotcoms.

We are the ones who make up the new story. When I say the story emerges, I don't mean it is on the other side of a curtain and comes out. It comes out through us, so it is a dynamic process. The new story has got to be global and its values have to be coherent in relation to our new identity. It also has to articulate our new identity. Its values can't be based on the old definition of what it is to be human. Inherently, it is also a new story of who we are, what the good is, what health is, and I mean that in the widest sense—spiritual, emotional, and physical. What is the new value that is the global equivalent of democracy?

What is holy, what is sacred? This is not directly about who or what is God, which is a theological question. It's about: What is it that is so precious that we should all care for it? And from that point we then move to: How do we instantiate our care? We build a system based on values that embody the care that we have for something. Then we institutionalize it with rules and ways of being.

We are at the very beginning, the Tom Paine stage. We haven't even written *Common Sense* yet, much less the Declaration of Independence. Much, much less the Constitution. At the moment I think society is way out in front of politics, but we haven't articulated it. We don't have a Martin Luther King. We don't have someone saying the words; we don't have the story. Our feelings are way ahead of politics, which is why we're so disgusted. Politicians don't seem to speak to our concerns because they're in a system that is smaller than our concerns. Politics are national, but our concerns— and much about our new identity and story—are global.

Part 3

Potential

Tomorrow's Tools
Technology

"Generally, when there aren't real arguments that something is impossible, we find ways to make it possible."

Danny Hillis

"Fuel cells will probably go forth and multiply first in stationary resource applications for individual homes. And then there'll be so many millions of them, it will be cheap."

Lee Schipper

"I think we have a global bandwidth shortage. Anyone who says, 'What are we going to do with all the bandwidth?' has no idea what they're talking about."

Paul Saffo

"People are taking technology—because they can and we're creative and are hoping to evolve humans—and applying it to things for which it wasn't intended."

Shaun Jones

"There's a perfect storm coming at the 100-nanometer level. Information technology, biotechnology, and nanotechnology are all converging on that scale."

Stewart Brand

"I think one of the lessons of the late twentieth century, in terms of astronomy and geology, is that the universe has turned out to be much more violent than we ever thought. We can wipe ourselves out with technology, but technology also is the key to protecting ourselves against the dangers out there."

Vernor Vinge

We now return to more familiar terrain for business—the domain of technology. Human history has always been shaped by our tools and evolving technological capabilities. From the creation of stone tools, through early agricultural innovations, right up to the explosive impact of the Industrial Revolution, we can identify a clear link between the introduction of new technologies and important changes in societies. Over the last few decades we have witnessed an unprecedented acceleration of technological change, and its increasingly pervasive reach. For most businesses, developments in information and communications technologies in particular have transformed the workplace, opened new markets, and reshuffled the economic players in many industries. But it is possible that the next 10 years might hold even more technology-driven change than we've experienced to date. In this chapter, we review some important and intriguing developments in technology, particularly in the fields of energy, telecommunications, computers, nanotechnology, and space (leaving biotechnology for the next chapter on science).

We begin with a general discussion about **Technology in Tomorrow's World**. Our network members consider a range of issues regarding the role of technology in our lives and our sometimes ambivalent feelings about it. One talks about how technological breakthroughs can dramatically alter the landscape, while another describes how technology subtly seeps into our lives. Another comments upon technology's potential for solving the deep intractable problems in the future—in fact, he says, given the problems we face, it is our only hope. This leads into a discussion of **The Next Wave in Energy Technologies**. Some of these are very practical and close to market, and others represent possible wildcard breakthroughs, such as the return of cold fusion. Taken together, these prospects could have extraordinary economic, social, and environmental consequences in the years ahead.

Next we consider **Telecommunications at the Cusp**. It's often asserted that today's telecommunications infrastructure is hugely overbuilt with excess capacity that will last for years. Here you will find a counterargument: that we might actually have a bandwidth shortage that will become obvious and more severe over the course of the decade as we solve the "last-mile" problem and unleash more of the Internet's promise. The last-mile solution, several network members contend, probably won't come from policymakers, but from innovators and entrepreneurs working within the largely unregulated spectrum of wireless broadband. Meanwhile, another network member points out that the field of photonics, upon which fiber-optic telecommunications are based, is just beginning to significantly refine its manufacturing processes and capabilities. The industry today is comparable to where the computer chip industry was during its vacuum tube stage—poised for far greater efficiencies and disruptive change.

The enormous impact of computing technology has already been felt over the last 20 years, but in our next section we focus on one of the more interesting issues on the horizon: **The Evolving Relationship Between Humans and Computers**. What might happen as the boundaries blur between people and computers? One network member points out how retail workers, using handheld computers and headsets, are already acting as the human interfaces between customers and powerful databases. But another speculates on the next step of implanting chips in people. Others push the boundaries even further and debate whether artificial intelligence will catch up to that of humans.

The final two technology fields head in diametrically opposite directions: toward the very small and the very large. In **Toward the Atomic: Nanotechnology**, contributors explore possible advances in tools at the molecular or atomic level. These might include the development of microscopic devices that can course through the human circulatory system and diagnose illnesses, send detailed internal images, and ultimately deliver appropriate therapeutics.

In **Toward the Cosmic: Space**, we hear why space exploration, a topic that has largely fallen from public discourse, may move back up the agenda in the coming decade. The large sums of U.S. government money likely to be dedicated to missile defense might seed practical business interest. At the same time, recent scientific findings suggest that life on Earth may be more vulnerable to a hostile universe than we ever imagined. This awareness may increase public support for investing in next-generation space technologies as well.

Technology in Tomorrow's World

Trust in Technology or Trust in Nature?

W. Brian Arthur ○ We're experiencing a collision at the moment on various fronts between two opposing views. One is that technology will save us—so you get genetically engineered crops and genetically modified organisms and so on. The other is in reaction to technology. Technology itself brings an anomie or helplessness—a smallness that we're starting to feel, a lack of control. People throughout history have relied on nature and so they trust nature. We've had two or three million years of experience with nature.

We haven't with the Internet. Nature works for us. We trust it. So we're at the start of a collision between trust in technology and trust in nature. It's not a new collision. We have a hope or trust in technology to get us out of predicaments and make our life better, but we have a reliance and a familiarity and a depth of at-homeness with nature. From time to time these huge unconscious forces just collide. If anything, America trusts technology more than any nation on earth. I see that as being one of the main ongoing stories of this century. The recent hullabaloo about stem cells is the same thing. Is this natural? Is this pro-life? Is this against life? Is it part of nature? Is this technology running wild or is this technology saving us? I favor technology, but I like nature too. It's not an easily resolvable thing.

Technology Is Our Only Hope for a Sustainable Future

Danny Hillis ∘ Look at some of the discussions of uses of technology. There's a big movement in the United States that says, "Technology has gone far enough." Maybe we should stop the development of technology. Maybe we shouldn't do things like nanotechnology. Maybe we should just freeze things right now. That's fine if you're rich and well-fed and free. If the whole world was as well-off as we are, I think freezing things for a while might be a perfectly reasonable thought. But we live in a world that is on an unsustainable path without new technology. In fact, if we didn't have a continuing stream of new technology, there wouldn't be hope of the world's surviving without a major population shrink. Just on the environmental level, what we're doing is unsustainable. The way that we supported industrialization, in the countries that industrialized early, is not going to work for the rest of the world.

We could just freeze things and have a few rich people and a lot of poor people, since the poor people are going to get poorer as we start taxing the resources of the earth more. I think that's a fundamentally unsustainable and unfair solution. You could say that we are going to have some sort of social revolution and we're going to take the resources we have and divide them equitably, in which case, we'll all be poor. Now that's a very hard sell, so I don't think that will work as a solution.

We could also do what we've done in the past, which is come up with new solutions and create our way out of this. That, to me, while it's difficult, is the only good solution. That means continued change and technology development, with all of the problems that come along with it. That creates its own set of problems, but compared to the other two alternatives, I think it's the one we should choose.

If Not Fundamentally Impossible, We Make It Possible

Danny Hillis ∘ Over and over, we've been in situations where people didn't see the solution and said we were doomed, and then people found a surprising set of solutions. All my life, I've read that we were about to run out of all the basic commodities. In fact, all my life, the price of basic commodities has been going down. Why is that? Well, it turns out that the real limit is not how much stuff is there, for the most part, but our ability to get and refine it. It's political issues, distribution issues, things like that. You have to really ask yourself if the limits are fundamental or just limits of our imagination.

I don't see fundamental limits that would create problems for us in the next century. It's like when people used to argue about whether humans could ever travel faster than 100 miles per hour, or faster than the sound barrier. There were a lot of superstitions, but no real arguments that they couldn't. Generally, when there aren't real arguments that something is impossible, we find ways to make it possible. I'm optimistic, in that sense.

If I looked at available energy and then at the energy required to keep people well-fed and happy and productive, and those were mismatched, then I'd say we have a fundamental problem. In fact, they're not at all mismatched. There is plenty of energy. But there are difficulties to getting at the energy. If there weren't enough acres of space on the earth for all its beings, then that would be a fundamental problem, but that's not the case.

On the other hand, if you look at the rate at which farmland is being destroyed and the rate at which new land is becoming available, we do have a problem. We're going to have to find out a better way of making what we don't consider farmland into farmland. Is that impossible? I don't think so. It's not that there aren't great difficulties to be solved and huge inventions to be made, but I don't see any deep reasons why it can't be done.

Tools for Entering the Territory of Zillionics

Kevin Kelly ∘ There's no question in my mind that a next step will be toward "the all," and that "all" is qualitatively different than "most." Having all the elements of the periodic table is different than having some of them. Having all the parts of a car is different than having only some of them. Having all the books available online via the Net is different than having just some of them. And having a map of the entire globe is different than having part of the map. So I think the destination of a complete global picture of things, that idea, is not new. What is new is the prospect and the feasibility of actually attaining some of that. The problem is that we don't have a lot of examples where we have done it because it is so difficult and big to do.

We haven't done much global accounting. What is happening at the global level? The answer is: we don't know. How much fresh water is there in the world? We don't know. How many feet of lumber are there? How many telephones are there in the world? The one question that we ask most often and with the highest degree of precision is: How many people are there in the world? And even with that I don't believe our numbers. What does the world look like to the resolution of a meter? We don't know.

I think we are developing tools and interest in asking about and compiling this information. These are tools of measurement and analysis, because part of the problem is that even if you have all this information, how do you look at it and what do you ask about it? What does it mean?

I think we're headed into dealing with vast amounts of information. I call it the territory of zillionics, where you have zillions of things. And zillions of things are different. That's one reason why "all" is different, because in many cases "all" deals with zillions of records. It's qualitatively different because it is in a different dimensional space—just by the sheer number of pieces. Things in the zillions behave differently than things in the millions do. It's not infinite. It's beyond billions.

And the reason why it's different is combinatorial. The number of possible combinations of those numbers is just beyond comprehension. You get to the point where you simply cannot even calculate or truly search that. There is not enough time in the universe. It's like if you had a Web space that, instead of having two billion Web pages, had a zillion Web pages. You would not even have an index to it, because the crawler would never get to all the pages.

Theoretically it's not unknowable, but there may be practical unknowabilities until such time as something else is invented—quantum computing or whatever. I'm just saying that it's a different territory. Along with it we'll have a different kind of thinking that's required to inhabit that territory. And a different kind of vocabulary: high-dimensional space and things like that. So as we start to deal with this space of "all" and zillions, as we try to get a global picture, our thinking space will also have to shift.

Beyond Moore's Law: The Orthogonal Spike of Invention

Vernor Vinge ∘ Science fiction writers, as well as a lot of other people, have gotten so caught up with Moore's Law (based on exponential change) that we have come to overlook that there is another model for spectacular technological progress, and that's the orthogonal spike: All of a sudden somebody does something that people have just talked about doing before. Contrast this with Moore's Law, where even the incremental things are smoothed by the marketplace.

For example, in the 1930s people talked about the someday possibility of nuclear energy. But in 1945, when the news came that an A-bomb had been dropped on Hiroshima, it was a very abrupt surprise. (My father told me that he went for days not believing the claim; he figured the journalists were just confused about some large new conventional bomb.) Up until the 1970s, many people, including me, had the notion that future progress would mostly happen in such orthogonal spikes; you'd get some terrific invention that would suddenly open up all sorts of new things. I think such orthogonal breakthroughs will always be possible, even though they are bumpy prospects for all of us who have been spoiled by Moore's Law.

The Street Finds Its Own Uses for Technology

Bruce Sterling • The ultimate uses of technology come from the street. My understanding of how this works, on a practical level, is based on the tremendous William Gibson insight that the street finds its own uses for things. Technological change happens. It's very rarely deployed in any kind of clean, top-down, ivory-tower fashion. It seeps out like water into a paper napkin. As with most important life developments, people explain and mythologize it after the fact.

The Next Wave in Energy Technologies

Wildcard Breakthroughs That Could Change the World

John Petersen • I keep running into these very interesting kinds of people who are on the fringe, working on mom-and-pop kind of stuff, who have got potential technological breakthroughs. Things like 300-degree Fahrenheit superconductivity. It's done with polymers and it's extruded to make wires out of plastics and it will be dirt cheap. It would change the whole world.

In energy, there's cold fusion. There are 150 different laboratories that have replicated the cold fusion experiment successfully. The problem with it is that it doesn't happen all the time. It isn't predictable. The example that I like to use is with Thomas Edison inventing the filament for the incandescent light bulb. He went through more than 1,000 experiments trying one combination, then another, trying to get the variables. He didn't understand the materials theory; he was just trying to get all the variables lined up until he finally got something that worked. When he finally did, he couldn't explain the underlying theory of why it worked. I think that's what's happening in the cold fusion area. Sometimes it works; sometimes it doesn't work. SRI has gotten to the point where they say that 70 to 80 percent of the time they're producing more energy out than they put in. Lately they've gone quiet and that probably means one of two things. Either they failed miserably and they don't want to talk about it, or they've really figured out how to do it and they're trying to get the venture money together. They also keep their heads down because the mainline science journalists would go crazy. They destroy careers when scientists speak up about cold fusion.

Here's another example. There's a guy in Michigan who says he's figured how to get 70 percent efficiency out of photovoltaic cells. Well, the average efficiency in a photovoltaic cell is somewhere around 10 percent. If it increases by 50 percent then that's a really big deal. By the way, it competes with grid-produced electricity at about 14 percent efficiency. It's about five cents a kilowatt-hour. If you got 70 percent, it would revolutionize how electricity is produced in this world. I don't know if it's for real. I haven't had a chance to look closely at it, but there are lots of interesting, breakthrough ideas around.

Solar Cells Are Dropping in Price and Rising in Use

Amory Lovins ∘ If all the economic benefits of photovoltaics (PVs) are properly counted, they're already cost effective in many, if not most, applications. Typically, they're valued only at the commodity cost of replacing a kilowatt-hour, which is one of their less important attributes. But if you also count the low financial risk of being able to build as you need, pay as you go, very short lead time, and the constant price attribute of the electricity, and its avoidance of distribution costs and losses, then PVs start to look much more attractive. And if you have, for example, a very efficient house, like ours, which uses $5 worth of household electricity each month, then it's cheaper not to hook up to the grid, because you can run the whole house on a few square meters of photovoltaics instead.

They continue to get about 20 percent cheaper for every doubling of cumulative production, like many other manufactured goods. But some kinds of plausible technical breakthroughs may cause prices to ratchet down faster and more abruptly than that historic pattern.

Photovoltaics have increased in use 26 to 42 percent a year in recent years. And wind power worldwide last year, which is already edging below three cents a kilowatt-hour, grew over 30 percent last year. In fact, wind in recent years has been adding over five gigawatts a year to global capacity, whereas in the 1990s nuclear power, with hundreds of billions of dollars and a half-century head start, added only three gigawatts a year. What does that tell you about relative economics?

Fuel-Cell Cars and SUVs Are Coming This Decade

Amory Lovins ∘ Last year, Hypercar, Inc., which I chair, developed a quintuple-efficiency uncompromised comparable-cost midsize SUV, running at the equivalent of 99 miles a gallon on a direct hydrogen fuel cell. What the U.S. government's Freedom Car initiative says it wants to develop has already been done with private capital, and is on offer to automakers for licensing. That is, we've got a complete and well-studied virtual design that is manufacturable and production-costed. There's still a lot to do to get it actually on the road. But we are highly confident, from the depth of analysis done with industry-standard simulation tools, that it does everything it's supposed to do. The key is, of course, to make the car ultralight and very low-drag, so it takes only about a third the normal amount of power to make it go. That makes the fuel cell, in turn, small enough to afford even at early prices, and it makes the hydrogen tanks small enough to package conveniently without interfering with the space required for people and luggage.

And the key to that, again, is to make it platform-efficient in the first place by giving it good design, so that it can cruise at 55 miles an hour on the power normally required in a car of that class just to run its air conditioner. So if the Freedom Car initiative takes the best learning from the Partnership for a New Generation of Vehicles (PNGV) and applies it to the cars first, so fuel cells go into very efficient cars, then it would be a wonderful leapfrog. An effort merely to adapt fuel cells to today's inefficient cars will be a failure.

Bear in mind that eight major automakers have already announced the beginning of low-volume production for fuel-cell cars between 2003 and 2005. And a lot of them already have fuel-cell cars on the road as experimental models. This is not that far off. And the reports you see in the press about how no one has solved the storage problem are terribly out of date. The storage problem was solved quite a while ago with tanks already on the market. These can hold enough hydrogen to run the car, as long as you make the car efficient. We now know how to do that. The automakers have done it. They just haven't put all the pieces together yet.

The Early Stages of Building a Hydrogen Economy

Amory Lovins • To get to a hydrogen economy in an orderly and profitable way, you need two changes. One is to make the car ready for the hydrogen. That's what Hypercar, Inc. already did. And second is to coordinate the deployment of fuel cells in buildings and vehicles so each makes the other happen faster and their integration gets you through the early stages of deployment.

The cars would not use on-board reformers. The cars would run on direct hydrogen, and that's perfectly feasible and the most attractive way to do it, but it requires that the car have a much lower tractive load. There's much less power needed to move it, because it's light and slippery. It turns out that has massive advantages to both the customer and the automaker, which means that superefficient cars can be marketed based just on value to the customer and competitive advantage to the manufacturer without policy intervention being necessary.

I would also add that when you design fuel-cell cars in the way I've described, they can easily be designed to plug in as mobile power plants when parked. Cars are parked about 96 percent of the time, typically. And a full fleet of such plug-in Hypercars—which send power to the grid, not the other way around—would have about six to 12 times the generating capacity that all the power companies now own. Doing this would save in the U.S. about as much oil as Saudi Arabia produces, or worldwide about as much as OPEC sells.

Homes, Not Cars—The First Fuel-Cell Target

Lee Schipper • Fuel cells will probably go forth and multiply first in stationary resource applications for individual homes. And then there'll be so many millions of them, it will be cheap. Preparing the distribution system, whether it's hydrogen or something else, is tricky. It may be that if you go to stationary resources first, you can strip the carbon out of natural gas and run that way. You can build a little reformer system for the home. That's my guess about what's going to happen first. So I just think it's a matter of time. But it does help to have high fuel prices to drive people toward thinking about how to use fuel better. And, again, that puts us at the mercy of a fluctuating oil market. The present oil prices are still way below their peaks in 1981.

I think by 2010 we will have several hundred thousand stationary fuel cell systems around the world. Small scale. And by 2020 there should be several tens of millions, if they turn out to be really economic. Why not make your own electricity in your home and sell what you don't need back to the grid?

The Overthrow of Bad Engineering and Design

Amory Lovins ∘ I have a wider ambition, which is the nonviolent overthrow of bad engineering. RMI is developing pedagogic tools that contrast optimization of components in isolation with optimization of whole systems. As a simple example, a supposedly optimized, in the conventional way, industrial pumping loop was recently redesigned with our help to use 12 times less pumping power but with lower capital costs and better performance in every respect. It didn't use any new technology, but it changed the design mentality, so we ended up with fat, short, straight pipes instead of skinny, long, crooked pipes.

This is not rocket science. This is good Victorian engineering rediscovered. And that sort of order-of-magnitude resource savings with lower costs and better performance has been demonstrated empirically now in a very wide range of uses and sectors. The general result is what we call "tunneling through the cost barrier," namely, making very large resource savings cost less than small savings. So when you invest in resource productivity, you get expanding returns instead of diminishing returns. That's important and needs to be spread around.

Telecommunications at the Cusp

New Fronts in the Communications Revolution

Paul Saffo ∘ The Internet and the Web have barely touched our lives. The Web arrived on the one piece of real estate we've been trying to get away from for the last 20 years: our desktops. It didn't get any further. This is what makes wireless and broadband so important. Wireless delivers the Internet in general, and the Web in particular, to where we actually live and work and play. That has profound implications for our life and also for the medium. The Web on wireless going to personal appliances is not the Web as we know it. It is something else.

The other big shift is in the nature of communications. Before deregulation, communications was synonymous with people talking to other people. The symbol was a telephone handset on a desk. Along come the Internet and the Web, and the growing edge of communications is no longer simply people talking to people—it's people accessing information and other people in information-rich environments. The real growth is in a third area. Communications is about to go through a big spurt, but it's not going to come from people talking to other people or people accessing information—it's going to come from machines talking to other machines on people's behalf. I think what you're going to see in 10 years, and really visibly in 20, is that the total communications traffic on the planet attributed to humans is going to precipitously drop. The vast bulk of communication will be machine to machine. In two decades, the amount of communications traffic attributable to human beings will be below the rounding error of your average corporate telecommunications account—maybe half a percent.

Nerds Not Wonks Will Finally Bring About High Bandwidth

Paul Saffo ∘ We need more bandwidth. We've got to get the bandwidth for our machines to talk and we need to give people bandwidth for entertainment and all the other things we want to do. The networks are too slow for what we already do and people want to do more. I think we have a global bandwidth shortage. Anyone who says, "What are we going to do with all the bandwidth?" has no idea what they're talking about.

Consider 3G and 802.11. 3G is third-generation wireless. Basically, it's wireless for watching video and accessing stuff, and it's regulated by the government. The phone companies had to pay huge sums for the licenses, and someone has to pay the bill for those. There's going to be a reality gap between what the phone companies want to charge and what people are going to want to pay. People are going to like the service, but they're going to say it's too expensive.

802.11 is a wireless standard for, in essence, wireless Ethernet. The important thing about 802.11 is that it's not switched, it's routed. In addition, it's not regulated in any meaningful way. So this is a space where entrepreneurs with big ideas, shoestring budgets, and not a lot of adult supervision can jump in and make stuff happen. The whole 802.11 world has the smell and feel of ISPs in the early 1990s. You buy an Apple AirPort modem and never have to worry about wires for your computer in your house.

Say you're living in a condo in San Francisco and you have friends above and below you. If you put in an 802.11 transceiver—one plug to your broadband line, the other plug to the power supply—your friends can use it as well. The telcos and the cablecos are all up in arms because people are pirating bandwidth. They don't get it. They somehow think that when you bring a line into someone's house—and this is classic circuit-switch thinking—only that family is going use it. Well, they're sharing it.

802.11 works inside the house. In addition, we're hovering on the edge of what is called mesh-routed 802.11, which is really interesting for neighborhoods. There are a couple of companies still running under the radar that have said, "Forget wired broadband. The big expense in that thing is pulling the wires. Let's do it wirelessly." There's one node that hooks your wireless network to the wired network, and one every half a kilometer or so. Everything else is wireless. They put up the node and offer the service, and you go buy an 802.11 transceiver, a little box on the side of your house. It picks up the signal from the neighborhood and also transmits the signal inside your house.

Here's the interesting thing. If your neighbor gets an 802.11 transceiver, the quality of your service improves. The more transceivers you have in the neighborhood, the more paths there are, and the happier everybody is. It's the exact opposite of cable modems, where you want to pay your neighbors not to subscribe because it's going to slow your service down. I think it's going to take off at a grassroots level, and then the establishment is going to finally cave in and do this stuff. The key thing is what happens with the phone companies trying to block 802.11 networks hooking up to broadband lines and the like. It's going to be messy. It's going to be ugly. It's going to be a scruffy, hippie-like thing that telecom executives will look down their noses at.

On some level we will always have a bandwidth bottleneck, because our expectations and our anticipation will always outrace reality. The bottleneck is going to be broken by nerds and entrepreneurs on Main Street and not by wonks in Washington. This is going to happen despite the FCC and despite the administration, not because of it. The phone companies are going to be humbled into seeing what the entrepreneurs are doing and then try to copy it. It's starting to happen already. The first mesh-route tests are underway. There are probably eight or nine companies funded in this space. We'll see stuff start to come out in the next 24 months. Within 10 years, wireless Ethernet could really make a substantial inroad.

Building a Wireless Broadband Network from the Bottom Up

Jaron Lanier ∘ There's a paper I circulated a long time ago called "How to Kill Microsoft and Make Billions of Dollars" that proposed three technology developments, one of which was peer-to-peer wireless. People have wireless routers, so they have short-distance, high-bandwidth devices that can receive packets at very short distances and pass along the ones that aren't theirs to other ones that are nearby so that they find their way to a destination.

That's a technology to watch. If each wireless home network talks to the one next to it, a lot of bandwidth could be delivered across distances. It's a way to get more bandwidth out to people without having to wait for the clearances to be able to drill new holes in walls and without the expense of hiring linemen to run around and patch new cables. And it also is a way of doing that without being limited by the bandwidth of a particular receiver station, because it's spread out over so many.

That scenario is not only the cheapest way to get bandwidth to people, but also the only way that can start small and grow gradually. It can make sense at each stage of growth instead of having to wait for some critical mass before it makes any sense at all, which has been the problem with connecting the last mile all along. Nobody's ever been able to finance the big initial investment. So this is a way of getting around that.

The system would sort of spread out gradually. It makes sense if it's just a few people, even inside one home, and then gradually the world fills up with these relays—just like with cell phones. Initially there weren't enough cells, but it gradually filled in to where cell phones can be used anywhere. Eventually there's enough distribution.

It's not necessarily the best technical solution, but the reason I'd originally proposed it, and the reason I think it still might come about, is it's the only one that doesn't require central finance. It's the only one that can grow from the grassroots. People would just buy little consumer devices that make sense in their own right, but then would gradually network with one another. Suddenly there's this wireless infrastructure where people can send high-bandwidth data to one another. It's a high-bandwidth but also a high-latency solution. There can be a lot of lag time. So it's not an ideal solution for real-time videoconferencing-like things. If you want to send somebody a movie that you've recorded, it's great. If you want to interact with them in real time, it's not great.

In order for us to see a low-latency solution, we have to see something that involves some degree of central finance, so that the path the signal takes is planned rather than just emergent. Bandwidth can grow without planning, but it's hard for latency to be reduced without planning. This was true with the Web. The Internet, as it grew wildly in an unplanned fashion, was functional. But somebody can come along and make it more functional. With the last-mile problem, there might be a distributed wireless solution that's able to grow from the grassroots with distributed consumer financing instead of central planning. Eventually that might create the market for low-latency services, and entities will spring up that provide centrally planned, low-latency paths that would allow for real-time communications.

The Baby Bells won't have much to do with it because no entity, either governmental or commercial, has been able to assemble sufficient finance at one time to do centrally planned solutions for high-bandwidth service delivery. We have a relatively small number of households with cable modems, which are asymmetric devices; they're more for content delivery than symmetrical streaming use of the sort you'd think of for teleimmersion or videoconferencing. And then you have DSL lines, but a very small number of them. Those have been financially difficult because they're too expensive to install and service.

Distributed wireless networks are the most likely solution. Consumers are paying for it gradually, so nobody realizes how much they're paying for it overall. If the government tried to say that we need flat screens, that could never happen. But if people are gradually buying screens that, in turn, finances better and better ones. Capitalism does its trick, and things happen. So distributed wireless is the way that can happen with bandwidth, but at the expense of latency. I predict that's what'll happen. When I talked about this stuff a decade ago, it was about killing Microsoft. Now it's too late for this stuff to kill Microsoft. But had somebody done it back then . . .

Those Dark Fiber Networks Are Waiting to Be Lit

Roger Cass • When the Qwests and Broadwings and spin-offs of the Bell system started laying fiber across the country they said, "Instead of just putting in one line we'll put down 20. Even though it's going to stay unlit for quite a long time, eventually it's going to be there when we need it." People at the time were saying, "Well, that's excess capacity." I don't regard it as excess capacity. It's not costing anything. It would have cost them a whole lot more to dig up the ground 20 times to put in one line than to put in 20 at one time, which most of them did.

So this is what we call dark fiber and it will be lit, primarily when we begin to resolve the last-mile bottleneck and demand goes through the roof. For the time being it's not costing us anything. It's not a big deal in my view. It's there and it's ready to be turned on, just like that.

Breaking Bottlenecks to Unleash Pent-Up Demand

Jeffrey Rayport • When you look at consumer demand for broadband and the incredible frustration consumers experience when they can't get it—and they can't get it because of the various regional Bell operating companies, basically the monopoly providers of the local loop reasserting themselves—there is every reason to believe that there's an enormous appetite for it out there. It's not reflected in the fact that 11 million American homes currently have broadband access, because if you look at the demand characteristics, that number ought to be double or triple what it is today.

In places like South Korea, where there is 42 percent broadband access from the home, we are starting to see a thriving broadband version of the Web. In Japan, there are between 12,000 and 15,000 new Web sites that exist solely to produce content for the NTT DoCoMo i-mode. Why? Because the i-mode, unlike your PC screen or mine, is actually a billable device. So I download my Hello Kitty screensaver and you charge me $1.50 a month. Ten million Japanese girls using those phones do that. That's a pretty good business on a monthly basis with near zero variable costs.

Huge Efficiencies Ahead for Photonics

Roger Cass ∘ We're actually in the vacuum-tube stage of the photonics industry. It's a very primitive technology with high failure rates in terms of manufacturing components. Right now in fiber optics you're lucky if you hit 10 out of 100, but we're moving toward automated processes, which will guarantee the same success rates in fabrication that we're now achieving in semiconductors. The technology is evolving dramatically in all kinds of areas. We're moving toward all-optical networks away from the OEO networks where you had to regenerate the signal. Now, light can be sent several thousands of miles. Avanex, for example, has developed systems where you can send the signal down 4,000 miles of fiber-optic cable without regeneration. Also the distortion rates are being reduced dramatically so you are getting less data failure.

Great Content Plus Infinite Bandwidth

Jeffrey Rayport ∘ It's not unlike what Bill Gates said a few years ago: Assume that bandwidth is infinite. That's got to be the operating and underlying assumption of everything you do. Let's just assume that we can light up the infinite bandwidth, because for all intents and purposes we now own it. It's in the ground. Then the question is, what do you put through that? It's kind of like the pigs in *Animal Farm*—all pigs are equal, but some pigs are more equal than others. All content is equal, but some content is more equal than others.

Disruptive Technologies in an Ad-Based Economy

Lawrence Wilkinson • In the '70s when the transition began, the three networks had a 95 percent share of the audience. Those three networks have 43 percent share today. Even when you stir in Fox, WB, and Universal, you're still down at 62 percent. And even as the advent of cable and satellite mean more choice, gross TV viewing is flat to down. Interestingly, it is down most sharply in households with PCs and Internet connections. And in that subcategory the biggest drop is in households with PCs and high-speed Internet access. And, by the way, they are multiplying at an incredibly fast rate.

And then you've got these destructive technologies coming along. TiVo is just one example. The remote control on this digital recorder box has a button that allows the viewer to skip ahead exactly 30 seconds. So, if you are willing to start a show a few minutes late, you have the ability to hit a button to skip through all of the commercials. Now TiVo penetration isn't huge—it's under 1 percent of the population—but the thing about TiVo is that you don't have to guess what people do. Because the TiVo is a big piece of electronic memory, and because that memory talks to the company's computer regularly to update the scheduling and such, the folks back at TiVo know exactly what you did. They know every keystroke that you made on your remote control, everything you stored, whether you erased it, how long you kept it. There are some real privacy issues there that are an important aside.

But the point here is that no one is yet taking into account the likely effects of this "skipping" technology. Eighty percent of these early adopters simply don't view commercials anymore. This is happening in an economy that is literally driven by advertising. This is not sanguine news. So that's why I think we're keyed up for a big change here.

The Evolving Relationship Between Humans and Computers

The Human Interface to Vast Data Networks

Jeffrey Rayport • We're going to see a bunch of hybrids of humans and technology that people will find compelling. We're starting to see the first signs of it. It's everything from the UPS guy and the Fed Ex person who show up with minicomputers strapped to their forearms, which allow them to be dramatically more effective in their jobs by knowing in real time all the time where packages are on the network—all the way to those kids who walk the drive-through window line at fast-food restaurants and take orders before you even get to the loudspeaker. They wear menus printed on their T-shirts and have little wireless handheld tablets that send orders back to the kitchen via an RF connection. Your order is sent five car-lengths—and, more importantly, 10 minutes—from where you actually would have placed it.

Now everything can be faster, and customers are more satisfied. My favorite version of this is what the Old Navy stores have been doing. They take a bunch of kids who are in otherwise not terribly stimulating jobs and they've wired them all, so these kids run around wearing headsets. They look like air traffic controllers, and the kid at the cash register can talk to a kid in the back room who can then check inventory for a certain item. So a bunch of things happened there. They look cool; they feel cool. But, maybe more importantly, they're able to be smarter, to perform or deliver more effective service by dint of richer kinds of information at the point of service. They can also all be available from anywhere in the store to do a very simple thing—answer the phone.

I think that increasingly we're going to see a lot of that, meaning this rather peculiar situation where you're dealing with a human being, but the human being is actually a human interface for either a database or a human or social network.

Wireless Humans and Other Unintended Tech Applications

Shaun Jones ∘ I think it's interesting to look at some of the things people are doing with technology for which it was not necessarily invented. For example, there are humans without physical disabilities who are trying to go from "wired" to "wireless." If I want to move my hand, I have to send a signal from my brain to my spinal cord and from my spinal cord down to my arm and hand. That's a "wired" system. The same movement could be achieved using a wireless "system" with technologies emerging today and available in the next 10 years. People are already experimenting with communications devices, integrated circuit chips, and other basic IT technology on and in their bodies.

The Singularity: When Computers Become Smarter than Humans

Vernor Vinge ∘ Computers are getting better and better, but it is a big leap to imagine a computer that is as creative and imaginative as a person. The really remarkable thing is a much smaller leap of the imagination, and that is what happens in two to five years after you reach the point that you have computers that are as competent as humans. It's very plausible to me that if we ever achieve that, in a short period of time we'd have stuff that is smarter. That is a technological development that is different than we've had before, because what has made us such hot stuff as humans is our creativity, our ability to do these internal simulations and figure out what to do next much faster than other animals can. The point where you get a computer better than humans is an event that is technologically analogous to the rise of the human race within the animal kingdom.

I call that point the singularity. I am not saying that anything has become infinite or anything like that, but it is a singularity in that our normal scenarios after that point are essentially impractical to do because we'd no longer be the driving forces behind creativity. We would no longer be at center stage, intellectually. It is like a physics singularity with relativity, in the sense that you can't see beyond it. You can't see into a black hole.

In my 1993 essay, "The Coming Technological Singularity," I said I would be surprised if the singularity happened before 2004. I still agree with that. I said I would be surprised if it happened after 2030. Many people have had these ideas earlier and independently. A lot of people use the term singularity, often with somewhat different meanings. But of the people that are talking about machines becoming in a broad sense our intellectual superiors or successors, most of the optimists are putting that date somewhat later than I am, mid-century or so. I still think the time range that I said is actually pretty plausible.

I think it is also plausible that it may never happen. The issue of software complexity is something really to watch. If we are still plunking around with software in 2012 or 2015, that would be a really bad sign for people who expect a real-soon-now singularity. On the other hand, if you begin to notice probabilistic models for computing, where we get very reliable performance of large numbers of nodes to do coherent tasks like air traffic control, or if you begin to notice biological models are coming to the fore in terms of dealing with large numbers of parallel processing units, these things would indicate a new paradigm for software on the largest scales. This would be a clear symptom that we're on a slide toward the singularity.

Artificial Intelligence Will Never Match the Human Mind

William Calvin • I don't take the general extrapolations of Moore's Law applied to competing with brains terribly seriously. So many of the people who comment on it have very little conception of where the modern mind has come from on the anthropological timescale. They just don't understand how recent and buggy it is. Psychiatry shows you an awful lot of the bugs. They also tend not to understand the stability considerations of why this brain doesn't just go into seizures all of the time. It's operating much more closely to the edge than most animal brains do in terms of getting hung up and crashing.

Toward the Atomic: Nanotechnology

A Fantastic Voyage Exploring the Inner Reaches of Our Bodies

Shaun Jones ∘ One of the things that will happen in the next 10 years—and it may just be around the edges—is the continuing evolution of Homo sapiens to "Homo technologicus." What does that mean? To a certain degree, it's both the use (for example, the wearing of technology) and the integration of technology into ourselves.

We've been doing that for years in a variety of ways using "dumb" inorganic materials—things like prosthetic hips, knees, and heart valves. In the next five to 10 years, "smart" materials will emerge with memory and logic in packages smaller than human cells. Do you remember the movie *Fantastic Voyage* where a tiny ship traveled inside a person? Do you remember *Tron*? In that film, Flynn gets beamed into the deathly game grid of a computer by the evil computer's master control panel. Inside the game grid is an entire electronic civilization complete with sophisticated devices such as racing light cycles. For its time, it was absolute genius in terms of visual imagery about the way information flows inside of a computer set against a heroic battle for mankind. So think about *Fantastic Voyage* meets *Tron* inside our bodies.

Today there is, of course, "nano" everything. There are groups creating devices that are hundreds of nanometers in dimension, that derive their power from ATP, or adenosine triphosphate, in the body. This nanopower drives little flagellar-like motors. The excitement is not so much because they are small and nanosized, but because their efficiency is 80 percent. If you talk to the macro industrial sector, they would be in seizures if they could get 35 percent for similar systems.

There are also groups creating molecular-based memory and logic circuits, or "moletronics." This is just in its infancy. The state of the art today is very reminiscent of the early integrated circuit days, when somebody now famous thought 64K would be all anyone would ever need. What are other folks working on today? Nanopower, nanomobility, nanocomputation, and processors, nanocommunications, nanosensing, and nanodelivery, and all of that stuff is put into nanoarchitectural systems. The *Fantastic Voyage* may very well be tomorrow but the ship is being built today.

If it's not yet apparent how amazing this is, let me give you a better idea of the scale. The terminal capillaries in the body are amongst the smallest places this "ship" would navigate through. Their diameter is about 10 to 12 microns, which is 10,000 to 12,000 nanometers. The diameter of a red blood cell is roughly 8,000 to 9,000 nanometers. Now this ship would be one-tenth that size and have power, mobility, computation, communication, and sensing in its architecture. We have each one of those capabilities today, but they're not integrated. So all the parts to the *Fantastic Voyage* ship are laid out but we haven't put them together. Once we do, we'll have something that circulates inside the body doing useful things. That something could be one-tenth the size of a human red blood cell. Applications will provide medical, biological, and health-related benefits as well as improved commerce and personal security. But human nature being what it is, all kinds of creative applications will emerge, both malevolent and beneficent.

What drives a lot of this is issues associated with health. The pharmaceutical companies are actually very creative and real future-thinkers. This is not a widely held view because most of what the consumer sees is that which makes a profit. Most of the companies, appropriately so, are focused on their P&L sheets. But the fact is, all of the parts to the *Fantastic Voyage* ship exist today and a proof of concept prototype could be assembled in as little as two to three years. That's how close it is. With what money, I have no idea. I can imagine a very long list of possible applications. One is a diagnostic laboratory inside your body, circulating. Take everything that's in the pantheon of modern medical technology and put it in something mobile that's moving through your bloodstream. You could have medical laboratories circulating. You could have medical imaging circulating. You could have pharmacies circulating. It could all be networked. It could be free if you didn't get it in 30 minutes.

It's not science fiction. I'll give you an example. The National Cancer Institute has a program called Unconventional Innovations. They're building multipurpose platforms, or inner-space ships. They can be in the nano or micro range, but they're small structures that have subsystems, which have components with different functionalities. These circulate in the body and hone in on a target pathology, in this case, cancer. When they get to the target, they will image it from the inside out, not the outside in.

They can already perform limited targeting and imaging. What they would like to do, in the next couple of years, is to deliver therapeutics this way. So go back to the *Fantastic Voyage* thing. You've got something that's circulating. It knows how to get to where it wants to go. Once it's there, it sends an image and relays a message about what it sees. Then it powers up the photon torpedoes and destroys it.

The Perfect Storm at the 100-Nanometer level

Stewart Brand ∘ As technologist Larry Smarr said, there's a perfect storm coming at the 100-nanometer level. Information technology, biotechnology, and nanotechnology are all converging on that scale. Quantum corrals are there and viruses are there. There's a lot of action. We are beginning to have the instrumentation that can work at the 100-nanometer level in biology. You can do information technology at that level. You can begin to do structural engineering at that level.

It's a space where there is going to be all kinds of news: new scientific information, new technological tools. It's an area of science technology that is now open to humanity that wasn't before.

Bioaccounting and Nanosatellites Monitoring Our Inner Space

Shaun Jones ∘ There is a trend line in medicine from external devices to internal devices. As the bio information space becomes internalized it will be readily available just like MPEGs or MP3s are, in terms of the communication sphere. I think this is on the cusp and could happen in 10 years.

I'm guessing there will be some very interesting business niches that will open up. Think about an individual's biological equivalent of a Quicken spreadsheet. You will have, given these converging vectors, the ability to essentially do bioaccounting. If I eat a piece of cheesecake, I get a debit. If I work out, I get a credit. We do bioaccounting in a crude way right now, except we call it a mirror or clothes or a friend's comments or a picture. What if those methods became internal? We'd be able to do it in a way that was derived from our own, real-time bio information.

How will it start? It might very well be that, just like the people in desperate straits got the very first mechanical hearts, there may be people who have certain types of health and disease issues who will have these inner satellites circulating in inner space. People will hear about it and say, "Wow, that seems to work pretty well. I'm not really sick, but I wonder if I could use it for this?" So things like bioaccounting will develop from it.

Suppose this inner-satellite business develops. The next step might then be people who want to free themselves of external communications devices. There may also be people who, instead of having outer tattoos on the skin, will want to do some kind of personal annotation based on the technology. Others may want to track and locate their family members or cherished pets. The migration from external to internal has already begun. Humans have implanted "chips" and animals have implanted "chips." There is Lo-Jack for your dog. And so many more things are possible if we look at cross-dimension mapping with very high fidelity.

What else is possible? If you have bioaccounting, then other things may fall into line: bioinvesting, biogambling. If you have a state of change, people will bet on it. Have you ever gone to Las Vegas and gone into a global gaming room? They bet on anything.

As for the possible dangers, especially with regard to national security, we should seek to understand as many of the implications of technology as possible before it becomes commonly available. That's something pretty straightforward for anything, anytime, anywhere.

The Similarities—and Dangers—of Nanotech and Biotech

Freeman Dyson ∘ I find Bill Joy's nanotechnology crusade very remarkable. I think he's misguided in that he's worried about the wrong things. He's saying that there's going to be a lot of terribly dangerous new technology coming out of nanotechnology. He's worried about when we'll be able to build artificial microbes, which can do all kinds of terrible things and replicate themselves, and we can more or less program exactly what they can do on a microscopic level.

Most of his ideas come from Eric Drexler, who is the prophet of nanotechnology. I don't think it has any substance. I took part in a big study on this, trying to figure out where nanotechnology might be going. There seem to be fundamental limits to what you can do. Suppose you want to try to make one of these machines that Drexler is talking about; he has a thing called the assembler. It is supposed to be a tiny little gadget that you can program to put atoms together in any way you want, and can replicate itself and perform all kinds of manufacturing operations, which could be put to evil uses too.

If you try to figure out how to do that, you're led back to John von Neumann, who studied self-reproducing machines in the abstract 50 years ago. Von Neumann was extremely interested in this whole subject. When he started on computers, he was already thinking of these self-reproducing machines. He wrote an essay about what is needed to make a self-replicating machine. It was published in 1951. Von Neumann was a mathematician; he thought in abstract terms. He proved that in order to have a self-replicating machine, you need four components: a machine shop that actually produces the hardware; a blueprint, which describes what the machine has to do—that's the software; a copier, which makes a copy of the blueprint; and a controller, which coordinates the machine and the blueprint and tells the machine how to execute the blueprint.

Two years after that, Watson and Crick discovered the double helix. It turns out the four components exactly correspond to what every living cell actually has. The machine is the proteins, the blueprint is the DNA, the copier is the replicase enzyme, and the controller is the ribosome, roughly speaking. That's what every cell has.

If you want to do the things that Drexler is talking about you have to reinvent the machinery that every bacterium already has. There's no distinction between nanotechnology and biotechnology. The dangers are the same old dangers that we've been worrying about for at least 50 years, like biological weapons. The United States had a huge biological weapons program. The Russians had one, too. The British had one. There have been many biological weapons programs. We know you can do horrible things. We know it's a real danger, but it's nothing new.

Toward the Cosmic: Space

The Cost of Getting Humans Back Into Space

Freeman Dyson ∘ One of the things that impressed me about the World Economic Forum that I attended was that you had these 2,000 tycoons talking for a week and they never once mentioned space. It's not something they take seriously. Obviously, they think it's irrelevant—and probably they're right as far as the next 10 years are concerned. Space is useful for communications and of course the GPS is now a tool that everybody uses. There's a lot of excellent science being done in space, but it doesn't dominate the scene in any way. I think it will be about 50 years before it does again.

It's a problem of whether you can find a cheap way of getting into space. At the moment, getting cargo into space costs around $10,000 a pound. Whether it's small or big, it's about the same price. A factor of a hundred cheaper, about $100 a pound, would make a huge difference. There's nothing in the laws of physics that says you couldn't do that. We just haven't been clever enough to figure out how to put together the machines. Space travel has to be in the range of a couple of million dollars rather than a couple of billion dollars if it's to be accessible.

New Technology for a More Dangerous Universe

Vernor Vinge ∘ It's interesting how getting something that is self-suffi-cient off the surface of the earth has faded from serious discussion. In a way, that's a great tragedy, because we're in a very fragile situation here. I think one of the lessons of the late twentieth century, in terms of astronomy and geology, is that the universe has turned out to be much more violent than we ever thought. We now know that there's a hierarchy of disasters that happen. Some of them are very specific, like an asteroid hits the earth. As you go to larger and larger astronomical levels, we have all sorts of evidence that greater disasters happen. There's just a lot of risk involved in being stuck in one place.

For example, if a supernova happened less than 50 light-years away it would very likely destroy civilization on earth. My recollection is that a par-ticle front would destroy a lot of the protective power at the top of the at-mosphere. If you wipe out things like the ozone layer, then you begin to get high radiation levels. This would go on for weeks. I think if it happened be-yond 50 light-years it might not be too much of a problem.

There is evidence of much larger explosions—explosions that, if we were in the way, would fry us out to thousands of light years. This possibility is just rising out of the "observational background noise" now. What's hap-pened in the last 30 years is that we've gotten better and better knowledge. But we've been flipping a coin, and we're convinced that it's a benign uni-verse because the coin always comes up heads.

We can wipe ourselves out with technology, but technology also is the key to protecting ourselves against the dangers out there.

The Missile Shield and Space Defense Are No Way Forward

Freeman Dyson ∘ I think the ballistic missile defense is technically total nonsense. It's hard to say that something is total nonsense; there are always a few things that may turn out to work. But it's never been spelled out what the program is supposed to do.

There was very good testimony given by Mike Cornwall, a physicist at UCLA, to the Senate Foreign Relations Committee about the Missile De-fense Program. He took a very hard-boiled view. He wasn't talking about politics; he was talking about the technology.

He said there were five parts of this program that Bush has been talking about. Two of them make sense and three of them don't make sense. The two that do make sense are the modest parts of it. One is essentially theater defense, local defense, where you're reasonably close to what you're shooting at. You have a chance at shooting it on the way up before it has time to deploy decoys. Those things could work. So, shooting down Iraq's SCUDs from some base in the neighborhood, as they tried unsuccessfully to do in the Gulf War, could work.

The other possibility is "boost phase" defense, which is something Dick Garwin has been advocating, where you have a defensive base, say, in Vladivostok in collaboration with Russia to cover North Korea. That would technically make a lot of sense. So you have your defensive missiles in Vladivostok a few hundred miles away from the launch sites in North Korea; you have a chance to shoot at them on the way up. Technically, that could be done. Whether politically it could ever be done of course is another question. So those are the two things that make sense, and they're both quite modest.

The first thing that doesn't make sense is the thing they were testing over the Pacific, intercepting a missile in midcourse, halfway across the Pacific Ocean. Even if the technology were developed, which at the moment it's not, there's no chance that it could prevail against decoys. There's no difficulty in deploying decoys if you have a long midcourse. That's one thing that obviously can't work. Another thing is carrying defensive rockets in orbit, which Bush has been talking about. The last item was the airborne laser, or spaceborne laser. I forget which it was, possibly both. It involves a high-powered laser, which is supposed to be a death ray that will destroy missiles at a distance. That's hopeless simply because you run out of power very quickly. That's roughly the score.

It's a welfare program for the aerospace industry. You never can tell, of course. You may find a new tool that comes out of this, but it's stupid to spend billions and billions of dollars in the hope that something might come out of it that you don't know about. If you want to do space science, this is clearly not the way to do it.

The Space-Age Equivalent of the Wright Brothers' First Flight

Freeman Dyson ◦ Leik Myrabo is a professor of electrical engineering at Rensselaer Polytechnic. He actually builds little model spacecraft that fly up a laser beam. It works very nicely. This is just a toy, but I think that's the most promising technology for cheap space travel.

The beam is the craft's power source. It's a pulsed laser that goes about 10 pulses a second. The machine is a little thing that looks like a fish. It has a mirror around its waist, which focuses the light backward so that the laser pulse comes to a focus behind the fish. It makes a little explosion in the air, and that drives the fish up the beam.

Outside the atmosphere you would have to do it differently. Then you couldn't use air as the propellant anymore because you're going into space, so you'd use water. You'd have to carry a tank of water and it would have to be slowly exuded from the bottom. It would have a flat plate with small holes on the bottom so the water would come through. The water would then be vaporized by the laser beam. It could work in the same sort of way, using water as propellant. You'd probably switch over from air to water as you got into space.

It's not really a model spacecraft. It's just a demonstration of the principle. I compare it to the Wright brothers' flight in 1903. It demonstrates that you can get off the ground. It's the first time anybody's done that. The first one Myrabo did was about two years ago.

I think this is quite possibly the way we'll go if you scale it up. This was a 10-kilowatt laser. The toy model weighed about two ounces. If you scale that up 100,000 times, you're talking about a gigawatt laser, which is not at all unreasonable. A gigawatt laser is something we know how to build. If it were used as a public highway, it could be very cost effective. Each payload could be five tons, if you multiply by 100,000. The acceleration would be modest, about three Gs or so. People could easily stand it.

The laser would point up into the sky and be a public highway. Anyone could pay the toll and up they'd go. Of course, the whole trick is to have enough traffic to pay for the laser. It's a chicken-and-egg business. You have to have a laser to do the job, and then you have to have the traffic to pay for it. It has to grow gradually.

The problem is that in order to make it really cheap you have to be using it all the time. It's like a highway. It takes about five minutes to get into space. You'd have to have a steady stream of customers standing in line, one going up every five minutes, to make it really cheap. It would have to be like a commercial airline. It could probably be as cheap as a commercial airline. Of course, a large airport costs you a few billion dollars, which is just about the same as the laser.

It may turn out to cost more. But roughly a gigawatt laser is around a couple of billion dollars. I think that this is the way the thing has to go in order to be cheap. It's got to be something like that, a public highway, so that you don't carry the fuel with you. The problem is, of course, where will they all go? You've got to have someplace to go to before you can go. So governments will probably have to get the thing started. You have to have a huge infrastructure before it becomes routine travel.

I would say it would take 50 years to get the thing technically developed, maybe 100 before it becomes an everyday commercial operation. The Wright brothers, of course, developed the technology pretty fast after their first flight. They went very quickly into commercial development. I think it could be a big deal. People have been talking about this, of course, for 50 years, but Myrabo is the first person who actually did it. He's a bit of a fanatic. You have to be a fanatic to do something like that.

Heavy Industry in Outer Space

Vernor Vinge ◦ One theme of science fiction in the '60s—again, something that's largely faded—is the idea of what heavy industry could really be like. Nowadays, everyone pussyfoots around about heavy industry. We talk about the post–Industrial Revolution era, but in fact we have the capability to undertake much heavier industry—if we had places to dump the thermal energy and some of the other pollutants. The asteroid belt was the favorite playing field of science fiction writers in the 1960s and 1970s. Out there, you could get an asteroid and, with solar or nuclear power, volatilize the entire asteroid and then send it through what amounts to a large mass spectrometer and mine the whole thing in a period of a few weeks. The mass spec would just sort of bend out the different elements. For instance, you could end up with 50 million tons of gold.

The idea of being able to undertake large industrial projects is something that has totally faded from our minds. What constitutes the most benign environment for a civilization depends on the level of technology of the civilization. Historically, we didn't have high civilizations in Northern Europe. I think part of the reason is that we had really cold and uncomfortable winters. However, at certain levels of technology, it's probably possible to run a comfortable civilization in Northern Europe better than if you were in Mesopotamia.

It's very plausible to me that at a sufficiently high level of technology, you can really dump into space large amounts of energy without having to get in anybody's way. You could probably have a wealthier civilization by far than anything we can manage here, where we and our effluents are all stuck in one small box. At some point in the future there would be operations on such a scale that you would get a sort of interplanetary green movement, but for operations that were merely 1,000 times larger than any earth site operation, there would be no problems. A solar system civilization would be a very different ballgame.

Communicating with Aliens Through Lasers

Freeman Dyson ∘ I've always been a strong advocate for searching for aliens. There's a delightful little project just starting up here at Princeton—it's called OSETI for optical SETI—which means search for extraterrestrial intelligence on the optical band, which hasn't been done much. Most of the searching has been done with radio.

The project involves looking for laser flashes, which could be a very good way of communicating over large distances. You can make nanosecond laser pulses. We could already do this with existing lasers so that for one nanosecond the pulse is brighter than the sun. If you want to shine at some colleague halfway across the galaxy and transmit a message, he can easily see your signal even against the background of the sun. We're looking for those now.

Optical is just another channel. It's about as cheap as radio with about the same bandwidth. They're more or less equally plausible. It could be a historical accident. We happen to have started out with radio, but the aliens might have started out with lasers. This was suggested by Charlie Townes about 40 years ago. We haven't done much searching so far. I don't expect that we'll actually find any aliens in the next 10 years. It's completely useless to try to calculate the probabilities. If we do find aliens, I'm quite sure that it'll have a profound effect. Whether this changes our way of thinking will depend on how far away they are and what kind of communication we have with them.

There's the general expectation that if we do find aliens that have any technology at all, they'll be millions of years ahead of us. I think that's reasonable. Whoever they are, they probably know a great many things that we don't know. The danger is that if they knew it all, then we'd lose self-confidence. This is the classic situation when primitive society comes into contact with an advanced civilization. The primitive society tends to suffer very badly. You hope that won't happen. I think it won't happen, because the chances are that the communication is very slow and that the aliens are many thousands of light-years away. It won't have any direct effect on us. Whatever we learn, we'll learn rather slowly.

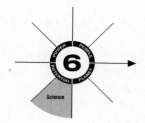

The Frontiers of Knowledge
Science

"We are in a period of major scientific and technological revolution akin to what happened at the beginning of the last century. In physics, chemistry, and biology we are seeing really revolutionary change, both theoretically and in terms of our capabilities. And as a result, we are going to see enormous advances in technology."

Peter Schwartz

"The human genome project was the equivalent of constructing a small village that's static, where every house is known and every street is clearly laid out. The human proteome is the equivalent of Manhattan on New Year's Eve, with millions of people flowing around different dimensions throughout the city, with constant reconstruction and construction of buildings."

Brian Sager

"I don't think biotech's going to make much difference in the world until it reaches the garage—the sort of street crossover point, where two guys in a garage can mess with genes and biology and do something useful. When that happens—which is inevitable—then we'll see the real revolution happen."

Kevin Kelly

"If you get molecular biologists drunk, or at least get a few beers into them, it's not rare for them to say they'll have aging solved in 20 years. That's not something they say in public."

Robert Carlson

"I'm thinking we will see energy crops, plants that produce gasoline, for example, instead of wood. You could have trees that would be genetically modified to produce gasoline or any other kind of liquid that could be used as fuel. That could really be a great equalizer for countries that have tropical climates. Essentially you need sunshine and water. That's about all."

Freeman Dyson

"The promise of biotech has been widely exaggerated. More importantly, not enough people understand that biotechnology is philosophically the opposite of biology. When I was last doing bench science, I thought science was a way of understanding how nature works. I didn't think it was a tool for changing what nature is."

Amory Lovins

More than 50 years ago Harland Manchester wrote in the magazine *Popular Science* that: "People must come to a better understanding of laboratory men and their methods, for science plans our future and sends us the bills." That insight may be even more true today than ever before. Science is creating new knowledge and opening up new prospects at an extraordinary pace, continually affecting our sense of what's possible. It seems that with each day, we can see new horizons—or new limits.

This chapter starts by looking at one way the horizon might expand through **The Next Scientific Revolutions**. GBN chair Peter Schwartz argues that we may be poised for major scientific revolutions encompassing physics, chemistry, and biology. This could be akin to what happened in the early twentieth century when Albert Einstein and Niels Bohr made their respective breakthroughs in the theories of relativity and quantum mechanics. In fact, the revolution in physics may involve finding an overarching theory that accommodates those two mutually antagonistic theories—as well as a raft of new experimental data that can't currently be explained. Such breakthroughs in physics may well take longer than ten years to unfold. But Schwartz does foresee revolutions in the other two fields happening within this decade, led by biology, which is breaking open right now.

In fact, biology and biotechnology make up most of this chapter. Advances in these areas could have a huge impact on almost all sectors of the economy and society although, as several members point out, general public and business understanding lags far behind the probable developments. In our second section, **Biology and Life Sciences**, we start with an overview of the key developments to monitor in biotech, primarily relying on two network members who are deeply involved in the field. One defines biology's theme for the coming decade as "embracing complexity." Cracking the human genome barely scratched the surface of understanding the complexity of humans and other organisms. In this decade our understanding will extend beyond genomics, the study of 30,000 human genes, to proteomics, the study of millions of proteins. The second scientist contends that we'll spend this decade watching biology become a "predictive" science, much like physics. In physics, the knowledge of laws and mathematical principles allows scientists to "predict" what will happen with a high degree of precision when, say, an object is dropped from a building. But because underlying biological systems are so complex and not fully understood, biologists don't have that predictive capability—at least not yet. That may well change as the decade progresses.

One of the factors causing the explosion of scientific knowledge is the development of new enabling tools. Current and future progress on this front are reviewed in **The Emerging Scientific Toolkit**. In fact, one network member argues that advances in tools, rather than theoretical breakthroughs, are the principal drivers of scientific progress. Another speculates that biotech will only reach its full promise when the tools get cheap enough and two people in a garage can innovate in this field. A third contributor says that day may not be far off.

We then move on to explore the **Human and Medical Applications of Biotechnology**. This decade will bring many controversial developments in this area, and some of them are just now entering the public's consciousness in both accurate and inaccurate ways. We look here at the critical distinctions between different kinds of stem cells and types of cloning, which almost certainly will evolve through the decade. We also focus on various efforts to slow aging and prolong healthy lives, let alone dramatically extend life spans.

Finally we shift to **Nonmedical Applications of Biotechnology**—innovations that don't directly apply to humans. This includes the future of genetically engineered crops, from making current foods more nutritious or prolific to extraordinary new possibilities. For instance, within the next decade we could be growing plastics from modified corn plants, or growing meat from stem cells in factory vats. Or perhaps we'll be growing modified plants that secrete an oil that tropical countries can use for fuel on the way toward becoming energy self-sufficient.

Although these nonmedical developments do not directly involve manipulating human biology, their indirect impacts could be profound. Woven into this section are arguments from both sides of a debate around the potential benefits and dangers of biotechnology. Some of the voices we hear are quite pessimistic, expressing concerns that we are in over our heads, knowing too little at this point to manipulate nature. Perhaps one important source of optimism, however, is the growing realization that nature has much to teach us, if we are ready and willing to learn.

The Next Scientific Revolutions

Three Scientific Revolutions Converging at the Atomic Scale

Peter Schwartz ∘ I have been doing some work on the idea that we are in a period of major scientific and technological revolution akin to what happened at the beginning of the last century. In physics, chemistry, and biology we are seeing really revolutionary change, both theoretically and in terms of our capabilities. And as a result, we are going to see enormous advances in technology.

Significantly, the three sciences converge at the very small scale, the molecular and atomic scale. Biological and chemical and physical systems have many, many properties and capabilities alike at that scale. What we're seeing is developments in these realms coming together and creating revolutionary ideas and capabilities. And the ultimate form is nanotechnology. So this is in many ways about the science that leads to nanotechnology, and many other scientific leaps and technologies along the way.

Passing the Baton from Infotech to Biotech

Paul Saffo ∘ Today, when we say "the future" or "the cutting edge," it's synonymous with information technology. But in the last 12 to 24 months, there's been an inexorable shift: The cutting edge is moving to biology. In the first third of the last century, the cutting edge was chemistry and chemists. Sometime around the 1930s, there was a very subtle shift, and it was no longer chemistry—it was physics. The next shift happened right around 1949, when we went from physics to electronics. Now we're doing the same thing, from digital to biology.

This doesn't mean that the earlier revolution is irrelevant; in fact, the early revolution sets the stage for the one to come. It was the experimental work of chemists like Marie Curie who made it possible for the physicists to develop their theories. And it was three physicists—Brattain, Bardeen, and Shockley—who created that foundational piece for the digital revolution, the transistor.

The same thing is true today. The indicator that we were going out of infotech and into biotech was the Human Genome Project. When it was first announced, it was something that was of the same scale, in terms of time and money, as the moon shot. Every year it got cheaper. That curve of cheapness, that was Moore's Law. Basically, computers turned out to be the personal intellectual bulldozers of biotechnologists; the genome got cheap because we had robotic sequencing systems using computers. So the computer industry helped launch biotech.

Ten years from now, we will be deep in the early stages of the biotech revolution. Computers and information systems will still be very important, but in a supporting role. There will be crossovers and synergies, biounderstandings that are applied to computer design, computer tools that are applied to biodiscovery and development. That very rich intersection between biotech and digital tech is going to be the place of fast water where major innovations are coming out, welcome and unwelcome in our lives.

Biology Broke Out First and Is 20 Years Along

Peter Schwartz ∘ In many ways developments in biology are further along because we really have had a scientific revolution that began 20 years ago in genetics and molecular biology. The clearest expression of it is the decoding of the human genome. But there are many other elements to it and what they've given us is a deep understanding of how biology works at a very fundamental level. Not only do we now understand it, we can manipulate it and control it in new ways. We can shape it and so on.

We have a new power over biology that simply never was imaginable, let alone doable. The recent advances in using stem cells are a perfect example, and there are many others. The new drug Glivec© is designed as a molecule targeting a particular molecule in a cancer cell. You just couldn't do that before. Until recently we just didn't have the technical means to even dream of that or understand the notion of how one molecule connected to another molecule. So in biology, we're very far along in the revolution. That's why it'll have such large effects in the near future, because a lot of the conceptual revolution has already happened.

Physics and the Next Theory of Everything

Peter Schwartz ∘ We're not as far along in physics and chemistry as we are in biology. In physics, we're about to go through a big conceptual revolution, like relativity and quantum theory were a huge conceptual revolution over Newtonian physics. Our perception of the universe changed when we understood that.

Scientific revolutions are always preceded by two phenomena. One is the old model gets weirder and weirder. That's what happened with the old model of the sun going around the earth. You could make the math work but, boy, it was hard, and it got stranger over time as we learned more. And it got really simple when somebody said, "Well, actually, suppose the earth goes around the sun?" Aha! Yes! All the weirdness went away in the math.

So now our models of both the very big and the very small have gotten weirder and weirder, and nobody seems to understand them. There was a great quote by a scientist at a recent meeting on dark energy: "We live in a preposterous universe." And I wanted to say, "No, we have preposterous models in a simple universe." I think that's where we are. We're finding many big anomalies. That's the other big thing—we find data that just simply doesn't fit the old model. A perfect example of that happened recently at the University of California at Berkeley—they discovered that the universe is expanding at an accelerating rate. That means there's another big force out there overcoming gravity. And this is a whole new form of energy we never even imagined. We're calling it dark energy. In fact, Einstein had a hint of it in his early work, but he said, "Naw, that's too stupid," and got rid of it. He called it the cosmological constant. The data now says he was right.

Now dark matter is another whole weirdness. That refers to the missing mass of the universe that our theories explain but that we can't find. We had to come up with a new name for it, so we call it "dark" because we don't know anything about it. That's because we can't see it, find it, imagine it. But there were radio waves before we had radios, we just didn't know they were there. Then we got this thing called a radio, and we now know there are radio waves out there. We haven't found the radio for dark matter and dark energy, though we did get a little hint, a tweak of reception recently. We actually got some direct connection to dark matter. And there is evidence that there is dark energy in the accelerating expansion.

So we are ripe for a new model in physics. Does that mean we will necessarily get one? No. Because, of course, this requires a great leap of imagination and rigor and science. But there are candidates out there that might prove string theory and other variations on that theme. We're nearing the point of a breakthrough, but it might be in 20 years. And it might not be in the United States. It might be an Indian, or Chinese, or Japanese, or Russian physicist who comes up with it.

In order for the breakthrough to happen, the mathematics for it has to also advance and be able to support the new fields. Einstein had to learn Riemannian geometry from his friend Grossman, and Riemann had to invent it, which happened just as Einstein was doing his theory of special relativity. Grossman learned about it, showed it to Einstein in 1912, and on the basis of Riemannian geometry he could come up with the theory of general relativity. So higher dimensional mathematics, computational abilities, simulation abilities need to continue to develop for us to be able to push these physics fronts, but they are in motion.

When it happens, two things are likely, one really big and the other almost really big. First of all, we'll reperceive the universe. I mean, it will all change again. When that happens, that's a big thing. You know, relativity had a huge impact on people's perception of human life and the human condition. What it will be, I don't know. But it's clearly going to shake things up again.

Second, it will create new technological capabilities. A good example that is very likely, but again unpredictable, is energy. Suppose there is dark energy out there. Suppose there is a way to overcome gravity using that energy. You could suddenly be in a world of completely new sources of energy, and maybe even antigravity vehicles. Now, I'm not saying that's likely. But it's not at all implausible to speculate that that's the kind of outcome that can come out of such a breakthrough. Just like you couldn't have solid-state physics and television without quantum theory and relativity. We wouldn't be able to get here. You needed that. If I had said to you in 1875 there would be pictures flying through the air in color and motion, you would have had no idea what I was describing. Is it magic? How can you send pictures through the air? Of course, we do it every day, every second, all over the planet. But it required new physics.

Because we know that one of the things that has to be explained is dark energy, and that dark energy is about overcoming gravity, it is not implausible that the technological expression of this could be some combination of new energy sources or antigravity devices. Again, I'm not making the argument that is what will happen, but you could speculate that it could happen.

Why Science Is an Unending Frontier

Freeman Dyson ○ Science is just an unending frontier. Every time you make a big discovery, it opens two more questions. I don't at all agree that once you have a set of equations to describe the universe, we're done. A good example of that is general relativity. Einstein had the equations right; it was a beautiful theory. It explains gravitation, but he never believed in black holes. Einstein not only thought that black holes were wrong, but he wasn't even interested in finding out. It was outside his way of thinking. He thought, "I've got the equations, that's all you need." The fact that they have these exciting solutions with qualities that he hadn't imagined wasn't interesting to him.

To me, you don't understand anything about gravitation if you don't understand black holes. In that sense, Einstein did not understand gravitation.

He had the right equations; that's all. To understand gravitation, you need to understand the solutions. That's in many ways harder and just as creative. That goes for all kinds of science. Having the basic equations is just a beginning. Finding the solutions is where nature really becomes creative.

A New Chemistry Will Congeal in the Next Five Years

Peter Schwartz ∘ The fundamental basis of chemistry has been thermodynamics. It's statistical. We have an understanding at a theoretical level of how molecules are formed, but the real world of chemistry is millions and billions of molecules bumping into each other under various conditions. We may apply catalysts or heat or cold or whatever it is, but what we're dealing with is statistical processes of very large numbers of things. So what applies here are the laws of very large numbers and statistics and thermodynamics.

We're now understanding and getting control of individual bonds, individual molecules, individual connections between them, and so on. Not only do we understand it at a more fine-grained level, but our level of control is gaining enormously at a fine-grained level. We can't do this yet, but we're close. For example, in the near future we should be able to use very small electric fields to disassociate an individual bond in a molecule and realign it around another electron.

So chemistry is moving from the realm of large numbers of things bumping into each other to finite numbers of objects being controlled individually. This fundamentally changes both our understanding and our capability—for designing new materials, for example. And it begins to overlap with the realm of nanotechnology because this kind of new materials stuff is needed before you can get to that space.

Today, if I want to take a steel rod and weld it to a copper sheet, I can use old or new welding techniques. I can use traditional methods and take a hot welder and some metal to bond the two together. Or I can use a superfine powder of steel and copper to electrostatically align these molecules so that one actually flows into the other. The result is a kind of flow between them of copper and steel that bonds the metals together. That bonding technique exists right now. But that's a step along the way. You could also form shapes that way. In fact, if you wanted that bond to have a structure around it of some sort that's performing some mechanical function—a gear, hypothetically—you could form that gear in the same way and have it be integrated with the metal around it.

So we might see new materials, new methods of manufacture of materials, new chemicals, new kinds of chemical processes, new ways of making plastics in the next five years. That's closer because a lot of the theoretical stuff is far along, but the physical capabilities are hard to do, and there's a feedback between the theory and the technical capabilities. So there's still some more theoretical work that has to be done.

Science Means Business: R&D Takes 10 Years to Play Out

Peter Schwartz ∘ We are moving fast toward a world of new science and technology. A good example is energy. We're making all kinds of assumptions about the future of energy. These could turn out to be fundamentally wrong because we will have really radical leaps in technology. Environmental issues are another example, as are manufacturing processes. All the different ways we make stuff—cars, semiconductors, furniture—could change. The new materials and the new manufacturing methods could be extremely significant.

R&D has a five- to 10-year time horizon. So in terms of R&D activities, it means you've got to be pushing the frontiers of science and technology now.

Biology and Life Sciences

The Gap in Public Understanding of Biology

Paul Saffo ∘ The most important thing is to recognize that, at the moment at least, biology is a lot harder to understand than computation and information systems. It's not too hard for an executive to get a sense of what a transistor is or what a chip is, but I find that senior executives are woefully unprepared for biotech. They don't understand what the genome is. They don't understand nucleic acids. They don't know the difference between DNA and RNA. They don't even have the vocabulary to begin to talk about this stuff, much less understand it.

Biology: From Reductionism to Embracing Complexity

Brian Sager ∘ In the 1940s, people were thinking about the substrate upon which genes are built and trying to figure out the structure of DNA. In the 1950s and 1960s, people were looking at the mechanisms through which genetic knowledge is transferred—in other words, the way genes interact with one another. Also in the 1950s and 1960s, there was an explosion of knowledge in semiconductors and electrical engineering, and in algorithms in general, which really gave the geneticists and biologists a framework for thinking about genetic circuits. Using those frameworks, they started to construct simple mathematical algorithms about positive feedback and negative feedback and self-regulating loops; a lot of the work was done at the Pasteur Institute in Paris by François Jacob and Jacques Monod. That was the classic paradigm for regulatory genetics. The simplicity of the circuit was what allowed a lot of rapid progress to occur in the field. And they were fortuitous in that they chose a simple circuit to study.

A lot of scientists in the 1970s and early 1980s were looking at simple circuits as well, or trying to be reductionist in the sense that they would reduce the complexity they see around them into something that's intellectually digestible. That worked to a certain extent, but as the amount of genetic knowledge dramatically grew in the late 1980s up to the recent sequencing of the human genome and the emergence of proteomics, we no longer can be reductionist. There's too much knowledge. We know too much about too little, in a sense, to naïvely or intentionally focus on a narrow band of knowledge in modern biology.

There are perhaps 30,000 genes in the human genome, but there are probably millions of proteins that arise from those genes in different combinations. Gene products impact each other, cutting proteins apart, gluing them together, modifying their structure in different ways. The permutations or combinations of all these cutting and pasting activities can create millions upon millions of proteins, and those can exist in a dynamic state.

People think the genome is a static set of genes that do not change—a library where all the books are in the right place on the shelves. The proteome is the equivalent of people flipping through those pages and reshuffling the books: Some of them go into the right shelves, some of them go to the tables where people are reading, and some people check those books out. And so at any point in time the holdings of that library change. Similarly, in a proteome, the number of proteins in its constitution will change, and so there is no such thing as a proteome. It's not a static structure—it's inherently dynamic. And at any point in time you'll have a snapshot that says what's going on in a cell at that moment, but that snapshot will change as time progresses.

This creates a complication for a lot of biologists and geneticists who are trained in the reductionist paradigm, because suddenly we're dealing with enormous, self-organizing, highly complex systems. Even to do the experiments requires multidimensional databases where the dimensionality is in the order of hundreds. A lot of biologists haven't been trained for that. And it's difficult for everyone, regardless of their training, to perceive a large number of dimensions at the same time. So there's the need now to have computer scientists, mathematicians, physicists, and engineers who deal with more complex systems enter into the field and work with biologists to look at complex systems and try to understand what's going on.

For example, studies of the human genome suggest that perhaps 2 percent of DNA is coding for genes. I can't imagine that's the case, that we would carry around 98 percent of any material that has no function in our body for long periods of time. It takes a lot of energy to create that, and I would think evolutionary pressures would have selected out a lot of that. If you look at viruses or other organisms that have very compact genomes, you see every DNA nucleotide is being used. You have maximum information compression. As you get to the human being, it seems to be very sloppy and loose and not very efficient. I think that's more a reflection of our current knowledge rather than what's actually going on. I think that 98 percent is probably doing something, and we just don't know what it is.

In the mid-1990s, there was an explosion in knowledge about expression patterns for many genes, because people were using DNA chips that you could purchase commercially through companies like Affymetrix or Synteni. And what you have as a result of that is huge amounts of knowledge about which genes are turned on when and under what conditions. But how to classify those into frameworks that allow us to ask why or why not has not been deeply thought out.

There have been some recent papers that have integrated mathematical perspectives in creating almost a reciprocal space of gene expression patterns. That's the kind of approach, a mathematical or biomathematical integration, that needs to take place in the next 10 years—looking at these gene expression patterns or protein expression patterns or proteome changes and trying to understand where the order is, how that order is manifest, what the rules of regulation are of these enormous numbers of moving parts and how they interact with each other.

I think that's going to lead to a general reformation or transformation in how people conceptualize disease. A lot of people in the last century thought of disease as something wrong with a body. I think that, if we move now to a high-dimensional space in which we have huge numbers of genes and proteins interacting with each other in very complex ways, we may think about human health as a phase space, almost like a phase diagram from chemistry. If there's a change of phase or a change of state in a phase diagram, we go from health to sickness, and we can be pushed from sickness back to health. It wouldn't be the actions of one gene that would be pushing us from health to disease or disease to health—it would be the interactions of thousands and thousands of components driving us away from one local attractor for health toward another local attractor for disease. So, for example, cancer or heart disease might be a change in the phase state in some high-dimensional phase diagram.

Intriguingly, there's precedent for this. The precedent is 5,000 years old, and it's Chinese medicine. I think we're going to see a reintegration between Chinese medicine approaches and modern medicine, in that Chinese medicine philosophically understood that there was a high level of complexity in the human body, and you would have different ingredients mixed together and different ratios to treat different diseases. Modern medicine takes the opposite philosophical approach. You have a single drug tuned as precisely as possible to execute on a single target in a human body and affect it in a highly predictable and known way. That works great when the source of the disease is something simple like Type 1 diabetes, where you have a lack of proper insulin—you can add insulin in and the diabetic patient is fine. That works quite badly when you have Type 2 diabetes, where the insulin reception is off for any number of genes, perhaps 20 or more, and you can't simply insert a single gene into a cell or add a protein or some small molecule that makes the patient better.

And so I think that if we embrace the complexity of this high-dimensional space that really is our metabolism, we may use more of the ancient Chinese philosophy of mixing together different herbs and roots and so forth in different ratios to treat disease. In this case, we would add together different drugs in different ratios as cocktails.

Proteomics: 10 Years of Building Immense Databases

Brian Sager ∘ The human genome project was the equivalent of constructing a small village that's static, where every house is known and every street is clearly laid out. The human proteome is the equivalent of Manhattan on New Year's Eve, with millions of people flowing around different dimensions throughout the city, with constant reconstruction and construction of buildings. So the folks in the village who think that being in downtown Manhattan on New Year's Eve is going to be the same thing are in for a surprise.

A proteome is almost a misnomer. It's a bad term because it suggests a static collection of proteins. A collection of proteins is anything but static. It's an incredibly rich broth where every element and every component is constantly changing—and it should, because that's the stuff of our metabolism. If it were static, we'd be dead. So we're getting closer and closer to dealing with our true level of complexity. That's why embracing it is so important.

In terms of the proteome work that's going to be done over the next 10 years, it'll be a lot of leaf collecting, just like the DNA sequencing was similar in some ways to chemical spectroscopy in the 1930s, when people collected line spectra associated with different metals but didn't know what it meant. We'll have to do that as well. We need a lot of data. That's the first thing that's going on right now.

Once we have the data, we have to have the databases. Once we have the databases, we have to have mental frameworks to allow us to digest high dimensionality and compress it into something a human being can understand. You have to remember that we humans are fairly weak intellectually in some ways. For example, most people can't remember more than seven digits at the same time. That's why phone numbers are seven digits long. If you think about Noam Chomsky's semantic studies in linguistics, humans have a hard time understanding sentences when there are more than two clauses. So we have fairly primitive amounts of buffer in our brain. And suddenly we're going to be dealing with millions or billions of interactions in a high-dimensional space. We have to have a mental framework that lets us as human beings understand it. Not a computer—us. We have to develop intuition, simple intuition, about inherently complex phenomena.

I think it's imminent—it has to be done. Once this data exists, it'll go out of the hands of the biologists and into the hands of the mathematicians and computer scientists, who will look for patterns. They will find patterns, and they might know what those patterns would mean. Those patterns will then go back into the hands of the biologists, and they will try to understand and predict experimentally how those could be changed or manipulated. And the results of those experiments will go back into the hands of the mathematicians, who will then look for changes and alterations in those patterns and feed the result back to the biologists. So it will be inherently a push and pull, back and forth, between different approaches. Ultimately, within proteomics, I think 10 years from now we'll be a lot less naïve about how complex a cell is or how complex metabolism is.

On the Cusp of Understanding the Brain and Consciousness

Brian Sager ◦ We certainly know that our neurons are not static. They're firing back and forth between each other at all kinds of different frequencies. There are spiral waves that bind together different parts of the brain in fashions that we don't well understand. There are collections of neurotransmitters between the individual neural cells that change in concentration and time.

We have to embrace the complexity there as well. In that field, for example, in the 1950s and '60s, they had a single neuron in culture on a glass slide, looked at it under a microscope, and used electrical devices to measure current or voltage or resistance across the cell. In the 1970s and '80s, people began to look at combinations of cells to see how one cell could impact the other. But only recently have people begun to look at the firing of large numbers of neurons simultaneously, which is in some ways equivalent to the expression of many genes simultaneously or the production or interaction of many proteins simultaneously.

With the neurons firing, people have created these multi-electrode arrays, where you can measure 100 brain cells or more all at the same time as, say, a rat wanders around some controlled environment, and actually monitor the neural system as it's processing information. So you can imagine that there's an enormous amount of data there as well. If we embrace the complexity of that, look for patterns in that, we'll be able to understand the beginnings of what consciousness really is—and the philosophy goes from a 2,000-year grandstand to an experimentally tractable problem of who we are as human beings.

We're just at the cusp. These multineuronal data-collection experiments began in the '90s, and now we have enough data to begin to look for really deep patterns. One could imagine looking at the difference between someone who's sleeping and awake, or dreaming versus not dreaming, and looking at how their neural processes change.

Again, we'll have to find patterns and mathematicians will have to be involved. But embracing the complexities is the first step toward understanding who we are as a species, and other species as well.

The Ramifications of Biology Becoming Predictive

Stewart Brand ∘ We're biological, we live in a biological world. If biology becomes predictive, then that's as consequential as the invention of satellites. We have these grand formulations such as ecological succession, but a whole lot of it is based on models. Models in ecology and biology are easy to find, fun to do, and that's sort of where the fads are. But the models aren't based on detailed data at all. Biology is not a predictive science because we don't know what's going on. Every time you look deeper, you discover new information. For example, you find a spider that has parasites. It turns out the parasites have parasites. Well, how many levels down do parasites go? Seven and counting. We might have only one-tenth or even only 5 percent of all of the species on the planet actually identified and documented so far.

How Biology Will Become Predictive Like Physics

Robert Carlson ∘ There's a difference in the ways stories are told in physics and stories are told in biology. When stories are told in biology, it tends to be a natural language story. I go out in the field and I see this organism does this thing. I see that worms come up when the ground gets wet and they go underground when they are not going to drown. They eat particular things. They behave in particular ways.

That same kind of story tends to be the way biologists describe molecular events as well. Here's a protein I see that is turned on under these circumstances. I know that this protein effectively is a wrench and it adds a nut onto another protein. Those are the kinds of stories you tell, but they're not predictive stories. It's not like you say, "I dump a hundred molecules of this into the environment around the cell and I know that cell responds by making a thousand molecules of this other thing." There haven't been models like that in molecular biology, but there are beginning to be some.

The physics model is as an equation, to some extent. What you're trying to do there is to make a quantitative prediction—that is, how much of this thing occurs when I twiddle the knob that controls the system by this amount? I have a ball in my hand. I drop it. I can predict fairly well how high it will bounce as a result of that. That's not a natural language description that provides me that power—it's calculus, and it's some understanding of the fundamental physical universe. If I have a ball and I throw it and I watch how it bounces, I know something about the ball's mass and, depending on how much physics you want to include, the shape and how smooth it is and that sort of thing. I can predict where the ball is going to go before I throw it because I know enough about the ball and the way it interacts with the world around it to be able to predict the trajectory.

It would be nice, for a variety of reasons, to be able to do that in biology. One is that such an understanding might lead to a better description of how drugs work, for example, or how disease works. Or say you have a genome for some organism and you can sequence that genome very quickly, so you find out what genes are there. You can go out in the world and see what genes that we already know about are like the ones in the organism that you just found. Well, even if you have that information, you still really can't say whether the organism is going to have two legs or four legs or whether it's going to fly or whether it's going to slither. That general kind of story, the ability to read the genome and understand how the pieces are going to interact and what that organism is going to develop into, would be useful from a scientific standpoint. If we could tell that kind of story, we would know how things work in a way that we don't now.

The ability to make quantitative predictions would also be useful when we think about design in biology. We already use biology as a technology. We have for tens of thousands of years as we've farmed and bred animals, etc. The manipulation of biology, of human interaction with the environment, just through the use of antibiotics, is an extraordinary example in itself of using biology as a technology. Penicillin is a biological technology. But these are not examples of "engineering" in the standard sense. Biological engineering doesn't currently exist in the same way that, say, electrical or aeronautical engineering does. The current flap about genetically modified foods, for example, is really more about the fact that we don't know what we're doing rather than there being something intrinsically bad about interfering with biology. If there were something intrinsically bad about interfering with biology, by that logic we ought not to be using antibiotics. Antibiotics, along with basic sanitation, basically by themselves, have changed the human life span by a factor of two in the last hundred years. In 1900, the life expectancy in the United States was about 47. Today, it's roughly twice that.

The ability to better engineer biological systems, to better design biological systems, to better describe how changes we plan to make in DNA or in the way a protein interacts with another, will affect the behavior of that biological system down the road. Quantitative prediction will be useful not only in the implementation of real biological engineering, but also in allaying fears about the organism that results being useful and not too detrimental. The ability for us to respond to any changes we might make is nil, effectively, at this point. We can't do anything about any changes we make that might be detrimental.

A lot of people said, when we finally sequenced the genome, that we were basically doing the quantum mechanics of biology. As someone whose background is physics, that just sounds totally wrong to me, because quantum mechanics is all about building predictive models. Really, all the genome provides is the parts list, and it's not even that developed because the genome is an incomplete list of the parts. How things interact is what's more important in biology than just the things that are there. The genome tells us very little, if anything at all, about how things interact.

One of the reasons that biology is making some strides now, the reason you see all these multidisciplinary efforts springing up all over the place between physics, biology, engineering, and computer science, is that the tools to measure biology have finally reached the point that you can begin considering building predictive models. The data has only just started to arrive that allows careful modeling at the molecular scale or simulation at any level in biology on a sufficiently parallel scale to describe all of the things that are necessary to keep track of a particular system.

For example, bioinformatics has developed as a way to deal with, in part, all of the gene expression data that is out there. There are something like 6,000 genes in yeast and they turn on and turn off in response to certain conditions. First of all, how do you keep track of all that information in a way that makes any sense? Secondly, how do you represent that data in a way that you can interact with it? No one had to face that problem in biology until recently.

No one knows, for example, how many genes you really have to keep track of to understand any particular given trait. One way to find out is to knock out a particular gene, thereby knocking out the protein, see what gets mucked up, and begin to make a list that way. While that strategy works, it is rather piecemeal. Often a gene we thought we understood is found to influence a trait or pathway that has nothing to do with what has been discovered previously. That's the way biology has traditionally been done.

Now you can go at it from the other way. You can keep track of everything and figure out from the top down what part goes where and when you wiggle which gene, how many other things are going to change.

Get Over Physics Envy and Think About the Whole System

Janine Benyus • Physics envy may be over. Physics envy started in the '20s when it was the science to go into. I think people are beginning to understand life more. I think they're getting more interested in biology and ecology. That said, I think even in those fields we kind of dove into the molecular level. Just as in physics, where we reduced everything down to the individual atom and the subatomic. Now we've put so much energy and resources into molecular biology, but we need to move back out to cellular and organismal and community ecology to understand how the system works together. I think that's a natural.

The Emerging Scientific Toolkit

What Drives Science: New Theories or New Tools?

Freeman Dyson • There are two styles of historians of science: the Kuhnians and the Galisonians, you might call them. Thomas Kuhn had this idea that the way science works is that you have a paradigm. He loved the word paradigm, which is everybody thinking the same way. Then you have evidence that conflicts with the paradigm and suddenly there's a paradigm shift and you have a totally new way of thinking. That's the Kuhnian model, which has become very popular. It applies to physics in the 1920s, and it applies occasionally to scientific revolutions. It doesn't really describe biology or apply very well to a lot of science.

What I call Galisonian science, which is driven by tools, is at least as important. Biology is much more like that. Peter Galison is still quite young; Kuhn is 50 years older. Kuhn held the field for 50 years, but Galison has a different point of view, that science proceeds in a more gradual way, mostly by people inventing new tools to approach the universe in different ways. The theories then limp along behind. So science is really driven by the tools, not by the theories. Both of them are true, but I think the balance is important.

New Measurement Tools Are Filling in the Biological Blanks

Robert Carlson ○ From my perspective as a physicist, it's really the measurement technologies that are driving where biology is going at the moment and how biology is developed in the long run as well. It's very easy to tell stories about a thing when you have no data; you can say whatever you like. In some sense, as a physicist, I'm a little more sensitive to that in biology than other people are because there's been a terrible history of physicists strolling into a biology lab and saying, "Oh, this problem is easy. I can solve that, no problem." A few years later they go away with their tails tucked between their legs in shame and the biologists laugh—the physicists couldn't solve the problem for whatever reason. There's been a lot of ink spent and trees cut down to tell stories in theoretical biology, especially from the physicist's point of view, when a lot of those stories were completely unconstrained by data. There was no way to test any of those models because you couldn't measure any of the parameters that were predicted.

Biologists have made progress, in contrast, by relying on data and relying on experiments and formulating what comes next based on the limits of the tools they had at hand, rather than the physics approach, which is to treat it more as a black box and say, "What's possible?" Now, because new measurement techniques are available, that means the physics approach is becoming ever more useful in biology. You can step back and say, "How does this thing work?" with the knowledge that you will be able to measure—

today, perhaps tomorrow—the thing that you're talking about, and biologists are not used to thinking about problems in that way.

Now the reason that theory works so well in physics is that there's this funny relationship between mathematics and the world that we see when we look out the window. For some reason that's still mysterious to many people, including myself, physics actually works. It's not at all clear why when you write down some equation that it has anything to do with the world we live in. It's a remarkable thing, actually. It works for that building you see out the window, for calculating all the stresses to ensure that it doesn't fall down. You have to have some kind of quantitative predictive model that allows you to make a pretty good estimate of what that building will withstand so that it doesn't fall down when a magnitude 7 earthquake comes along. Those same kinds of mathematical descriptions don't allow you to say very much about the tree you see out the window. There are all kinds of things happening in the tree that are much more complex than what is happening in a building.

We don't have the theoretical framework to figure that out. We're only just developing the measurement tools that allow you to say a lot about the molecular details of what's going on inside the tree.

The Real Biotech Revolution Will Happen in the Garage

Kevin Kelly • I don't think biotech's going to make much difference in the world until it reaches the garage—the sort of street crossover point, where two guys in a garage can mess with genes and biology and do something useful. When that happens—which is inevitable—then we'll see the real revolution happen.

As long as it requires a Ph.D. to do this stuff, it's a priesthood. It's going to be more of the same, and continue at the fairly slow rate that it's been going. As soon as two high school guys can purchase the tools and start to do things in a garage, then this will be truly revolutionary. The question is when.

I don't think people will move to stop biotech as long as it's the domain of Ph.D.s, because the regulatory powers will remain in place. But it's going to proceed very slowly; I don't think that the genetic revolution, so to speak, is going to happen very soon with that setup. The drugs will trickle out and the changes will be very, very moderate until there's a democratization of the tools.

Can you imagine if you needed to have a Ph.D. to build a steam engine? Or to build any kind of engine? The reason the Industrial Revolution took off is that anybody could come in off the field and start fixing and inventing engines. But there's a qualitative difference in the level of knowledge you need for biotech compared to inventing engines and that's why it hasn't taken off.

But I think eventually we'll have the tools. If you had said in the 1940s that everybody in the world will have a computer, people would have responded, "Do you think just anybody can have the knowledge to deal with a computer? It's very complex." You'd say, "Well, yes, but there's all kinds of tools and interfaces that hide the ignorance." They call it operational literacy. So we have operational literacy, but we don't have the tools yet to allow operational literacy for biology.

Biological Tools Are Accelerating Faster Than Moore's Law

Robert Carlson • It's very difficult to predict the course of technology. One of the important lessons about sequencing the genome is that when that project was started in the early '90s, there were some people who said, "This is absurd; it will never get finished. It's just too big and too hard." They were saying that in the context of the tools that existed at that time. There were other people who disagreed. They could conceive a situation where, using the tools that existed—in particular the ABI 377, a kind of sequencing machine—they would buy a lot of those machines and hire a lot of people to sequence the genome. There was always the thought out there that you could spend a lot of money and solve this problem, using those tools. In fact, people were imagining $3 billion. Some people were imagining $10 billion. Some people were imagining $15 billion and 10 or 20 years to even make a dent in the problem.

Then along comes Craig Venter, who says, "Well, actually, technology is moving fast enough. There's a new machine that not only operates more quickly than this previous machine, but it can be automated in a way that was not possible before." They could remove human labor from a lot of the process. Moreover, the ability exists to take a different strategy for removing DNA from organisms to sequence it. So suddenly Craig Venter starts, and 18 months later he's finished. The human genome is effectively finished in 18 months. It's true that he used data from the government project to help provide landmarks for his efforts, but nonetheless, he finished that project for something like $200 million, and it was finished long before even the original optimists said it could be done and for much less money—because of the way technology changed.

It's not just that things will happen that we can't predict, but that things will happen that we can't predict. Here's what I mean. The world is going to change a lot faster than we can imagine. It's not just that I don't want to look out into the future and say what will or won't happen. What I am trying to say is that things are going to be wild and crazy much sooner than we expect.

One reason is that our ability to manipulate biological systems is accelerating. If you look at our capability to either sequence DNA or synthesize it from scratch, then both are improving much faster than Moore's Law. Assuming those trends continue, within five years all of the sequencing effort that went into the human genome project will be accomplishable by one person on the laboratory bench in about one day. That is, in five years' time, one person in a day could sequence the human genome on their bench because of improvements in technology.

There's no reason to think that won't happen. That's just the way the trend is going. We're already beginning to use biology to manipulate biology—we have for some time—but now the power, in terms of the biological widgets we use, to further manipulate biology is really moving quickly. What I see is that within just a few years we are going to have to contend with organisms that have been modified in fairly sophisticated ways. This is particularly important when you think about bioterrorism.

I'm a physicist, so I have my own particular perspective on biology. In truth, what I really do best is build things, so biology for me is another set of widgets for building. And as people like me, as people like engineers get involved, we are going to learn a lot more about biology.

Carlos Bustamante, a professor in physics and biology at UC Berkeley, likes to make the analogy to synthetic chemistry. In the early 1900s, chemistry was about understanding how things that were already out in the world were put together in a chemical sense: how chemical reactions happened, the structures of things, the chemical makeup of things. There weren't that many people who were interested in making new things. Then along came someone who synthesized urea from scratch. Suddenly, the way chemistry was done changed because you actually have to understand more details about the system to build a thing than to simply look at it and poke at it and figure out how it works.

It was the process of moving to an engineering of chemistry that radically changed the way people understood chemistry because they had to learn lots of new rules that weren't apparent before. In the same way, as we move into engineering biological systems, we will learn a lot more about the way the pieces work because challenges that aren't obvious just from watching things happen will arise and we will have to understand them and solve them.

Human and Medical
Applications of Biotechnology

Brain Science Will Make Education More Like Medicine

Bill Calvin ° People are always asking me about the sort of genetic engineering you could do to improve intelligence and so forth. My usual answer is that it's possible but I bet education gets there sooner. Education is where medicine was about 100 years ago. A hundred years ago, most of medicine was empirical—somebody tried it and figured out whether it worked or not. Of course, it didn't work very often but they couldn't figure that out. They were trapped into thinking it worked, like with bleeding and purging.

Gradually, over the last century, medicine became half scientific and half empirical. Over the next few decades I suspect the same thing will happen with education. In its present state of affairs, science is not really contributing very much to the subject. We're going to understand a lot more about how the brain works, how brains develop, and what the critical windows of opportunity are for introducing concepts. We are going to understand a lot more about the strategy of introducing new material versus rehearsing what you've already been exposed to versus sprouting out the creativity. We will know at some point the basis for how about half of these different aspects—of the way we try to get children to learn—really work.

Understanding them will lead us to making considerable improvements. They will suggest to us new empirical things to try out, and it will go a lot like medicine has gone. We'll be able to educate children to grow up and be better thinkers. For example, there are some basic limitations that you see now. That's a lot about what IQ tests are measuring. Most people can juggle at least a half-dozen different concepts simultaneously. For example, a multiple-choice question, "A is to B as C is to D or E is to F," is juggling six things at a time. You remember seven-digit telephone numbers, but you have a lot more trouble with 10-digit telephone numbers. That surely is amenable if that's one of your goals, to make everybody capable of doing a dozen things at the same time. I suspect that with the right kind of childhood education we could probably achieve that.

The second big part of IQ tests is the speed with which you can make decisions and move on to the next one. That, too, is probably amenable. Modern physicians have to make decisions quickly, bear a lot of possibilities in mind at the same time, and sort through them within a 15-minute office visit. I think that the educational system will produce many more people who are capable of operating at that level. It won't be genetic changes that do it. It will be changes in the way you go about education.

This is one of those things that could take a while but could also happen very quickly. I can easily envisage somebody developing the technology in all the private schools within 10 years. It could also, of course, produce a catastrophe. I don't want to present this as something that is inevitably good, because people operating faster and faster can dig themselves into deep, dark caves.

Parents will do the experimentation for us. My guess is that as these techniques begin to become available, parents will pick them up and run with them and produce various disasters along the way. Instead of speaking in complete sentences by age three, maybe some of the kids will do this by 11 months. But the side effect of doing it may turn out to be that they can't think straight about anything else. You just don't know how these things hang together. Just what it does to their later development we don't know. Science probably won't be able to predict it.

The Real Possibilities for Stem Cells and Therapeutic Cloning

Brian Sager ∘ The language and the semantics surrounding regenerative medicine are muddied right now. I'm not even talking about a philosophical framework or a value system conflict. I'm just talking about apples to apples and oranges to oranges. Having people talking about the same things is challenging; it's an inherently difficult linguistic task.

For example, therapeutic cloning versus reproductive cloning—most people think of cloning as cloning, but those are two very different approaches. Reproductive cloning is what most people see in science fiction movies and what they're afraid of in the legislatures of most countries. That's where this primordial germ cell becomes a blastocyst upon fertilization, and those blastocyst cells are used to breed a clone of the original patient, so you make more of yourselves. That's what Dolly was. That's what people have been working on. But all of the benefits are actually in therapeutic cloning. That's when you're taking different kinds of stem cells and using them to replace tissue that's been damaged. Now the most extreme form of that would be using stem cells from an umbilical cord. And the most extreme example of that is from your own umbilical cord.

These are your stem cells; they were used to create you. Fifty years later, if you have some disease, your baby self could end up saving your own future self by taking those cells out of deep freeze and using them to create a new organ or tissue to replace one that's damaged. You're using your own cells for your own body. This isn't a nightmare scenario of some military force creating thousands of soldier clones. You're saving your own life. Is that an ethical conflict or not? I'm not going to argue it either way. But I will say that that is distinctly different than taking an aborted fetus and creating a stem cell line and using that for many different patients. In the one case you're helping yourself, and in the other case a resource is being used to help many people.

As to the level of semantic confusion that exists right now, there are actually four kinds of stem cells: embryonic stem cells, embryonic germ cells, umbilical cord stem cells, and adult stem cells. They all have different ethical implications, different regulatory implications, and different value propositions for healthcare or for a biotechnology company that's producing those.

Embryonic stem cells are the cells you would get from a fetus. They're incredibly powerful, in the sense that they can be transformed into almost any type of tissue or any type of organ. That's why a lot of people are concerned about fetal tissue, because it's the primary source. Embryonic germ cells are a little bit less controversial. This is fetal tissue that's been transformed into a germline cell. They're not as ubiquitous in their ability to differentiate into different cell types. But since they were a certain class of cells that are normally ejected from the body either as sperm or eggs in the course of normal life, they may be less controversial than taking the cell from a heart or a brain.

Umbilical cord stem cells should be even less controversial because people are helping themselves for the most part, although it's possible that they could be used to help other people as well. And the final level, which is the least controversial, is adult stem cells found in different parts of an adult body. The great thing about them is you can take them out of fat tissue or what have you, and there are no ethical issues for most people about the challenges. But it's much harder to get them to differentiate into the cell types you want.

The potential uses that I see—replacing damaged cardiac muscle cells in arteries, insulin production for Type I diabetes, replacing damaged nerve cells in spinal cord injuries and Alzheimer's patients, new skin for burn victims, adding nerve cells for Parkinson's disease—I think those are realistic, because they address unmet needs that a lot of patients are suffering from right now. There are strong patient advocacy groups and a lot of political forces at work to try to help these people. People who have been paralyzed with spinal cord injuries want to walk again, and there's going to be a lot of pressure on different legislative bodies in different parts of the world to let those people walk again if the technology is there to do so. Same thing for heart disease, same thing for burn victims or people suffering from neurological and metabolic disorders like Alzheimer's, Parkinson's or diabetes.

What you probably won't see is a lot of therapeutic work or cosmetic work to change someone's hair color or eye color or skin color, work that would be considered elective surgery or elective genetic therapy. I think that's going to take much longer because the value proposition of an unmet need is not as clear if the ethical issues are just as strong. So the sense of exploitation might be greater.

Will Aging Be Solved in 20 Years?

Robert Carlson ◦ If you get molecular biologists drunk, or at least get a few beers into them, it's not rare for them to say they'll have aging solved in 20 years. That's not something they say in public. It's not something they speculate about in print because aging is extraordinarily complex; development is extraordinarily complex. But when they scratch their chins and let their guard down a bit, they speculate that we'll have a sufficient understanding of those complex systems within 20 years to really make significant changes in how those systems operate.

It's also true that people tend to estimate that it will take between two to five decades to solve the problem that they're working on because beyond that timeframe gets to be beyond when they'll be working on it, so it then becomes someone else's problem. That certainly is true in physics. If you ask an older person when the problem will be solved they will tell you, "Well, about 50 years." They give you a timeline that is within your career but past theirs—to give you some hope, maybe.

When a molecular biologist says it will take 20 years to solve human aging, they're kind of looking back and saying, Wow, 50 years ago we didn't know that DNA is the carrier of genetic information. Twenty years ago we were just beginning to learn about AIDS and HIV. We have learned a tremendous amount of biology from studying HIV. Eighty years ago we barely understood viruses and bacteria and infection on a very descriptive basic level. Penicillin only happened in World War II, at least at a level where it became useful.

If you're really talking about solving human aging, it's not going to be simple like it's just the telomeres or an enzyme that controls aging. It seems the length of telomere, the structure at the end of a chromosome, has something to do with aging, but it's still not clear what it is. At one point the suggestion was that all we have to do to control aging is switch telomeres on or off. Well, that's not true. There's a much more complicated model now where the length of a telomere is a probabilistic function of this and that and the function of the enzyme is modified by all sorts of complicated things. Even with remarkable results in yeast, fruit flies, and mice, it won't be trivial to transfer such results to humans.

Can Aging Be Altered Through Genetic Manipulation?

Brian Sager ∘ Stopping aging is not a natural process. It's actually a negative thing, from an evolutionary point of view, because you have too many people who are no longer reproductively useful and are not susceptible to evolutionary pressures because of that. In a way, evolution works best when the breeding cycle is as fast as possible, so that adaptation can occur as fast as possible. And so we are not only slowing the breeding cycle dramatically, but also creating the population of nonbreeders who are buffering the population in different ways. So mathematically it's not a good thing.

Of course, any individual facing the prospect of their own mortality would prefer to live, including myself and likely any reader of this book. So certainly there's a need there. But I would say there is a natural precedent for different rates of aging. In the past, people have thought about aging as a cellular wear and tear of some kind of oxygen radical that was destabilizing the metabolism of the cell through free radicals that were essentially acting like little bombs inside the cell, disrupting its apparatus in unpredictable ways. That is probably happening at some level. But fundamentally aging is a genetic effect.

How do I know that? Well, dogs may live 20 years. Humans may live 80. Trees may live for 1,000. Yet we all have essentially the same metabolism, in the sense that all the fundamental elements of our biochemical makeup are essentially identical in everything from bacteria to plants to animals to human beings.

However, we all have different genetically encoded rates of decay. Even though fruit flies and humans have a similar genomic makeup, they live for two weeks, and we live for 80 years. There must be something in the genetic makeup, in this high-dimensional structure, that is responsible for aging. And so while there's not a precedent for stopping aging, there's a precedent for controlling it genetically because different species age at different rates. And, in fact, within a species different individuals age differently. You've probably met people who aged very slowly and looked incredibly healthy and vigorous in their 50s or 60s or 70s, and other people who seem to age overnight in their 20s or 30s. Some of that may be lifestyle decisions, but a lot of it is genetic as well. So I think that both of those precedents suggest that there is a genetic component.

I should say too that in the lab people have dramatically changed the life span of the C. elegans nematode, and also fruit flies. They've actually doubled the life span by altering a single gene. What I was arguing before was simple correlation, but now we have a causative effect, where you can double the life span of an organism by knocking out a gene. And that work is really in the last 10 to 15 years.

I think the challenge in delinking aging from breeding is that you get a massive increase in population growth, which is not inherently natural for a species that needs to evolve. I can imagine people who weren't aging because they were wealthy enough to take these anti-aging drugs being a source of resentment for those who were aging because they couldn't afford to take those drugs. I think that would generate enormous social unrest and a high level of risk.

I think what we might see instead of that is something a little bit less socially disruptive, but in some ways very pleasurable, which is decreasing the effects of aging without necessarily decreasing too much our current life span. So, maintaining our health at a high level so that we can run a marathon, even as very old people. I would certainly like that.

Diseases of Age Might Simply Be Caused By Viruses

Robert Carlson ∘ It wouldn't surprise me if a number of the things we call diseases—things that are just kind of mysterious now, ailments we say are just part of aging—are actually caused by pathogens, meaning a virus or a bacteria or something. We recently have added to the list of things that I would call pathogens prions, for example, which may have something to do with Alzheimer's, or mad cow disease. Before 1980, no one had a clue that a protein molecule could cause an infectious disease, but it can. That's kind of an extreme example in some sense, and it's an obvious big red flag hanging out there.

In slightly more subtle discussion—and it's sufficiently sophisticated to have reached the pages of *Nature*—if you look at a disease like multiple sclerosis, it is not really a single disease but a syndrome, a collection of symptoms. When you display enough of those symptoms, a doctor says you have MS. In a rather strikingly large number of cases of MS, particular viruses also appear in people's blood samples. There's no cause and effect listed yet, but there is a remarkable correlation. It's not a pathogen that anybody knew of or thought a lot about 10 years ago.

Before 1990, ulcers were just ulcers. It was just a problem of bad diet, or you were genetically susceptible because your father had ulcers, or some such thing. Of course, now we know ulcers are caused by bacterium, and that's treatable with antibiotics. There's a bug that's causing a disease that for hundreds if not thousands of years was just thought to be some trait of being human and growing older.

How Long Is a Long Life?

Vernor Vinge ○ Since the beginning of the human race, we've wanted to be free from hunger and we've wanted to live a long time and have lots of children. Well, as you push the idea that technology can do good things, you eventually push it so hard that you must confront the true meaning of your desires.

For example, one of the most fundamental is the notion of living forever, the persistence of the soul. What happens when you near that goal? Then the question is, What does it mean? I could imagine that ordinary people could live and enjoy 1,000 years if they were in good health. It's hard to imagine how a person could live 1 million or 1 billion years and get very much out of it. It seems to me that after a while your personality would be like a tape loop or your personality would change so substantially that it would be laughable to talk about it being the same person.

If you took as your goal to live forever, one consequence of that is that you would probably have to become a larger-souled person. That means that you would become superhuman. So you find that you are asking for things that are sort of scary.

Nonmedical Applications of Biotechnology

Corn Fields Growing Plastic and Other Feats of Bioengineering

Brian Sager ○ I think there are going to be a lot of advances not only for therapeutics, but also for nontherapeutic products. An example is using bioengineering or biomaterials in new fabrication processes or new information processes. I think that we can do the same thing with materials. In fact, at the library yesterday I picked up a paper that just came out about creating plastics in crops. There's another paper that just came out on getting rid of those same plastics. So you could see a situation where you grow a source material, like a plastic, in corn or what have you, harvest your crop, and use that plastic to create a chair for an office. At the end of the life cycle of that chair, you sprinkle some enzyme on it and the chair dissolves.

You get the raw material to create the chair, but you don't have to synthesize it in a chemical lab, which is much more energy intensive and creates costs and has end-of-life issues. That means the furniture industry is suddenly being powered by biotechnology. That's inherently complex, and I'm certain that most furniture manufacturers are not thinking of themselves as biotech companies right now.

You can imagine using biomaterials for architectural frameworks for houses, for example. Ironically, that's a very old technology; that's been done for at least 10,000 years. Spider silk is so strong that material the size of a thumb could hold up a jumbo jet by itself. It's got five times the tensile strength of steel. Yet spider silk is grown inside a spider that may have just eaten a cricket. That may be the source material for this incredibly strong stuff. And this is happening in its belly at room temperature. Kevlar, which isn't as good as spider silk, is produced in boiling sulfuric acid. It's not very environmentally benign.

Now, I'm not saying we have the ability to produce spider silk today, but if spiders can do it, we should be able to learn how they do it eventually. If we embrace the complexity of the process and don't oversimplify the mechanical aspect and the biochemical aspect and understand what is really required to do that, we will be able to create those types of silks—and improve them. In fact, someone has just put a patent on a mechanical device that mimics the silk-producing organ in spiders. So we're getting close. I mean, this is probably not as little as 10 years off, but I don't think it's 50.

Biomimicry Rather than Bioengineering Is the Answer

Janine Benyus ∘ When I look at some transgenic engineering, I don't see that as that much of an advance. Let me give you an example. People study spider silk and they study the way the spider processes the silk. Biomimicry would be finding a way to use abundant carbon materials and create three-dimensional organic molecules that self-assembled into a fiber and process that fiber at room temperature—in other words, to literally mimic that organism's processing.

Instead, what people are doing is taking the gene from the spider and inserting it in a goat. The mammary glands of the goat then milk out spider silk, and then they clone that goat. To me, that's not an evolutionary leap. That's just creating a different kind of milk cow. We're right back to using nature to do what we want to do. It's really not imitating.

Reengineering Trees to Secrete Liquid Fuel Out of Sunshine

Freeman Dyson ∘ I'm thinking we will see energy crops, plants that produce gasoline, for example, instead of wood. Wood is not a very good energy crop. It's the most important energy crop; much of the world depends on firewood. But it's a bad crop because you have to chop down the tree to get the wood. Harvesting the wood is harmful to the environment and it's also expensive and, generally speaking, ugly.

The carbon release from wood is not a problem at all because you're taking it out of the air when you grow the tree and putting it back. It's sustainable from that point of view. But if you could directly produce liquid fuel and feed it into a pipeline, it would be far more economic. You could have trees that would be genetically modified to produce gasoline or alcohol or any other kind of liquid that could be used as fuel instead of wood. It's certainly conceivable. It's not yet practical. People have been much more interested in the medical applications of genetic modification. But I think with a bit more science, one could create an energy crop. The science isn't yet done. You'd have to understand a lot more about the genome of trees, and I don't think a single tree has yet been sequenced.

We know there are plants that produce liquid fuel. Of course, there's a thing called jojoba, which produces liquid oil, which is supposed to be quite good, but it's just on much too small a scale. It's clearly not trivial to reengineer a tree to do something like this, but I think it could be an enormously cost-effective way to produce fuel if you could figure out how to do it.

We could see this much sooner than getting people into space. Probably a decade to do the science and another decade to develop the technology. That could really be a great equalizer for countries that have tropical climates where it would work best, where you have lots of sunshine. Essentially you need sunshine and water. That's about all.

The End of Agriculture and Growing Steaks in Steel Vats

Kees van der Heijden ∘ There's no doubt in my mind that in 10 years' time we may have done away with most of agriculture. Just as the world got rid of the horse and buggy as soon as the horseless carriage was invented, we will get rid of farm animals as soon as we figure out how to produce the same products from stem cells. When we understand how genes work we'll start building factories that do the same thing. We will produce steaks in factories. If we know how to make spare organs for humans from stem cells, growing steaks in factories will seem easy. The incentive is huge. The agriculture sector is such a problematic area of our economy. If we can get rid of it techno-logically, I think we'll get rid of it in the economy—very quickly. The coun-tryside will be redesignated as a recreational resource.

The repercussions will be enormous. It means the end of hunger, doesn't it? Because once we make agricultural products in factories, without any need for land-connected production, then there is no reason why this wouldn't spread quickly across the world. Now, that's another interesting question: What happens to the world if hunger has been eliminated? Why does hunger exist? Apparently it's not because we can't produce the food. The reason is that the agricultural system is too complex. We still haven't learned how to distribute across the world. But if we can manufacture this stuff in factories, then we can actually overcome these problems, and we can get the food to whoever needs it and is able to pay.

I think some people will say, "I want the natural steak." There will be or-ganic farms. So in the supermarket you will have the organic stuff, which will be twice as expensive, but there will be some people who will buy it. But most of us will buy the factory steak, which is just as good. It will be impossible to make any distinctions in quality or substance or taste or anything. The tradi-tionalists will pay twice the price only for sentimental reasons.

The worry about genetically modified agriculture is when it is set out in nature and it cannot be controlled. There are some rules about minimum distances around experimental plots and so on, but already it's very clear that this stuff spreads out beyond these distances, and it cannot be con-trolled. So we're setting out mutations in nature at a rate that's unprece-dented. The origin of the basic worry is that we are sort of entering an evo-lutionary experiment here that nobody has any clue where it can possibly end.

Now, that's essentially different from what I'm talking about. I'm talking about something that happens in steel vats, in factories, and it has nothing to do with mutations in nature or anything like that. It doesn't interfere with the evolutionary system. It just creates good, cheap steaks.

Africa's Desperate Need for Genetically Modified Crops

Freeman Dyson ○ You can produce artificial crop plants with genetic en-gineering. The question is, Who needs them? What we found out in the world economic forum at Davos is that the Europeans don't need them. The Europeans are violently opposed to what they call GM food, genetically modified food. They have a really strong ideological aversion to this, which of course coincides with their own economic interests. Europe is self-sufficient in old-fashioned food and likes to protect the farmers. The interesting thing was that Africa is firmly in favor. In fact, several of the Africans there said, "We really need this stuff, and what's more, we don't need you to do it. We can do it ourselves." It's actually very hard to grow things in Africa. That's one of the reasons that Africa is so poor. The climate is mostly bad and the soils are mostly bad. They have big problems just trying to feed themselves. These GM foods are a godsend for them.

Biotech's Promise Is Exaggerated and Its Dangers More Profound

Amory Lovins • What the ag-transgenics folks are trying to do won't work for very basic biological reasons. Many people in the genomics business don't seem to understand biological fundamentals. Very few of the people in what they call life sciences have studied such important aspects of life as ecology and evolution.

I also see disturbing cultural issues all over the industry. It means not only do people try to do things that won't work, but they try to do things that, if they did work, would be a terrible idea. I just ran across an example where certain women have a genetic defect that kills human sperm, so somebody had the bright idea of trying to find that gene and splice it into corn plants so that corn could grow contraceptives. Given gene drift from corn, this seems a rather disadvantageous trait to start spreading around uncontrollably. We now find BT-toxin-making genes in wild Oaxacan corn in the remotest parts of Oaxaca, 60 miles from any place where genetically modified corn is known to have been. Spreading around a gene for human sterility could be a very unexpected solution to the population problem.

There is an aggressive effort to reinvent botany. What we understand as botany evolved over 3.8 billion years, where everything that didn't work got recalled by the manufacturer after rigorous testing. There now is an effort to reinvent it with two basic changes. One is to speed it up by something like nine orders of magnitude so that there isn't time in the development process to test whether things are a good idea before they get spread around. Second, the objective of the process is changed from survival of the fittest to survival of the fastest—that is, from biological fitness to economic profitability—which is a very different goal and, I think, at odds with how nature does business.

Some technologies tend to go through stages, such as, say, nuclear power. They are vigorously promoted but shielded from market and political accountability, so they become able to screw up on a really big scale. And transgenics is well along in the same process, unfortunately.

The other thing that strikes me about ag-transgenics is the insubstantiality of the benefits claimed for it. I have yet to see one that isn't by much simpler and more benign means already available, but outside the orthodoxy. The work on the human genome is similar—as somebody said, it's like a several-billion-dollar telephone directory. It tells you everybody's name and address, but you haven't the foggiest idea who they are, what they do, or how their interactions make up the functioning society.

The promise of biotech has been widely exaggerated. More importantly, not enough people understand that biotechnology is philosophically the opposite of biology. It's not a use of biology. When I was last doing bench science, I thought science was a way of understanding how nature works. I didn't think it was a tool for changing what nature is. That's a much more fundamental or profound difference in the enterprise, and not one that I'm at all comfortable with.

The Five Key Areas of Bioconvergence to Watch

Brian Sager ∘ There are about five dimensions of bioconvergence that I'd watch closely. There's biomaterials, or just genetically modified or biologically produced materials that are used in traditional products, not in human therapeutic products. They could be used in clothing, they could be used in creating the sail for a sailing ship or rope to hold a box in place during shipping—a wide variety of uses.

Bioengineering would be more like nanotechnology, where we would use enzymes to manipulate small molecules or clusters of molecules, which is what enzymes do best anyway. They are, in fact, already nanotechnology, so using them in this fashion certainly makes sense. And I think that'll become more common. In fact, some research was recently done where some folks in Texas found a set of antibodies that bound to metal, which means that you could use the antibodies to place electronic structures on, say, a gold wafer. That is an example of the use of bioengineering—using antibodies rather than soft lithography to pattern an electronic circuit.

Environmental remediation we've briefly touched on with the dissolving plastic. It's interesting. The biotech industry's very first patent was for an oil-eating bacterium to get rid of oil slicks. Then the industry moved away from environmental remediation. But I think we'll see a swing back to that, where we'll be tackling a lot of environmental problems partly using biology. But again, we have to embrace the complexity of what's going on, not view things narrowly. If we understand that, then we can use these products in a context where their use is not dangerous, which is the primary reason it wasn't adapted. People worried about these things getting out of control. So we have to fine-tune the specificity in the complex environment such that they don't do that.

Another example is industrial biotechnology, where you use enzymes to replace chemical processes that require caustic compounds that may be environmentally toxic, or high-temperature or other energy-intensive processes that are costly and have their own secondary environmental impacts. So, in a sense, green manufacturing could be driven in some part by biological processes. There is a precedent to create an exquisitely complex organism or a device, namely, a human being, in a way that is environmentally benign. And I think we can adapt that for a lot of different classes of products.

Another area would be agricultural biotechnology, of course. Genetically modified organisms are highly controversial. But I'm even thinking about things like edible vaccines, where you would have, say, a vaccine in an apple: You eat the apple, and you're immunized. Agricultural biotechnology is similar to the controversy around therapeutic versus reproductive cloning in the sense that therapeutic cloning is highly focused and reproductive cloning can get out of hand. If you plant crops freely and let it get out of hand, and you have clones of organisms growing wildly, that's what a lot of people consider a nightmare scenario. The flip side of that is if you have highly focused growth of plastic, for example, in a factory area that is completely contained, it can't possibly grow outside of that because the environmental conditions or nutrition factors are such that they would never exist naturally. You can constrain it.

Oftentimes the genetically modified organism issue arises because it's going into a person's body. If it's not going to be put into a human being's body, but used to create the chassis for a stereo system, I don't think people would be as frustrated. It was a very bad idea for the industry to focus on foods as the first products because of the emotional issues associated with food. But if we focus on textiles or materials, I think agricultural biotechnology becomes less contentious.

Another bioconvergence area is biocomputing, the information technology component. Certainly how our brains work is much more elegant and highly analog relative to the way most modern computers work. If we understand better how our brain works at an algorithmic level, we might be able to use some of that for redesigning an operating system that is incredibly robust. The other side of this area is to use biological molecules like DNA or proteins to carry out chemical reactions in a way that allows us to have a high level of computational efficiency at low cost and low energy.

People thought that was impossible, but I've seen repeated breakthroughs in that field since 1994. In the last seven years people have made dramatic advances, and they're now leveraging the same kind of gene chip technology that people have been using for the gene expression experiments to create simple computers.

The Dangerous Game of Creating Organisms with Libidos

Janine Benyus ∘ I'm terrified of the fact that we are manipulating the genome. Genes evolve and travel in assemblies of genes, in a network in which other genes are turning them on and off. We cannot, from our vantage point, predict what's going to happen. But we can predict that when something that we create has the ability to self-replicate, then we will have no control. Getting into that game frightens me. We're creating something and it has a libido. It wants to pass itself on. Holy mackerel. Yeah, I'm worried.

Directed Evolution Works 10,000 Times Faster than Nature

Brian Sager ∘ Directed evolution's fundamental tenet is that the purpose of sex, from a genetics point of view, is to create variability, so that evolution can act on that variability and select the organism that is best adapted for the current environmental niche. That requires a breeding cycle. Breeding cycles are typically long. In human beings, they may be 20 years or more. But in the lab you can create a breeding cycle in the equivalent of a few minutes. And the way you do that is you take a gene that codes for a certain protein and you take other genes from other organisms that are similar—that mimic the effect of different breeding partners from unrelated families. And you take a restriction enzyme, which cuts apart those genes, all at certain predictable places. You've got all these fragments from these closely related but not identical genes, and you mix them all up in this little soup of fragments.

And you do what's called a polymerase chain reaction, which amplifies out the full sequence again. When you do that, you've reshuffled these parts. That's the equivalent of a certain type of genetic event that occurs during meiosis in a human being or other cell, where you actually have genetic recombinations going on at the chromosomal level. Here, we're doing it with a single gene. This kind of molecular breeding can go through 10,000 breeding cycles in two or three months in the lab.

Several companies have been developing products based on this, some of which are on the market. The way they create these products is they define what they want based on their ability to measure a certain property. Then they take a gene that doesn't do a very good job of serving that property, and they reshuffle a bunch of variants and look for a new one that works better than the parent genes did.

I'll give you a really simple example, which is a green florescent protein that comes from jellyfish. The jellyfish glow in the open ocean because they have this protein that fluoresces in the green light spectrum. Scientists have been using this for years in the lab to tag genes and to see their expression levels. The problem is, they didn't glow very brightly, and you'd have to use a really sensitive microscope in a really dark room with dark-adapted eyes. Well, some folks took the gene coding for this green florescent protein, did molecular breeding and selected highly bright gene products. They got a 400-fold increase in fluorescence emission, which tells you that the local physical chemistry of the protein was not optimized, or it was optimized locally. What they did with molecular breeding was optimize it globally. So instead of being suitable for a certain environmental niche, it was suitable for whatever use. They maxed out its potential. There have been proven examples of as much as 32,000-fold increases in functional activity done in a matter of days in the lab.

This is a field poised to take off in the next 10 years. Say you had a protein-based drug that didn't work very well—for example, EPO, a drug from Amgen that does a certain type of blood-cell stimulation. If you do molecular breeding to make that work substantially better, you've suddenly taken a blockbuster drug and made it massively more effective. That's going to be done on virtually every drug.

This creates a complication, though, because as you change the genetic sequence, you obviate the intellectual property at some level. So some biotech company could take another company's blockbuster drug, restructure it, resequence it, make it work better, and patent it themselves, and at minimum cross-license it with the original company. I think we're going to see this over the next decade.

The Genius of Nature's Technologies Compared to Ours

Janine Benyus ∘ The more-than-human natural world is full of incredible technologies and incredible engineering feats, so I'm very pro-technology and pro-engineering. The question is always: What is adaptive and what is maladaptive? When we talk about biological technologies, we need to discriminate about that too.

Let's call technology "tools for living." All organisms on earth have to solve a certain number of problems; they have to power themselves and house themselves and heal themselves and find food. I don't see any real difference between what other organisms have had to solve—the physical design challenge of staying alive and keeping your offspring alive—and what we're doing. But organisms other than humans have solved things in a different way than we have.

It's as if, through evolution, we're climbing toward optimal solutions. We've climbed different peaks, very often, than other organisms in the natural world. For instance, when we make materials, we tend to take a bulk material and carve it down into what we want with a lot of waste left over. We use what material scientists call "heat, beat, and treat." We'll heat a petroleum product up to high temperatures. It'll undergo incredible pressure—that's beating it. Then we'll treat it with chemicals. We force it into what we want. We wind up with something like 94 percent waste and 6 percent product.

Now that's predicated on the fact that we believe that we don't manufacture in or near our own body. When an organism has to create a material, it has to do it in or around its own body, and it can only use raw materials that are locally and readily available. So it has chosen a different strategy. For instance, a spider making silk in its body cannot afford to heat it up, beat it with high pressures, or treat it with toxic chemicals. So nature makes a miracle material in a silk that's five times stronger than steel, but it chooses a different path.

If you heat up petroleum to 1,400 degrees Fahrenheit in bubbling sulfuric acid, drawn out under high pressures, you end up with Kevlar, a really tough material that will last 20,000 years in a landfill. The spider takes flies and crickets, breaks those down, reforms them into a couple of proteins that self-assemble in the abdomen, then squeezes it out through a spinneret to create a fiber that is five times stronger than steel and that the spider can eat if it needs to make more webbing. So it's different. There are certain limitations that the spider is living within, and those limitations are, "I have to live in or near my own manufacturing plant." And we're realizing that so do we.

How nature has decided to solve a problem is 180 degrees different from how we have decided to solve that problem. We've climbed different mountains in the landscape of possibilities. Look at synthetic chemistry, which is how we make everything. Terry Collins of Carnegie Mellon says that we basically use every element in the periodic table with very simple reagents and reactions, because we can. But carbon-based organisms like us use very few elements in the periodic table and very complex reactions and reagents. That's the difference. There's basically biochemistry, and then there's synthetic chemistry, or industrial chemistry. It's like two paths in the road.

We're looking across to the other mountain and we're saying, "Hey, wait a minute." We're realizing, first of all, that the products that nature makes and the processes by which nature operates are not inferior to ours. We are talking about materials that are tougher, stronger, and more resilient, in many ways. They also tend to be biodegradable. They're pretty amazing things. The way they're made, the energy that they use during their lifetime, and what happens to these natural materials at the end of their life all wind up creating conditions conducive to life. That life cycle analysis is the envy of anyone trying to manufacture sustainably these days. Now we're looking across at that mountain and seeing that it's brilliant on all levels, not just from a design standpoint. The processing and the way that it fits back into the circle of life are incredible.

It's an auspicious time right now. We have this push toward biomimicry, or toward looking for new ways of doing things because of our biological vulnerability. The pull is the fact that biological knowledge is doubling every five years. We really are beginning to get a glimpse of how nature does what nature does. We certainly don't have it all figured out, but we're beginning to understand it. Since the early '80s, we've come to understand photosynthesis better. You have to understand something well enough to start to try to mimic it, and we are. We're starting to try to create molecular-sized solar cells that self-assemble. What every leaf and every grass frond has already done is self-assemble incredible solar packs.

The timing is right in terms of us really beginning to understand how nature does what nature does. We're also realizing that those operating conditions, both the limits and the opportunities of our habitat, are exactly the same as what these organisms have realistically been dealing with for billions of years.

Part 4

Planet

The Earth as a Whole

Environment and Sustainability

"When climate change happens in five or 10 years, there's no time to build roads, relocate agriculture, and resettle people. In the meantime it's sort of like the Four Horsemen of the Apocalypse. Even if no one sets out to make war, you get into a mode of operation where the population collapses with the agriculture. The whole world could resemble something like the Balkans today. The survivors all hate one another and for good reasons."

William Calvin

"I think by any rational standards you'd have to say that the proposition we call China is a mass of almost insoluble contradictions. I could be wrong, but 1.3 billion people trying to have a lifestyle like Orange County? Can you imagine just the environmental consequences of that?"

Orville Schell

"The one-liner is that the environmental movement is redesigning everything. Through the next 10 years the indicator will be how well humans can organize their activities. It's that simple. It's not going to be about technology. It's not going to be about economics. It's about organizational skills and helping people organize."

Peter Warshall

"The energy system is heading for its most radical and deep-rooted change in centuries."

Amory Lovins

"Biomimicry has to do with using nature's ideas, not using nature. There is a line there. Using nature's design principles in our own manufacturing is very different than using organisms to do our work for us."

Janine Benyus

Mounting anxiety about the state of our environment coupled with increasing interest in the concept of sustainability has reshaped public debate and policy over the past 20 years. And that momentum appears likely to grow in the decade ahead. This chapter looks ahead at how critical environmental problems might evolve, how various actors might respond, and where promising solutions might be found.

We start with **The Global Problem of Climate Change**, drawing heavily upon the scientific and societal perspectives of evolutionary neurobiologist William Calvin and environmentalist Paul Hawken. Calvin refutes the commonly held belief that climate change will be gradual and will result in uniformly hotter temperatures. He argues that the climate could flip quickly, causing another Ice Age—and that the beginnings of this shift could conceivably happen this decade. Hawken suggests that climate might soon become a serious limiting factor to the success of the human race, and that this realization could have the unexpected effect of knitting humanity together in a new way. Both believe that the issue's magnitude and complexity demand immediate attention and new approaches—and they offer some thoughts on the way forward.

Next we look at some **Mounting Regional Problems**. Apart from the global climate that we all share, most parts of the planet are also experiencing their own particular forms of environmental degradation. The developing world faces some of the most pressing problems, particularly in mega-cities with inadequate infrastructures to support huge populations. Various network members also consider the challenges in rapidly industrializing China, in Africa, which is more dependent than most on the natural environment, and in the Middle East, which could soon face the prospect of water wars.

We then move from understanding the problems to considering **Grassroots and Institutional Responses**. One network member gives a fascinating overview of how the environmental movement transformed itself into a broader sustainability movement—starting with an unexpected confluence of events in 1986–1987. Another argues that the notion of protecting the environment is almost a new American religion, a bedrock belief that cuts across political persuasions. Other network members consider the impacts of culture and politics on national policies and priorities. And we also look at some of the changes underway in the business response to environmental issues.

Next we consider the prospects for finding effective, well-integrated approaches to environmental problems. Indeed, virtually all of our network members stressed the importance of viewing both the problems and their solutions from a systemic perspective. In **Systemic Solutions: Energy**, we discuss significant shifts in the world's energy system, which is fundamental to any long-term environmental solution. In chapter 5 we looked at some specific energy technologies that may come to market this decade; here we focus on the design of the system as a whole. In particular, our contributors debate the timing and impact of a transition to a much more benign hydrogen economy, what one calls the most deep-rooted change in centuries.

Finally, we look at **Systemic Solutions: Biodesign**, drawing upon the vision and insight of Janine Benyus, a naturalist and life sciences writer. Benyus argues that we must consider how to redesign our economic activity by following the lead of Mother Nature. She thinks that the concept of biomimicry, or imitating the elegant design solutions that nature has evolved over the eons, will become almost common knowledge five years from now. And widespread acceptance of this approach over the decade will provide an important foundation for practical solutions to our environmental problems in the long term.

The Global Problem of Climate Change

Global Warming Won't Just Go Away

Paul Hawken ○ I think there's a sense that because the Cold War just went away, maybe this environmental thing will go away too. People think that somehow everyone is going to wake up one morning and two bald men will sign a document with a photo op and it will be enough. But it won't go away in this century, and it won't go away in the next century—even if we took every measure we could starting right this second.

What will be the political and social response to climate change? You can surmise fairly reasonably that as the climate changes so will the social/political atmosphere that surrounds it. There is a high correlation between climate and civilization. We see it archaeologically and agro-archaeologically, and we're fascinated when we discover those connections. We're going to be even more fascinated when we discover we are a civilization in the very midst of being dramatically affected by our climate.

There's a tendency to disconnect politics and culture and society from living systems. The question is how global climate change will affect the world. It's the first time, I believe, that global civilization, as opposed to a specific culture or place, is subject to an environmental phenomenon.

The Ice Age Cometh: The Probability of a Climate Flip-Flop

William Calvin ○ Most of the things I think about in terms of climate are low-probability events that happened so often in the past that you're pretty sure they're going to happen again. The question is when. The way warming may accelerate some of these sudden lurches in climate means it could happen at any time. We've probably known that for 10 years, but the public has not heard about it.

There are both regional and worldwide climate changes that happen in just five to 10 years. They're like droughts that don't quit. They're widespread and pretty traumatic, the sort of thing where you go from a warm and wet climate like today's into a cool, dry climate. It isn't the cold that hurts so much as the dryness, the dust storms, and the high winds that go with it. This cool, dry, windy, dusty mode of climate is rather typical of both Ice Ages, but you can flip into a warm and wet climate like today's worldwide in just five to 10 years. You can also flip back. Since we're in the warm and wet today, the next flip is likely to go back.

There are also regional modes of this. The Sahara could switch to a vegetated, almost lush, environment in just a matter of decades. There are some people who think that, at the same time, the Amazon Basin could dry up. This could happen in just a decade or two. So there are regional versions, but it's the worldwide ones that I've been most concerned with because that's what most of the debate is on.

People's general sense of climate is fixed on this global warming notion that we've been sold—that the climate ramps up like a dimmer switch rather than flipping from one mode to another, like an ordinary light switch. What we've been discovering is that there are a lot of flips. The notion that climate is gradual is based upon good physics in the sense of predictions about how greenhouses act. But it hasn't encompassed the knowledge that the earth often just flips into a new mode of operation. There are quasi-stable climate modes both regionally and worldwide and they are the real threat. They tend to happen so quickly that agriculture collapses, countries go to war with one another over the remaining resources, and serious trouble can happen pretty quickly.

If the same change had taken 500 years and you knew it was happening, there would be all sorts of things you could do about it. When it happens in five or 10 years, there's no time to build roads, relocate agriculture, and resettle people. In the meantime it's sort of like the Four Horsemen of the Apocalypse. Even if no one sets out to make war, you get into a mode of operation where the population collapses with the agriculture. The whole world could resemble something like the Balkans today. The survivors all hate one another and for good reasons. Getting out of that could be very slow.

The Gulf Stream Fails and Turns Europe into Siberia

William Calvin ∘ A planetary shift in climate is like most things in medicine. You have a long chain of causation. Let's take the global stuff. The Gulf Stream keeps the North Atlantic a lot warmer than it ought to be. There's nothing equivalent to it in the Pacific. This keeps Europe about 10 degrees Celsius warmer than it ought to be compared to, say, Canada or Siberia, which are at the same level of latitude.

The Gulf Stream fails with some regularity. Over the past 100,000 years, there have been about two dozen failures. When this happens, not only does Europe get hit badly—which is what you'd expect given the way the winds blow and carry the warmth from the Gulf Stream to Europe, keeping it wet as well—but so does the whole earth. The Antarctic might be a slight exception, but the failure affects basically everything else.

It goes into a regime of about 25 percent less water vapor in the air, and that lowers the greenhouse into a new mode. The air/sea temperature contrast tends to become much greater, and you get high winds and a lot of dust blowing around. If you look at the ice cores in Greenland, you see that just within a few years you can flip from a warm and wet regime like today into a cool, dry, windy, and dusty regime. There is dust in Greenland that came all the way from China. Dust storms in China will send dust all the way around the world.

At the same time, you see indicators that the tropics are changing. The wind strings around the equator have changed in lock step with changes recorded in Greenland. The air bubbles that are trapped in the ice tell you what the atmospheric methane and CO_2 are. The methane starts popping up very soon after the Greenland temperature does. Back before agriculture, methane was a gas produced in the tropics, showing you that the tropics are warming up and cooling down very quickly.

Like I said, this is a worldwide change. The impressive thing is that these have happened every few thousand years. There hasn't been a big one since about 12,000 years ago, although there was a minor one about 8,200 years ago. Classic ones tend to cool down suddenly, stay down for centuries—sometimes as much as 1,500 years—and then pop back up faster than they cooled down. The warming is even faster than the cooling. No one knows quite how that works. If one happened today, with the population having expanded about 6,000-fold since the last one, just the sheer number of people would make it very different.

There's this old adage in geophysics that earthquakes don't kill people—buildings do. In essence, civilization has built a huge house of cards. We are very dependent upon efficient agriculture and an efficient transportation system to go with it, so that 2 percent of the population can feed all of the rest. This business of living in the cities could collapse almost completely under one of these. We could wind up with farmers able to provide for themselves or two or three times their population, but not 50 times their numbers.

Climate is not the only way that could happen. You could do it with an economic collapse. You could do it with a widespread disease. There are any number of things that make civilization precarious because of its sheer size. If you have 500 years to make changes, you can survive all sorts of things. If things happen in five years, it's quite another matter. Things really do tend to collapse.

But it's clear that global warming could trigger these abrupt chills. We've known that since 1987 or so, when the first computer simulations of the Gulf Stream failure were done, and there have been a half-dozen simulations performed since then confirming it. The mechanism is very simple physics. It's not anything exotic. If you're going to bring all that warm water north on the surface, you've got to get rid of it somehow to bring more north. There is a mechanism that sinks the North Atlantic current, the Gulf Stream. Up in the area around Greenland the water falls to the bottom of the ocean and then it flows south. There's a sort of conveyor belt that brings warm water north and takes the cold water south. Basically, cold winds from Canada blow across the surface, and they evaporate a lot of water and take the heat with it.

This is what keeps Europe wetter and warmer than it ought to be. But in the process it cools down the surface water. Furthermore, because of all the evaporation, you leave a lot of salt behind. The surface waters become rather salty and because they are denser than the underlying water, they sink. They tend to sink as a giant blob of water to the bottom. In the late winter, you can see 15-kilometer-wide whirlpools in the North Atlantic that are funneling surface water down to the bottom in this big column. There are high-efficiency mechanisms like that in both the Greenland Sea and the Labrador Sea. Counting everything, the flow totals about 100 Amazon Rivers.

This is the normal Gulf Stream operation. The problem is that it's vulnerable. You'd normally think rain falling into the ocean would not cause you any problem, and in most parts of the world it doesn't. But it can. If the surface waters don't get dense enough to sink, warm water can no longer flow north. The stuff just sits there instead of sinking and being flushed and gotten out of the way. Fresh water from rain or from floods out of Greenland or Norway or Iceland can affect it. So can increased rainfall in the northern latitude, which spills out into the north-flowing rivers and into the Arctic, then flows out into the Greenland or Labrador Sea. Any of those mechanisms are quite capable of killing the circulation.

It's not clear that this is how it typically happened in the past, but it's certainly clear that it's the way it might happen next time.

How Climate Might Limit the Human Race

Paul Hawken ∘ Global warming is the mother of all environmental issues. One of the unintended side effects of *Limits to Growth*, the groundbreaking report from the Club of Rome, and the debates that followed, was that businesspeople began to think of resources in a component way. Even though the modeling of Donella Meadows, Dennis Meadows, and Jørgen Randers had been based on Jay Forrester's work on system dynamics at MIT, the way the book was interpreted and portrayed in the press was often about fear. It was about running out, shortages. People began to think of resources not as a part of a system but as distinct components—the way you think of light bulbs, toilet paper, and white bread.

What happened was that resource prices from that time until today have fallen. What the modeling didn't predict was the fact that the methods of extraction were going to improve exponentially. It didn't mean that there was more of anything; it just meant the economic availability increased. Economists responded to the arguments of *Limits* by arguing for substitutability: If we run out of copper, we have fiber optics. If we run out of oil, we have natural gas for 200 years. If we run out of natural gas, we can gasify coal for 500 years. There was a sense of, "What's the problem?" In fact, economists pointed out that when you run out of something it can lead to new growth—new jobs, opportunities, innovation, patents.

What was forgotten and not discussed was complementarity. A complementary system is very different from a substitutable system. Economics, because it's all about fungibility, thinks in terms of substitutability. But in fact, living systems are complementary and they're not substitutable. The best example for a layperson of complementarity is to imagine being marooned in winter on a mountain. You need three things—food, water, and warmth—but none is substitutable. The limiting factor to your survival is going to be which of those things is in the least supply. You can have PowerBars and you can be in a snow cave, but if for some reason you couldn't drink anything you would die fairly quickly. If you had all the water you wanted and all the warmth you wanted and no food, you'd die. If you had the food and water but were exposed to the elements, you'd die. You need all three.

When we're faced with a situation, we automatically inventory what we need and we go right away to the thing that is the limiting factor to our survival or development. Humans are brilliant at that. The environmental issue confronting the world is not resource shortages, although there are water issues and such, but the loss of living systems. One of those living systems, if you will, is climatic stability. If you lose climatic stability, you start to lose oceans, fisheries, and agriculture. It has a domino effect. You can't substitute air conditioning and sprinklers for climatic stability. Perhaps you can for a decade or so, but at a certain point there is no substitute.

That's why, if you look at all the systems that compose a healthy environment, you'd have to say the one thing that's in most limited supply now is the carbon sink of the atmosphere. If it continues to be overloaded, it can have the greatest effect on human well-being. The effects would range from warmer oceans and run-off of the Greenland ice pack to stopping the North Atlantic gyre such that European agriculture fails from Ireland to Russia. That's possible.

Climate becomes a limiting factor to the success of the human race on this planet, which is why I think it's the mother of all issues. One of the things that was not reported last year was that all of the major climatic models, which are empirically recalibrated on an ongoing basis, started to converge for the first time. Before that, some were divergent. I'm not saying that the models are correct; I'm not a climatologist. I'm saying that rather than being divergent, from the perspective of long-term effects of 50 to 100 years, they are now in alignment. That should have been front-page news.

Preventive Medicine for Our Climate: The Need to Act Now

William Calvin ∘ We're discovering a lot of climate cycles that we didn't realize existed. To call them cycles lends more of a notion of predictability than they deserve. It's like El Niño. Yes, they happen every few years, but they can also go for decades. The climate cycle that's driving all of this may be a 1,500-year cycle and no one knows where it comes from yet. There's a whole batch of real scientific uncertainties.

These things are always Rube Goldberg chains in causation, but that also allows you to intervene at any number of points. Even though you may not understand the basic mechanism that's setting off a cancer in the first place, you may understand how to intervene to slow things down and head it off. I think that we're heading toward a preventative medicine of climate. I am not sure that anybody in the climate business sees it that way, but that's my analogy. I think that we'll have the knowledge to at least buy time in the same way we do in medicine. Everybody dies of something someday, but life span has been more or less doubled in the last century. I think we might be able to slow down at least the rapid parts of climate change and make them more survivable.

Scientists are mostly saying, "We don't understand this yet." The people in climate science are not used to thinking in terms of interventions like physicians. They're quite right, we do need to understand it, but consider this adage from medicine: "If you wait until you're dead-certain about the diagnosis, you may wind up with a dead patient." There's a problem with waiting for scientific certainty; you just can't let yourself get distracted by that.

This sort of thing is happening with global warming. As far as I can tell, the oil people and everyone else whose pockets might be hurt by doing something about climate have discovered that the science is uncertain, so they say we have to wait until we're more certain. I think they understand that the way science normally works is that for every question you answer you turn up two new questions. The thing is never finished. If you have to act, you're going to do it on the basis of uncertain knowledge. It's going to be just like medicine, and you're going to have failures along with the obvious successes.

A Lush Sahara: The Mechanisms for Regional Climate Shifts

William Calvin • Regional shifts, like the Sahara Desert becoming as lush as the Congo, are triggered by different phenomena. You have to understand that droughts and recovery from droughts are somewhat random events. A drought gets started in an area just because by chance the storm tracks don't go through the region for a few years, so the plants wither and dry out and the soil beneath them gets a lot hotter because it's not shaded. This is a sort of self-sustaining system of decline. Once it gets started, things can collapse down to where it really takes a couple of good years of rain, and all of a sudden everything recovers. Soon you go through the cycle of grasses to shrubs, from small trees to forests.

The Sahara is sort of like this. In the cooler-and-drier mode, there is a lot of dust being generated that blows off the continent. By drilling ocean cores off the Canary Islands, you can monitor what the changes have been like over the last 100,000 years. One of the things that you see is that the winds and the dust can dramatically change within a century or so, and it corresponds to the Sahara getting vegetation back.

When the closest approach to the sun is in June (it's currently in January), the Sahara gets hotter summers and cooler winters. As afternoon temperatures increase, the monsoons penetrate further and further into the Sahel and Sahara. As perihelion drifted into May, about 14,500 years ago and again about 9,500 years ago, it reached a point where all of a sudden the

African Sahara got grass and grazing animals and elephants back. About 5,500 years ago, as summers cooled somewhat with autumn perihelion, all of a sudden things collapsed, apparently within just a few decades. When one of these drought cycles gets going it may be hard to reverse it—until by chance you get a lot more rain somewhere, and then it just stops happening. You can have these rapid flips in regional climate.

I use that as an example to show how gradual drivers can cause revolutionary changes. The feedbacks in the system are such that you can really flip. It's like pushing on a light switch slowly, slowly, slowly. All of a sudden it pops into the on position. That's climate.

Practical Solutions: Include Seeding the Sky and Preventing Floods

William Calvin ∘ The notion that global warming is caused by humans is probably the wrong way to frame the issue. Whether or not it's our fault we still have to do something about it. This is sort of like doing something about floods or smallpox—just because it's natural doesn't mean that something can't be done about it.

The mechanisms for doing something about it are not apparent yet. In the climate-change mechanisms there are slow aspects and there are very fast aspects. We might actually be able to do something about the fast aspects even if we can't get a handle on the slower ones. For the fast ones, their mechanisms are crucially located—the Labrador and Greenland seas. We might actually undertake a regional climate project, just trying to make sure that the waters continue sinking even if we have to help them along.

This could involve cloud seeding, to make the rain fall elsewhere. I think that we'll probably have some high-tech ways of approaching this in the future. Right now, I tend to use analogies from nineteenth-century technology. If floods from Greenland are a problem, you can undertake to make sure that floods don't happen in Greenland. The floods occur because fjords get blocked by an ice dam, so they build up one or two years of melt water behind them. Then one day the dam breaks and it all comes sluicing out; you get 100 times the runoff in a week.

That's easy to prevent. You just make sure that the ice dams don't last very long. You send in helicopters and highway-construction amounts of dynamite, and a week after the dam forms you break it open and make sure that it keeps running. There are ways to prevent some of the causes and that buys us time to discover better ways. As I say, there are a lot of regional climate floats that are also possible, like the Sahara or the Amazon going in opposite directions, that we don't know very much about yet.

Multiple Weather Disasters That Might Make People Act

Paul Hawken ∘ The trigger that would make people understand the severity of climatic instability would only occur if there was something external like two Category 5 catastrophic hurricanes marching up the East Coast in the same season. I think that would have an effect. At GBN, Peter Schwartz did a study on Hurricane Andrew for an insurance company that simply moved the vector over 11 miles or so. It didn't change the course of the hurricane. If I remember correctly, it took down most of the American and European insurance industry. The damage and the claims were many times greater.

Hugo was like that, but it was down in Central America and we mostly ignored it. If you had two Hugos making landfall on the East Coast of the U.S., especially if they got a little bit further north—Philadelphia, New York, Connecticut, Rhode Island, where there are large population centers—I think that you could see a sea change in attitude. The overnight thing occasionally happens in the world. How did smoking become déclassé? I don't know, it just did. Where was the inflection point, the tipping point?

You also have things like the fall of the Berlin Wall, which was very sudden and sharp and completely unpredicted. What was the cause of that? There are lots of theories, but there really is no explanation for it in the end. The same thing could happen with global warming, which is that people could see that inactivity is in fact corrupt.

The most expensive thing we can do is what we're doing. That's the high-cost solution. In fact, moving toward radical resource proactivity and renewable energy is actually the cheapest thing. We try to make a case for that in Natural Capitalism. What we're saying is that the current thinking is upside-down and backward. The idea that somehow reducing carbon emissions is a cost to the world is a red herring. It's simply not true. Those voices are not heard because there's no money behind them, no lobby. There's no power, no political oomph to saying that.

Reducing Carbon Dioxide Is Our Only Leverage

William Calvin ∘ My attitude about CO_2 is that it's not so much a matter of whether it's our fault or not, but CO_2 is the only handle we've got on the system. If we want to do something about all of the climate changes that will result if CO_2 levels keep going up, then CO_2 controls and reduction are at the moment the only way we can grab hold of the system. So even if it wasn't our fault, CO_2 reductions would still be the name of the game.

This may change as we understand a little bit more about pollution of the atmosphere and the extent to which we can turn some of it to our own gains to stabilize systems. Industry has been throwing an awful lot of stuff into the atmosphere and we have been relatively lucky up to this point. If industry had been producing bromides rather than chlorides, for example, that would have wiped out the ozone layer long ago and there would be a worldwide hole.

Nobody really realized until the study of the atmospheric chemistry progressed to where it has today just what a catastrophe it would have been if bromides had been used. We don't know how many other things like that are brewing. You can get away with a lot in a world where you don't have this huge house of cards that is so vulnerable to just a couple of bad years. It's like that phrase attributed to Woody Allen: "Time was invented to keep everything from happening at once. Space was invented to keep everything from happening to you."

As it stands, the East Coast bails out the West Coast when it has earthquakes and the West Coast bails them out after hurricanes. These events have this virtue that they're over and done with and the next day people can start recovering. In a situation where crises aren't over the next day and they happen everywhere at once, nobody can bail out the others.

The Commonality of Volatile Weather May Knit Us Together

Paul Hawken ∘ One of the problems with global warming is that it's a misnomer. It's global climatic instability. It's global climatic volatility. In some places it will get colder. In some places it will get hotter. Some places won't have any temperature change but will be affected dramatically by run-off. It's a deceptive term, but it's a real thing.

We all have a looming weather problem. It will manifest itself differently in different places—too much rainfall here, too little there, too hot there, too cold there. It's not that everything is going to be hot and humid. It's going to be more volatile. If North Dakotans have two 500-year floods in a decade and England has two hurricanes in a decade, one of which destroys much of Kew Gardens, then in a way a North Dakotan has a lot to say to a Londoner. There is a shared condition, even though one might be flooding and one might be wind. I do think that it could knit humankind together in an odd way. It will seem that their dilemmas have commonality.

Mounting Regional Problems

China's Attempt to Become Orange County

Orville Schell ○ I think by any rational standards you'd have to say that the proposition we call China is a mass of almost insoluble contradictions. I could be wrong, but 1.3 billion people trying to have a lifestyle like Orange County? Can you imagine just the environmental consequences of that?

Environmental Crises Will Become Security Issues

Peter Warshall ○ Kenya's economy is based on tourism. We have already seen the economy go down after al-Qaeda blew up the embassy in Nairobi. But what happens now if the climate changes? It'll be more severe in areas with low soil moisture, as in parts of Kenya. Suddenly the huge migrations of antelope and wildebeest and lions can't occur anymore. Or when they do occur they will have to go through cities like Nairobi. So all of a sudden another part of the tourism industry begins to collapse, the cash inflow to Kenya stops, and more people become unemployed. You begin to see environmental security affecting political and economic security.

We'll also see a lot more insecurities if the theory that clearing rainforests releases more parasites and viruses into the human environment is true. This is one theory about how AIDS spreads so rapidly. A good American example of the environmental security concerns is downstream from all pharmaceutical companies, in the effluent from their factories, in a soup containing discarded antibiotics. Inside that soup the great microbes of the future are growing, becoming resistant to all the antibiotics that we've created since World War II. And so in that little vat, just downstream from the corporation, we are creating an incredible environmental insecurity. All of a sudden one of those resistant microbes will get into a water supply. At a minimum we'll see huge new public health costs. Worse, we could actually see a body count—a large body count. So you can't separate your environmental security from your political/economic security. That's a new way of looking at the environmental movement.

The Potential Wars over Water in the Middle East

John Petersen ○ One of the things that we watch on a regular basis is the possibility of wars over water. In one sense it's not a wildcard because it's almost a certainty, but it has this very explosive aspect to it. When you don't have water you die, you know? It is a very serious situation where people do extraordinary things in order to provide drinking water. If you think the

Middle East is a mess now, just wait. There are limited places like the Jordan River where they can get water. And there are lots of ways in which the Turks, the Syrians, and the Jordanians can all shut off Israeli water. That's one of the reasons why, for instance, the Israelis have figured out how to do drip irrigation. They use the water 10 to 20 times more efficiently than Americans, who just throw it all over so much that great amounts evaporate. Water is also a really big problem in China. In the Beijing area, they're going to run out of water in five to eight years. Right now that's what it looks like, at most something like 10 years.

But if you got an energy breakthrough, particularly zero point energy, or cold fusion, you could do desalinization of ocean water cheaply and easily. The Saudis do that now just because they've got all of that petroleum and burn it to boil and reconstitute the water. There's also the possibility—and I have scientist friends who are really pitching this—to do this with small-scale nuclear power. In any case, water shortages are the kind of thing that could really explode. Even though people anticipate it coming, they haven't put any measures in place or responded appropriately. So we keep an eye on that too.

Prolonged Drought Could Bring Environmental Devastation

Peter Warshall ∘ When I worked in Ethiopia, they were suffering from 16 years of drought. Can you imagine 16 years of drought in California? There would not be one free-flowing river left. We'd start reversing the river protection laws. Wilderness sections would become places for dam sites. America's only seen a three—or four-year drought. It's nothing compared to what's been seen in the Sahel of Africa.

The Desperation in the Mega-Cities in Developing Countries

Lee Schipper ∘ I've been working in cities in developing countries that are so desperate that they're willing to change everything. They are polluted, congested, and messed up politically. Beijing, Bangkok, Cairo, Delhi, Calcutta are much worse than L.A. ever was. I spent half an hour in a hotel in Bangalore picking the dirt from Calcutta and Delhi out of my pores. I couldn't believe how filthy I was. My white cap was brown from all the dirt and grit. A lot of the problem is poverty. Poor countries accept lower standards. And the question is whether one can tunnel through that kind of gap. Bangkok, Manila, Delhi—all probably lost. But Bangalore, India, really wants to do something and is trying to grow a bus system. Brazilian cities are, by Indian standards, very wealthy, and some of them are trying to avoid the huge mess that you have in Rio or in São Paulo. Indonesia still has a lot of pedal rickshaws, guys on two-wheelers with two seats behind them. But they also have cars and Surabaya has an exciting transportation plan. Bogotá, Colombia, now has a bus-only freeway down the middle that's attracting a half a million riders a day. These are small initiatives, but they tend to have a big impact.

Grassroots and Institutional Responses

From the Environmental to the Sustainability Movement

Peter Warshall ◦ The years 1986–1987 are what I consider the beginnings of the twenty-first century for the environmental movement. In 1986, Chernobyl exploded. And with that, faith in the communist regime of the Soviet Union fell apart, leading to the eventual downfall of communism. For environmentalists, who had always said, "Think globally, act locally," that phrase disappeared. Now you had to think and act locally and think and act globally. Fallout was everywhere. It truly globalized the environmental movement. In 1987, the Montreal Protocol on ozone set the first clear, global precedent for planetary law.

The same year, what's known as the Brundtland Report put the word "sustainability" on the map. Commissioned by the Organization for Economic Cooperation and Development, it set out what became the new basic global principles of the environmental movement. What happens to this word "sustainability" is an indicator to watch in the next 10 years. Previous to the Brundtland Report, the environmental movement worked on doom/gloom scenarios: Paul Ehrlich's *Population Bomb*, nuclear winter. Sustainability said that we had to create a world with intergenerational equity. That means that one generation had to take responsibility for the next, and that we should leave the world as good, if not better, for the next generation, as we have it right now. You can get very elaborate about the definition, but that's it, essentially. And sustainability has been adopted as a word and a phrase by everybody from Royal Dutch/Shell to the Rainforest Action Network. And like all words—even like democracy—it's going to have a thousand interpretations and a thousand forms. But it is the new word that gets us from a doom/gloom scenario to a positive-futures scenario.

The early environmental movement was basically fragmented. In the U.S., it had a bunch of white, middle-class people saving species in the North, fighting for their own water supply locally. It got together nationally to protect special places and habitats, but it did not have a broad view. It did not have any minorities in it. It surely didn't include the southern countries. And so the environmental movement of that era was very effective regionally and locally, but was not a globalized or a comprehensive movement. It was bound to fail because, for instance, whales are global. They go all over the place. Warblers, the new world songbirds, fly from Canada down to South America.

The world had already been globalized by the creatures on the planet, except it was not recognized. So the environmental movement began to understand—through global warming, through the ozone hole, through acid rain, through fallout, through the Gaia hypothesis that microbes helped regulate the atmosphere—that the planet was a whole earth. As the dust from Mongolia wound up in the United States, or the dust from the Sahel wound up in Florida, we began to understand that this is a global system that needs to be looked at globally. The movement also began to understand that it had to incorporate those who are marginal and impoverished. And it had to give up its ideology: the ideology of doom and gloom. Its style had worn itself out. Those three things—a whole earth, impoverished people, and more optimism—suddenly catalyzed and became the sustainability movement.

Another milestone came in 1987 in Brazil when Chico Mendes organized the Forest People's Alliance of rubber tappers and indigenous people to oppose the clear-cutting of rain forests and joined internationally with many environmental groups and human rights groups. He was assassinated two years later, but became one of the martyrs of the new sustainability movement, not because he denied the need for rubber nor advocated perfect little museum Indians in museum rain forests, but because we needed to figure out how to use commodities in a way that would be intergenerational.

We could go on and on about product substitutions since the 1970s. The most interesting recent product substitute wasn't even intentional—Viagra. The Asians were killing off Asian rhinos and grinding up their horn to get hard-ons. So along comes Viagra. It's much more reliable and predictable, costs a hell of a lot less, and all of a sudden the Asian rhino is saved. No more poaching—there's no market. So the understanding of product substitution and conservation has evolved quite a bit.

Let me not be too idealistic here. The African rhino is still endangered because it's used by men from Yemen for knife handles, and so that's a cultural barrier. And it turns out that the cultural barriers are much more difficult. So how do we get Yemeni men to switch to a new kind of knife handle to take the pressure off the poaching of African rhinos? That's another important thing to notice, that sustainability brought in the necessity to look at culture.

The New American Religion: Thou Shalt Not Harm Nature

Kevin Kelly ◦ I'm noticing that environmentalism is becoming a foundational, religious viewpoint, a dogmatic and motivational framework—it's sort of like the new American religion. If you ask people why they do certain things or what their beginning assumptions are for what they do, often at the root will be this idea of doing no harm to nature, the protection of nature, the restoration of nature.

And that statement is really astounding in a certain sense because it's the foundational premise, which is not to be questioned. It's the one that you take for granted, and all the other things are built upon it. It's sort of the prime directive. And it's very universal. In my observation it cuts across all economic backgrounds, races, and geographies, particularly among the educated. I think it's very, very profound because this was not the universal stance 30 years ago, and I don't think we've seen all the consequences of this shift. I think that it has become embedded into the American psyche in a way that I don't think any of the environmentalists could have believed, nor maybe do believe right now. But I think it will go on and continue in the next decade to play out its full consequences.

I'm guessing that this spiritual stance will be absorbed by the traditional religions. For a long time I could not see why environmentalism would not be something advanced by the fundamentalist Christian churches. Why is it being promulgated by the liberal atheists when deep ecology had a lot to do with the same mindset that fundamentalist Christians would have too? Thou shalt not this and that. It could be that the eco stuff becomes a politically conservative movement. I don't know. But I do know that it's become mainstream in a way that we haven't yet fully appreciated.

The environment is a basic, fundamental stopping point for everybody. It's like world peace. What do you believe in? "World peace. And don't harm the environment." It's a starting point for many people for how they think about the world and what the world needs. And if you ask them why, it's like asking them why it's good to be alive. It's unanswerable.

Part of this is generational. It's taught in schools. It's insidious. It's reached into the fabric of the culture in a way that the acceptance of God would have a couple hundred years ago. It's something you don't question. That's another point with this. You cannot question the validity of the statement that nature is not to be harmed. It's like the Hippocratic oath, that thou shalt not harm nature. This is not a debatable premise.

Traditional Religions as a Driving Force for Ecological Change

Peter Warshall ∘ The environmental movement is definitely, in part, a religious movement. Go back to the mid-1980s again. The first environmental conference of the major religious leaders of the world was held in Assisi in 1986. It was their first summit on the environment. Finally, all the major organized religions met and said that we have to include the environment or ecology in our liturgy and reinterpret our texts. They were losing members because the ethical—or I would call it the spiritual—labor of earth healing was not in their books.

If you look at what people do, they love to go out and plant trees. They love to go out and watch birds. The biggest and fastest-growing U.S. sport in the 1980s was not golf, but birding. And so the religious frameworks, the religious infrastructure, suddenly realized it was out of touch. A fact I love is that the average size of Catholic families is smaller than the size of Protestant families in the United States. Now, is someone listening to the Pope or not? And so we have this odd situation of the hierarchy, of the bureaucracy of the major organized religions, trying to feel relevant again.

Religion and the environment are one of these "interactive threshold effects" and they could be the big one. We could suddenly see a revisioning of religion as a major driving force in environmental issues, maybe not in the next 10 years, but in the next 10 to 20 years. In other words, recycling aluminum cans, which many churches do and are encouraging now, will evolve into making sure that your work space is ecologically sound, making sure that the corporation you work for is following particular ethical principles. In other words, you've moved from the crushed can to the corporate shareholder. You're saying, "Now we're going to put these religious understandings, our new ethical understandings that come through our church or through our synagogue or through our mosque, into our practice of business."

Every American family wants to take the kids to certain places: the Grand Canyon, Yosemite, Yellowstone, to see the redwoods. That has become an American family ritual. People save up to do it. It's a big deal. Flash back to India, where that's been going on now for 3,000 years. You see religious pilgrimage fusing with ecotourism, this obligation within the family to make a certain circuit. It doesn't matter how you get there. It flattens the economic class structure into this structure of love of nature. Americans are paying homage. Everybody has a different way, different levels of sincerity, and different degrees, but we're beginning to see the structure of the pilgrimage route.

We're also seeing a plethora of books coming out on the subject of religion and environmentalism. Ten years ago you'd never see a book like *Judaism and Ecology*; now *Whole Earth* magazine gets one a week. Or you'd never see a book on Hinduism and ecology; now Harvard is running conferences on it. What you're beginning to see is the new generation of religious bureaucrats, of priests and rabbis now studying this. So what's the generational time on that? It's not clear; that's why I say it's more like 20 years than 10 years. This takes a lot of time, but it's already rolling.

Another good indicator of change is Rabbis for the Redwoods. It's an amazing group—they'd be called radical rabbis. The guy who owns the Headwaters, the last remaining private large chunk of redwoods, happens to be Jewish. So Rabbis for the Redwoods went and held a completely nonviolent ceremony among his trees. They reinvigorated an old, old Jewish ceremony, which has to do with the Tree of Life. Then they went to Houston, where the guy is from, and tried to convince the rabbi who runs his synagogue that this guy is not quite a good Jew. And the reason he's not quite a good Jew is because he's wrecking the last remaining redwood forest in America and he should have a greater sense of generosity and holy spirit.

Another group is called Evangelicals for the Endangered Species Act, who have adopted Noah's Ark as a metaphoric symbol for saving all species. They say, "It's hubris against God to eliminate any species because He hasn't told us to do it. We can't destroy His creation."

The strongest environmental consciousness in the world is in the strongest Lutheran country, Sweden. Which caused which? There's no doubt in my mind that the emphasis on conscience in Lutheran doctrine has been very influential in Sweden becoming one of the leading green thinkers. And the Danes are not far behind.

Searching for the Rock Hudson of the Greenhouse Effect

Bruce Sterling ◦ We've been looking for the Rock Hudson of the greenhouse effect for a long time—the kind of martyr, bloody-shirt figure who can change societal sensibilities so radically that people agree to whatever.

In a funny kind of way, George W. Bush is probably the Rock Hudson of the greenhouse effect. He was willing to radicalize Europe on the issue by refusing to go along with the Kyoto accord. In a sense, he's made so many unilateralist moves that he's actually managed to make Europe unite as a political bloc. It's odd to see them doing it over an environmental issue because they generally quarrel over everything. When you think about it, this issue is actually a pretty good one for the Europeans to be asserting themselves over because they do have the lead in developing green technologies. It's also a thing that they can do that makes them feel cozy and together, although everyone always points out that the United States does something like 25 percent of all carbon emissions. Hey, the rest of the world does 75 percent, OK? It doesn't matter how virtuous the Yankees are unless everybody else makes something happen.

The on-the-ground stuff that's happening in the way of green energy and pollution controls is generally being spearheaded by Danes and Germans.

They've underwritten it a lot better. They've developed more popular support. The Danish windmill movement has been really interesting—seeing these co-ops and labor unions and these other sorts of weird, goofball, lefty kind of enterprises willing to erect their own windmills in order to own a means of energy production. It's like: "We're tired of paying those Arabs. We're tired of paying the state. Let us own it."

Think about it. If you're a Danish guy, why the hell are you exporting huge amounts of revenue to volatile Muslim states? What's in it for you? Why don't you just pay a little extra and give it to your uncle who owns the shoreline or wherever you're putting that thing? It costs more than fossil energy, but you're keeping that revenue stream in the community. I would guess that to be some kind of viable business model. But I question whether it can compete with natural gas, which is just the cheapest stuff in the world. It's unbelievable how cheap that is. What makes the Danish movement interesting is the patriotic angle to it. Nobody is going around beating up Royal Dutch/Shell there. They're not having a "Stop Esso" campaign in Denmark. It's more like people are saying to themselves, "Look, we can actually own the means of production here. We're going to write our names on the windmill. We'll be happy about it."

The issue around releasing greenhouse gases is more like plumbing. If you argued about plumbing the way that the American coal companies argue over the Kyoto accord, nobody would have plumbing because it's a lot cheaper to simply urinate on your lawn. So why do you have all these pipes and flushing toilets and everything? It's sort of an expensive luxury. People react with a natural sense of loathing at the idea of people excreting on the lawn and exporting this disease risk to other people, but people don't think that way about tailpipes and smokestacks yet.

George Bush As an Unwitting Friend of the Planet

Paul Hawken ○ A lot of environmentalists were understandably upset when George Bush was elected. I wasn't as upset. He represents a large number of American people and the thinking that informed his campaign and his candidacy has been there for years. Having Bush elected means it's out there for people to see. This kind of retrograde thinking needed to come out and be seen for what it is.

George Bush's extreme position with respect to the Kyoto protocols changed everything. He took what was once the marginal position and made it mainstream, which is that the countries of the world should figure out how to reduce carbon emissions. Today, there's hardly a country left in the world that doesn't think that's true and Kyoto, as anemic as it is, is a step forward. In a way, we can thank George Bush for his extremism.

The Fait Accompli: That We'll Be Natives in a Greenhouse World

Bruce Sterling ∘ We in the Viridian movement are trying to become natives of a greenhouse world. We're not interested in denying it or saying that it might happen and we can divert it. In our opinion, it's very much here. What we really need to do is understand what it means and what it means for our children and what it's actually going to do and what daily life is going to be like with a radically altered global weather scheme. It's a question of how radical it gets, I guess. I believe it's a fait accompli because the twentieth century has banked up enough carbon dioxide now that even if we all switch to solar and nuclear by next Wednesday, we're not going to get out of the climatic build that is already coming due. That doesn't mean the end of the world. It doesn't mean apocalypse. It doesn't mean even the breakdown of civilization.

Eventually we will win our way through to some kind of sustainable economy. It's just that a sustainable economy and sustainable technology are going to continue to change just as radically as the unsustainable one did. Eventually we might be in some kind of tech fix position where it's like, "OK, well, get all the carbon dioxide out of the air." But that's by no means the end of the story. It's going to continue. The secondary and tertiary effects of what we've done with carbon-based industrialism are going to continue to play out over the rest of my lifetime. Point of fact, it's really an issue for my children and grandchildren. By the time my grandchildren are involved in it, it's going to be the most boring thing in the world. Everybody will know the climate is messed up. People will be watching Hollywood movies and just marveling at the way things used to look.

How Different Nations Handle Environmental Problems

Peter Warshall ∘ Culture is essential to solving the environmental problems we face. Acid rain is a good example. The Japanese studied acid rain because the public sued the government for health benefits to cover eye irritations. The United States and Canada got into a big skirmish because of acidified tourist and trout lakes, and it was affecting the Canadian tourist industry. When Sweden started the whole acid rain transboundary globalization treaty, it was looking only at its forests because of its timber industry. It noticed that power production in the United Kingdom and other countries was killing its forests and ruining its essential industry. For Sweden, it was a battle between two industries, not a battle about human health. In Italy the major sculptures and building exteriors were deteriorating, and so Italians became concerned about their cultural-artistic heritage being eaten up by acid rain.

Notice how different their motivations were. Each culture had a little piece of the pie. And what it took was for the scientific community of all those different countries to get together to write a single treaty that was willing to cover all of it. And the United States balked, of course. Acid rain was the beginning of its continuing lack of vision on these kinds of issues. Originally, the UK also balked, because its power generation would be hurt if it had to reduce sulfur emissions. What was interesting is that there were no environmental groups really involved until the UK decided that it wouldn't sign the treaty. And then, all of a sudden, there was environmental lobbying. Friends of the Earth and Greenpeace in Europe came to the fore and started pressuring the UK government to reduce sulfur emissions.

Then this odd thing happened—every culture decided to handle the solution differently. It was brilliant. Japan went to China, where all its acid rain was coming from, and said, "We want an exclusive contract with you for our technology to improve your coal power plants, and we'll subsidize it." So Japan grabbed the whole Chinese market in pollution control, in exchange for getting rid of acid rain in their country. The United States worked completely differently. The Environmental Defense Fund became almost a shadow agency to the EPA, doing a lot better research than the government could afford or do, and came up with the tradable-emissions scenario in which companies can market their pollutants. They came up with a market-oriented solution for the Northeast that was a completely different solution than Japan's. In terms of sustainability there will be cultural differences, and that's something that the cookie-cutter attitudes of the WTO or the IMF don't seem to understand.

European Business Leads Toward Better Energy Policies

Lee Schipper ∘ I think the problem is that businesses in Europe, as well as their leaders, are not afraid to say that a better long-term energy policy is something that's worth paying for. In the United States everything is passed on. Let me give you a good example. We have a problem at airports. We have a lot of congestion. For years economists have been begging to charge more to land at congested times. Can't do that. Why? Well, we just can't do that. It would cost the business traveler. It's always a cost—me, me, me, me. And the costs and benefits are never measured together by the same person.

In the political sphere, Europe is much more prepared to use the best tools to do the job, whether it's environment or climate, and the U.S. is not. And I think that's why we're so totally stalled in climate, because no president wants to get up and say, "It's worth paying a little now to get a lot back later." It was American companies who were leading the anti–global climate accord coalition. When I was in Kyoto, I was amazed at how many of my buddies from GM and Chevron were running around with little global "badges of convenience"—Global Climate Coalition or International Business Roundtable—who were basically there to stop Kyoto, in Kyoto. Not to learn what the rules would be so they could respond as corporate citizens.

When the World Business Council first started looking at sustainability in the early '90s, before Rio, the Europeans would say, "How come, when we have these meetings, the American guys are always opposed to everything? They don't want to admit there is a problem." The policy landscape of the last 15 years is littered with the blood drawn by American companies trying to stop these movements of global change.

France, Germany, and, to some extent, Britain are so weighted down by history and regulation that it's taken a long time to shake loose entrepreneurs and outstanding intellectuals. Yet maybe that's not so bad. They may have lower GNP growth, but maybe in the end they have more stability. Maybe they can deal with these important, very long-term global issues with a very long-term, global perspective and not just with the "me, me, me" U.S. perspective. Americans are getting rich so fast that we figure we must be doing the right thing. George Bush said Kyoto will hurt us. It's going to hurt everybody a little. That's not an excuse. The Europeans didn't say, "We reject climate accords because they will hurt us." What they say is, "We'll set goals, and then we'll do our best to meet them, and we'll minimize the hurt."

Will We Start Accounting for Externalities in the Economy?

Peter Warshall ∘ One definition of a corporation is an organization that has neither a soul to damn nor a body to kick. Ambrose Bierce said it is "an ingenious device for obtaining individual profit without individual responsibility." But the sustainability movement now says: You can't have individual profit without individual responsibility. The "sense" of responsibility has always been held within businesses; the responsibility has usually been to the shareholders or to the accounting book.

A great indicator for the next 10 years is to watch what happens to international accounting rules, especially after Enron and Andersen. The idea now is to create a sense that there are no externalities to economics, so that you are responsible for anything that leaves your property as a manufacturer.

And you have to pay for the whole life cycle of the product. In other words, the polluter rather than the polluted pays the principal. And the more efficient you can get, the more that you have green manufacturing processes with fewer toxic residuals, and the less resource-intensive you are, obviously the better that is for cost control. If the accounting profession starts to change its methods to include externalities and efficiencies, you're going to see a major, major change in how businesses operate.

Business Is Starting to Emulate Nature's Symbiotic Alliances

Janine Benyus ◦ I think cooperative alliance is a lot of what we're talking about here. We're talking about aligning with other companies that you might not normally hang out with because it'd be cheaper to do so, as well as being environmentally hip. Those cooperative alliances are forming more—at least I'm seeing them more—than they did before.

It's interesting as a biologist to look at that because when you take a plant system that is going to stay in an area for a while, a mature system that's going to put down roots, that system has a higher percentage of cooperative alliances and symbiotic, very tightly coupled alliances than an annual plant system that is moving from spot to spot.

In business, people are starting to hook up and research together; they are cooperating in the lab and competing in the showroom. That is very interesting to me. Isn't that interesting, that cooperation is becoming an important thing to teach someone in business school—as important as competition? To me, that signals a maturing of the successional system.

The Crucial Need for Political Sustainability

Lee Schipper ◦ When defining sustainability one thinks of social sustainability or equity: What you do isn't going to hurt certain groups. One thinks of economic sustainability: profitable in the macro social sense, but also businesses won't go broke doing it. And environmental sustainability—we won't leave crud around for other generations. But there's a fourth, very important level of sustainability that I've defined called political sustainability. When a president can pull out the rug from a very important but very fragile negotiation, and almost upset the whole world, that's not politically sustainable. Something is wrong.

I'm driving at this because corporate strategies face all of those sustainability pressures. Whether it's Occupational Safety and Health Administration rules or hire-and-fire rules, companies have been forced to be more socially sustainable. Economic sustainability is a given; with few exceptions you can't go into business and expect to be bailed out anymore. Environmental sustainability is still being tested; some corporate leaders swear that we don't have a greenhouse problem. But the fourth pillar has to be political sustainability. Companies and institutions have to do things that are politically robust, and that's very, very, very difficult.

The Decade's Challenge: How Well We Reorganize Everything

Peter Warshall ∘ The one-liner is that the environmental movement is redesigning everything. Through the next 10 years the indicator will be how well humans can organize their activities. It's that simple. It's not going to be about technology. It's not going to be about economics. It's about organizational skills and helping people organize. By that I mean reorganizing the World Bank, the IMF, and the WTO, or redesigning a small town like Norco in the Louisiana Delta where the poor, racially segregated population believes it is being poisoned by a Shell petrochemical plant. It's about reorganizing the border crossings for jaguars and how Mitsubishi does business in Guerrero Negro in Baja California. It's about salmon and hydroelectric agriculture in the Pacific Northwest and organizing the timber business in Indonesia so it's not rape-and-run. Those are the skills and leadership that will be required.

By the 1990s, the Environmental Protection Agency started the Green Chemistry Awards. Now, that may seem like a silly thing, but everything since World War II had been based on industrial petrochemistry and its toxic pollutants. The Green Chemistry Award rewarded corporations for creating different ways of doing the same thing. They could produce the same product, but were now doing so in a way that caused no outside harm or used less energy. And it was amazing. Chemists had just never really thought about redesigning. And it wasn't that it was all that hard; you just had to refocus people's thinking.

Systemic Solutions: Energy

Changing the Way We Do Energy Changes Everything

John Petersen ∘ Energy is underneath everything. A number of years ago, for the Department of Energy, I did a strategy for the United States on the possibility that fossil fuels become obsolete. What do we do? How do we do it? I was working on this in a little cabin up in Pennsylvania. I had papers strewn all over the floor when it suddenly hit me, that if you fundamentally change the way you do energy, everything else changes. I looked across the room at a hinge—you'd mine the metal differently. You'd refine the metal differently. You'd certainly make glass in a different way. Just walk around and everything you see—food, everything—changes fundamentally if you change energy because energy is the underpinning that supports it all. A breakthrough like that would be the equivalent of the discovery of fire.

A Hydrogen Economy: The Most Radical Change in Centuries

Amory Lovins ∘ I think the energy system is heading for its most radical and deep-rooted change in centuries. Look at the latest Shell Global Scenarios that came out in the fall. The business-as-usual case shows the world getting a third of its energy and all of its new energy from renewables by 2050. The more radical, and I think very plausible, case is one of technological discontinuity and a rapid shift to a hydrogen economy. It's called "The Spirit of the Coming Age." And it has world oil demand stagnant until 2020 and then dropping steeply.

Bear in mind that we've been decarbonizing fuels for over a century, shifting from coal, which is basically CH, to oil, which is CH_2, to methane, which is CH_4, to direct hydrogen and electricity and so on as carriers for renewables, which is either H_2 or maybe just electrons, maybe just heat, but no carbon. And if you look at the world fuel mix right now, you'll find that slightly more than two out of every three fossil fuel atoms we burn are hydrogen. Only the last one is carbon, which is the climate problem. So the next step is to eliminate both the carbon and the burning by going to hydrogen fuel cells, and that's well on the way.

The future energy system will tend to deliver energy at the quality and scale suited to the task, rather than doctrinaire giantism supplying highest quality for every task, whether required or not. That's just a logical way to save money and hassle. The system will become increasingly dispersed, diverse, renewable—all the attributes that minimize both cost and vulnerability.

I guess you could draw a larger theme out of Hunter's and my work, and that is convergent benefits. In energy, what you would want to do to save money or to protect the environment or to enhance security are all the same things. In Natural Capitalism, the same things you'd want to do to protect the environment also make you more money and are more fun. Better costs less. It's not a completely new idea, of course. We're accustomed to this notion in consumer electronics, which get constantly better, smaller, faster, cheaper. For some reason, however, we've been brainwashed by economic theory that in resource policy better must cost more or it would have happened already.

It's the usual fallacy that markets are essentially perfect, so anything that should have happened at present prices has already happened, and if it hasn't happened yet, all you need to do and all you can do is change the prices. This is a really impoverished intellectual landscape that an organism with a central nervous system, let alone a cerebral cortex, should be able to improve upon.

Our Centralized Energy System Is Vulnerable to Attack

Amory Lovins ∘ The problem of energy security has been misframed. Twenty years ago Hunter and I wrote for the Pentagon what is still the definitive unclassified study of domestic energy vulnerability called "Brittle Power: Energy Strategy for National Security." It points out that although Mideast oil is a national security risk, it is equally or more risky to substitute highly vulnerable domestic resources. What makes an energy supply secure is not where it is, but how it's designed. For example, the Trans-Alaska Pipeline, which is the only way to get Arctic National Wildlife Refuge oil south, is even more vulnerable than the Strait of Hormuz. It's easier to shut off for longer, harder to fix, and would carry more oil. Substituting one for the other doesn't solve the problem; it just transfers it.

In the narrow sense of interruption of supply, the highly centralized and concentrated energy flows and facilities that we've built up for decades in this country both reward and invite devastating attack in asymmetric warfare. The only real surprise is that more of it hasn't happened. There are many layers to the issue. The whole architecture of our modern energy system is inherently brittle. It's easy to disrupt by accident or malice on a very large scale. On the other hand, if it were designed to be efficient, diverse, dispersed, and renewable, major failures would become impossible by design. That is, large-spread failures wouldn't happen, and local failures would be benign. And this is the direction in which the market is taking us if we let it, because it turns out that the decentralized systems have much better cost and risk attributes that the market is starting to recognize.

To put it another way, the central power plant and grid solution, for example, cannot in principle deliver really cheap and reliable electricity. It can't be cheap because the grid now costs more than the power station—and because such big, lumpy, long lead time facilities carry too much financial risk that's reflected in a premium on their cost to capital. And it can't be really reliable because 98 or 99 percent of the failures and glitches in power supply originate in the grid, mostly in distribution. So if you want really reliable supply, you have to make it on the premises or nearby.

American Consensus Around a Centrist Energy Policy

Amory Lovins ∘ There are many broad areas of agreement about energy policy that are seldom articulated because most people's attention is focused on detailed wish lists about which they disagree. For example, there is broad consensus on the importance of improving energy productivity across the board, although there's disagreement about how much you can do that way. There is broad agreement on the primacy of markets, structured in a transparent way that rewards entrepreneurship and protects the public interest. There is broad agreement on the desirability of reducing dependence on Mideast oil. And, of course, there are many ideas about how to do that. What if we built energy policy around our objectives and principles?

If you asked people how they want their energy services met, and what attributes they want, they'd probably say something like secure, reliable, safe, healthful, fair, affordable, durable, flexible, innovation-friendly. It's hard to get disagreement that those are desirable objectives. And to a lesser but still very important degree, one can get a similar consensus on the principles that ought to be followed in shaping policy instruments to those ends. There is also a broad sense, among almost all private sector leaders, that there is a climate experiment going on, and we probably won't like it and ought to stop doing it. A well-ordered exploration of those objectives and principles is an indispensable foundation for a centrist consensus on what should be the content of energy policy, that the more we push on things people agree about, the less we'll need the things they don't agree about.

Replacing the Energy Infrastructure Will Take Many Decades

Gerald Harris ∘ When you think of replacing the energy infrastructure in any comprehensive way, you're talking about decades for it to play out. There's no other way you can do it because of the sheer scale, the slow turnover in housing stock, and the rights of people to resist those changes. For example, take an office building that was built in the 1930s and is still usable. If someone says, "This building is highly inefficient and needs to be redone," what is the owner of the building going to do? Unless you're going to buy it from her, crash it down, and build something new and more efficient, then nothing's going to happen. Given that the turnover rate of housing stock is around one-half of 1 percent, it may take 200 years or so to turn all this over.

The Good News: Surprising Progress in Recent Years

Amory Lovins ∘ Two-fifths of the energy services in the United States are now delivered by reduced energy intensity compared to 1975. And we've already doubled our oil productivity in the past quarter-century. But almost nobody noticed. If you treat energy savings since 1975 as a resource, it's 1.7 times as big as oil consumption, three times oil imports, 13 times Persian

Gulf imports. It ought to get more respect. It's our biggest and fastest-growing energy source.

Some of the changes in usage are changes in the structure of the economy. Most of it, however, is technical improvements in how much work you get out of each unit of energy. A tiny bit is behavioral change. The fastest-growing energy sources on the supply side are renewable. Europe plans to get 22 percent of its electricity from renewables by 2010. That's twice the current U.S. share. In some countries it's pretty spectacular. Denmark is now one-sixth wind-powered, headed for half by 2030.

And for that matter, I've just been in a meeting on climate policy where people were asking, "Well, let's see. Do we have to diverge from business-as-usual trends in 2010 or 2020 to stabilize CO_2 at various levels?" Well, guys, look at the numbers. It turns out in 1998 the world economy grew 2.5 percent. CO_2 emissions fell half a percent. In 1999, the world economy grew 2.8 percent. CO_2 emissions fell 0.8 percent. In 2000 the world economy grew about 3.5 percent. We don't have the numbers yet because China and the U.S. have a two-year reporting lag. So you can take your pick whether CO_2 emissions rose 0.1 percent or maybe fell. We don't know yet. But the point is, starting in 1998, world economic activity and CO_2 emissions started heading in opposite directions.

We need to give credit where it's due. Some countries, including China and the United States, have been doing remarkably well. From 1996 through 1999—maybe through 2000—the U.S. economy grew something like nine times as fast as its CO_2 emissions. So there is some good news out there, and we just need to capture a lot more of the cost-effective energy savings. Doing that will not be easy—but it's a lot more attractive than continuing to waste money and then pay for the consequences.

The Prospect of Free Solar Energy

Janine Benyus ∘ I have a lot of feelings about energy. Obviously, we need to get to current sunlight as the source of our energy. I like the idea of storing it in the form of hydrogen. I like the solar hydrogen economy very, very much.

As a biologist, I am looking at systems that have unlimited renewable energy coursing through them. They are open, energetic systems, meaning unlimited abundant sunlight comes through them. The system works to enhance the place—in other words, it's building soil, it's building capacity. If our economic system is a depleting system, a machine that depletes, and we add more energy to it, it will just deplete faster. The answer for me is not just add free energy—it's fix the system and then add free energy. We absolutely do need to be able to hook it to the sun.

Systemic Solutions: Biodesign

Our Species Finally Realizes We Need Nature as Much as Science

Janine Benyus ∘ For the first time there's this species that's aware of itself as a species. There are a couple of things going on. We're beginning to be aware that we need other species like pollinators, like plankton in the ocean, like the filtering organisms that are in the soil. There was a time when we really thought we could replace all of this stuff—we could hard engineer our way out of anything. I think we are beginning to realize we really can't.

There was a time in which nobody would have guffawed at the term "better living through chemistry"—when we actually believed that industrial, synthetic processes would replace natural ones, that we truly wouldn't need nature. We would eat pill food and not really need agriculture anymore. I think we're starting to wake up out of that little dream. The blanket belief that scientists in white coats are going to take care of us and they know best—we're way beyond that.

Biomimicry Copies Nature's Simple Rules and Complex Designs

Janine Benyus ∘ Biomimicry has to do with using nature's ideas, not using nature. There is a line there. Using nature's design principles in our own manufacturing is very different than using organisms to do our work for us. It's a matter of continually repeating that differentiation.

When you're mimicking, "structure grants function" is the mantra. Nature tends to put a lot of energy into design, shape, structure, and relationship among parts. Information is what allows nature to make the most of a limited pool of resources. So the structure in a natural forest or in a prairie is more than just a scientific curiosity—it's actually an answer to a very specific question. If you want to know what the soil thinks, ask a plant. If you want to understand what the demands and opportunities of your habitat are, ask the organisms that have solved the riddle—not as individuals only, but as a whole system. Suddenly you begin to see a system that is making the most of where it is. On top of that, it's improving the place so that its offspring has somewhere rich and fecund to live.

We're starting to realize simple rules, just like people in chaos theory are realizing that very simple rules lead to beautifully complex results. Well, the simple rule for an organism is "keep yourself alive and keep your offspring alive," meaning your offspring a thousand generations from now. An organism can't really predict the future. It's not like it's literally designing things the way we do with forethought. What happens is evolution basically x's out the organism that doesn't take care of its offspring or its place. An organism doesn't really take care of its offspring generations out; it takes care of the place that takes care of its offspring. That's what we don't do.

It's such a simple rule: Keep yourself alive and take care of the place that will take care of your offspring. Organisms don't do it on purpose, but the ones that did it wrong are no longer with us. As a biologist, I see us as a species in the midst of this experimentation. Some of our technologies are really well adapted. Others of them may be clever, but they're not well adapted. Eventually, evolution will judge them to be very maladapted. But we're in the midst of this huge lag before we get judged. Then the big brain comes in, because with the big brain, we can play out the scenario. We could stand in for natural selection and we could decide which of our technologies are well adapted and which are maladapted, and we could kill out the ones that are maladapted. That's an amazing place for a species to be.

What's amazing is that we are rather late to the game of evolution. We are a rather young species. Homo sapiens showed up a very short time ago. One of the adaptive qualities that could save us is the ability to mimic. Imitation is beginning to be recognized as a cultural form of evolutionary advancement. The ability to imitate what something else does allows you to adopt that without having to evolve it yourself. It's a huge time-saver.

I feel that, as a species, we are starting to use this adaptation—the fact that we are uncanny mimics—and also use the fact that we've developed the scientific method, which allows us to accumulate over the generations all of this knowledge.

New Paradigm for Manufacturing: Self-Assemble Like You

Janine Benyus ∘ I really do think that self-assembly is going to be a major new paradigm of manufacturing. I don't know when, but I see it happening. We're going to start in a liquid form. We are going to pour our products into a mold and evaporate away water so that what's left self-assembles into a layered structure or a three-dimensional structure of some sort. Right now, when I talk about self-assembly, people go, "What's that?" But I think in five years, people are going to know about it. People are going to ask businesses: "Why are you heating this up and adding all of this energy? Why don't you just have it self-assemble?"

Self-assembly is what the abalone shell does when it lays down that beautiful mother of pearl. It self-assembles this really tough ceramic that is a three-dimensional architecture of a mineral and a polymer in alternating layers. Sandia National Labs studied the abalone, and they figured out a way to make a hard optical coating that self-assembles. The same thing is now happening with organic solar cells. They've taken a layer of material that is sensitive to the sun, and another layer that conducts the released electron away. Think of what Silicon Valley does when it makes silicon chips, think of how toxic that whole process is. Now imagine instead the paradigm being that you pour material out and water evaporates away. The three-dimensional molecules that are left are such that they jigsaw together and they layer out—sort of like oil and water—and solidify into a solar cell on your roof or highway. That's the next paradigm.

Life has been doing this all along—that's what's hysterical. Your bones self-assemble. Your tendons self-assemble. Your hair self-assembles. Self-assembly is everywhere we look. We're composed of self-assembled materials and yet, because the mountain that we climbed in the adaptive landscape has us heating and beating, we took earth and heated it up to make ceramics. If we had walked over to the ocean's edge and asked the abalone, "How are you making that ceramic?"—which is twice as tough as the high-tech ceramics on our missile cones—the answer would have been no heat whatsoever. We just climbed a different mountain.

The Economic and Biological Disconnect

Janine Benyus ∘ I think feeling vulnerable as biological beings is still very much a core feeling. It's one that we don't acknowledge right now. But if we can get in touch with that feeling, it might help us focus on what is important work for us as a species. On the one hand, we're very much operating out of those biological imperatives of needing clean air, clean water, and a good place to live. On the other hand, we're in this schizophrenic mode in which profitability isn't yet synonymous with the biological wealth that we evolved to value. The disconnect between our economic system and what's valued there and our biological system and what's truly valuable is one of the things that is threatening our existence as a species.

We obviously have been in flight from the biological imperatives for a long time. We've gotten to the point where we now realize that our industrial technologies are not just our saviors on a white horse—they are actually, in many ways, threatening us. We are starting to discriminate now between well-adapted technologies and maladapted ones.

Preparing for the Long Term

Civilization and Infrastructure

"We have a global economy without a global body politic. We're developing a global body politic and we're developing a global society and a global civilization. The global economy is forcing that. At least a third of this century—maybe half, maybe the whole thing—will be spent sorting out the global society in terms of global governance and the global frame of reference."

Stewart Brand

"I'm sanguine that human imagination may well be able to get us out of this mess largely in one piece, even though many bad things will still happen and there is much suffering in the universe. On the other hand, the jury is still out in evolutionary terms on whether this radical experiment of combining a large forebrain with opposable thumbs was a good idea."

Amory Lovins

"We're getting world government, but it's not happening from the top down in a hierarchical way. Instead, it's percolating through a lot of different technical areas, like air traffic control, product standards, and safety standards—a zillion areas with a lot of governance."

Frank Fukuyama

"Social entrepreneurship—that's where the action is. That's where the real innovators are. That's where you'll find the people who will be remembered 50 to 100 years from now. We won't remember a single person who's in business except as a footnote."

Paul Hawken

"We need wise and philosophical thinking from business leaders. They have only had to think strategically and tactically in the past. They've never had to think on behalf of the whole. The best businesspeople I have met are certainly up to the task. I am glad the world is in their hands at this point in history."

Betty Sue Flowers

In this chapter we gather our network members' insights and provocations on the issues relating to the whole world over the long term—essentially the future of civilization. "Civilization" has been understood historically as the total culture of a particular people: its philosophy and arts, science and tools, forms of governance and community, and innovations and advances of all kinds. Civilizations of the past have often been remembered for their physical infrastructures—grand buildings, roads, public works—but equally by the intangible infrastructures that allowed them to function and thrive. These included educational systems, political institutions such as representative democracy, and even cosmologies to make sense of their world. Going forward, our thinking about civilization and infrastructure may have to become even more comprehensive, more global and systemic. As one network member puts it, this decade might even seed the first global civilization, one that evolves gradually over the rest of the twenty-first century.

Taking a very broad and long-term perspective can result in a profound sense of challenge, including, at the extreme, the possibility of civilizational collapse. Certainly history would suggest that all civilizations eventually lose their power and vitality, ultimately succumbing to new challenges. With that in mind, this chapter opens with an overview of the **Profound Challenges Ahead**. Here we explore some reasons for pessimism—including the possibility of economic collapse, the spread of epidemics, and even madmen wielding weapons of mass destruction—but also offer some counterbalancing arguments supporting a more optimistic view.

In **The Need to Think Systemically**, we share our network members' observations about the complexity of our current situation. With so many problems and issues on so many fronts, each can't simply be thought about in isolation and dealt with individually. The only way to deal with them, several members argue, is to embrace them all and understand how they interrelate. This will require systemic thinking, new ways of understanding the whole and not just the parts—a big departure from how we generally think and operate.

We then turn to some areas where we expect to see some constructive innovation in the coming decade that could position us more favorably for the future. In section three we explore **The Evolution of Governance**. Different network members talk about the simultaneous moves toward global and local governance, while making the key distinction between world government, which few see as feasible, and world governance, which some see as essential to keep pace with the global economy. We also take a particular look at an issue of growing importance—the future of intellectual property rights. In a knowledge economy, who owns ideas is critically important not just to business, but to society. Today there is much confusion and conflict regarding these rights—and how this plays out over the decade could have far-reaching consequences on everything from the level of innovation to wealth distribution around the world.

Next we look at **The Impact of the Third Sector**, variously understood as the realm of nonprofits, non-governmental organizations, and mass movements of citizens. These people are deeply engaged in building the civil society upon which our future may increasingly depend. Here we confront some core issues such as our treatment of "the commons," that which is shared by all in society, and how we handle the concept of social justice in a world in which four billion people live in extreme poverty. And we hear encouraging reflections on practical solutions such as how philanthropists and foundations can provide fluid social venture capital that enables social entrepreneurs to spur innovation and widespread change.

Our final section of this chapter, which also concludes the conversation with the network members, returns to the world of business, and makes **The Case for Greater Business Leadership**. Businesses are not used to leading on large-scale and long-term issues regarding the future of the planet—in the past they did not have a clear role in such domains. Going forward, however, that might change. Several members point out that the increased power and reach of business, and particularly global corporations, brings new responsibilities. They argue that businesses will need to assume greater leadership in concert with other sectors, not only because it is the right thing to do in moral terms, but also because it makes good business sense. Good corporate citizens will be expected to be part of the solution rather than part of the problem.

Profound Challenges Ahead

The Long View in Millions of Years: Collapsing Timescales

William Calvin ∘ Certainly our general progression during human evolution is not what we thought it was—a series of gradual changes in intelligence and brain size and cultural complexity. These things happened in a disjointed way. There's two and a half million years of occasional progress. You can go for a million years without much change in tool-making technology while the brain is growing. Up until about 50,000 years ago, it is not clear from any of the evidence that our big-brained ancestors were thinking very much differently than chimpanzees. They could stage their tool-making and food preparation better than chimpanzees, but in terms of producing anything to look at, you couldn't say, "Those people thought a lot like we do," until about 50,000 years ago.

Six thousand years ago is when we started getting cities and differentiation of occupations, the subtle existence of civilization. There wasn't anything that looks like modern science or philosophy until about 2,500 years ago and then it was spotty until things took off about 400 or 500 years ago. The stage we're at in terms of total population, movement of people around the earth, movement of disease organisms around the earth, all these things have largely happened in the last 200 years.

Two hundred years ago there was almost no knowledge of medicine. It was all bleeding and purging, no real understanding of how things work. We're really living in a time when there has been enormous acceleration in our capabilities, largely due to culture. This is not a genetic change. Culture has accelerated everything—particularly the technological aspects and the political organization.

With a background like that, you have to say, "Does 50,000 years ago represent the first worldwide distribution of the beta software?" It looks like minds like ours happened first in Africa, then spread around the world immediately afterward. The major bugs that are left—psychiatric disorders, epilepsy, all these things that you just don't see in other animals—really suggest that we're on the edge.

I'm using the word culture here to cover education, technology, science, politics—the whole thing. Some of these operate on fast tracks and others operate slowly, and you can get into big trouble that way. Physical systems go into oscillation when you have setups like that, and there's no reason to assume that problems with economics, epidemics, or the climate won't substantially collapse the whole house of cards. The chances of losing an awful lot of what we've gained are high—much higher than they were 200 years ago. There's just an enormous increase in the population, which makes us very vulnerable. A hundred years ago, farmers made up 30–40 percent of the American population. Now it's 1.3 percent. That alone tells you how vulnerable we are.

I find the speed as exhilarating as other people do. This last decade has been a great ride and I have learned a great deal from it. But nonetheless, it is a house of cards. It is rather vulnerable to the breezes. When you're moving people and disease organisms around the world as fast as we are, you've just got to expect trouble.

The Long View in Thousands of Years: Collapsing Civilizations

Stewart Brand ∘ The really long view—1,000 to 10,000 years—makes the prospect of total collapse seem thinkable. Every now and then, civilizations decline steadily or come to relatively sudden ends. It's normal. In the perspective of centuries, there is nothing special about it. The sense that "that's something those poor fools in history did" goes away because you realize that, in their way, they were just as smart about what was going on as we are about our times. The fragility of things becomes interesting.

Another thing that emerges is Ray Kurzweil's idea of the self-acceleration of technology and, thereby, of the pace of history, which has been a pretty secular trend of logarithmic increase for many centuries. There is no reason to expect that acceleration to suddenly turn into an "S" curve that levels off on its own terms. Technology accelerates itself and is accelerating itself more and more, and the idea that a singularity is coming is a way to think about the present that is helpful. A whole bunch of technologies accelerate themselves and each other to the point where basically it's a new world every week.

There are countervailing intelligent and sometimes not-so-intelligent forces against the pace of change. As Jaron Lanier said recently, all of the rhetoric of the hyper-acceleration of technology absolutely freaks people out. People feel that engineers are messing with their essence and they're not going to stand for it. They think: "I've got to protect my children. I've got to protect my family. I've got to protect my church. I've got to protect all of these things against the nitwits who think they'll just give us a pill so we can live forever."

They've got a point. The rhetoric is overwrought. Nevertheless, the statement made by Paul Saffo and others that we overestimate how rapidly change is coming in the short term and underestimate how much change is coming in the long term continues to be the case. While the country is focused on stem cells, eight other things are swarming ahead with no attention paid at all. A while back somebody created an advanced birth control pill without asking anyone's permission and it changed the world.

Doom is plausible when you take a long-term view, and acceleration matters when you take a long-term view. These were actually called megatrends once upon a time—large trends with sudden manifestations. A major acceleration of everything in 10 years' time is a sudden manifestation. Tipping over some edge into a place you can't get back from could be a sudden manifestation. There's a mild form of that going on in Japan at the present. They fell out of their bubble economy into a place where they can't pick themselves up.

There's a malaise of progress going on that I think is somewhat part of the long view. It was, in a way, predicted by cyberpunk science fiction writers. The Bruce Sterlings and the Bill Gibsons saw it coming—that there would be a noir version of high-tech that was not going to be glossy; it was going to be ugly. It was not going to be freeing; it was going to be enslaving. It wasn't going to make everybody rich; it was going to make some people rich.

All those are ways of saying that technology acceleration goes on and that all these other things go with it. There's the deepening of fundamentalism, liberal resistance, conservative resistance. Liberal resistance is found in preservation of old buildings. Conservative resistance is found in attempts to stop stem cell research or cloning or whatever.

People who say that this is sort of like resistance to Darwinism are absolutely accurate. Darwin knew that he was basically saying, "God is not only dead, he never existed. Humans weren't designed by a great designer; all of life was designed merely by a very long sequence of lives." People said at the time, "You may be the grandchild of a monkey, but I'm not." That debate hasn't changed a bit.

The Mismatched Paces of Technological and Political Change

William Calvin ∘ Relative timescales matter enormously. For example, it took less than 10 years after physicists realized that an atomic bomb was possible to make it. It took 50 years for the European community to reach the point of having a common currency. The technological stuff and the political stuff that could be done to make the world safe for the technology operate on very different timescales. There's nothing in nature to guarantee that you won't shoot yourself in the foot this way. The political timescale of consensus-building requires the old generation to retire and get out of the way, making political changes slow. I think what the Europeans have done is perfectly miraculous in terms of bringing people together under a common framework that had not existed before, but it did take 50 years. Compared to the timescale of technological change, that's pretty slow.

What really causes ruptures is when things operate on different timescales. What makes an explosion an explosion is that other things can't get out of the way in time. The chances for our technology to dig us into deep holes are pretty considerable. Whatever general trends there might be, whether it's in computing power, economics, or whatever, I don't see us necessarily overriding any of these dangers. I don't necessarily see technology as solving more problems than it creates. It's not that technology is inherently evil, but I have no faith in the ability of society to react in time to the changes it makes. I think human institutions change much more slowly than the technology does, and the chances of producing a world that we seemed to have headed off—of weapons of mass destruction, computer viruses, and so forth—will not follow the wave of change fast enough. Just from the speed of technological change, we are heading into a period of substantial instabilities, quite aside from nature's instabilities. Technology is not automatically going to be very stabilizing. It will take a large human effort to do that. So far, it's not one that we're doing very well.

A Centuries-Scale Project: Building a Robust Global Civilization

Stewart Brand ∘ It's possible that we'll face a global recession or some other form of back-to-basics era. The '60s were supposedly a back-to-basics time, and to some extent they were. The '60s crowd was both revolutionary and extremely conservative; they wouldn't even use fertilizer on their gardens, which as a result did not grow. Frankly, I think that it's a completely valid scenario, but I don't think it's going to happen. I think we are, in fact, in a long boom. The opportunities of globalization drastically outweigh the downside. It is going ahead and can't be stopped. There will be other avenues that will emerge for managing it. The issue is how to make a global system that can progress pretty rapidly without breaking.

I'm talking about civilization. We have a global economy without a global body politic. We're developing a global body politic and we're developing a global society and a global civilization. The global economy is forcing that. At least a third of this century—maybe half, maybe the whole thing—will be spent sorting out the global society in terms of global governance and the global frame of reference. We may have one big currency or just a few big currencies. Do we all see the same entertainment? What things are increasingly unique, and how fine-grained can uniqueness go? Not everyone can be a nation and have its own currency, its own parliament, and its own airline.

It's a centuries-scale project, building a global society. In the past, when civilizations have failed, other civilizations have taken up the slack. When Europe was in a dark age, Islam was having its own renaissance, which eventually helped the European Renaissance. Once it's an all-encompassing civilization, you've got all your eggs in one basket. If you drop the basket, all of your eggs are broken. You have to build in the comeback capabilities internally. There's a certain rent you have to pay to have a relatively safe global civilization and we don't know what that is yet.

Democracies are very conservative; they're on the increase, but there's a present-oriented conservatism that goes with that. So you will probably get crises—some that aren't real, and maybe others that sneak up on you that are really deep, with no easy fix. What are the crises that change behavior? A lot of it is perception. I think that the Seattle/Genoa type of ruckus looks like a crisis, but it's not. Not yet. But it probably refers to something that is real.

Shoring Up the House of Cards to Absorb the Inevitable Shocks

William Calvin ∘ If you value what civilization has brought us, you have to do things to help stabilize it and keep it from being so vulnerable. It's akin to realizing that buildings kill people in earthquakes, in which case you better not have shoddy construction, like they do in most of the world. You have to design buildings and bridges to be earthquake resistant.

I don't think we've even begun to do that in other areas. I don't think that economics has the brakes available. We're moving organisms around the world on airplanes and in ships, and most of them don't do very well in the new environment and just die out. But occasionally one of them will flourish, and without any natural predators or controls these things can take off pretty badly in the same way that smallpox and tuberculosis took off among American Indians. You can quickly wipe out nine-tenths of the population that way without warfare at all. The chances for either economic collapse or epidemics are high. In the next 50 years, we'll get hit by one of them on a fairly broad scale.

Science Gives Us the Knowledge and Tools to Think Long Term

Stewart Brand ∘ On the other hand, scientific knowledge is increasing and archaeology never stops. We know more and more about everything. We will know what happened to the Maya. We already know pretty much what happened to the Easter Island civilization—basically an ecological collapse. That civilization had mastered going anywhere in the Pacific, navigating super-large catamaran canoes. They were great engineers building these statues; they were on an island that wasn't even an archipelago. They must've seen what was happening when they had 40,000 people on 40 square miles. Then it all collapsed.

We're getting those stories and science is increasingly able to tell us things like global warming is real, methane at the bottom of the ocean is released or not released and has this effect. These are multi-century, deeply important trends. As soon as you take seriously the idea of the oceans rising X feet in your lifetime, or the Gulf Stream turning off in the period of a couple of years and freezing Europe, it's a different story.

I think that science is giving us this long-term perspective and it gets out there through the media, through the schools. Kids care about it. That starts to yield a long-term frame of reference in terms of responsibility. One nation alone can't unilaterally fix it or be ignored by the others if they're part of the problem. There's a globalization of concern, and one has reason to think in century terms because science gives you both the need and the tools to do that.

I think part of long-term perspective is the increasing life span. If an eight-year-old starts to assume that 150 to 200 years is a plausible life span—personally—that's going to change thinking and probably behavior. People never used to know their great-grandparents. Now everybody does. That will go on to great-great-grandparents. In turn, they're going to know their own great-great-grandkids. They'll start thinking: "What's life going to be like for them? What will I do now about that?" That creates a personal lengthening of the frame of reference. The "now" of one's life is extending. Things will change around that.

The Power of Madmen: The Unabomber As Molecular Geneticist

William Calvin ◦ Globalization's virtue—making everybody dependent on one another so that they don't go to war—is more obvious, but whether this will wipe out and demoralize cultures is much harder to foresee. Analyzing this just in economic terms of personal income and educational opportunity is not enough. I think you really have to look at issues. What do you do when a country is so far behind in terms of average education for its people and still doesn't have a system of free schools? How do you bring a country like that up to a global standard? Even if you didn't have the problem of politicians pocketing aid money, you'd still have an enormous psychological problem. When people don't understand how things work, they can only try to do what they're told and not improvise because they will get into trouble.

I worry that the whole world could find itself in the position of the colonial-era Africans—feeling like they don't have any control over things, that there's no point in doing anything or planning for your future. Fatalism is about all you can do, and it makes for a very dull life. If you have the rich getting richer in the educational sense, where there's a very smart class that tries to run things successfully for the rest of the world, you've still got the problem of a lot of smart people with no jobs to go to, and they probably will get the world in trouble.

It's like Bill Joy's comment that we're lucky the Unabomber was only a mathematician and not a molecular geneticist. There's a sense in which technology empowers the disaffected to do a lot of damage. The easiest analogy is: If you were disgruntled and only had bare fists, there's a limit to the damage you could do. But with a knife or a gun or a bomb on an airplane, you could do a lot more. With nerve gas, you could wipe out a whole city.

There are going to be people who are mad like that, no matter how good the economics get. The amount of damage that a single person can do is growing with our technology, even though their percentages are very small. People like the Unabomber don't come along every day and I don't see any way of heading them off in terms of genetics. We will continue producing a lot of variability.

I'm very impressed with a lot of things about our technological confidence but I also see the opportunities that technology gives to people who would do damage. Society's responses to them operate on a slower timescale than the technology. That will create problems and is likely to get us into a lot of trouble. I don't know whether it will happen in the next 10 years or the next 50, but it's hard to imagine how we are going to head all of them off.

The Scientific Oath: Still No Evidence of Rogue Scientists

Stewart Brand ∘ The thing I keep expecting, and that keeps not happening, is the sale of that which is forbidden in some countries by other countries—whether it's mind-altering drugs, surgery to make you smarter, even terrorist bioweapons. If it's easy for a terrorist to make something scary, it's also increasingly possible, using the same tools, for an overseas startup to make something new and desirable.

Freeman Dyson says that scientists all talk to each other globally. They certainly have national loyalty, but they have a greater loyalty to the soundness of science and the well-being of humanity. And they're all connected. He thinks that a technological determinism will not drive all of these things. There is a constant permission-giving, which is not giddy; it is reluctant. Scientists want to prove things five times over before they feel OK about going ahead. There are no rogue scientists out there worth mentioning. Dyson's often been right and I've been wrong. Chances are he's on to something.

The Pessimistic Perspective: Does Civilization Flicker Out?

William Calvin ∘ The intelligent species that solve problems are the ones that survive. In the SETI (Search for Extra Terrestial Intelligence) business, it's called the lifetime civilizations factor—how long they'll last, what sort of window there is for communicating with civilizations elsewhere. Does it

flicker on and off for such short periods of time that it's essentially unde-
tectable? The jury is still out on that.

We've always been aware that economics could go up and down and bust.
We have some notion that epidemics could do that; we lost 30 percent of the
population to the plague over a matter of a couple of decades. We now know
that climate changes are not only just regional droughts and unseasonable
weather but major changes that last for centuries before they pop back into
a new mode of operation. Learning how to live with that is going to be a matter of figuring out how to slow them down as well as how to build for them.

Civilization is not really a matter of going faster and faster; it's a matter
of flying safer and safer. You've just got to assume that some idiot will do
something wrong and you've got to figure out how to keep things from col-
lapsing when he does it.

It's much easier to be a pessimist than an optimist in some sense because
the things to be pessimistic about are so obvious and the things to be optimistic about require such a large amount of hope. While my work has led
me into a consideration of a fair number of catastrophic things, I also recognize there's a much harder-to-find long boom, I hope, in operation here,
which I don't think we can trust to happen all by itself. I think we've got to
keep heading off the catastrophes in order to enable it. That means very serious planning as to how to stabilize society against collapse, whether it's
climate or economics or epidemics.

The Optimistic Icon: The Whole Earth from Space

Stewart Brand • Going to the moon at the end of the 1960s was a global
event. We saw a photographic view from space, but there was a sense that
we, humanity, went to the moon, not just Americans. In a period of about
five years, the image of the earth really did replace the mushroom cloud as
the governing icon of thinking about the big, strange picture. It was an optimistic versus pessimistic icon.

The Human Species is Heading Toward Graduation Tests

Amory Lovins • I'm sanguine that human imagination may well be able to
get us out of this mess largely in one piece, even though many bad things
will still happen and there is much suffering in the universe. And since
brains are evenly distributed one per person, and most of the brains are in
the south, then most of the good ideas will come from the south, and we'd
better have the humility to get used to that idea. On the other hand, the jury

is still out in evolutionary terms on whether this radical experiment of combining a large forebrain with opposable thumbs was a good idea.

Until our wisdom catches up with our cleverness, we need to be alert to how adroitly we can do stupid things, some of which we may wish we'd never heard of. So you could say our species is heading for its graduation tests, and right now we're in the prelims. The student shows promise, but is not yet well disciplined.

The Need to Think Systemically

The New Mind-Set: Adapting to an Out-of-Control World

Danny Hillis ∘ We are going through a shift in our attitude about how the world is supposed to be. I can identify three modes that civilizations go through cyclically. One is viewing the world as static. When you're in that mode, your zeitgeist is about fitting into the system. The system is a given, so how do you make sure you are operating within the rules? How do you stay harmonious with it? How do you maintain consistency and order? The organizational symbol of that is the monastery. The monastery will be the same if you look at it in 100 years. Every day there is a ritual that is a device for denying change. You preserve consistency.

Another attitude, which is the one that I think we're just coming out of, is the attitude of progress—getting control of it and forcing it to go in the direction you want it to go. That's the old model of the Ford Motor plant that took the steel in at one end and produced Ford cars at the other end and controlled every single element in between. You take in the raw input and push it in and form it into what you want. The zeitgeist is about exercise of power. How do you get efficiency? How do you put the right metrics in place? How do you manage? How do you order people to do things you decide they should?

The third attitude—the one that we're shifting into—is viewing the world as chaotic. It's a jungle out there and you've just got to live in it. You're never going to understand it. You're never going to control it. Instead, you have to be responsive. You have to go with the flow. You have to make sure that when an opportunity arises you can take advantage of it. That's much more the attitude behind network economies and learning companies, the kind of agile organizational structures that are emerging. What's important about them is not that they're in control, but that they're able to adapt quickly, to redefine themselves. That's a different attitude about the world, and maybe its symbol is the Internet. There's nobody in charge of the Internet. There's no place to call up and say, "It's not working," because it just kind of happens.

To make a music analogy, the cyclical version is the Gregorian chant; the control version is the symphony, where everybody is working together under a conductor; and this new world is jazz. You've got to pick up on the latest riff and make your variation. I think we'll look for global principles of understanding complexity and if we're lucky, we may find some. I also think we'll just develop a different attitude about how much we expect to be in control. We're moving out of an age of control and entering an age of adaptability—out of an age of coherence and into an age of combinatorial richness.

It's frightening to make one of these transitions. I'm sure it was very frightening to go from an age of constancy to an age of progress. In fact, there are still people who are dealing with that fright. But we got through that to the point where we could see progress as a positive framework.

I am an optimist. I believe that humans are becoming something better. I think we're at a halfway point right now between being animals and being something else. I believe that if you stepped back far enough, you would see this evolution that's gone all the way from raw chemicals sitting on a rock to living things to intelligences to culture—to whatever this next unnamed thing will be.

Wildcards as Catalysts for Systemic Change

John Petersen ∘ I got into this business because it became obvious that there was a collision of huge trends, these driving forces, that were already in place. There was also the possibility of wildcard events—big surprises that you know are going to show up, you just don't know which one it's going to be. The quality of these wildcards is very different from any other time in history. They're global in scope. They're potentially very disastrous or disruptive. And they're intrinsically out of control in chaos theory and complexity terms.

Simply put, wildcards are low-probability, high-impact events. They are either so big or they come so fast that the underlying social structure can't effectively deal with them. The book I wrote lists 85 big things that run all the way from an asteroid strike, to the Internet melts down, to ET shows up, to a global epidemic. They go from economics to a crisis in the United States that results in a strongman president. They are something that just explodes and everything changes. These surprises could also be extraordinarily positive like an energy revolution that makes fossil fuels obsolete.

You look at these kinds of convergence and then at the big negative trends like the have and have-nots situation and the possibility of a global epidemic, and you realize that this is a systems problem. They're all tied together in different ways: Concentrations of very poor people in large urban areas without public health support increases the possibility of disease. Then you've got airplanes flying across the world, and if you've got a disease with a latency of a week, it could literally be distributed everywhere in the world before you even figured it out.

Qualitatively, it seemed to me, this was different than anything that humanity had dealt with before, in terms of the scope, the discontinuous nature, and the absence of traditional mechanisms for effectively dealing with these things. A real central issue here is that a lot of people are concerned about certain specific problems but they are never concerned about all of the underlying problems. They're concerned about the environment or energy or their particular thing, but few people are looking at this as a whole system.

What humanity has to do, almost in Darwinian terms, is to evolve. Culturally in the past and biologically in the far past, life on this planet has, in relatively short periods of time, undergone major shifts that moved everything to a new plateau. It's called punctuated equilibrium. We're at a place where the existing way we operate—the economic system, capitalism, and a variety of other things—has no fundamental incentives to solve the big, deep-seated problems. You get big change by humanity hitting the wall and saying, "Wow, we can't keep doing this!"

Look at education—at the huge numbers of poor people that are uneducated around the world. With the present economic model there's no way that the schoolhouse model—paid teachers in buildings—is ever going to happen in Zimbabwe. I've been there; I've talked to the people there. They say the only hope is a breakthrough in information technology that allows wireless distribution of high-quality information through some kind of new device. It isn't a laptop, but maybe something like a joystick that enables uneducated, illiterate people to start to learn. The point is that somehow there's got to be a breakthrough.

There have to be breakthroughs not only in the tools we have available to solve some of these environmental and economic issues, but also in ideas, in values, in the way we think. Otherwise, you're going to keep throwing money at the same old stuff. And for that we need to have a punctuation. You then start asking what would facilitate or catalyze that, because it's not going to be evolutionary. There is no way that suddenly people are going to come around. There's not enough time. The incentives are all wrong.

That's where wildcards come in. September 11 was the latest of a growing size, number, and amplitude of such events. If we haven't gotten the word yet, there's going to be another one that's even bigger. I really do believe that.

The Secret to Systemic Thinking: Everything Is Connected

Paul Hawken ∘ If there's a problem in a systemic sense, then every node of the system, so to speak, needs to be addressed. The answer is everywhere but it has specificity, and the specifics change according to what it is you're addressing—whether it's agriculture, education, or technology. Whatever subject you bring up, there is a way of thinking that embodies an awareness and a connectivity to other dilemmas, issues, problems, and trends that exist in the world, but still has a great deal of granularity with respect to the subject.

I'm not of the Archimedean school that there's a lever somewhere, and if we could just find this leverage point then somehow we would change the world for the better. I don't believe that's true, whether it's in technology or business or media or art or education. I do believe that with a more comprehensive understanding people can become very effective doing what they know best, whether they're a kindergarten teacher, a carpenter, a docent, a single father, a farmer, or a poet.

I think the shift is to relax back into what we've always known, which is that everything is connected. That sounds New Age but I don't mean it that way. I mean it in a Batesonian way, a Buddhist way. I mean that you cannot disconnect your life from those of others. Again, it's a matter of seeing the world as a system. The only difference between those who work toward sustainability and ecological and social justice and those who don't, is the way in which they see the world. They're not better people. They're not nicer people. They're not smarter people. They're just people who've had some sort of moment where they began to see their world as a system. It is an "aha." Once that happens, you can't act the same or be the same.

No Way to Wall Off the Rest of the World

John Petersen ∘ Buckminster Fuller said that in 1984, for the first time in history, there were resources available on this planet to feed and provide a modicum of quality of life for everyone. Before that people had to compete because of scarcity. You could argue that capitalism has, at its core, this notion of scarcity. Competing for these resources is the basis upon which the United States and the developed world have accumulated what they have, saying if you don't work for it, and you don't get it for yourself, the system is not going to provide it. In one sense, they were right. The problem is that the have-not situation has gotten so large it's approaching instability. No longer can you isolate and insulate yourself from the rest of the world. Think of it in systemic terms. Fuller talks about "Spaceship Earth"; others say we're all in this lifeboat together. We're all connected. In the past, if you built the walls high enough you could keep all of that out and you didn't have to worry about it, but you can't do it anymore.

The Need to Communicate About No-Fooling-Around Questions

Alex Singer ◦ Almost anybody who is a thinking person in the sciences or technologies has a feeling of profound misgiving about the enormous mismatch between the understanding of the public—and I'm not speaking of just the American public, but the vast number of people in the world—and the level of problems that we face as a species. The problems are many-sided and multidimensional, and have to do with all the things we can name: how we use the tools that emerge from computation, how the changes in our understanding of biology and genetics are going to affect every part of our lives, how nanotechnology affects it, how the environment is responding or may respond to the things we are doing. How the planet continues functioning at all is subject to a series of real questions now—genuine, no-fooling-around questions, requiring at the very least some information and some processing tools that seem to be alarmingly in short supply. I am struck by what I think is going to be the need for all of us to be communicating.

The American Penchant for Opting Out of the System

John Petersen ◦ We've got to get around some of the fundamental ideas that shape all of the policy and economic alternatives, one of which is sovereignty of nations. Clearly it's getting eroded all over the place, but a whole lot of people still say, "We're Americans and we're not going to do what anybody else says. We're not going to give our military to the UN and have them work for some raghead general from over there. We're Americans. We don't work for them, they work for us." We don't work by the rules of the rest of the world. If the world court comes up with something that we don't like, we discount it, we ignore it. Somehow we, as a nation, as a culture, have got to figure out that this is a system, and we are all involved. And, by the way, we have the ability to make changes and affect the outcomes far more than anyone else so we have a larger responsibility for the outcome of the system.

The Evolution of Governance

Devolving Power: The Resilience of the Desire to Create a Country

Kevin Kelly ◦ Civilizations come and go, although in the grand scheme of things, the memetic aspects of civilizations are passed on from one to the next. They accumulate. It's hard to imagine, but we have to say that Western civilization ain't going to be around forever. It will have to succumb to something else at some point. When and to whom, I wouldn't think to suggest. But while the civilization has tremendous amounts of things that are decadent and not working and it's easy to imagine it failing, I can't see anything around that could supplant it. So I think that for at least the next 50 years, if not longer, we're going to see the continued prominence of Western civilization.

There will certainly be some aspects of civilization that will be global. But for the next couple of hundred years, while we still speak different languages at home and have different ethnicities in terms of genetics, I think that the neighborhoodness of each nation will still play a huge role. They may not even be countries, but the idea that the people living in Kurdistan will want to by and large do things together with other Kurdistanis or whatever, and they may even want to try to do things a little differently—that will remain.

Think about it this way: Today there is a tremendous interest in starting your own company, to have your own set of values, your own way of tackling the problem of selling a service. I think there's also a similar appeal to making a country. The people in a country won't have the same power that they used to have, but the idea will remain of "Let's make a country. We can make a country better than other people."

Unbundling and Reassembling Governments

Danny Hillis ∘ I think this may be a theme for the decade—that we're going to take packages of things and unbundle them and reassemble the parts. It happens with cultures and biological organisms. It also happens with governments. In the past, because people mostly interacted with people that they were physically next to, it made sense to organize things spatially. You drew a border around a certain area of the earth and said that all of these people were going to be in the same government. That government did a lot of things—it was your economic system, your defense system, your educational system, your healthcare system. All of that came together as a package.

I think those functions are already beginning to be deconstructed a bit. I may get my defense from NATO and my trade laws from the WTO. I may get my post delivery from FedEx, my health insurance from a private carrier, and my education through a network of homeschoolers. Those are all functions that maybe I would have turned to the government for, but now I'm getting them from alternative sources. When you use alternative sources, that lets you shop for the best in each. In fact, I sort of like my American government's system of civil rights enforcement, but I don't much like their system of postal delivery. So I'll keep them for what they're good at, but I'll throw them away for what they're not good at. I don't think that nation-states are going to go away. What's going to happen is they're going to stop doing things that they're not good at. So they're going to do less; they're going to be less all-encompassing and less universal.

This doesn't mean that there will be a world government. That's just reapplying the old model at a new scale. To me, the EEC is very retro—it's that idea of trying to build a giant, omnipotent nation-state on a larger scale. That's a silly idea. Having a common currency is a great idea, but I think having a new uber-bureaucracy is a terrible idea.

On the other hand, there are a lot of functions that make sense to do internationally instead of spatially. Take product safety standards. I think Underwriters Limited does a better job of establishing product safety standards than each of the individual governments. Or take censorship. A lot of people subscribe to the Disney Channel because the Disney Channel only allows a certain kind of content. They are, in some sense, subscribing to a private censor to provide material to their children. I like the idea of subscribing to my censorship because I can choose, for different purposes, what censorship I want. I'd much rather have that situation than have the government choose a censorship for me.

We're heading for a world where it's unsustainable for the government to even do that. The government won't even have the tools for censorship. That's not to say that there won't be international control in some cases and private control in other places. I think we're going to replace a unitary system with a kind of mix and match—again, a menu. Everybody will choose from a much larger menu of possibilities, and they'll assemble the combinations that make sense for them. It ends up being much better because good solutions can emerge that aren't a part of the package that dominates.

The New Institutions: Our Global Era's United Nations

Betty Sue Flowers ∘ The people who have to face the challenges of globalization most are multinational corporate leaders. An issue that really concerns them is "the international system." What system will support prosperity in the future? You can't just think in terms of countries anymore.

Most businesspeople, and certainly Americans, are very wary of anything that smacks of global governance. I spent some of the summer with the former European head of the Trilateral Commission, Georges Berthoin. He was at a seminar in Aspen run by Harlan Cleveland, who assigned all the international participants to different countries and Berthoin, a Frenchman, was assigned to be the U.S. representative. As soon as he began acting in this role, he realized that everyone ganged up against him. Although he was supposed to be leading the world, he found that he couldn't speak on behalf of the world and the U.S. at the same time. At that point, he came up with an idea that he called "extranational institution building," involving a non-national group that would propose solutions for the common good that individual nations could then accept or turn down. The power to propose and the power to execute would be situated in different spaces. You wouldn't have to give up national sovereignty but, on the other hand, you would have some way to come up with proposals on behalf of the common good of people, not just of certain nations.

The only institution we have now that can make proposals is the United Nations—but it's made up of nations, whereas this would be a body of representatives that were not representing their nations. Then you wouldn't get the politics, for example, that were involved in Kyoto. In any case, we set up the League of Nations after World War I and the UN after World War II, but we haven't set up anything different since the Cold War. What are the new institutions we need to be setting up now?

I think that the corporate leaders at this meeting began to see that somehow there have to be global rules to the game—but without losing national autonomy to the UN or some other international body. That's why I thought that separating the power to propose from the power to execute was a very useful concept.

Leaders are congenitally indisposed to hopelessness. All of the leaders at this conference were looking for solutions and expressed a deep desire to tackle this problem in some way. There was a sense of urgency—that now we have a window of opportunity. People weren't making predictions about how long we have. But there was a strong sense that we have to do something now for the sake of business as a whole. Long-term self-interest demanded it—but what "it" is, nobody knows.

We're Getting World Government from the Bottom Up

Frank Fukuyama • I said in one of my books that it was the end of history. I still think that on a political level, that's right. I don't really see any momentous shifts in political paradigms that are going to upset the legitimacy of markets and liberal democracy. In that sense, I think it's still the case. The globalization aspect of it has gotten a lot more controversial over the last couple of years, but ultimately I don't really see that going anywhere. When there is socialism in the world, there is a positive program that is an alternative to capitalist liberal democracy. I just don't see any of the anti-globalization people having anything coherent to offer as an alternative.

We're getting world government, but it's not happening from the top down in a hierarchical way. Instead, it's percolating through a lot of different technical areas, like air traffic control, product standards, and safety standards—a zillion areas with a lot of governance. It comes through standards-setting committees that are done industry by industry. And it happens in a fairly non-politicized way. I see that as a positive thing. If you don't have standards, you don't have trade and commerce and communications.

The Global Version of the Interstate Commerce Clause

Michael Hertz ∘ I do think you're going to have a global movement toward uniformity in the laws. In the U.S. Constitution, there's something called the commerce clause, which was put in there because the drafters knew that there would never be a true national economy if each state could basically have its own set of laws that governed interstate commerce. A whole series of decisions have been rendered that uphold federal power over interstate commerce. And then there's the Uniform Commercial Codes and other uniform codes that basically try to create some legal uniformity across the states. The same thing is happening and must happen internationally.

Non-Governmental Organizations as Informal Watchdogs

Frank Fukuyama ∘ I'm looking at international governance, because I think that no one country can really hope to write the rules. You've got to think of creative new ways of dealing with it at an international level that avoid heavy-handed international regulatory agencies and so forth. The most obvious development in the last few years is the direct participation of civil society in setting up things like corporate codes of conduct. A good example is Nike and Adidas and sweatshop issues. You can try to legislate within the WTO rules on environment and labor, which I think is a formula for killing the WTO and free trade. Alternatively, you can do what's been going on in quite a number of sectors where an NGO that's interested in workers' rights in Honduras stages a protest and then Nike accepts a code of conduct regarding the kind of labor its suppliers can use. That's happened in labor, the environment, and quite a number of different areas. In fact, this issue is at the heart of Peter Schwartz's book *When Good Compa-*

nies Do Bad Things—that companies can do well by doing good. Companies have an interest in their reputations and don't want to be singled out like Shell was for dumping an oil rig into the North Sea.

This needs careful thought. Nobody wants overt international regulation because no one has figured out how to do it in a way that is remotely responsive and doesn't end up being overbureaucratized. On the other hand, more informal kinds of self-regulation by the private sector have problems because in many areas it's hard to bring pressure on companies to improve their conduct. In other cases it's not clear that the NGOs that are pressuring them to adopt the codes of conduct actually represent the real interests of the people.

Ethan Kapstein, who's been fairly sympathetic on labor and the environment, points out in a recent *Foreign Affairs* article called "The Corporate Ethics Campaign" that it's not clear that Nike adopting an anti–child labor corporate code is actually doing these countries any good. They promise not to hire anyone under the age of 17, but mandatory schooling in most of Central America ends at about age 12. In effect, Nike is saying that they are not going to employ all of these kids that are not in school and were supporting their families by working for a Western multinational. It's a complicated issue. It's nice to say you have these more flexible ways of, in effect, doing global governance, but how to do it equitably and legitimately is something that we haven't really figured out yet.

In the U.S. we have these democratic institutions like Congress, elections, and political parties that evolved over a long period of time because that was the best way anyone could figure out to represent all of the different societal interests and to make them accountable. You can un-elect your representative if you don't like what he or she is saying in your name. The problem with the NGO sector is there's not that kind of accountability. There's some question about whether you could make them accountable, but then you start regulating them and they become part of the problem rather than part of the solution.

It's really hard to balance the need for a system that's flexible and participatory versus one that is legitimate and representative. Often the two are enemies. The reason we have formal, hierarchical, well-established institutions is to make them transparent and legitimate. But once they become formalized and hierarchical, they also become slow, inflexible, and hard to modify. There's not an easy way to reconcile those kinds of competing demands.

Global governance is going to be a big political issue for the next few years. We have actually created a system of global governance, and the WTO is probably the most institutionalized form of it. It has more teeth than any of the UN agencies, apart from the IMF and the World Bank, simply because everybody's got a big economic stake as a member of the WTO. Some forms of global governance will grow out of that, but it's also, therefore, a big target of everyone that is upset with the system. So that issue is going to be central, certainly from the standpoint of any multinational corporation. They're going to have to spend a lot of time worrying about how to deal with NGOs, how to deal with the backlash against globalization, and how to make their activities seem legitimate in all sorts of different markets.

Networks Can't Supplant the Legitimacy of Governments

Bruce Sterling ∘ What governments have that networks don't have is legitimacy. If you're an agent of the state, you've got a uniform and a badge, you're trained, and you take an oath. In the case of a network, if somebody turns out to be a criminal, say a computer criminal or a fraudster of some kind, everybody immediately disowns him. They don't have a self-policing facility, especially not a legitimate one, where people are heard out. A network can shun people and they tend to be very fractionalized. Flame wars break out easily, but you don't get justice. There's no legal system. There are no civil rights. Though they're very street level and electronically fast, these ad-hocracies, as I like to call them, have severe organizational weaknesses. It's sheer bohemian arrogance to think that networks are the future or that everything is going to be arranged like that.

Governance Through Peer Collaboration and Best Practices

Robert Hormats ∘ The change that will occur globally will be the result more of what is called peer collaboration. This means you don't get the IMF or the World Bank telling you what to do; it doesn't come down from up high. Individual finance ministers, central bank governors, or attorneys general work across borders among themselves and review what one another is doing to promote best practices. This is the practical way of cooperation. If you are in an environment where people are reluctant to have global government and to have multilateral institutions play a more extensive role, you have to find a more purposeful way of cooperating. Governments have an interest in helping other governments improve economic governance and growth.

The Human Rights Legal Framework as the Original Global Law

Dorothy Q. Thomas ∘ In the human rights arena, you have a transnational system of standards and supporting institutions that has been in place since the late 1940s and has evolved over time fairly dynamically and expansively. Although it's not the be-all and end-all and there is no human rights army—the enforcement mechanisms are pretty minimal—you still have in place a globally acknowledged, established consensus about what basic rights standards are regardless of virtually anything. Regardless of your geography, your ethnicity, your class, your gender, your sexual orientation, or your nationality, there are basic standards in all arenas of life that must be met.

The historical moment at which the Universal Declaration of Human Rights was articulated was in the wake of World War II. You had a moment when parties from a variety of different countries and backgrounds and perspectives understood that there was an obligation to establish minimums that had clearly been abrogated in the course of the Second World War. It's an extremely inspirational document, very hopeful. There are billions of criticisms of the human rights system, but I would say its most profound challenge is less about which rights are or are not rights than the degree to which any given government is actually willing to uphold and enforce those rights.

You can see how the failure of the United States government to hold account to these standards has a very great ramification for the entire human rights system. If the most powerful country in the world, at least in its own eyes, says we don't have to be bound, it doesn't send a particularly compelling message to the rest of the world about its obligations.

From Individualistic Human Rights to Common Responsibilities

Mary Catherine Bateson • The Universal Declaration of Human Rights basically deals with the rights of individual persons. It makes sense in the context of a highly individualistic society, but I think we desperately need to learn some of the values of other societies. What's wrong with the Universal Declaration of Human Rights is not that they are not all valid and good, but that they are not balanced by concern for communities and ecological systems. The Universal Declaration of Human Rights is a culmination of a long process of ethical development, but it is lopsided. To the extent that we push it without balancing it, I think it's going to be destructive.

There are people in this society, for instance, working toward rebuilding community, saying that the solitary individual is not the be-all and end-all. What the anti-globalization movement is saying is that there are elements in globalization that are having unethical effects on communities and on the environment. We tend to put it in terms of individuals because that's the language we have. We need to take the notion of individual rights and build off it a notion of responsibility. You can't have one without the other.

The Law for Corporations Already Is Becoming Global

Michael Hertz ∘ On the corporate commercial level, law is becoming totally global. Because as globalization occurs, there is a very strong interest by multinational corporations to have at least the commercial rule of law implemented in the places where they're investing. You want to be able to protect your intellectual property, and you want to be able to protect your investments, and the only way to do that is if there's some world law that exists in that country. The place that this is happening big time is in the huge infrastructure projects: power plants, telecommunications, airports in places like China and Indonesia. Those are all being developed largely by construction companies that are headquartered in the West. And they've got to have a legal regime in place that protects them if the government changes or Indonesia goes into crisis because of its currency. And so you're seeing a lot of countries basically copying our securities laws or our commercial code.

Here's what now happens in most sophisticated, big international transactions. Take an example of a big power project where you have different banks from different countries financing it. You've got multiple construction companies that are all cooperating to build it—some Italian, some Korean, some Japanese. You've got all the local contractors in the country where the thing's being built. All of that framework is contracts. And generally what they've done is contractually agree that any dispute will be governed by X law, usually U.S. law, and will be heard in an international arbitration setting, a contractually created court that has rules, procedures, and enforcement mechanisms. It's not like a U.S. court. You have arbitrators whom you select, and there's a set of procedures around doing that. They are the decision-makers, and their decisions are binding. They listen to evidence. It looks almost exactly like a court proceeding.

Nobody's going to invest billions of dollars if they think disputes are going to be decided in a court that's corrupt or doesn't have established procedures. You can leapfrog the problem areas, but ultimately you're going to have to have a global legal structure, which already exists in a lot of ways.

From a global meta-perspective, one of the big tensions is that the rule of law is mostly available to corporations. Individuals, especially poor people, do not necessarily live in a world where the rule of law exists. Let's take the United States, where the rule of law is kind of assumed. If you don't have meaningful access to a good lawyer in many contexts, you don't have access to justice. You don't have access to the rule of law. You can be screwed and can't do anything about it. And that's the reality in the richest country in the world with one of the most extensive judicial systems and more lawyers than anywhere else in the world.

So then you think about what a poor person in Bangladesh faces in terms of the rule of law. They don't have it. Exxon has it if they're in Bangladesh. So in some ways, the legal arena has been turned into something that is really serving institutions as opposed to individuals. And I think that's problematic, ultimately.

That's one of the reasons you have these protests now at big global conferences, because the people who are in the conferences are generally representing big institutions—big government, big corporations, big multinational organizations like the IMF and the World Bank, global institutions of all sorts. Individuals don't have really a voice in a lot of those—or let me say they don't perceive themselves as having a voice, although they do theoretically. And so what are they doing? They're taking to the streets. They're throwing trash cans at people.

Changing Property Rights Changes the Foundations of Society

Steven Weber ∘ Property rights are the foundation of every economy and every society. Even more important and more fundamental is what ownership means. What does it mean to own something? What can I do with it? What can't I do with it? Can I sell it? Can I give it away? Can I break it up?

Property rights are the foundation of every community, every economy, every society. When property rights shift, it's revolutionary. In the '90s we talked so much about the e-economy, how the Internet economy was reducing transaction costs for business, and how that was going to revolutionize the way the business world worked. Transaction costs are nothing compared to property rights. When you change property rights, you completely remake the foundations of a community. That's a core economic insight, and it's potentially much more disruptive than anything having to do with the reduction of transaction costs.

There are a lot of notions of property rights out there. The notion of property rights being exclusive—I own something so I can keep you out of it—is one sort of core notion. And there are others. I've been talking to Rabbi Irwin Kula, one of the more interesting religious thinkers, about what property rights religious leaders have over traditions. If I decide that I want to take a religious tradition like lighting candles on Friday night, and I want to recombine it with a religious tradition of taking communion, who can tell me that I can't do that? Religious traditions are sort of open source, right? You can create a new religion. You can freely take whatever you want, all these traditions, put them together, and then you can repackage and re-distribute it out there in the world. Rabbis don't own traditions in the same way that you own your house. But there is a property right that makes them a leader in the community built around those traditions. The open-source community has begun to articulate what rights a leader has around the software that he or she creates or writes. The religious community is start-ing to articulate what it actually means to be the steward of a tradition.

This is starting to happen in the environmental movement as well. People, particularly in environmental economics, are becoming increasingly disillu-sioned. Some think the reason the environment isn't taken care of correctly is ownership. The property rights are not correct, and the pricing isn't right. So the reason the ocean is polluted is because nobody owns it and has the incen-tive to keep it clean. It's the tragedy of the commons. There's an increasing sense among environmental economists that maybe property rights around environmental issues need to be thought of in a different way. Maybe there's a stewardship notion that's something closer to what religious traditions have, or what the open-source movement has created.

What I'm trying to say is it's important to watch the creation of alternative systems of exchange, of community, of relationships that are built up around a different notion of property rights. And as they spread, and as people exper-iment with them in different places, they're going to create all sorts of new things that are going to be really, really different in a way that the Internet economy reducing transaction costs didn't even get close to.

Intellectual Property Rights: The Frontline Global Legal Battle

Michael Hertz ◦ Intellectual property is the big piece that's out there where there's not a lot of agreement. You have countries that are engaging in outright piracy of intellectual property: software, drug patents, the whole bit. Think about that in the context of something like Napster or other peer-to-peer technologies, where you have fairly large groups of the population spitting in the face of obvious legal principles. Everybody who used Napster knew that they were violating the copyright laws. It was clearly a violation of law. It's undeniable that traditional intellectual property rights are being blatantly ignored in a global way.

So now some argue that the law should be changed. I think it'll be a huge battleground, and I think the people who are in favor of changing the cur-rent structure in the next 10 years will lose. The people who have the money and the power are going to fight like hell to keep their intellectual property protected. And it's going to take a lot of time to erode that power. It's not going to be easy. The tip of the iceberg is the whole Napster fight. Those record companies just squashed them. I'm just saying it's going to be very difficult for people to go to Congress and say, "Change this."

The Impact of the Third Sector

The Parallels Between Philanthropy Today and 100 Years Ago

Katherine Fulton ∘ Like many people, I am fascinated by the parallels between the beginning of this century and the beginning of the last century. When the United States made the transition to an urban-industrial national economy, when waves of immigrants were coming in, and new massive business organizations were taking on the corporate form.

Look at the number of social and political innovations that happened in that period of time. You had breakthroughs in ways of thinking about public health and ways of conquering and preventing different kinds of disease. You had lots of breakthroughs in public education. You had different kinds of groups wanting to be empowered in new ways. You had workers organizing labor unions. You had women looking for the vote. You had whole movements to win victories we now take for granted, like child labor laws and limits on the amount of time people can work. With the distribution of more mass media in the late nineteenth and early twentieth centuries, investigative reporting came about and became a big force. Then you had people—including Andrew Carnegie and Woodrow Wilson—dreaming about different ways of achieving peace internationally.

If you look at the new ideas and institutions that had to be invented to go along with the transition to an urban-industrial national economy, you start to say, "Are we at that same exact kind of moment, where the big story in the next couple of decades is the nature of social and political innovation—why it happens, where it comes from, does it take hold?" In a very dramatic way, it's a parallel course. It's worth looking a bit more methodically—and that's what I'm trying to do—at where these areas of innovation are and need to be. Solving the problems that face us in the environment and in conflicts of values is going to require new ideas. Going back to a knee-jerk kind of governmental regulation is not going to fix a lot of the problems. For instance, universal health insurance is a great idea, and I don't think any country in the world can pay for it at any sort of high level.

Since this is an age that's going to require questioning old assumptions and inventing new ways of solving problems, then you naturally turn to the philanthropic sector, which is social venture capital. It's the only flexible social R&D money that exists. What I'm trying to understand and help to accelerate is how philanthropy doesn't do the old things the old ways, but figures out new ways to tackle new challenges. I think that it's a very exciting opportunity, and a fascinating story to follow.

Right now in the United States, about $200 billion a year is given away, and there are about 56,000 foundations. Globally, philanthropy has grown quite rapidly in the last 10 years, but we don't have numbers for it. The low estimate for the intergenerational transfer of wealth in the next 50 years is $40 trillion. If past trends hold true, something like a third of that will go into the voluntary sector. In addition, the explosion of wealth that's part of the transition to the knowledge economy has resulted in a generation of people who've made money and are now living donors, and they're giving away money in all kinds of new ways. Pierre Omidyar, who invented eBay in his apartment, has created what may one day be a great new foundation, called Omidyar. He's in his 30s. He could easily be guiding his foundation for 50 years.

That's just one of many stories like that. Bill Gates is the most famous one. He's in his 40s, and he has already created the largest philanthropic institution. In a funny way, he's doing for twenty-first century public health what Rockefeller did for the beginning of the twentieth century, only he's doing it globally. He sees that money invested and resources leveraged in very creative ways can fill gaps that neither the government nor the markets are going to fill.

These people are at the very beginning of their careers. You have George Soros and Ted Turner making fortunes in media and finance and giving away lots of money in their lifetimes. Our estimates are that the total amount of money given away in the U.S. in year-2000 constant dollars will be closer to $300 billion on an annual basis by 2010. Because the installed base of money is already higher, the cumulative amount of money given away by American foundations in the next 10 years will be greater than the 25 years previous, even with the downturn.

When you look at the system of philanthropy, you've got many—and much more diverse—players. You have not only givers in the United States, but lots of rich people in other countries getting involved in philanthropy in their countries. You've got Hispanics and African Americans getting involved in philanthropy. You've got women involved in philanthropy in new ways. You've got celebrity sports figures increasingly involved in philanthropy. What it means is that the image of American philanthropy as the boring, bureaucratic foundation in New York City run by an older academic white male is just getting exploded. Lots of these new givers aren't going to set up foundations at all. They're going to participate in giving circles like

Social Venture Partners or they're going to have donor-advised funds. They're going to have multiple vehicles for giving money away.

Even though it's larger, more diverse, and more complex, social capital is still, relatively speaking, a very small amount. In their lifetimes, Rockefeller and Carnegie together gave away the equivalent of a federal budget. They gave away something like $13 billion, and the federal budget was roughly $11 billion at the time. Today, to equal one U.S. federal budget, the 400 richest people in the world would have to give away all of their net worth—twice.

Philanthropy's Fluid Money Can Move to Solve Problems Fast

John Petersen ∘ One of the wonderful things about America and the United States is that unlike any other country or society in the world, we have this stratum that's built around volunteerism and philanthropy. Nobody else has those kinds of mechanisms and foundations. They have extraordinary resources and increasingly they're starting to talk to each other and coordinate. This is part of what gives me hope because if you can start to articulate an alternative to an underlying problem and communicate it effectively, then you can start to move resources in this new direction. Then there are corporate foundations and corporate giving as well as corporate policies and decisions about where they invest and spend their money. This is fast money that can turn quickly; particularly in business, people can make decisions in weeks or months. Governments can't make a decision; it takes forever.

Our Gilded Age's Social Innovations Will Come Too

Katherine Fulton ∘ One hundred years ago, when the country was making the transition to an urban-industrial national economy, there were three important philanthropic inventions. One was the invention of the private foundation by Rockefeller. There had been various kinds of trusts set up in other ways, but the notion that you could set up a general-purpose endowment in perpetuity, that controls its own funds, was a new idea when the twentieth century began.

A few years later, in the Midwest, two other kinds of institutions were invented. One was the precursor of the United Way, which I once heard jokingly called "putting all your begs in one ask-it." But the notion of putting a portfolio of organizations together and aggregating donations was a new one. It was suited to cities that were growing and new organizations that were coming about to solve these new problems in cities. Then you had the invention of the community foundation. Obviously, most people aren't as rich as John D. Rockefeller was, but people have enough resources to not necessarily want to give their money to a single nonprofit. Maybe they want it to serve their community in perpetuity. So the notion of a community foundation came into existence. People could give a small endowment and keep it in trust at a community foundation. Other people would do the same, and the resources would then be used to benefit that community.

There's a lot of debate about the actual influence of tax policy, but it certainly is clear that a lot of very wealthy people get into philanthropy because their tax advisors advise them to.

I believe we are now living in another transformative moment in philanthropy. We're going to see new kinds of regulations, and we're seeing the birth of new institutional forms. It's the emergence of a new definition of organized philanthropy. That system that was created by foundations, community foundations, the United Way, and tax deductions was a system that grew through the twentieth century and came to define what we thought of as organized philanthropy. My hypothesis is that while that system will continue to exist, it is now morphing into something else that we can't yet fully understand or see. I think there's a chance that it could be much more effective, and could actually catalyze and accelerate social and political innovation. But it's not a no-brainer. The system could change in ways that could do new harm.

The dominant philanthropic institutions were invented by the last great Gilded Age donors. We're in a new Gilded Age. A lot of these people have a lot of money, and they're trying to think about the meaning of their life and their legacy, and how to leave their mark. And we now have new technology that makes it possible to connect people and ideas in completely new ways.

A Marketplace for Social Entrepreneurs

Katherine Fulton • There are great people in business; there are great people in government; there are great people in the third sector, which some people call the voluntary sector, the civil sector, the social sector—there are all kinds of names for it. What's really interesting is not where they are, but what they do and are able to do together. As a social investor, you don't care. You care about whether the person has a good idea, will he be able to make it work, will it scale. It doesn't matter what kind of organization she's in. You're going to see much more of that.

The dream a lot of people have is to create a marketplace that pulls together people who want to invest money in social things. Can there be metrics to measure the performance of these organizations, and therefore could you aggregate money in a way that makes life easier for the nonprofits, not harder? Nobody knows whether the metrics can be created or not. In the for-profit world, the metric is profit. What's the metric to measure the performance and the impact of a nonprofit?

A great invention of the twentieth century was to allow individual small investors to be able to pool their resources with other investors and get a good return, with very little investment of their own time and without having to be experts. Could that mutual fund model work for philanthropy? Right now, if you want to give away $5,000 for an issue, you give to whoever asks you or to who you know, and that may or may not be very connected to what would really make a difference. What if there were a way to know that very good, knowledgeable people had put together this portfolio of organizations that each have a piece of the problem of solving homelessness? It's a $50 million fund that foundations and individuals are contributing to, and it could be very strategic, connected, and effective.

Realigning Socially Responsible Pension Funds and the Economy

Hunter Lovins ∘ Most people feel profoundly disempowered. Take, for example, pension funds. Pension funds have assets equivalent roughly to 46 percent of the U.S. GDP. If you could get those funds shifted in a sustainable direction, you could have an enormous impact on how companies do business. This is a pool of capital that could be used to implement the ideas of natural capitalism. And it's not. If anything, it is being invested in the most conventional ways imaginable.

Why? If you look at pension funds, they're made up of people who would want to be value-driven investors, who ought to care about issues like sustainability. And yet, the guys who make the decisions, the pension fund trustees, feel disempowered. They may care about the values of their union, but they have no idea how to implement them, so they have hired professional investment experts to manage their money, believing that this is obedience to fiduciary responsibility. These experts disempower the trustees even further by saying that fiduciary responsibility not only means that you have to hire us to make your decisions, but you cannot invest with your values in mind because you have to, as a trustee, receive the highest rate of return in a short period. They erroneously claim that socially and environmentally responsible investments are not as profitable. Recently, such firms as Domini have disproved this.

At a recent conference, the chair of the California Public Employees Retirement System said it best: "If you think about what a pension fund needs, we really don't care if one company does spectacularly well in the next quarter as against another company. We're so big, we're invested in essentially every company in the economy. What we care about is that the entire economy is healthy 20, 50 years from now." As a result, CALPERS has undertaken to screen its investments. This is a first step to shifting some of the biggest blocks of capital in the economy to more restorative investments.

The Third Sector Will Initiate Change in Other Sectors

Katherine Fulton ∘ Confusion is an important part of the story. It used to be very clear that there were for-profit organizations, nonprofit organizations, and governmental organizations in this country. In other countries, those sectors don't exist in the same way. Part of the story is that the boundaries among these things are not so neat anymore. A non-governmental organization often gets money from the government, which is why sociologist Manuel Castells calls them "neogovernmental" organizations. It's not unusual in any way for there to be substantial government funding. Partly that's because the government has tried to outsource to the social sector or the voluntary sector some things that are better done in more traditional charity models than by government bureaucracy.

Then you have the confusion between institutions and movements and citizenship. Those are really three quite different things. When people talk about civil society, they're often talking about what it means to be a member of a democracy, not a customer of a business. Civil society is an umbrella that covers me as a citizen, and it might cover me as a giver to a nonprofit organization or a participant in a movement of some kind. In general, people think of the third sector as anything that isn't business or government. So there are lots of definitions going on.

When you think about where change will be initiated, it's most likely to be initiated outside of government and business. Why does a big corporation change its behavior? Sometimes it's through visionary leadership, but usually it's because they've been pressured to do so somehow by a constituency. I think it's fabulous that BP and Shell and some of the great companies in the world are now deeply engaged in issues of sustainability. Twenty-five years ago, they didn't do that. It took the pressure of a global environmental movement to get that to happen. The same is true about regulatory laws being passed by governments in the environmental area. As

Frederick Douglass once said, "Power never conceded anything without a demand. It never has and it never will."

History Will Remember the Social Entrepreneurs

Paul Hawken ◦ The constraint of capital, the constraint of growth, the constraint of competition, and the constraint of time to market or time to profit—these are huge constraints that encumber what corporations can and cannot do. There is an underlying assumption that we do what we can within the constraints that are imposed upon us. I understand that. It's why the truly innovative acts of entrepreneurship that are occurring now and will continue to occur are no longer in business.

Social entrepreneurship—that's where the action is. That's where the real innovators are. That's where you'll find the people who will be remembered 50 to 100 years from now. We won't remember a single person who's in business except as a footnote. Every single person who runs a corporation today, including Mr. Gates, will be forgotten. Their names may live on as a foundation or a residual pool of capital but nothing they've done will be seen as valuable 50 to 100 years from now. Nothing. The real value being added today is by people who are outside of the business framework.

The world needs to take care of itself. You know the numbers. Nearly 3 billion live on less than $2 a day, 2 billion on less than $1 a day. A billion people cannot work who want to work. That number has been growing faster than employment for the last 25 years. Eight hundred million people are malnourished. Twelve million children die every year because of malnutrition and disease. It is the people who devote their lives to addressing these issues who will be remembered.

The Case for Greater Business Leadership

The New Reformation: The Shift in Power to Business

Jay Ogilvy ◦ I call it the new reformation. The first reformation was the separation of church from state. The Pope really was calling the shots prior to that and health, education, and welfare were in the hands of the church. Then you had Martin Luther banging the thesis on the door and got a separation of church and state with a tremendous amount of power passing from the heads of church to the heads of state: kings, presidents, prime ministers. Now we're going through a second reformation. Just as we saw in the transition from the religious era to the political era, in the transition from the political era to the economic era we're seeing this tremendous gushing of power from the heads of state to the marketplace. That's where the power is. That's not Democrat or Republican; that's historical. A long-term secular one-way door. It's a shift. This isn't to say that politics goes away any more than the churches have gone away. They just kind of take a back seat.

I think we are solidly in the economic era but that some folks in the marketplace have not really woken up to the fact that the old boundaries between the public sector and the private sector have really shifted. Along with that increased power come increased responsibilities. For example, healthcare, education, and welfare are largely run by the private sector. The old model was that you would get your education from the public sector at the beginning of your life, and that's good all the rest of your life. Now, partly because of the pace of change and partly because of the inadequacy of that education, corporations have to spend billions and billions of dollars on educating their workers.

If I were to throw out a guess for the successor to the religious-to-political-to-economic era, my candidate would be aesthetic or environmental. Here the sources of value are not religious. It's not about political categories like justice or the freedom of slaves or colonies. It's not just economic categories either—value in wealth as we would ordinarily measure it in terms of head of cattle or acres of land or tons of steel. The sources of value would really be more aesthetic: beauty, laughter, and cultural and artistic value. But that's too ridiculously long off to entertain.

Not Government, Religion, or Academia, but Business Leads

John Petersen ∘ The only people who are going to solve the world's problems are people who metaphorically dress like us, who wear suits and ties. That's because we're the ones with the resources and the intellectual capability to solve the problems. If you look within the social system, business is the place that really makes the difference. Businesses have the shortest response time. As the world changes, they adapt. They have a profit motive and quarterly processes for feedback. They have the most resources and the most to lose in the short term. Government, academia, and religion never lead; business leads. That's why it's so cool that the chairmen of BP and Shell are getting out there on environmental issues. They're saying, "We're in the energy business and we have to look out for a future where there isn't any petroleum," and they're investing in renewables and alternatives. They're the ones with the long view.

Global Commerce and Collapsing Space Can Distribute Wealth

Danny Hillis ∘ I believe that we're beginning to address the issue of wealth distribution. Too slowly, yes, but it is starting to happen. One of the problems has been that we've been so dominated by our spatial organization. In the past, if you had a lot of resources near you or you had a good system around you, you could be very rich. People who didn't have such an effective system with so many resources were poor. That's the sort of seed that created this inequity in the first place. I see lots of signs that the spatial division of things is becoming less and less fundamental and less and less viable. I see more and more people interacting with people all over.

When my friend Nathan Myhrvold built his house in Seattle, he went to the Internet to look at stone vendors and found one in India. He bought directly from India. You have one of the richest people in the world interacting with one of the poorest countries in the world. All of a sudden, two people who wouldn't have been able to interact directly before are now doing so and exchanging resources and becoming a part of the same system. That's a physical resource example.

Information, which is becoming the commodity of the most value, flows even more easily across space. Encyclopaedia Britannica is finding that somebody in India can edit an article just as well as someone in Chicago. In fact, there's a flow of that work to India because they're doing it more cost effectively, and over the long run that will cause an economic balance. The people in Bangalore will become more like the people in Chicago, in terms of the resources they have access to, the people that they're connected with, the system that they're a part of, and so on. That, to me, is a very positive sign of some of these fundamental problems getting worked out.

Competing Capitalisms and the Limits of Market Mechanisms

Jay Ogilvy ∘ From having been pretty involved in lefty politics in the '60s and '70s, I came to the realization that this is just not where the action is. The action is in the marketplace. So, in living out that transition from trying to make the world a better place by political action to saying, "No. What really changes people's lives is the market and the corporate world," the next stage is to begin to see the limits of the marketplace.

What became clear to me, indeed partly by accident of doing a bunch of work in telecom and education and healthcare, is the following idea: Wherever you have a mandate to universal service, market mechanisms alone will not be adequate, for slightly different reasons in different industries. In telecom, it's elegantly obvious in the idea that telecom is a kind of natural monopoly. It's absurd to have two telephones on your desk—one on one end to contact half the people you know and another one on the other that hooks you into the other half. The ideal communications system hooks everybody to everybody. I don't want a system that some people can't afford to join. I want everybody on that system.

There are slightly different reasons in education and healthcare. In education, we're all worse off the higher the level of illiteracy in society. In healthcare, we're all worse off if a bunch of people are walking around either sick and therefore infectious or without health insurance, causing my health insurance bill to be higher because I'm cross-subsidizing their trips to the emergency room. In these three industries—health, education, and telecom—you have these fairly clear demonstrations of the limits of market mechanisms. Then you ask, "OK, what is the residual role for the public sector? How do we want to influence or manage markets?"

It's the underlying drama of competing capitalisms. The U.S. is the Wild West: unrestricted, privatize everything. Japan and Southeast Asia are too far in the extreme of "let's pick winners" and "we will thumb our noses at marketplace mechanisms" in order to keep our crony network in place. Over the long, long run Europe may have got it right, with a fairly strong welfare state where you keep the safety nets in place. You do try to look out for people and you don't have 44 million people running around without health insurance.

A Framework for Corporate Social Responsibility in the World

Betty Sue Flowers ∘ I have never had an academic model arise out of a meeting of businesspeople. But one actually did emerge at a meeting I recently attended in Aspen—a model of corporate social responsibility that began with an idea from Roger Martin, dean of the School of Management at Toronto. The idea was then developed into a model in the seminar, and Roger developed it further for an article in Harvard Business Review.

Imagine three spaces and call them A, B, C. Think of A as the space of rules and laws. In countries like the U.S., we have very well-delineated rules of the game that allow us to prosper; sometimes American business forgets that. In that space you can call the corporate leader "a good citizen" if he or she is someone who obeys the rules and practices. In underdeveloped countries that A space is very thin.

The B space is very interesting. It is not yet part of the common structure of rules, but you can come up with new ways of doing business in that space that both benefit the society as a whole and make money. In the B space you might call someone "a leader in corporate social responsibility." That's the space of leadership.

The C space deals with society's needs, too, but in this space, meeting society's needs means that you would actually lose money. I called that space "hero/martyr" because you can be a hero and your company could also be martyred. For example, if you are a multinational company, and you decide to divulge all the extra payments you're making to a host country to do business, the host government will boot you out, and you'll lose your investment. That may not be socially responsible for your stockholders.

A corporation should want a large A space that allows a big B space and relatively few unmet needs in the C area. How do you migrate from C to B or from B to A in society as a whole? There are two ways to migrate from C to B. One is technology. For example, if you decide to build fuel-cell vehicles, but you don't have a good fuel cell, you will go out of business because it isn't economically viable. But if an invention makes the fuel cell really viable, then the leader of the pack breaks out in the B space. C can also become B when the rules of the game—in A—are changed. If tax policy began to favor fuel-cell vehicles, the first-mover martyr would become a first-mover leader. You migrate from C to A by making new laws or rules.

All three boxes exist in each country, but the amount of space in each box differs. We have a pretty good A space in this country. But if you operate globally, the boxes look different: A is small, B is not so big, and C is huge. There are a lot of social needs, but because the rules of the game aren't established, you'll be a martyr if you try to meet them. Globally, what you want are healthy B and A spaces. We have this in some countries but not others. That's why corporate leaders have to start thinking in terms of global governance—not government, but governance.

The Corporation as Cult: The Limits to What Business Can Do

Paul Hawken ○ There are some very good people in big corporations doing great things. But the fact is that everybody who works for a corporation lives within a belief system that prohibits the First Amendment. There's no free speech. If anybody thinks there is, they should test it out and see if I'm wrong. What most don't see is that they live within what has been traditionally known as a cult. In this case, these are commercial cults. You can distinguish a cult by the fact that they usually have charismatic leaders, either dead or alive. They have a tendency to have the tallest building in town. They use borrowed language—that is to say, language that is specific to a place or an institutional belief. There is sleep deprivation and a dress code that is particular to their belief system. You go right down the list, and there's no difference between a corporation and a cult.

The Two Ways to Spark Change: Crisis or Lighting a Candle

Katherine Fulton ∘ Let's be clear what we're talking about. Can there be a fundamental shift in the absence of a crisis? I believe it's possible, but not likely. Yes, you could imagine that all of this gets accelerated by horrible things such as the terrorist attacks. But what we've been looking at is philanthropy, the civil sector, the creation of a global civil society to match the global economy. We've been looking at a number of sources of hope.

When Eleanor Roosevelt died, Adlai Stevenson said something that I am sure has been uttered through the ages in other contexts, which is that she would rather light a candle than curse the darkness. What I'm most interested in, in my life, is finding the people who are lighting those candles, and helping them turn those flames into a roaring blaze. In the absence of a crisis that would spur and mobilize forces in a different way, that, to me, is the source of the greatest hope.

The Three Levels of Change: Macro, Organizational, Personal

Hunter Lovins ∘ What we're really looking at is: How do you implement big-scale social change? The ideas contained in the notion of Natural Capitalism make so much sense. What does it take to get an idea like this into practice? Obviously, all ideas are implemented by people. So people are going to be a big component of getting any big idea implemented.

So how do people go about change? It seems to us that it occurs on at least three levels—sometimes simultaneously, sometimes one level has to go first. They're all interrelated, and you have to understand the dynamics of all of the levels and be prepared to work on all the levels to get a big idea implemented. For example, there is the macro level of systems: legal, political, economic, the whole influence of globalization on companies. These all have huge implications for how, say, a corporate decision-maker makes decisions.

Then there is the mid-level of organizations—how each organization is different, learns differently, accepts change differently, how change proceeds through an organization differently. And understanding the sort of work that Peter Senge does with organizational learning and dynamics is just as critical as understanding the big political systems. Understanding how the organization with which you're dealing differs from another organization that you may have dealt with successfully in the past is critical to getting these ideas implemented.

At the same time, there is the personal level. Each of us, as individuals, is more or less amenable to change, to new ideas, to learning, to doing things in a different way. At the same time, particularly in today's environment, we think there is a hunger in people for what is real, what is authentic, a hunger to feel motivated, to want to be a part of something that's bigger than they are. So at the individual level not only is there a whole host of barriers, there also are motivating forces. And understanding those in today's society—what is it that makes people afraid of change and what is it that makes people hungry for change—is critical to getting an idea like natural capitalism implemented.

The Need for Wise Business Leaders to Will the Good

Betty Sue Flowers • Whether business leaders want it or not, they have a leadership role in the world. Leaders have certain responsibilities, and one is to "will the good." Now our problem is that we are having a pause of will at the moment, while events cascade around us. We don't know what to will because we don't know what the good is. That's a deeply philosophical question: What is the good?

In the past the business of business was business. Now we are all linked together. You can't just do business anymore because you're connected to everything else. Real business leaders have always known this, but they could do things in their local communities. If you are running a company in Detroit you try to do X, Y or Z in Detroit. What happens if your responsibility is the entire world and not just Detroit? Can you possibly do anything, and, if so, what is it you can best do? What is it to will the good in a global context?

We need wise and philosophical thinking from business leaders. They have only had to think strategically and tactically in the past. They've never had to think on behalf of the whole. The best businesspeople I have met are certainly up to the task. I am glad the world is in their hands at this point in history. But it takes all of us, including other kinds of thought leaders, to articulate the ideas and create the tools that help everyone think about the whole.

Typically people transform themselves and think in a wider way when they face crisis. As Dr. Samuel Johnson said, "When a man knows he is to be hanged in a fortnight, it concentrates his mind wonderfully." True, perhaps, but I hope it won't take that. We are not in a true crisis yet. I hope people will not just wait to respond to crisis but will proactively do the kind of work that's required. This includes real work on the self, too. It requires spiritual discipline individually—like training for the Olympics, only spiritually. You have to start that now to be in shape when the time comes.

I would also hope that people will see a true crisis or huge opportunity in advance so they can be ready for it. That's why I want to develop this way of thinking out ahead of what actually happens in the world. That's why we should have a sense of urgency even if things seem to be pretty good right now. My sense of urgency doesn't come from impending crisis; it comes from a need to be prepared for anything—including opportunity.

Much Will Depend on Who Will Empower People and Lead

Katherine Fulton ∘ I'm really fascinated by how everywhere I go, in every context, people feel powerless. From the outside, corporations look really powerful and have tremendous resources. But when you do work with large corporations, you often hear from people about the ways in which their choices are constrained, the ways in which power is constrained. It's the same in other, very different places. From the outside, foundations look really powerful. From the outside, NGOs look really dangerous. They can force big oil companies to rethink their plans for disposing of oil platforms. They have a lot of power because they have the press behind them and the citizens behind them. From the outside, the federal government looks really big and has a lot of money and ought to be able to do a lot of things—and occasionally, like in the case of the military, it does. But from the inside, everybody feels that they don't have anything like the power or control they feel they need.

One of the big questions for the next period of time is where leadership comes from, where it is that people step out. Remember the movie *Network*, where the guy throws his window up and says, "I'm mad as hell and I'm not going to take it anymore!"? I have this fantasy of people standing up in the business community together, not just alone, and saying, "The rules of the game aren't serving any of us anymore, and we're not going to play by them anymore!" Occasionally there are business leaders who say that to the investment community. They usually get punished, but not always.

We're caught in this funny kind of paradox of power and powerlessness. We see how complex these systems are and how daunting the challenges are at this moment in history, and so every person individually feels small and unable to do anything. I think that going forward a lot will depend on the leaders who do emerge and where they emerge from. Much will depend on the degree to which those leaders can inspire people to see how much power we actually do possess, both individually and collectively.

Continuing the Journey
Implications

"We're moving out of an age of control and entering an age of adaptability—out of an age of coherence and into an age of combinatorial richness."

Danny Hillis

"The more-than-human natural world is full of incredible technologies and incredible engineering feats, so I'm very pro-technology and pro-engineering. The question is always: What is adaptive and what is maladaptive?"

Janine Benyus

"The attitude that we're shifting into is viewing the world as chaotic. You're never going to understand it. You're never going to control it. Instead, you have to be responsive. You have to make sure that when an opportunity arises you can take advantage of it. That's much more the attitude behind network economies and learning companies, the kind of agile organizational structures that are emerging. What's important about them is not that they're in control, but that they're able to adapt quickly, to redefine themselves."

Danny Hillis

"We're starting to realize simple rules, just like people in chaos theory are realizing that very simple rules lead to beautifully complex results. Well, the simple rule for an organism is 'keep yourself alive and keep your offspring alive,' meaning your offspring a thousand generations from now."

Janine Benyus

"Whether business leaders want it or not, they have a leadership role in the world. Leaders have certain responsibilities, and one is to 'will the good.'"

Betty Sue Flowers

Fifteen years ago GBN set out to persuade business leaders that the future was unpredictable and would not be a straight line projection of the past. It has been increasingly easy to make that case in these turbulent times. A second challenge was to demonstrate that exploring the future required fresh ideas and insight as much as rigorous data and facts, creative synthesis as much as logical analysis, and diversity of perspective as much as focused expertise. This book embodies these ideas.

Our journey began in the more familiar field of finance and economics, where we contemplated the patterns behind the turmoil of the past few years, before venturing into the decade ahead. We then traversed the terrain of geopolitics with its many crosscurrents, delved into cultures and societies around the world, and entered the realm of values and beliefs, including religion, spirituality, and the outer reaches of human potential. We examined emerging technologies that ranged from manipulating atoms to searching for signs of aliens in space. We became immersed in the complex world of science, and zeroed in on controversial developments in biology. Then we roamed the domain of the environment, coming to terms with the very real possibility of severe climate change. And we ended by contemplating our era from a civilizational perspective, taking a long view that extends not just decades but centuries into the future. We hope you found this journey through the new terrain stimulating and along the way you picked up some new ideas and insights into how the future may unfold.

At the start of the book, we promised that we would reach no definitive conclusion, offer no distinct prediction, and provide no step-by-step methodology for success. You chose to join us on this journey just the same—so perhaps we can make some assumptions about you. You are probably deeply curious, comfortable with ambiguity, able to grasp the mounting complexity of the world, and inclined to be suspicious of simplistic approaches and easy answers. We expect that you, along with other readers, share another characteristic—a deep desire to help make a real and positive difference in your organization as it navigates through an era of uncertainty. Whether from positions of power and leadership, or from more modest platforms of personal influence, we believe that every reader can help their business or organization adapt more effectively to the changing environment. And we believe that this need has never been greater—and will surely grow in the decade ahead.

Over the last 20 years, the need to build *competitive advantage* has become increasingly accepted and understood. More and more sophisticated tools and approaches for market analysis, industry modeling, customer intelligence, and competitive positioning have been developed and applied with ever-increasing effectiveness. This did not occur in a vacuum, but in a context that demanded such focus: a world of market deregulation, converging industries, mounting customer choice, increasingly demanding financial markets, and ever fiercer competition.

Competitive advantage is rooted consequently in understanding your marketplace. In the years ahead, we believe the new terrain for business will introduce an additional imperative for continued success, namely, *adaptive advantage*, which is rooted in understanding the world. Adaptive advantage will come to those best able to adapt swiftly and wisely to the changing external environment that we've explored in the last 300 pages. This requires significant improvement in two linked areas: the ability to anticipate and sense change, and the capacity to respond quickly and coherently. These twin demands, neither of them easy, will set the developmental agenda for many organizations in the coming decade.

Within the next 10 years we will surely see the invention and evolution of increasingly sophisticated tools for making these improvements and securing adaptive advantage. While we have been developing our own approaches for the last 15 years, we do not pretend to have any easy answers. There still is a great deal to be learned, much of it involving trial and error. But in the spirit of shared learning, we will describe some of the approaches that GBN uses. We won't tell you what to do, but rather, tell you what we do. With this in mind, we see three main areas that could help you achieve adaptive advantage: thinking differently, learning differently, and acting differently. In each category we offer a few tools and approaches worth considering.

Thinking Differently

For sustained effectiveness, business leaders will have to increase the complexity of their thought to mirror the complexity of their environment. There are three related ways of evolving one's ability to do just that: *outside-in thinking, connective thinking*, and finally *scenaric thinking*.

Outside-In Thinking

For years GBN has used the simple bulls-eye graphic on the next page to depict three different levels of focus that apply to any business organization. The inner ring refers to internal focus—the values, sense of purpose, organizational structure, proprietary systems, and talent that define and differentiate the organization and bring it to life. The middle ring we describe as market focus, which directly relates to competitive advantage. This focus concentrates on market size and dynamics, new products, customers, competitors, partnerships, and so on. The outer ring represents external focus—looking at the broader issues of geopolitics, economics, governance, society, sustainability, technology—in short, the terrain described in this book.

OUTSIDE-IN THINKING

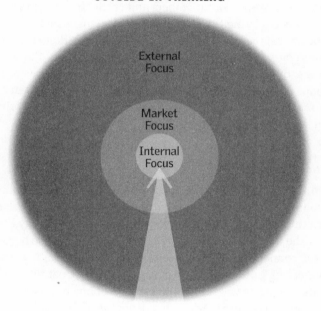

Figure 1

Most strategy or thinking about business development adopts an inside-out trajectory, starting with the organization's purpose and core strengths, and then exploring its marketplaces and competitive positioning, and only then looking externally for broader shifts that might matter. Much of the time that trajectory is entirely appropriate, but not when you are seeking to boost your sensitivity to changes in the external business environment. That's because there is one consistent problem with inside-out thinking. By the time you get to the external focus, you have subconsciously introduced so many filters that you're not seeing the whole external world at all—you're only seeing a very small subset of it. As a result you can miss the big changes that are going to matter the most.

These unintended filters are your implicit assumptions, based on your past experience, about what matters to your organization. They define what you perceive to be relevant. These assumptions may prove increasingly flawed in the decade ahead as more and more external factors from far outside your experience impinge profoundly upon the business environment. But no matter how hard you try to let your assumptions go, if you start from the inside-out, you'll probably never accomplish it.

At GBN, we encourage our members and clients to think from the outside-in, to start by considering the kind of external changes that might, over time, impact our markets and our organizations. Of course, there are still some parameters and filters on our thinking, otherwise we would suffer from an overload of ideas. But they are much less restrictive and allow us to think more openly about the many potential changes that could be important. By starting from the outside-in, we get a fuller list of issues that we can prioritize according to which might matter most to us over time.

Connective Thinking

Another thinking skill that is becoming more critical is the ability to make creative connections between apparently separate ideas. This is closely related to systems thinking, the topic of superb theoretical work by Jay Forrester and others over the past several decades. But when applied to the terrain of future possibilities, connective thinking becomes a different creative challenge. It is about connecting dots in new ways to discover new patterns of possibility. Chances are the future will not unfold because of one big change but because multiple changes converge. Adaptive advantage, therefore, will partly come from making quicker, smarter connections across varied domains.

Many of you will have already started to make some interesting connections between the ideas contained in different parts of this book. Let's explore one example of how "connecting the dots" can reveal a radical possibility of enormous potential consequence over the next 10 to 15 years—the reversal of the globalizing industrial production and distribution system that has been established over the last several decades. Start with John Arquilla who gave a one in four chance that a terrorist group would set off a weapon of mass destruction in a major city this decade. Let's say that does happen. There's one dot: Americans might become more isolationist and fearful. Paul Hawken argued that what today looks like a rag-tag anti-globalization movement might grow into a powerful global coalition aimed at multinational corporations. That's dot two: Carrying out far-flung business operations around the world could suddenly become much more difficult. Next Kevin Kelly talked about how environmentalism is almost becoming a new American religion, a bedrock belief held by people of all persuasions. Dot three: What happens as people become acutely sensitive to the environmental impact of global transport and industrialization in developing countries? Then Amory Lovins argued that the energy system is poised for a radical shift to a decentralized hydrogen economy. Dot four: If energy becomes radically decentralized, surely other operations will follow suit. Janine Benyus argued the case for biomimicry—that humans will start to emulate how nature self-assembles in a benign, sustainable way. There's dot five: The ability to build things cleanly and cheaply in small-scale operations. And finally, add Steven Weber's speculation that an American biotech-led economic boom this decade might require much lower levels of foreign trade.

Connect these apparently random dots and we can see the glimmer of a very different future in which the current logic of production at the locus of lowest cost, followed by complex global distribution, becomes less important. Instead, production could occur much, much closer to the point of consumption—a switch that would pose new challenges and opportunities for regions, governments, corporations, and citizens alike.

Scenaric Thinking

Thinking with an external focus, and making new connections between disparate developments, inevitably leads you to contemplate many "What-ifs" about the future. And the more we explore the future, the more obvious it becomes that we cannot predict it—there are simply too many variables in play, too many embedded uncertainties. But that does not mean we should focus exclusively on the short term. Indeed, much of our work at GBN continues to involve helping organizations tackle two different issues. One is denial of uncertainty—assuming that the future will look pretty much like a projection of the past. The other is overcoming the fundamental challenge of paralysis by uncertainty—abandoning all attempts to take a long view because everything is too complex, too crazy.

GBN continues to refine a well-tested methodology that enables us to anticipate the future without committing either the folly of trying to predict it, or the mistake of ignoring it. Our approach to taking a long view involves "scenario thinking"—a process of developing several very different but plausible stories of how the future might unfold in ways that are relevant to organizations. Scenarios are not forecasts, based on single models of the world, with perhaps a best-case and worst-case adjustment. Rather, they are internally consistent stories, structured around several crucially important uncertainties about the future. By providing multiple plausible perspectives on what could happen, scenarios enable our clients to better understand and challenge the dominant assumptions under which their organizations operate. Moreover, each individual scenario (we generally write three or four) can be used as a "wind tunnel" within which we can test and refine existing strategies and imagine new ones. Scenarios, therefore, help to boost our preparedness for different credible futures, while also providing innovation spaces for discovering new opportunities for the future.

Above all, scenarios are stories. Stories are an ancient and remarkably powerful form of communication. They are the vehicles through which values and beliefs are communicated in myths. They are how communities, even cultures, are sustained. Scenarios, stories of the future, are narratives that create meaning and convey possibilities to others, which they can then evolve and re-tell to new audiences. Scenarios enable new ideas about the future to take root and spread across an organization—helping to overcome the inertia and denial that can so easily make the future a dangerous place.

How are these scenarios constructed? Actually, the interview project that led to this book was designed to inform a set of scenarios that we built with and for GBN members. Every year GBN hosts meetings that bring together our corporate members and remarkable thinkers. In the fall of 2001, we gathered to explore "What's Next?" with a special focus on the external environment through 2010 and its implications for the business agenda. We began by brainstorming dozens of the big uncertainties for the coming decade. After much discussion and debate, we selected two themes that were both highly uncertain and important. One focused on the zeitgeist or global consciousness in 2010—would the world be more fragmented or more integrated? Would people describe the prevailing spirit of the time as cohesive or fractured? The other uncertainty revolved around the values shaping society 10 years from now. Would market values predominate, leading businesses to concentrate exclusively on profit and market share? Or would non-market values like community, the environment, and social justice rise significantly—even becoming equally important? These became our two intersecting axes of uncertainty with the four quadrants of the matrix defining four scenario worlds, as seen on the next page.

For each of these worlds, we created very different stories about how the future might unfold—complete with names, characters, and timelines—and thought through how businesses would fare. One world situated in the quadrant defined as fragmented and driven by market values was titled "I'm

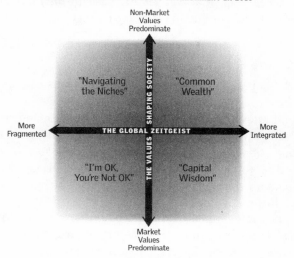

Figure 2

OK, You're Not OK." This is a volatile world of weak government and social turmoil in which successful businesses create their own order. On the other hand, in "Capital Wisdom" (integrated and market values), globalization helps pull the world together with business leading the way. "Common Wealth" (more integration, non-market values) is a world where severe crisis leads to the invention of new institutions to address global inequities—and business corporations play an important part. "Navigating the Niches" (fragmented, non-market values) is a radically decentralized world where people cluster around communities defined by beliefs. In this scenario, trade slows, multinational corporations suffer, and business is bleak.

These quick and dirty scenarios were developed in one day—and were brought to life on stage that same evening by an improvisational theater group. Every few years, GBN also engages its members in a more rigorous and intensive process to produce a new set of global scenarios. We're currently in the midst of that work, which is drawing upon many of the ideas expressed in this book.

Learning Differently

Gaining adaptive advantage requires that business leaders not only think differently, but also learn differently. There are three ways we think this can be achieved: developing what we call *literacies for the future*, establishing *learning networks*, and conducting *learning journeys*.

Literacies for the Future

With so much happening in the world, so many drivers of change, so much uncertainty, how can we identify what we "don't know we don't know"—but actually should know—without being overwhelmed by information? This concern is frequently expressed by overworked executives, and has been the focus for much of our work at GBN. We have come to use the term "literacies for the future" to describe those major external developments that may have low impact on your business today, but might be hugely significant in defining your future. Typically, it is possible to learn enough about these areas to become more familiar with their potential impact upon your business without having to acquire great depth and expertise. It is a bit like learning enough of a foreign language to feel comfortable visiting the country, without pretending to have acquired true fluency.

Many of these literacies for the future are quite specific to a particular organization, and—as with scenarios—they are best developed in a customized exercise. However, given the significant shifts in the business environment that we anticipate will occur in the coming decade, we believe that there are also some common "literacies" emerging today. With that in mind, and as part of the GBN meeting mentioned above, we identified common topics that were likely to become more central to the business agenda—and therefore should become a focus for additional organizational learning. Three topics emerged very clearly as being major external developments that would shape the future but about which businesses are not sufficiently informed. Not surprisingly, there is some relationship between these three literacies and several of the domains in our new terrain map.

The first literacy is *BioFutures*, which essentially is a look at the convergence of many technologies—biotechnology, nanotechnology, computing and communication technologies, sensing technologies—at the molecular level. Just as technological convergence at the digital level created the platform for much innovation and disruption over the last 20 years, we expect convergence at the molecular level to create a platform for even more significant innovations and challenges over the coming decade. The second literacy is *Emergent Global Politics*. The next act in the drama of globalization may well lack a single consistent theme, such as the liberation of market power. But it will undoubtedly feature new actors interacting in unpredictable ways. There will be many geopolitical issues to track, including understanding the key hot spots, the motivations of the main regional and institutional actors, and sources of tension as well as sources of potential alignment. Our third generic literacy for the future is *Values and Cultures*. Western businesses have tended to assume that their values and dominant cultural norms are in the ascendancy, and that others will conform to them. That has proven to be only partly true over the last 20 years, and may prove to be even less reliable over the coming decade. We need to explore more rigorously that changing cultural landscape.

Today most organizations are underinformed about these aspects of the evolving global context for business. Achieving higher levels of understanding in these areas makes sense—at least for now. That brings up a final point about literacies for the future: They will keep changing as the future unfolds, and we catch glimmers of new surprises on the horizon.

Learning Networks

Identifying several core areas for focused learning is a beginning, not an end. It is equally important to remain open to a broad range of developments that might not fit within the chosen areas of focus. One way to achieve that breadth of exposure is by developing learning networks, both internal and external, that include members with a wide variety of expertise. These networks can consistently challenge and inform you. And because networks are among the most adaptable forms of organizations, they can quickly add members to address new needs and changing circumstances. Although effective people and organizations have always leveraged professional and personal relationships, we now have an unprecedented ability to grow global networks, and to use them productively.

At GBN our experience in creating and maintaining networks of both organizations and "remarkable people" has confirmed their value as sources of ideas and community. Making them work effectively, however, is not straightforward. Networks are not easy to design. In fact, there is something paradoxical about the idea of "designing" a network, precisely because they work best as emergent, free-flowing communities. Addressing this paradox requires both humility and nimbleness. You need humility to appreciate that any network you help establish will, if it succeeds, set its own agenda and grow in ways that you may not have anticipated. And you need nimbleness to ensure that the network serves its interests as well as your own—by generating ideas, insights, and knowledge about themes that matter to your organization. To be productive, networks require some form of facilitation. In an ideal world, your networks would be entirely self-directed and self-facilitated. However, in reality they will almost certainly require some nudges to catalyze, sustain, and conclude the conversations. There is a subtle balance to be struck between honoring the autonomy of the network to explore, and providing occasional direction to ensure purposeful communication.

There are other lessons that we have learned over 15 years of nurturing networks. For instance, in an increasingly diverse and complicated world, one pragmatic way to deal with complexity is through diversity. But by their very nature, networks tend more than hierarchies to be self-defining, and so are often rather homogenous. Because they emerge and hold together around some commonality of belief, interest, or concern, they can easily tend toward a uniformity of perspective that doesn't effectively stretch learning and challenge assumptions. This homogeneity requires constant attention, including turnover of membership. People's interests wax and wane, morph and reform over time. Your most active contributors may gradually lose interest in the topics your network chooses to explore, or might find their priorities shift significantly in view of life or career changes. It is useful to have an easy way for them to withdraw or place themselves on inactive status until they are motivated to re-engage more fully. At the same time, you must keep introducing new members as original ones fall away to ensure that a critical mass—in terms of numbers, perspectives, and active involvement—is retained.

The best networks are generous insofar as people share ideas openly and without explicit promise of return. But don't assume that anyone in your network will have an infinite capacity for unrewarded generosity. Whether it is access to the ideas of others, accelerated learning, explicit acknowledgement of contributions, plain good fun, or some other more commercial rewards for their input, over time everyone must see the mutuality of benefit if they are to remain motivated.

Although many members of a network will be very comfortable with the primary forms of interaction you have chosen, others will have different preferences. It is important to offer multiple ways in which members can choose to participate. Some are happy in online conversation, reading the thoughts of others and responding with their own in writing. Others like real-time interaction either through telephone conferences or face-to-face meetings and conversations. Inevitably considerations of economy and efficiency will force you to prioritize certain forms over others—but where possible it makes sense to design several different ways in which members can interact over the course of each year.

Finally, sustaining a networked learning community may call for some clear principles informing behavior, governing attribution, or establishing expectations. Ideally, rather than delivering them as centrally imposed rules, they should emerge from the network, and violations should be dealt with firmly but amicably by fellow members of the network as opposed to the initiating organization. By paying attention to all of these issues, it is possible, as we at GBN have discovered, to create networks that will provoke, inform, and accelerate learning—both in intended and unimagined ways.

Learning Journeys

Adaptive advantage also requires new, creative processes that accelerate and stimulate learning. Probably the most powerful learning process that we have developed is the highly immersive, experiential "Learning Journey." We have been conducting Learning Journeys with senior corporate executives and leaders of public agencies for 15 years and consistently find that they have a strong and lasting impact. Unlike fact-finding missions or benchmarking expeditions that often seek to substantiate preconceptions or prove hypotheses, Learning Journeys are truly exploratory. They push the envelope on what is known and redefine the boundaries of what is possible. They are designed with the explicit intention of introducing the participants to striking new experiences, places, people, and ideas. We strive to take people into situations that they would never experience in their normal daily lives—in a personal or professional capacity.

The British writer John Le Carré once wrote: "A desk is a dangerous place from which to view the world." It is crucial to get out into the world and be exposed to forces that might shape the future—or are already shaping the present in ways that are invisible to most of us. A Learning Journey is typically designed around a particular theme, but deliberately stretches far beyond the obvious and the everyday, providing an assortment of different visceral experiences. If the theme is technological change and the emergent generation, then the group might go into the physics lab of a university to view atoms through an electron microscope with graduate students who are breaking new ground in nanotechnology. The next visit might be to a detention center where incarcerated youth who produce an award-winning newspaper recite and discuss poetry about their lives in the inner city. The group might then proceed to the dilapidated but well-wired offices of a youth organization that coordinates anti-globalization protests around the world. The last stop might be a tiny startup to try out state-of-the-art virtual reality goggles designed by techies in their early twenties.

At the end of each day we reflect together upon all that we have observed. We share our biggest surprises, what we think is truly meaningful, and what is probably superficial. We identify the assumptions that we brought into the experience and now must challenge, make connections between our current business and what we have just witnessed, and imagine ways we might create new opportunities for the future. Finally we distill the core meaning from our journey, the most relevant learning for our business, the ways these insights must be taken back into the organization. And we explore what might now be done differently as a consequence.

The impact is often profound and permanent. Over the years we've undertaken many such journeys, bringing participants to people and places they are highly unlikely to have visited of their own accord. Not once has a group come to the end of the process and said, "We wasted our time." Regardless of how uncomfortable a visit might be, the participants invariably come away energized. Sometimes they even come away with an idea for a new business. In the spring of 2000, before the dotcom valuations finally peaked, we ran a Learning Journey in the San Francisco Bay Area entitled "Is the New Economy Getting Real?" Most of the participants were from so-called old economy companies who were unsettled by the dramatic rise of the startups extolled in the press. Many began the journey with a sinking feeling that their large, slow-moving organizations were doomed. However, after several days of deep immersion, most traded their sense of doom for a sense of excitement and opportunity. The more established companies, not the dotcoms, seemed better positioned to translate some of the ambitious ideas into real businesses. One participant in particular, the director of business transformation programs at a major aerospace company, had a specific idea for a new business as he sat on the bus driving back from Silicon Valley at the end of the day. A year later his company launched a web-augmented engineering solution business, which was able to leverage the firm's brand and engineering strengths, and open up a new market.

Acting Differently

Thinking and learning differently will have little impact in the absence of changed behavior. So the third pillar of adaptive advantage is acting differently. Here we highlight three important areas we expect to become increasingly important for business success: *acting ethically*, *acting inclusively*, and *acting experimentally*.

Acting Ethically

In the industrial era, businesses produced widespread economic advances and quality-of-life improvements through mechanizing, standardizing, and automating their processes, and scaling up their operations over time. This progress was not entirely benign in terms of its social and environmental impacts. In fact, it was at least partly responsible for triggering challenges in most parts of the world to the moral legitimacy of capitalism, and in some countries it led to the rise of communism as an alternative system. However, in most capitalist societies, civic expectations of business remained modest and businesses were considered morally neutral. It was assumed that they would not deliberately cause harm or act with wanton carelessness, but neither would they be expected to pursue a greater social good. Unintended negative consequences of commercial activity—so-called "externalities"— were by and large tolerated, even expected. The benefits seemed to outweigh the costs.

With time, however, there became a growing disconnect between "economic wisdom"—doing the profitable thing—and "moral wisdom"—doing the right thing. Today that trend may be reversing. We may see a realignment of economic and moral wisdom for businesses—enabling and encouraging them to "do well by doing good." Why? A number of factors are coming together to drive this realignment. The sheer scale and reach of market-based business activity has reached the point where its fundamental significance to life on the planet is clear and acknowledged. And there is also accumulating, incontrovertible evidence of the enormous environmental, social, and cultural consequences of business activity.

At the same time, we are experiencing an unprecedented level of transparency—accelerated by the spread of communication and information technologies and the global growth of media—that makes it much harder to hide or disguise business activities and their impacts. Add to that a growing sense of public concern regarding the role of corporations and their impact on the world, and it seems inevitable that we will see a continued growth of public scrutiny by governments, media, NGOs, and citizens. This means that there will be fewer places for transgressors to hide, and more ways for their transgressions to be discovered and communicated. Once these are exposed, governments, citizens, and consumers will be predisposed to punish the economic actors who appear to violate common moral wisdom.

As this new climate unfolds, the potential for catastrophic ethical failures in business will increase, while public tolerance of such failures will decrease. We may already have witnessed the first major indicator of this phenomenon. For many years to come the names Enron and Arthur Andersen will probably bear posthumous witness to the devastating consequences of ethical violations. But in the coming decade businesses won't even have to act unethically to be suspect. The same forces of increasing transparency, scrutiny, and accountability, combined with the growing complexity of the business world, will lead to mounting public suspicions—some justified, many not. Every business could find that its reputation and credibility is constantly in play and at peril. The safest strategy will be to strive for impeccable behavior that over time becomes embedded in your business brand.

This means that business leaders will have to instill a deep ethical consciousness throughout their organization—not as an adjunct to business strategy, but as a core organizing principle. Anything less will result in risk that will become increasingly unacceptable to shareholders and other stakeholders. This growing imperative for business is not simply a defensive measure. It will also help enhance adaptive advantage because a clear, shared ethical compass will be essential to quickly navigate through the complex terrain of the future business environment. The ability of people at all levels of an organization to develop appropriate options, make rapid decisions, and act swiftly in a changing world will increasingly require a common set of ethical imperatives.

Instilling such an ethical consciousness will take more than putting a statement of values beside the corporate logo on computer mouse pads. Paying lip service to ethical behavior will not suffice—the commitment must become truly embedded in the DNA of the organization. Fortunately, promoting ethical behavior does not run counter to the personal instincts of most employees and stakeholders. Most people want to act ethically, and do so in their personal lives. The vast majority of businesses simply have to articulate their ethical commitment explicitly, and design their systems to support the personal values of their people. By working with the grain of existing values and ethics, and consistently encouraging everyone to meet the same ethical standards in their professional lives as they do in their private lives, the establishment of ethical consciousness may prove surprisingly easy to achieve. Moreover, those who move early in this direction can expect to attract and retain great people.

A case in point: Several years ago we ran a Learning Journey in the United States for a dozen European managers from traditional businesses. We visited a Saturn auto dealership to see some of the innovative approaches of this fairly new player in a very traditional industry. Just before leaving, we asked the franchise owner how his work experience at Saturn differed from his previous experience working in automobile retail sales.

"That's easy to answer," he replied. "This move has changed my life. It has brought the person I am at work into harmony with the person I am in the rest of my life. Previously, I was one person at home—father, husband, church volunteer, coach—and a quite different person in my world of work. I didn't even know how much I had to change personality twice a day—in the car on my way to work, and again on my way home—until I made this move. Now I'm the same person everywhere, and I've never been happier."

Acting Inclusively

A consistent theme throughout this book, referenced by almost all of our network members, is growing interconnection and mutual interdependence. It surfaced in every domain: the fusion of cultures, the systemic nature of environmental crises, the impact of biotech development on national and international politics, and the global ripple of financial problems in Japan. Likewise we heard repeatedly about the importance of a more holistic and inclusive approach to thinking—and acting.

For businesses, an inclusive approach could take several forms while also conferring a clear adaptive advantage immediately and in the years ahead. For example, simply taking a more inclusive view of the purpose of your business—beyond making profit and creating shareholder value—could reveal new opportunities for alliances or long-term investments. Similarly, adopting a more inclusive definition of your stakeholders and being open to broader opportunities for dialogue and collaboration with them could enhance your business intelligence, standing, and relationships.

Perhaps the most promising—and challenging—long-term opportunity to create adaptive advantage by acting inclusively involves engaging the excluded billions of the world's poor. As many of our network members observed, the growing scale of inequity, the mounting divide between the "haves" and the "have nots," appears to be unsustainable. As UN Secretary General Kofi Annan has stated, "If we cannot make globalization work for all, it will work for none." Despite the relentless march of economic globalization over recent decades, around two-thirds of the world's population remain disconnected from the economic mainstream. They are largely untouched in any positive way by economic progress, while they may be negatively affected by corollary environmental or cultural changes. The businesses that have played a key role in spreading opportunity across one-third of the planet's population appear daunted by the seemingly intractable problems of the other two-thirds.

Yet addressing the needs of the four billion poor could become a new business priority in the decade ahead. This notion has been gaining ground in recent years and has even resulted in a new acronym: "B24B," short for "business to 4 billion." There are two main reasons why this could rise in importance. One involves direct self-interest: These could be the new markets that will allow businesses to sustain high growth in the coming decades as more mature markets evolve toward different patterns of demand. The other reason involves indirect self-interest: To create a sustainable business environment for the long-term, businesses need to do their part in addressing the deep problems found in many parts of the world, by helping lay the foundations for appropriate economic growth at the local level. Only when faced with a sense of meaningful opportunity and hope will those currently excluded become engaged. The alternative may be bleak. As our network members described clearly, continued exclusion makes the prospect of significant disruptions for society and business very real.

Moving seriously in this direction will involve enormous challenges and changes—in attitude, strategy, product development, marketing, and financial arrangements. However, as the highly regarded management guru C. K. Prahalad has observed, moving into—and often creating—these new markets is by no means impossible. The very process of understanding different needs, creating new solutions that are appropriate and affordable, and forging very different sorts of relationships could also serve as a catalyst for innovation—and hence adaptiveness—in businesses.

Whether making B24B a reality or beginning to tackle big environmental and civilizational challenges, business need not act alone. Many of the most exciting opportunities of the next decade will revolve around projects that invite partnerships between business, government, and not-for-profit organizations. Indeed, the boundaries that separate these sectors themselves are blurring. And the complex problems that need to be solved will require participation from them all. At GBN we work extensively with all three sectors, and often observe in each a lack of understanding of the others. Yet their respective concerns and aspirations for the future are much more similar than different. The means that they each use to make a difference in the world are much more complementary than clashing. And their objectives and priorities are typically closer to alignment than they might realize. An important challenge for those seeking to act inclusively will be to discover creative ways to exploit these synergies more fully.

We can already observe real progress being made in integration between sectors, at least at the level of new dialogue and shared principles and commitments. The United Nation's Global Compact, for example, is aimed at getting businesses to commit to sustainable goals that benefit the whole world and are shared by non-business actors. The World Economic Forum in recent years has invited participants from sectors outside business into their high-level discussions, which include the broader role of business in society. While much remains to be achieved in terms of concerted action, this will surely become an increasing focus for many businesses in the decade ahead—and a powerful source of change in the world.

Acting Experimentally

We have set out above some important new ways in which business behavior may have to change. There will be many others—in fact, it is probable that in the coming decade businesses will have to change even more frequently, more rapidly, and more dramatically than has been the case over the previous 20 turbulent years. To do so effectively they may have to acquire a critical new capacity—the ability to *act experimentally*.

In the process of evolution, nature experiments through speciation, trying out frequent small-scale changes, or genetic variations, that iterate and compound over time. Science is also based on experimentation, as hypotheses are tested and refined through frequent, small experiments. Although most of these experiments will fail, they cost relatively little yet yield valuable learning. Just as widespread, small-scale experimentation is the paradigm of nature and science, it may well become the paradigm of business in the next 10 years.

Today, however, few businesses have mastered the art and practice of experimentation. Rather, most changes in business are introduced through large projects and initiatives (sometimes preceded by "pilots" designed to prove the need for the full-blown approach). Such projects typically are based on a single approach, consume considerable resources, take a relatively long time to carry out, and have little room for course correction should developments go wrong. And because these high stakes make it hard for those responsible to acknowledge failure, everything must somehow be positioned as a success. This approach often works against adaptation—it might even be an adaptive *dis*advantage.

A better approach aimed at adaptive advantage might involve importing the well-tested techniques of experimentation from the scientific context into the business world. This would require the design of many more initiatives, and at much smaller scales, to make progress toward your goals, and a clear commitment to capture learning and feedback at every stage to inform the next steps. Network member Michael Schrage, author of the book *Serious Play*, explains this process as "rapid prototyping," a far more effective way to iterate your way toward new products and services. Critical new core competencies in the coming years, then, will be the abilities to imagine, design, and execute small-scale experiments in new opportunity spaces; to systematically extract the learning from both success and failure; and to move swiftly on to the next iteration. With that skill set and cultural attitude deeply embedded, businesses could find themselves much better equipped for the challenging but opportunity-rich decade ahead.

The experimental approach is useful in its own right and also reinforces the other concepts that we have laid out in this chapter. *Thinking differently* is largely predicated on gaining a multiplicity of insights and viewpoints rather than relying on one big idea. Scenaric thinking, in essence, is about creating many thought experiments about how the future may unfold. *Learning differently* requires us to design many different experiences and methods of study in order to maximize learning and to keep nudging our knowledge forward in new directions. And *acting differently* may well require huge changes in the behavior of business. By acting experimentally, we can adapt incrementally, taking small steps toward the big changes required for survival in our rapidly changing world.

Rising to the Challenge

At Global Business Network we have the privilege of working with many of the world's great enterprises, and we are convinced of the powerful role that business plays in shaping the future. Over the last 20 years we have seen businesses large and small, global and local, help create the economic, social, and environmental conditions that profoundly impact the way we all live. We have watched private enterprise help create a complex, interconnected, interdependent world, while helping spread wealth and opportunity globally.

As we have looked ahead to the future it has been easy to imagine scenarios of increasing complexity in which technology gets increasingly elaborate, products and services increasingly sophisticated, global markets increasingly diverse, financial instruments increasingly complicated, collaborative relationships increasingly numerous. But it has been equally easy to imagine businesses rising to these challenges, and innovating effectively as they continue to thrive.

Today, however, informed partly by the interviews for this book, we sense that the changes in the world may soon become more than the sum of the parts—creating a more disturbing challenge ahead. We can all too easily imagine scenarios in which the increasing complexities and accelerating pace of change that business has helped create actually compound to undermine the economic, social, and physical environment on which we all depend. As many of our network members passionately and eloquently argued, we may now be facing deep and difficult issues across all of our domains that are reaching critical proportions and must be addressed systemically.

So there is now a new set of challenges facing all of us in the business community. In addition to better understanding the world, we will need to more actively contribute to addressing the problems of the world. Collectively, the business sector now holds too much power to be morally neutral in its activities. We cannot focus solely on profitability and shareholder value. We cannot ignore the plight of billions of people untouched—or worse, harmed—by the economic progress of the last century. We cannot, in short, simply *adapt* to the changing world—we must seek to use our strengths to influence that change for the better.

These are easy words to write, but more difficult for individual businesses to act upon. No single business can easily provide leadership in engaging the world more fully with a new and broader agenda. Few business leaders will relish, on top of their many existing burdens, the additional weight of reconsidering their organization's role and impact in the world, and adjusting their practices accordingly. Taking on broader responsibilities will involve significant costs—especially if competitors fail to engage in a similar spirit. However, some of the best businesses on the planet are already making impressive early strides in this direction, dedicating some of their attention and creative energy to new responsibilities, and taking a broader view of their role and purpose. In the decade ahead, they undoubtedly will help lay down new paths for others to follow.

And business need not act alone. The world is blessed with visionaries, innovators, and people of action—those with the imagination, the passion, and the talent to make a real difference. And many of them are working outside the business sector. If we more effectively align the mainstream business agenda with their efforts, then surely we will see creative solutions emerge for the big, complex, long-term problems of the planet.

The next stage in the evolution of business is beginning. Having done so much to create a remarkable new world, we now must play a more active part in nurturing and improving it. This may prove to be the most profound source of sustained success in the twenty-first century. We can, we should, and we will rise to the challenge.

Acknowledgments

The first acknowledgments in this book go to all of the people who have created the community of Global Business Network. These include the visionary founders **Stewart Brand**, **Napier Collyns**, **Jay Ogilvy**, **Peter Schwartz**, and **Lawrence Wilkinson**, and the outstanding team of people they attracted; the remarkable thinkers who saw the potential of this new type of organization and were willing to enrich it with their insights and ideas; and the corporate members and clients whose willingness to experiment and collaborate made it all possible. Over the years, new players have arrived with different ideas and energies to keep the momentum going, grow the organization, and move us in new directions. Together, all these people have created an enduring community of learning and foresight without which this book simply could not have come into existence. To all of our colleagues past and present, as well as to our new colleagues within the Monitor Group, especially **Jim Cutler** and **Alan Kantrow**, we give our heartfelt thanks.

Next we gratefully acknowledge all 50 of those network members and other remarkable thinkers who agreed to be interviewed for this project. Each of them rose to the challenge from the moment they were asked to engage in an expansive conversation about their fields and the state of the world in the next 10 years. They carved out time from their busy schedules and were generous with their ideas—and often with hospitality in their offices or homes.

For outstanding help with this project, we thank GBN's **Dawn Warfield** for her ongoing organizational assistance, as well as her painstaking transcriptions of the interviews and fact-checking. Monitor's **Jenny Johnston** and **Jennifer Sturak** transformed the interviews from spoken to written English. We thank them all for their impressive turnarounds and enthusiastic feedback, as well as **Alyson Weir** for so effectively coordinating the authors' schedules during a very hectic time. **Laura Likely's** strong editorial talents and tough-mindedness also served the project well. Many superfluous phrases and some lame ideas were removed from this book thanks to her keen eye.

Above all, we are truly indebted to **Nancy Murphy** for her amazing work on this project. She was absolutely central from the first moments to the very last—from helping identify the right people for us to interview, to managing interactions with them, to crucial editorial feedback and practical line-editing of the book. And as if that was not enough, her optimism and energy kept us going whenever ours flagged. Thank you, Nancy, from the bottom of our hearts.

Thanks also to **Nick Philipson**, our editor at Perseus, who saw the potential for this book from the first time he heard about the interview project. Eamonn Kelly also expresses his deep gratitude to **Katherine Fulton** and **Eric Best** for their intellectual and professional comradeship and their help over the years in arriving at many of the important ideas that underpin this book. And **David Bank**, as he often does, consistently helped Peter Leyden evolve key concepts and think through the project's problem of the week. His insight and friendship were both appreciated.

Finally, and most importantly, we want to acknowledge the forbearance and support of our families. Peter thanks **Sharon Hawkins Leyden** and daughter **Emma** for their incredible tolerance for late nights and lost weekends. Not only did Sharon generously give me the time and space required to create this book, but she would listen to me talk endlessly about the ideas. Through it all we managed not only to stay connected, but to grow closer—mostly because of her. Eamonn thanks **Rita Kelly**, without whose many, many years of loving support and encouragement none of my modest achievements could have come to pass, and **Adam, Sam**, and **Leona**—my amazing family who patiently endure my hectic and far-flung schedule, and make my every return a true joy. With every passing year, I count my blessings that you are all in my life.

About the Authors

Eamonn Kelly is CEO and president of Global Business Network, the renowned California-based, future-oriented network and consulting firm. He has been central to sustaining GBN's thought leadership about the future, and is also head of its consulting practice. He has consulted at senior levels to dozens of the world's leading corporations in most sectors, including health care, energy, telecommunications, transportation, financial services, manufacturing, computing, professional services, and consumer goods. Eamonn has also worked with key global and national public agencies, as well as major philanthropic foundations. For more than a decade he has been at the forefront of exploring the emergence of a new, knowledge-intensive economy, and the far-reaching consequences for society, organizations, and people—and has been invited to present his provocative ideas frequently all over the world. Prior to joining GBN, Eamonn was head of strategy at Scottish Enterprise, one of the world's most respected development agencies, where he led the creation of new and effective strategies for economic and social development in a new era. He has also established successful community-based business initiatives, and served on the boards of numerous organizations. Eamonn studied drama, sociology, and economics at the University of Glasgow, and also holds a Masters of Business Administration from Strathclyde University. He lives in San Rafael, California, with his wife, Rita, and their children Adam, Sam, and Leona. Contact him at WhatsNext@gbn.com.

Peter Leyden is the knowledge developer at Global Business Network, helping identify what GBN and its extended network know and should be learning about. He makes connections between ideas and helps communicate them throughout the network and to the world at large. Peter is coauthor of *The Long Boom: A Vision for the Coming Age of Prosperity* (Perseus 1999), now translated into seven languages. He was the former managing editor, and a longtime senior editor at *Wired* magazine, covering digital technologies and the new economy in the 1990s. He watched the rise of Asia as a special correspondent for *Newsweek* magazine in the late 1980s. During his 15 years as a journalist, he wrote for many publications, including the *New York Times*, *Chicago Tribune*, *San Francisco Chronicle* and *London Guardian*. Peter received two master's degrees from Columbia University, one in comparative politics and political economy, and one in journalism. He did undergraduate study in intellectual history at Georgetown University. Peter has spoken frequently in the United States and Europe about new technologies, economic change, and the future. He lives in Berkeley, California, with his wife, Sharon, and 10-year-old daughter Emma. He can be reached at WhatsNext@gbn.com.

About the Network Members

Here are more detailed bios of the GBN members and other remarkable thinkers who appear in this book. You may also find out more at the GBN Web site at www.gbn.com.

Laurie Anderson

One of the world's premier performance artists, Laurie Anderson has consistently intrigued, entertained, and challenged audiences with her multimedia presentations. Anderson's artistic career has cast her in roles as various as visual artist, composer, poet, photographer, filmmaker, ventriloquist, electronics whiz, vocalist, and instrumentalist. Her work includes CDs (*O Superman, The Nerve Bible, Bright Red, Strange Angels*), a 20-year retrospective book, *Stories from the Nerve Bible*, and many multimedia shows, including *Stories from the Nerve Bible, Moby Dick*, and *Happiness*. She has also created film scores, dance pieces, orchestral compositions, live theatrical and cyberevents, and art installations.

John Arquilla

John Arquilla is associate professor of defense analysis at the United States Naval Postgraduate School in Monterey, California, and a consultant to RAND. He and David Ronfeldt were among the first to explore the issue of information technology in warfare and coined the terms "cyberwar" and "netwar." His most recent books include *The Emergence of Noopolitik: Toward an American Information Strategy*, and *Networks and Netwars: The Future of Terror, Crime, and Militancy*, with David Ronfeldt.

W. Brian Arthur

W. Brian Arthur is Citibank Professor at the Santa Fe Institute. From 1983 to 1996 he was dean and Virginia Morrison Professor of Economics and Population Studies at Stanford University. Arthur pioneered the modern study of positive feedbacks or increasing returns in the economy—in particular their role in magnifying small, random events in the economy. His work on increasing returns won him a Guggenheim Fellowship in 1987 and the Schumpeter Prize in Economics in 1990. Arthur is also one of the pioneers of the new science of complexity. His main interests are the economics of high technology, how business evolves in an era of high technology, cognition in the economy, and financial markets. Arthur was the first director of the Economics Program at the Santa Fe Institute and he currently serves on its board.

Mary Catherine Bateson

Mary Catherine Bateson is a writer and cultural anthropologist who divides her time between New Hampshire and Massachusetts, where she is currently a visiting professor at the Harvard Graduate School of Education. She has written and coauthored numerous books and articles, lectures across the country and around the world, and is president of the Institute for Intercultural Studies in New York City. For the last decade she has been Clarence J. Robinson Professor in Anthropology and English at George Mason University. Her most recent book, *Full Circles, Overlapping Lives*, looks at how our concepts of personal identity and shared fulfillment are changing. Bateson explores her theme by weaving together words of a group of remarkable women whom she taught at Spelman College and at George Mason University. The lives of these women—young, old, black, white, married, single—offer a prism through which we all can glimpse facets of ourselves.

Janine Benyus

Janine Benyus is a life sciences writer and author of six books, including her latest— *Biomimicry: Innovation Inspired by Nature*. In *Biomimicry*, she names an emerging science that seeks sustainable solutions by mimicking nature's designs and processes. She has worked as a backcountry guide as well as a "translator" of science-speak at several research labs. She now writes popular books in the life sciences, consults with sustainable business and government leaders, serves on the Dream Team at Interface, Inc., and gives talks about what we can learn from the genius that surrounds us. Janine's next book will explore home as habitat, taking a biological look at human habitat selection.

Stewart Brand

Stewart Brand is a cofounder of Global Business Network and the Long Now Foundation. Best known for founding, editing, and publishing the *Whole Earth Catalog*, he also has a long-standing involvement in computers, education, and the media arts. Stewart is the author of *The Clock of the Long Now*, *How Buildings Learn*, and *The Media Lab*. He founded, edited, and published *CoEvolution Quarterly* (now *Whole Earth*), and was founder of The WELL (Whole Earth 'Lectronic Link) a computer teleconference system based in the San Francisco Bay Area. Stewart is also a cofounder of the All Species Foundation, a nonprofit organization dedicated to the complete inventory of all species of life on earth within the next 25 years, and of the Long Bets Foundation, bringing accountability to predictions.

Albert Bressand

Albert Bressand is the managing director and cofounder of Prométhée, a nonprofit, Paris-based international think tank. Prométhée spearheads an international effort to analyze the emerging global networked economy and its implications for corporate strategies, markets, and international economic relations. He is a member of the board of economists of *Time* magazine and an adviser to the *International Economy* magazine in Washington, D.C. He is also a fellow of the World Economic Forum in Davos, where he has been chairing sessions on electronic finance, "networked markets," the Euro, and globalization. Albert previously served as economic advisor to the French foreign minister, as deputy director of the French Institute for International Relations, and as a member of the policy planning staff of the World Bank. Albert also served three terms as the president of the Services World Forum, a Geneva-centered network of experts on international services issues.

William Calvin

Bill Calvin is a theoretical neurophysiologist and affiliate professor of psychiatry and behavioral sciences at the University of Washington. He is a member of Emory University's Living Links Center, the science advisory board for a NOVA television series on evolution, and the board of advisors to the Foundation for the Future. He is the author of 11 books, mostly for general readers, about brains and evolution, including *The Throwing Madonna, The Cerebral Symphony, The River that Runs Uphill, The Cerebral Code, Conversations with Neil's Brain* (with George Ojemann), and *How Brains Think*. His book with Derek Bickerton, *Lingua ex Machina: Reconciling Darwin and Chomsky with the Human Brain*, is about syntax. His new book, *A Brain for All Seasons: Human Evolution and Abrupt Climate Change*, focuses on paleoanthropology, paleoclimate, and considerations from neurobiology and evolutionary biology.

Robert Carlson

Dr. Robert Carlson joined Applied Minds as a scientist in 2002, where he continues to work on biology as well as projects as diverse as fuel-cell design and hydrogen fuels, new display technologies, and machine vision. Formerly, he was a research fellow at the Molecular Sciences Institute. His interests include discovering what kinds of problems single cells can solve and how they interact with their environment. He is also interested in the related question of how information flows from the environment into the genome and is currently working on techniques to measure internal states of cells, such as quantifying the expressed protein complement, and the related problem of quantifying protein-protein interactions. Carlson's previous experience includes single neuron recording in a fly, experiment and modeling of human leukocyte behavior after physiological deformation, and developing new microfabrication techniques for use in biology, optics, fluorescence microscopy, and spectroscopy.

Roger Cass

President of Cass Research Associates since 1974, Roger has written and spoken widely on global strategic issues, and has for the past 20 years served as a consultant on portfolio strategies as well as on international economic, political, and military trends to many of the world's leading corporations and financial and investment institutions, including Anglo American De Beers, Atlantic Richfield, E.I. Du

Pont de Nemours, College Retirement Equities Fund, Deutsche Bank, the Harvard Endowment Fund, Royal Dutch Shell, M&G Investment Management, Morgan Stanley, the United Nations Pension Fund, UBS Asset Management, Volvo Corporation, Wells Fargo Bank, and Westinghouse Electric Corporation. He has also served as a consultant to GBN on global economic and political trends for the past 14 years, and is the creator of the WorldStats scenario quantification service.

Catherine Distler

Catherine Distler is deputy director and cofounder of Prométhée, a nonprofit, Paris-based international think tank working on the global networked economy and its implications for corporate strategies and for policymakers. She served previously as Chargée de Mission at the Centre de Prospective et d'Evaluation of the French Ministry of Research and Technology and as research associate at the French Institute for International Relations (IFRI). In addition to her role as contributor or co-editor of Prométhée publications, her personal publications build on her studies in telecoms to reach into the broader world of networks. They include *Global Superhighways: The Future of International Telecommunications Policy* (co-authored with Vincent Cable), and *La Planète Relationnelle* (coauthored with Albert Bressand).

Gwynne Dyer

Gwynne Dyer is a freelance journalist, broadcaster, and lecturer. His syndicated columns on international affairs appear in a dozen languages in nearly 200 newspapers published in more than 40 countries around the world. In 1980, he and Tina Viljoen collaborated on a seven-part television series for the National Film Board of Canada, *War*, first telecast in Canada in 1983. *War* was shown in 45 countries and one episode, "The Profession of Arms," was nominated for an Academy Award. With Viljoen, Dyer wrote a book based on the series, *War*, published in 1985. Dyer and Viljoen again collaborated on *Defence of Canada*, a three-part series that aired in 1986. Their book, *The Defence of Canada: In the Arms of the Empire*, was published in 1990. In 1994 Dyer completed a four-part series, *The Human Race*, which looked at the roots, nature, and future of human politics. In 1995, his three-part series on peacekeeping in Bosnia, *Protection Force*, first aired.

Esther Dyson

Esther Dyson is chair of EDventure Holdings, a small, diversified company focused on emerging information technology worldwide and on the emerging computer markets of Central and Eastern Europe. As an active investor and commentator, she focuses on emerging technologies and business models (peer-to-peer, artificial intelligence, the Internet, wireless applications), emerging markets (Eastern Europe), and emerging companies. Esther is also active in industry affairs; she was a member of the U.S. National Information Infrastructure Advisory Council (advising Vice President Al Gore) and vice chair of the Electronic Frontier Foundation. She also sits on the boards and executive committees of the Santa Fe Institute, the Institute for EastWest Studies, and the Eurasia Foundation. In 1997, she wrote a book on the impact of the Net on individuals' lives, *Release 2.0: A Design for Living in the Digital Age.* She has also worked as a reporter for *Forbes* magazine.

Freeman J. Dyson

Freeman J. Dyson is professor of physics at the Institute for Advanced Study, Princeton. Professor Dyson has received many awards during his distinguished scientific career, including the Wolf Prize in physics in 1981. He has made seminal contributions to quantum electrodynamics, the theory of interacting electrons and photons. His work explained the equivalence of two approaches to the theory put forward independently by Julian Schwinger and Richard Feynman. He also developed the theory of random matrices, which describes random energy spectra of complex systems: nuclei, atoms, and small particles of metals and insulators. Professor Dyson is the author of a number of books and popular scientific articles, including *Disturbing the Universe, Weapons and Hope, Origins of Life,* and *Infinite in All Directions.* He was honored with the National Book Critics Award for nonfiction in 1984, the Gemant Award by the American Institute of Physics in 1988, the Britannica Award for dissemination of knowledge in 1990, and the Templeton Prize for progress in religion.

Betty Sue Flowers

Betty Sue is a poet, editor, educator, and business consultant. Before becoming director of the LBJ Presidential Library, she was the Kelleher Professor of English at the University of Texas at Austin and director of creative writing. Her publications range from poetry therapy to the economic myth, including four television tie-in books in collaboration with Bill Moyers, among them *Joseph Campbell and the Power of Myth.* She hosted *Conversations with Betty Sue Flowers* on the Austin PBS affiliate, KLRU, and has served as a moderator for executive seminars at the Aspen Institute for Humanistic Studies, a consultant for NASA, a member of the Envisioning Network for General Motors, a visiting advisor to the secretary of the Navy, and a writer of Global Scenarios for Shell International in London and the World Business Council in Geneva.

Francis Fukuyama

Francis Fukuyama is Bernard L. Schwartz Professor of International Political Economy at the Paul H. Nitze School of Advanced International Studies (SAIS) of Johns Hopkins University. He was formerly Omer L. and Nancy Hirst Professor of Public Policy at the School of Public Policy at George Mason University. Dr. Fukuyama has written widely on issues relating to questions concerning democratization and international political economy. He has, in recent years, focused on the role of culture and social capital in modern economic life, and on the social consequences of the transition into an information economy. Dr. Fukuyama's book *The End of History and the*

Last Man has appeared in over 20 foreign editions and was awarded the *Los Angeles Times'* Book Critics Award as well as the Premio Capri for the Italian edition. *Trust: The Social Virtues and the Creation of Prosperity* was published in 1995, and his most recent book is *The Great Disruption: Human Nature and the Reconstitution of Social Order.* His latest book *Our Posthuman Future: Consequences of the Biotechnology Revolution* was published in 2002.

Katherine Fulton

Katherine is a partner at GBN-Monitor where she works with private, nonprofit, and public sector organizations to better anticipate and shape their futures. Her lifelong interest is in leadership, learning, and the connection between the two. Her current work focuses on philanthropy and the nonprofit sector, but while at GBN she has also worked with leading organizations in publishing, financial services, law, education, health care, social services, telecommunications, broadcasting, computers, consumer products, and national security. Katherine has also taught scenario planning at Harvard University's executive programs. Before joining GBN she taught at Duke University, where her courses explored the future of leadership and organizations, the future of communications, and the future of democracy. Her innovative teaching was featured in *Time* magazine. Previously, Katherine cofounded a publishing company and edited its award-winning weekly, which won her a Southern Foundation Prize and a year at Harvard as a Nieman Fellow.

Joel Garreau

Joel is a student of culture, values, and change. For the last three years, his main interest has been hinges in history enabled by technological upheaval that produce seismic social change. He is also fascinated by human—as distinct from electronic—networks. Joel is the author of the best-selling books *Edge City: Life on the New Frontier* and *The Nine Nations of North America.* Joel is CEO of the Edge City Group, Inc., a senior fellow at the school of public policy at George Mason University, a staff writer for the *Washington Post*, a frequent television and radio talking head, and the troll of a small forest in the foothills of Virginia's Blue Ridge.

Gerald Harris

Gerald is a senior practitioner with GBN, specializing in the energy sector. Prior to joining GBN, Gerald spent 13 years at Pacific Gas and Electric Company, northern California's largest utility. As director of business planning for engineering and construction, he was responsible for providing strategic and business planning services to a 4700-person business unit. Before joining PG&E, Gerald was a financial analyst in international project finance at Bechtel Corporation. He has written and spoken extensively on the future of energy markets, especially concerning the integration of new technology, and the application of scenario planning processes to strategy development.

Paul Hawken

Paul Hawken is an environmentalist, educator, entrepreneur, and best-selling author. He is known as one of the leading architects and proponents of corporate reform with respect to ecological practices. His writings and work have caused CEOs to transform their internal corporate cultures and business philosophies toward environmental restoration. He has founded several companies, including Meta-code, a B2B infrastructure company; Groxis, a portal and search engine interface software provider; Smith & Hawken, the garden and catalog retailer; and several of the first natural food companies in the U.S that relied solely on sustainable agricultural methods. He is author of six books, including *The Next Economy, Growing a Business*, and *The Ecology of Commerce*. His latest book is *Natural Capitalism: Creating the Next Industrial Revolution* with Amory and Hunter Lovins. His books have been published in more than 50 countries in 27 languages and have sold more than 3 million copies.

Michael Hertz

Michael Hertz is the cofounder and president of Pro Bono Net, Inc., a startup non-profit that makes innovative use of the Internet to increase access to justice for low-income and other vulnerable communities. Pro Bono Net has developed a powerful set of tools that can be used by public interest and legal services organizations to increase the amount and quality of legal services provided to low-income individuals and communities. Its goal is to build virtual communities of public interest lawyers that bridge the private, legal services, and academic sectors of the profession and publish legal information for low-income people. Legal aid programs in nearly 30 states have adopted Pro Bono Net's technology platform. Michael is on an extended leave of absence from a national law firm, where he is a litigation partner.

Danny Hillis

Danny Hillis is the founder of Applied Minds, an invention and R&D Laboratory in southern California and a former Disney Fellow and vice president of R&D at Disney. He is also cofounder of the Clock Library with Stewart Brand. Previously, Danny cofounded Thinking Machines Corporation, producer of massively parallel computers. The design of Thinking Machines Corporation's major product, the Connection Machine, was the topic of Danny's dissertation at MIT, where he was awarded his Ph.D. in 1988. Danny's long-term interests include designing a true thinking machine. He is the recipient of ACM's Grace Murray Hopper award, the Spirit of American Creativity award, the Ramanujan Award, and the Dan Daud Prize. He holds over 50 U.S. patents and is an editor of several scientific journals. He is a member of the science board of the Santa Fe Institute and the advisory board of the ORSA *Journal on Computing*, and is a fellow of the American Academy of Arts and Sciences and the National Academy of Engineering.

Robert Hormats

Bob Hormats is an economist who has had a distinguished career in international trade, diplomacy, and investment banking. He is currently vice chair of Goldman Sachs International Corporation. He previously was vice president of international corporate finance. Before joining Goldman Sachs, Bob was a presidential advisor and helped prepare eight economic summit meetings. He served in the State Department as assistant secretary for economic and business affairs. He is also a former staff member of the National Security Council. Bob has been a guest member of the Trilateral Commission and is on the board of directors of the Hungarian-American Enterprise Fund, Englehard Hanovia, and the Council on Foreign Relations, as well as being on the board of overseers of Tufts University.

Shaun B. Jones

Dr. Shaun B. Jones is a Navy captain and physician and an advisor to senior advanced technology and concept groups throughout the national security community. Shaun earned his medical degree at the Uniformed Services University of the Health Sciences. He completed a residency in otorhinolaryngology—head and neck surgery—at the National Naval Medical Center and was a resident research fellow in the divisions of Cytokine Biology and Monoclonal Antibodies, Center for Biologics Evaluation and Research of the FDA. Shaun is a diplomate of the American Board of Otolaryngology, a fellow of the American Academy of Otorhinolaryngology, and an FDA consultant, division of ear, nose, and throat device evaluation. In addition to numerous chapters and publications, he is an internationally invited speaker and active participant on multiple editorial boards for peer reviewed journals on advanced medical and surgical technologies, and biological warfare defense.

Kevin Kelly

Kevin Kelly is editor-at-large of *Wired*, the award-winning monthly magazine about digital culture based in San Francisco. He has edited the *Whole Earth Review*, a quarterly journal of unorthodox technical news, and he co-initiated the Hackers Conference, a yearly gathering of maverick computer programmers, young code dudes, and teenage crackers. He was involved in the startup of The WELL, a legendary outpost on the new information superhighway. He also published *Signal*, the first sourcebook for cyberpunk culture, and is author of *New Rules for the New Economy: 10 Radical Strategies for a Connected World*, and *Out of Control: The Rise of Neo-Biological Civilization*. His current passion is a campaign to make a full inventory of all living species on earth. This project, called the All Species Foundation (www.all-species.org), hopes to make a Web-based catalog of all species on earth in one generation, or the next 25 years.

Jaron Lanier

Jaron Lanier is a computer scientist, inventor, musician, composer, visual artist, and writer. He coined the phrase "virtual reality," founded the VR industry, started the first VR company (VPL Research, Inc.), and is the co-inventor of fundamental VR components such as interface gloves and VR-networking. He is currently serving as lead scientist of the National Tele-immersion Initiative (a coalition of research universities studying advanced applications for Internet) and codirector of Project GUMBO at Caltech, which explores the collaborative process of very large-scale scientific simulations science. Music is Jaron's first love and he has been an active composer and performer in the world of new classical music since the late seventies. He is also a pianist, a specialist in unusual musical instruments, and a composer of chamber and orchestral music for performance, film, and video. He writes on numerous topics, including high-technology business, the social impact of technological practices, the philosophy of consciousness and information, Internet politics, and the future of humanism. His book *Confessions of a Closet Human* is forthcoming.

Amory Lovins

Amory Lovins is the founder and chair of Hypercar Inc., a new company established to promote hypercar research and development. He, with Hunter Lovins, is also the cofounder, CFO, and research director of Rocky Mountain Institute, founded in 1982 as an independent nonprofit resource policy center. Together they founded E source, which provides technical information on new ways to save electricity. A consultant physicist educated at Harvard and Oxford, Amory's visionary work in energy, sustainability, and resource management and policy has earned him six honorary doctorates, a MacArthur Fellowship, the Heinz Award, the Nissan Award, the Mitchell Prize, the Right Livelihood Prize, and the Onassis Prize. The *Wall Street Journal's* Centennial Issue named him among 39 people in the world most likely to change the course of business in the 1990s, and *Car* magazine called him the 22nd most powerful person in the global automotive industry. Amory's newest books are *Natural Capitalism* (with Paul Hawken and Hunter Lovins) and *Small is Profitable: The Hidden Economic Benefits of Making Electrical Resources the Right Size* (forthcoming with André Lehmann).

L. Hunter Lovins

L. Hunter Lovins, Esq., is the cofounder and CEO-strategy of Rocky Mountain Institute. A member of the California Bar, she helped establish and for six years was assistant director of the California Conservation Project (Tree People), an innovative urban forestry and environmental education group. Since 1982 she has directed RMI, a 50-person, independent, nonprofit, entrepreneurial applied research center. Lovins has coauthored nine books and dozens of papers, and was featured in the award-winning film *Lovins On the Soft Path*. Her latest book, *Natural Capitalism*, coauthored with co-CEO Amory Lovins and Paul Hawken, was published in 1999 and is in its fourth printing. Work has begun with social entrepreneur Walter Link on a new book, *The Human Dimensions of Natural Capitalism*. She has shared a 1982 Mitchell Prize for an essay on reallocating utility capital, a 1983 Right Livelihood Award, a 1993 Nissan Award for an article on Hypercars, and the 1999 Lindbergh

Award for Environment and Technology. In 2000, Ms. Lovins was named a Hero of the Planet by *Time* magazine. In 2001, she received the Leadership in Business Award.

Michael Murphy

Michael Murphy, founder of the Esalen Institute, is an educator, author, and pioneer in the human potential and transformation movement. In 1962, Michael cofounded Esalen Institute (with Richard Price) in Big Sur, California. The institute became the source of the human potential movement of the 1960s and continues to contribute new thinking in humanistic psychology, holistic health, spirituality, and mind-body awareness. Michael was instrumental in establishing the Institute of Humanistic Medicine (1968); the Department of Confluent Education at the University of California, Santa Barbara (1967); the Esalen Sports Center (1973); and the Esalen Soviet-American Exchange Program. He recently formed the Esalen Center for Theory and Research to initiate a sustained global inquiry into human potentialities and help overcome the fragmentation of knowledge that isolates pockets of vital discovery regarding human transformative capacity. Michael is the author of *Golf in the Kingdom*, *The Future of the Body*, *The Life We Are Given* (coauthored with George Leonard) and the recently published *God and the Evolving Universe*, with coauthor James Redfield.

Jay Ogilvy

Jay is a cofounder of Global Business Network. His research and consulting experience revolves around the role human values and changing motivations play in consumption, purchase decisions, communications, health, and education. He has pursued these interests at SRI International, as a consultant to Royal Dutch/Shell, and since 1988 with GBN. At SRI International Jay split his time between developing future scenarios for strategic planning and serving as director of research for the Values and Lifestyles (VALS) Program, a consumer segmentation system used in market research. Jay's work in future studies and values research builds on his background as a philosopher. He taught at the University of Texas, at Williams College, and for seven years at Yale, where he received his doctorate in 1968. He is the author or editor of many articles and six books, most recently *Creating Better Futures* and *China's Futures* (with Peter Schwartz).

Walter Parkes

Walter Parkes is a writer and producer of motion pictures and television shows. In 1994, he became president of Amblin Entertainment, Steven Spielberg's production company at Universal Studios, and in July 1995 was named director of motion pictures for Dreamworks SKG. He was a producer of *Gladiator*, which won the Academy Award for best picture in 2001. His first feature-length film, *The California Reich*, was nominated for an Oscar, awarded a special citation at the Cannes Film

Festival, and shown at film festivals around the world. Walter is a four-time Academy Award nominee including for *War Games* (best original screenplay, 1983) and *Awakenings* (best picture, 1990). Other screen credits as producer and/or writer include *True Believer, Sneakers, How to Make an American Quilt, Twister, Men in Black,* and *Minority Report.* Walter also created and was executive producer for the ABC drama "Birdland," starring Brian Dennehy. In addition to his work in film and television, Walter is involved in the development of new interactive products for DWI, the joint venture between Dreamworks and Microsoft.

John L. Petersen

John Petersen is a futurist and long-range strategic planner. He is president and founder of the Arlington Institute, a non-profit policy and research institute in the Washington, D.C., area specializing in the dynamics of global transitions and identifying and preparing for wildcards—discontinuous events that are fast moving and could have profound global impact. His government and political experience includes stints at the National War College, the Institute for National Security Studies, the Office of the Secretary of Defense, and the National Security Council Staff at the White House. He was a naval flight officer and is a decorated veteran of both the Vietnam and Persian Gulf wars. He is the author of *The Road to 2015: Profiles of the Future* and *Out of the Blue!: How to Anticipate Wild Cards and Big Future Surprises.* John works with organizations, corporations, and government agencies helping them to develop new images of possible futures, often by leading groups through scenario design processes.

Jeffrey Rayport

Jeffrey F. Rayport is CEO of Marketspace LLC, a content and consulting business that helps information industry companies create advantage in the networked economy. Marketspace is a unit of Monitor Group, a Cambridge, Massachusetts–based strategy services and merchant banking firm. Until recently an associate professor at Harvard Business School, Rayport focuses his research on new information technologies and their impacts on services and marketing strategies, particularly in information-intensive industries. With coauthor Bernard J. Jaworksi, he has published three leading MBA-level textbooks on strategy in the networked economy (*e-Commerce, Cases in e-Commerce, and Introduction to e-Commerce*) with McGraw-Hill/Irwin. At Harvard, he developed and taught the first e-commerce course at a top-tier business school. Business plans produced by students in the course resulted in dozens of Internet startups, including Yahoo! Until he went on leave from HBS, the Harvard Business School Association voted him Outstanding Professor in 1997, 1998, and 1999. Rayport serves as a director of several public and private corporations, including Andrews McMeel Universal, CBS MarketWatch (MKTW), GSI Commerce (GSPT), International Data Group, and ValueClick (VCLK).

Richard Rodriguez

Richard Rodriguez is a prominent writer, an associate editor with Pacific News Service in San Francisco, a contributing editor of *Harper's* and the *Los Angeles Times*, and a regular essayist on the *Jim Lehrer News Hour*. He is the author of *Hunger of Memory* and *Days of Obligation: An Argument with My Mexican Father*, and *Brown: The Last Discovery of America*. Richard received a 1997 George Foster Peabody Award for his *News Hour* essays on American life. The Peabody Award is designed to recognize "outstanding achievement in broadcast and cable," and is one of television's highest honors. Richard's awards include the Frankel Medal from the National Endowment for the Humanities and the International Journalism Award from the World Affairs Council of California.

Paul Saffo

Paul is a technology forecaster studying long-term information technology trends and their impact on business and society and a director of Institute for the Future, a 30-year-old foundation that provides strategic planning and forecasting services to major corporations and government agencies. His essays have appeared in numerous publications, including the *Harvard Business Review*, *Wired* magazine, *Civilization* magazine, the *Los Angeles Times*, the *New York Times*, and *Fortune* magazine, as well as other more specialized periodicals. Paul is the author of *Dreams in Silicon Valley* and *The Road from Trinity*. He was a 1997 McKinsey Judge for the *Harvard Business Review*, and in the same year was named one of one hundred "Global Leaders for Tomorrow" by the World Economic Forum. Paul serves on a variety of boards and advisory panels, including the AT&T Technology Advisory Board, the World Economic Forum Global Issues Group, and the Stanford Law School Advisory Council on Science, Technology and Society.

Brian Sager

Brian is a strategy consultant, scientist, composer, and the founder of a new nanotechnology company. He has more than 14 years of experience in scientific and management consulting focused on advisory services for high-growth, entrepreneurial companies. His strategic engagements range from valuations, scenario planning, competitive strategy, and market entry strategy to research and development portfolio management, corporate development, and merger and acquisition advisory services. He is currently leading GBN's Biofutures program. As a composer, Brian writes and produces new classical music, and has recently released a CD containing two symphonies for full orchestra, four piano sonatas, and a piece for string quartet (http://www.newclassical.com). Brian is currently writing his third symphony.

Orville Schell

Orville is dean of the Graduate School of Journalism and research associate at the Center for Chinese Studies at the University of California, Berkeley; a member of the Council on Foreign Relations in New York, the National Committee on U.S.-China

Relations, PEN, and the Author's Guild; and a board member of Human Rights Watch/Asia and the Yale-China Association. He is the author of 14 books—nine about China, including *Virtual Tibet, Mandate of Heaven,* and *Discos and Democracy.* Schell has also written widely about Asia for *Wired,* the *New York Review of Books,* the *New Yorker, Harper's, Newsweek,* and other national magazines. He is the recipient of Guggenheim and Alicia Patterson Foundation fellowships and numerous writing prizes. Schell has also served as correspondent and consultant for several PBS *Frontline* documentaries as well as an Emmy Award–winning program on China for CBS's *60 Minutes.*

Lee Schipper

Lee Schipper is the director of EMBARQ, the Center for Transport and the Environment established by the World Resources Institute and the Shell Foundation. Until recently, he was visiting senior scientist at the International Energy Agency in Paris. He is also staff senior scientist at the Lawrence Berkeley Laboratory (LBL), University of California, Berkeley, and co-leader of the International Energy Studies group. He is also associated with the Stockholm Environment Institute. In 1986–1987 he was a visiting researcher with Group Planning, Shell International Petroleum Company, London. He spent six months at the Swedish Heating Society in Stockholm and was a Fulbright Scholar at the Beijer Institute in Stockholm. He also served as information specialist at the Energy and Resources Group, University of California, Berkeley, and remains as a faculty affiliate of that group. He has consulted for the UN, the OECD/IEA, the World Bank, and many other international organizations, and is a senior associate of Cambridge Energy Research Associates. Schipper was also a faculty member of the San Francisco Conservatory of Music and is a jazz vibraphonist and pianist.

Peter Schwartz

Peter is a cofounder and chair of GBN and a Monitor partner. Peter is also a venture partner of Alta Partners in San Francisco and serves on the advisory boards of numerous organizations and companies ranging from the Highlands Group to USC's Institute for Creative Technologies. Before cofounding GBN in 1987, Peter headed scenario planning for the Royal Dutch/Shell Group of Companies in London and directed the Strategic Environment Center at SRI International. He is the author of *The Art of the Long View* and coauthor of the books *When Good Companies Do Bad Things, The Long Boom, China's Futures* and *Seven Tomorrows.* Peter publishes and lectures widely, writes the monthly "Scenarios" column for *Red Herring,* and has served as a script consultant on such films as *Deep Impact, War Games, Sneakers,* and *Minority Report.*

Alex Singer

Alex Singer is a film director based in Los Angeles. In his 40-year career he has directed more than 280 television shows, and five theatrical features. His body of

338 - **About the Network Members**

work includes some of America's foremost TV series: "Profiles in Courage," "The Fugitive," "The Bold Ones," "Police Story," "Lou Grant," "Cagney and Lacey," "Hill Street Blues," and the three recent forms of "Star Trek." Alex's many honors include an Emmy and a Humanitas award. He has lectured and taught film production, cinematography, and directing at UCLA, USC, private institutions, and the Directors Guild of America. Through the DGA's Special Projects, he has explored the development of scenarios for the entertainment industry with GBN colleagues. Under contract to MCA/Universal Studios, he headed a task force assigned to integrate established motion picture technologies with the new computer-mediated forms of entertainment at its Orlando, Florida, theme park and continued as principal consultant applications of virtual reality technologies. Alex continues to explore these themes with the National Research Council, the active arm of the National Academy of Sciences; DARPA; the Engineering School; and the Institute of Creative Technologies at USC.

Huston Smith

Huston Smith is Thomas J. Watson Professor of Religion and Distinguished Adjunct Professor of Philosophy, Emeritus, Syracuse University. He also taught at Washington University in St. Louis, MIT, and the University of California, Berkeley. Smith has been awarded 12 honorary degrees. His writings include more than 80 articles in professional and popular journals, and 12 books, of which the best known is *The World's Religions*, which has sold over two and a half million copies. His discovery of the capacity of certain specially trained Tibetan lamas to sing multiphonically (solo chords) is considered a landmark in the study of music. His documentary films on Hinduism, Buddhism, and Islam have all won international awards. In 1966, Bill Moyers devoted a five-part PBS special, "The Wisdom of Faith with Huston Smith" to his life and work.

Bruce Sterling

Bruce Sterling is a science fiction and technology writer and a chronicler of the cyberpunk movement. His latest novel is *Zeitgeist* and he is also the author of *Holy Fire, Heavy Weather, Islands in the Net,* and *Schismatrix.* He coauthored *The Difference Engine* with William Gibson and edited *Mirrorshades: The Cyberpunk Anthology.* His nonfiction books include *The Hacker Crackdown: Law and Disorder on the Electronic Frontier.* Bruce has contributed fiction, columns, and nonfiction to a wide variety of publications, including *OMNI, Wired,* the *New York Times, Newsday, Whole Earth Review, Interzone, Computerworld, Details,* and *Boing Boing.* His short story collections are *Crystal Express, Globalhead,* and *A Good Old-Fashioned Future.* Sterling is a board member of the Austin Electronic Frontier Foundation and he also founded the Dead Media Project, a mailing list and discussion group dedicated to studying the "life and death" of now-defunct media. In 1999, he began the Viridian design movement, which advances environmental consciousness through revolutionary art and design.

Hirotaka Takeuchi

Hirotaka Takeuchi is dean of the Graduate School of International Corporate Strategy at Hitotsubashi University in Tokyo. His research interests are focused on the knowledge creation process within organizations, the competitiveness of Japanese firms in global industries, new product development processes, and competitive strategy. His business experience includes consulting at McKinsey and advertising at McCann Erickson in Tokyo and San Francisco. An April 1996 *Fortune* article introduced him as "among the intellectual leaders of the younger, globally-minded generation that is coming to power in Japan." He recently coauthored *Can Japan Compete?* with Michael E. Porter. His coauthored book *The Knowledge-Creating Company* (Oxford University Press) won the "Best New Book of the Year" award in 1996. He was also named one of "The Stars of Asia: 50 Leaders at the Forefront of Change" in the July 2001 issue of *Business Week*.

Dorothy Q. Thomas

Dorothy Q. Thomas is an independent consultant on human rights in the United States. From 1990–1998 she served as the founding director of the Human Rights Watch Women's Rights Division. She is a 1998 MacArthur Fellow and a 1994 Bunting Fellow of the Radcliffe Institute for Advanced Study at Harvard University. In 1998 she received the Eleanor Roosevelt Human Rights Award from the president of the United States. She is the author of several articles and reports on human rights, including "We Are Not the World: U.S. Activism and Human Rights in the Twenty-First Century," "Making the Connections: Human Rights in the United States," "All Too Familiar: Sexual Abuse of Women in U.S. Prisons," and "Advancing Rights Protection in the United States: An Internationalized Advocacy Strategy." She serves on the advisory boards of the International Council for Human Rights Policy and the Open Society Institute's Program on Reproductive Health and Rights.

Nirav Tolia

Nirav Tolia is cofounder and CEO of Epinions, a company founded in 1999 to help consumers make better buying decisions by offering unbiased customer advice and reviews on over 150,000 products. Prior to Epinions, Nirav spent three years at Yahoo!, where he was an early member of the marketing group and frequently appeared on CNN, MSNBC, and in other media as a company representative. Nirav began his career at McKinsey & Company. Nirav is also a founder and president of Round Zero (www.roundzero.com), a not-for-profit organization that brings Silicon Valley entrepreneurs, venture capitalists, and professionals together to discuss high-tech issues.

Kees van der Heijden

Kees is the director of the Center for Strategic Planning and Future Studies, Strathclyde University, Glasgow. He is coauthor of *The Sixth Sense*, the author of *Scenarios: The Art of Strategic Conversation*, and a GBN cofounder. His practice focuses on the emergence of institutional strategic thinking and learning. Prior to 1991, he headed the business environment division of group planning at Royal Dutch/Shell, London, where he oversaw scenario planning. This included monitoring and analyzing the business environment and communicating with top management on strategic implications. Previously, he headed Shell's internal strategic consultancy group, assisting management teams in strategy development and implementation. Kees joined Shell in the Hague in 1957 and spent many years abroad in operating companies in Manila, Singapore, and Curaçao, mostly in activities concerned with commercial planning, economics, and corporate planning and strategy.

Vernor Vinge

Vernor Vinge sold his first science fiction story in 1964. During the late 1960s and early 1970s he was active in science fiction short fiction, selling stories to *Analog, if, New Worlds*, and Damon Knight's *Orbit* series. He is best known for *True Names*, *The Peace War*, and *Marooned in Realtime* (which were nominated for Hugos), and *A Fire Upon the Deep* and *A Deepness in the Sky* (which both won Hugos). Vinge holds a Ph.D. in Math from the University of California, San Diego. From 1972 to 2000, he taught mathematics and computer science at San Diego State University. He has now retired from that position to write science fiction full-time. His current interest is in distributed and embedded computer systems.

Peter Warshall

Peter Warshall's work centers on conservation and development. He has worked at the United Nations High Commission for Refugees, in 11 African nations, with the Tohono O'odham people of Arizona, with municipal governments, and as a consultant to major transnationals such as Volvo, Senco, Clorox, and SAS Airlines. His training and experience include natural history, natural resource management (especially watersheds and wildlife), conservation biology, environmental impact analysis, conflict resolution, and consensus building among divergent economic and cultural special interest groups. He is editor of *Whole Earth* magazine, runs his own small consulting firm, and lectures, writes, and guides natural and cultural history tours throughout North America. Peter received his B.A. in Biology with a minor in French Literature and a Ph.D. in Biological Anthropology from Harvard. As a Fulbright scholar, he studied cultural anthropology under Professor Claude Lévi-Strauss at L'École Practique des Hautes Études (Paris), specializing in Native American history.

Steven Weber

Steve is a consultant with GBN, a professor in the department of political science at the University of California, Berkeley, and a member of the Berkeley Roundtable on the International Economy (BRIE). His areas of special interest include international political economy, United States foreign policy, the political economy of European integration, and theories of cooperation. In 1992 Steve served as special advisor to the president of the European Bank for Reconstruction and Development in London. Steve received a B.A. in History and International Development from Washington University in St. Louis. After several years of medical school training at Stanford University, he moved to the political science department at Stanford, where he received an M.A. and a Ph.D. His current research projects include the examination of changes in the business cycle, and implications for firms and governments; a project on globalization and the development of new stock markets in Europe; and a book (forthcoming next year) that examines the economic and social logic of open-source software as a window into new production processes of the Internet economy.

Lawrence Wilkinson

Lawrence Wilkinson is cofounder and vice chair of Oxygen Media, Inc., and cofounder and chair of Hemming & Condell, an investment and advisory firm. He serves as advisor to and director of Ealing Studios, Ltd., Design Within Reach, and the Character Development Lab. Prior to joining Oxygen, Lawrence cofounded and served as president of Global Business Network. He has also served as president of Colossal Pictures, as director and chief architect of Wired Ventures, and as a director of Broderbund Software, Direct Medical Knowledge, and Lieberman Productions. Lawrence has authored and edited numerous publications and Harvard Business School case studies ranging from *Broadcasting in the U.S.* to *The Cambridge Milton*. He has produced and executive-produced numerous television programs, multimedia titles, and feature films, including *Crumb*. He also has contributed regularly to general and business periodicals and national television, cable, and radio business news programs, including *Wired, Advertising Age, Backstage, Business Times, Nightly Business Report*, and the *Wall Street Journal Report*.

The GBN Book Club

In addition to offering consulting and training services, Global Business Network has for the past 15 years run a membership organization called WorldView that provides organizations with a blend of experiential learning, original content, personal connections and innovative tools and methodologies. Many products and services help member organizations to engage in long-view thinking, but one particular service might be of interest to readers of this book—the GBN Book Club. Each month since 1988, GBN has sent members selected books and other media accompanied by short reviews. GBN cofounder Stewart Brand made the choices for more than 10 years based on his criteria of what books appeared to be most prescient about the future, most insightful about how organizations learn and adapt, and most revealing of the hidden patterns and deep structure behind current events. Starting in 2000, we invited a different network member each month to select books that had made a profound impression on them, influenced their thinking, and might stimulate others. What follows are their selections, and a brief description of the books, starting from the beginning of the millennium. They might provide a useful departure point for further inquiry on many of the topics discussed in this book.

Kevin Kelly, Founding Executive Editor, Wired

Nonzero: The Logic of Human Destiny—Robert Wright. How mutual self-interest ("non-zero sum" outcomes) created civilization and is accelerating economic and cultural globalization

Rembrandts in the Attic: Unlocking the Hidden Value of Patents—Kevin G. Rivette, David Kline. The role of patents in measuring, protecting, and managing innovation

Kevin Kelly, Founding Executive Editor, Wired

The Tipping Point: How Little Things Can Make a Big Difference—Malcolm Gladwell. Delightful mix of theory and examples of how tiny changes within networks can change whole cultures

The New New Thing: A Silicon Valley Story—Michael Lewis. A look at the new economy's craziness and velocity through the speculative dealings of technology entrepreneur Jim Clark

The Futures of China—Jay Ogilvy and Peter Schwartz. Four scenarios for China's possible emergence as an economic and political power

Brian Eno, musician and artist

Philosophy and Social Hope—Richard Rorty. Replacing the eternal search for objective truth with a pragmatic approach to politics, ethics, class, love, and money

Mother Nature: A History of Mothers, Infants, and Natural Selection—Sarah Blaffer Hrdy. A scientific and personal analysis of motherhood as a complex calculus, beyond mere instinct

Don Michael, social and policy theorist

The Spirit in the Gene: Humanity's Proud Illusion and the Laws of Nature—Reg Morrison. Why denying the power of genes blinds us to their influence on human behavior, culture, and the possible destruction of our species

The Passion of the Western Mind—Richard Tarnas. The evolution, interconnection, and expression of the ideas that have shaped the Western worldview

Peter Schwartz, GBN chair

Natural Capitalism: Creating the Next Industrial Revolution—Paul Hawken, Amory Lovins, L. Hunter Lovins. Valuing nature as a critical source of capital in both theory and practice

The Change in the Weather: People, Weather and the Science of Climate—William K. Stevens. A balanced look at both sides of the global warming debate with practical implications for behavior and policy

Peter Warshall, biological anthropologist

Kurdistan: In the Shadow of History—Susan Meisalas. Stunning photo-documentary of the history and tragedy of the Kurdish people

The Song of the Dodo: Island Biogeography in an Age of Extinctions—David Quammen. Real-life adventures in nature reinforce the importance of biological diversity and healthy ecosystems

Pamela McCorduck, science writer

Genes, Peoples, and Languages—Luigi Cavalli-Sforza. The interdisciplinary causes and effects of human migration around the globe

The Adventures of Ibn Battuta: A Muslim Traveller of the 14th Century—Rose E. Dunn. The spread of trade, ideas, and learning through the Islamic world through the incisive eyes of a holy scholar

Peter Schwartz

The Rise and Decline of the State—Martin Van Creveld. The history and future of political power and the role of the nation-state

Telecosm: How Infinite Bandwidth Will Revolutionize Our World—George Gilder. The story and characters behind the communications technology revolution that is transforming our future

Joel Garreau, cultural revolutionary, the Washington Post

A General Theory of Love—Thomas Lewis, Fari Amini, and Richard Lannon. A new theory of social interaction premised on our genetic need for love

The Social Life of Information—John Seely Brown and Paul Duguid. Exploring the social context of information—and the technologies that shape and deliver it

Steve Barnett, anthropologist and business strategist

Freud's Megalomania—Israel Rosenfield. A novel about chaos, complexity, and the impossibility of controlling or predicting our futures

Against Race: Imagining Political Culture Beyond the Color Line—Paul Gilroy. Scholarly, if controversial, analysis of racial and ethnic assimilation into Western culture

Bo Ekman, business executive and humanitarian

No Future Without Forgiveness—Desmond Tutu. Tutu's stewardship of South Africa's Truth and Reconciliation Commission reveals broader lessons for humanity

Humanity: A Moral History of the Twentieth Century—Jonathan Glover. Examining the brutality of man and the need for a new political, personal, and moral imagination

Eric Clemons, economist

Voltaire's Bastards: The Dictatorship of Reason in the West—John Ralston Saul. How the hyperrationality stressed at most elite business schools erects strong barriers to learning and change

The Armchair Economist: Economics and Everyday Life—Steven E. Landsburg. An amusing, yet grounded, look at the value of economic rigor in research, analysis (and even scenario planning)

Mary Catherine Bateson, cultural anthropologist

And Keep Your Powder Dry: An Anthropologist Looks at America—Margaret Mead. Classic analysis of the "American character" and need for self-knowledge that still resonates after 60 years as we observe Mead's centenary

Continuities in Cultural Evolution—Margaret Mead. The process of cultural continuity and innovation, including the critical roles of environment and leadership in social change

Peter Schwartz

When Genius Failed: The Rise and Fall of Long-Term Capital Management—Roger Lowenstein. A costly and cautionary tale of hubris and overdependence on financial models

Six Nightmares: Real Threats in a Dangerous World and How America Can Meet Them—Anthony Lake. A scenaric look at the big threats facing America: crime, terrorism, political instability, and dysfunction at home and abroad

Napier Collyns, GBN cofounder and network architect

Reframing Business: When the Map Changes the Landscape—Richard Normann. A lifetime of experience and insights into business by one of Europe's top management scholars

Twenty-One Leaders for the Twenty-First Century: How Innovative Leaders Manage in the Digital Age—Charles Hampden-Turner and Fons Trompenaars. Stories of 21 business leaders who have succeeded—and failed—at reconciling opposing cultural values and dilemmas in their organizations

Bruce Sterling, science fiction writer

Bobos in Paradise: The New Upper Class and How They Got There—David Brooks. A meticulous, often hilarious, portrait of the new, brainy bourgeois bohemians whose SUVs sport Save the Whales bumper stickers

The Diary of a Political Idiot: Normal Lie in Belgrade—Jasmina Tesanovic. A Serbian war diary, first circulated on the Internet, that asks what went wrong

John Petersen, futurist

Catastrophe: An Investigation into the Origins of the Modern World—David Keys. A scientific detective story about an ancient catastrophe that plunged the world into twilight

The Cosmic Serpent: DNA and the Origins of Knowledge—Jeremy Narby. An anthropologist's amazing journey of discovery from talking plants to intelligent DNA

Adam Kahane, organizational transformation consultant

Leading Systems: Lessons for the Power Lab—Barry Oshry. Understanding the structure and patterns of power relationships through stories from the Power Lab

Civic Dialogue/Civic Scenarios Workshop—Bettye Pruitt. Lessons from groundbreaking, cross-institutional, civic dialogues in 17 countries

Jay Ogilvy, GBN cofounder and philosopher

Emergence: The Connected Lives of Ants, Brains, Cities, and Software—Stephen Johnson. Understanding emergent systems in nature and then creating them in culture

The Springboard: How Storytelling Ignites Action in Knowledge Era Organizations—Stephen Denning. A minimalist, cocreative approach to storytelling for organizations

Peter Schwartz

Unrestricted Warfare—Qiao Liang and Wang Xiangsui. Two Chinese colonels fundamentally redefine the aims and methods of war in the current age

Long-Term Global Economic Trends: Reshaping the Geopolitical Landscape—Central Intelligence Agency. How demographics will shape geopolitics in the decades ahead

Energy Needs, Choices, and Possibilities: Scenarios to 2050—Shell International. Two very different pathways toward energy and environmental sustainability

Alex Singer, film and television director

The Diagnosis—Alan Lightman. A novel about the human dimension of information overload and mediated relationships

Einstein, Picasso: Space, Time, and the Beauty that Causes Havoc—Arthur I. Miller. Intertwining science and the arts to illuminate the singular creative process

Gerard Fairtlough, biotechnology executive and scenario planner

Creating Better Futures: Scenario Planning as a Tool for a Better Tomorrow—Jay Ogilvy. Explicitly incorporating values in scenario planning to design the futures in which we want to live

The Power of the Tale: Using Narratives for Organizational Success—Gerard Fairtlough and Barbara Heinzen. Storytelling as an effective tool for aligning, enriching, and changing organizations of all kinds

Ged Davis, head of Shell International's scenario team

The Earth from Above—Yan Arthus-Bertrand. An oversized book of extraordinary aerial photographs taken over sixty countries on every continent, with analysis on the state of the world

Panarchy: Understanding Transformations in Systems of Humans and Nature—Lance H Gunderson and C. S. Holling (editors). An attempt to develop an integrative, systemic theory to help understand changes occurring globally

"People and Connections: Global Scenarios to 2020," Global Business Environment—Shell International. The latest scenarios from Royal Dutch /Shell Group explore the world through 2020

Katherine Fulton, GBN-Monitor partner, heading philanthropy practice

Leadership on the Line: Staying Alive through the Dangers of Leading—Ronald A. Heifetz and Marty Linsky. Exploring the emotional, intellectual, and moral risks leaders take when they put themselves on the line

The Radical Center: The Future of American Politics—Ted Halstead and Michael Lind. Imagining how America could fundamentally rethink its public philosophy and institutions to catch up with an Information-Age economy

Lawrence Wilkinson, GBN cofounder and vice chair, Oxygen Media.

Brown: The Last Discovery of America—Richard Rodriguez. A memoir reflecting on the meaning of Hispanics to the life of America

"Gorillaz"—Gorillaz. The music CD of an animated British rock group that has won two Grammies

No Man's Land—directed by Danis Tanovic. A DVD film documentary on Bosnia that won the 2001 Academy Award for Best Foreign Language Film

Index